VEGETARIANO

400 Regional Italian Recipes

VEGETARIANO

400 Regional Italian Recipes

Slow Food Editore

Translated by Natalie Danford

RIZZOLI
NEW YORK

New York · Paris · London · Milan

Photograph Credits

Front Cover: istockphoto.com/vicuschka

Lorenzo Borri: Page 35

Giuseppe Cucco: Page 337

Davide Gallizio: Page 6, 9, 10, 15, 21, 27, 29, 33, 43, 53, 61, 67, 77, 105, 113, 119, 125, 133, 141, 149, 157, 165, 173, 191, 229, 233, 247, 279, 285, 291, 303, 307, 313, 327, 333, 343, 345, 353, 371, 379, 387, 395, 403, 411, 417, 423, 433

Marcelo Marengo: Page 83, 297

Alberto Peroli: Page 79, 213

Barbara Torresan: Page 63, 71, 73, 91, 193, 239, 261, 265, 267, 269, 275, 299, 339, 383, 389, 393, 405, 409, 421, 425

Slow Food Editore

Originally published in the Italian language as
Ricette vegeteriane d'Italia
© 2015 Slow Food Editore, S.r.l.
Via Audiso, 5 – 12042 Bra (Cn) Italy
www.slowfoodeditore.it

First published in the United States of America in
2018 by Rizzoli International Publications, Inc.
300 Park Avenue South
New York, NY 10010
www.rizzoliusa.com

© 2018 Rizzoli Publications, Inc.

For the Italian-language edition:
Editor: Bianca Minerdo
Assistant Editors: Grazia Novellini, Eugenio Signorini
Layout: Roberto Fidale
Many thanks to LeeAnn Bortolusi and Brunella Tiso

For the English-language edition:
Translator: Natalie Danford
Typesetter: Lynne Yeamans / LYNC

2018 2019 2020 2021 / 10 9 8 7 6 5 4 3 2 1

Distributed to the U.S. trade by Random House, New York.

Printed in Italy

ISBN: 978-0-8478-6181-1
Library of Congress Catalog Control Number: 2017948439

TABLE OF CONTENTS

INTRODUCTION

Italy is an earthly paradise for vegetarians. Italy's culinary culture is one of endless invention—it is also based on a wealth of diverse ingredients, but not material wealth, so for decades meat was reserved for holidays and special occasions, rendering most Italians accidental vegetarians much of the time. The need to make much out of little left an indelible mark on regional cooking traditions, which were born and developed largely in the face of poverty, in rural areas, by the farming families that as recently as fifty years ago still constituted the majority of the country's population rather than from fancy restaurants. In the absence of meat, Italians creatively crafted satisfying vegetarian dishes.

Living in humble circumstances taught valuable lessons about reuse and recycling, identifying the best times to purchase or harvest ingredients, and making the most of all produce, including those fruits and vegetables available at the beginning or the end of the season. Even in the modern era, Italian food maintains its seasonal ebb and flow. In her infinite wisdom, Mother Nature arranged for comforting, filling foods that warm our bellies to be available in winter and lighter foods suitable for summer to be available in the warmer months. Italians are also masters at canning, preserving, drying, and other methods for storing foods long-term.

Additionally, the nation has many advantages when it comes to vegetarian cooking. Its mild climate makes it a fertile place to grow an almost infinite range of various types of produce. Grains flourish in Italy's fields and are treasured in its kitchens. They are eaten in whole form, as well as being ground into flours that expand the culinary possibilities exponentially, paving the way for the creation of pizza and bread—not to mention Italy's signature food, versatile, quick-cooking, and endlessly adaptable pasta, a vegetarian's boon companion. The Italian way with cheese—cow's milk, goat's milk, sheep's milk, buffalo's milk—is justly world-famous and diversified to a granular level. Yet the greatest vegetarian Italian ingredient of all may be what can only be called ingenuity. Italian home cooks and restaurant chefs make magic with simple, fresh ingredients: eggs, a handful of herbs, a few tomatoes. The result is a trove of interesting and exciting vegetarian dishes from every one of the country's regions.

Slow Food, which collected the recipes in this book from restaurants and home cooks, celebrates local, artisanally made food. Today a global, grassroots organization,

Slow Food was founded in 1989 to prevent the disappearance of local food cultures and traditions, counteract the rise of fast life, and combat people's dwindling knowledge of where the food they eat comes from and how food choices affect the world around us. The movement began in Italy in 1986, when McDonald's wanted to open a franchise at the base of the Spanish Steps in Rome. A group of Italians gathered to protest, but rather than marching and chanting, they brought a big bowl of pasta and served it to those in the crowd. That gathering was the foundation for the birth of the Slow Food movement. For decades now, Slow Food has been promoting environmental sustainability and social justice for consumers and producers, but above all it highlights robust flavors.

While not a strictly vegetarian organization, in its push for good, clean, and fair food, Slow Food believes that responsible meat consumption means eating less meat. Among its other activities, Slow Food has a program called the Ark of Taste that collects small-scale quality food products: fruits, vegetables, cheeses, breads, sweets, and more. A product that is at particular risk of extinction may be safeguarded through the creation of a specific Slow Food Presidium. At the time of this writing, there are 199 vegetarian presidia, representing the breathtaking biodiversity of Italy's crops. These focus on everything from the Altino sweet peppers of Abruzzo (horn-shaped peppers that are harvested, sewn together, then air-dried), to the sorana

beans of Toscana (a thin-skinned variety of shell bean that flourishes in land drained by the Medici family in the sixteenth century), to the traditional fiore sardo sheep's cheese of Sardegna (dried in the heat of a brazier and rubbed with wine vinegar, olive oil, and salt). For Slow Food—indeed, for Italians—ingredients are more than mere puzzle pieces to be assembled into dishes. Each has its own etymology; each tells its own story, and each meal is a poetic narrative where those stories intertwine. In addition, each recipe includes its Italian or local-dialect name, its contributor, and its city, province (unless from the capital), and region of origin. Explore the recipes geographically via a regional index at the back of the book.

One needn't be a strict vegetarian to enjoy the recipes in this book. Just as there are few vegetarian restaurants in Italy, as meatless food is not considered particularly outside-the-box, this is as much an Italian cookbook as it is a vegetarian one. If you are vegan, you will discover a large number of suitable recipes, all marked with a V symbol. If you are interested in culinary traditions that have been around for centuries, you will find examples in these pages, but there are some modern inclusions as well. Italian cooking, like any great cuisine, is always evolving, even as it rests on a rich underlying heritage. And if all of this sounds too intellectual for your taste and all you want to do is prepare and then enjoy some really good food, you're in luck, because most of all, this is a book intended to help you do just that.

SLOW FOOD PRESIDIA
VEGETARIAN PRODUCTS BY REGION

ABRUZZO

Abruzzese Apennines Solina Wheat
Altino Sweet Pepper
Casoli Intosso Olive
Castel del Monte Canestrato (Cheese)
Dried Atessa Reale Fig
Fara Filiorum Petri White Onion
L'Aquila Appennine Honeys
Montonico Grape
Navelli Chickpea
Paganica Beans
Santo Stefano di Sessanio Lentil
Turchesa Potato

VALLE D'AOSTA

High Mountain Honeys

BASILICATA

Basilicata Podolico Caciocavallo (Cheese)
Ferrandina Baked Olive
Pantano di Pignola Red Bean
Sinni Valley Signora Pear

CALABRIA

Ciminà Caciocavallo (Cheese)
Pizzo Calabro Zibibbo (Wines)
Saracena Moscato al Governo (Wines)

CAMPANIA

Acerra Dente di Morto Bean
Caiazzana Table Olive
Casalbuono Beans
Castellammare Purple Artichoke
Cicerale Chickpea
Cilento Cacioricotta (Cheese)
Cilento Cracked Salella Olive
Controne Bean
Heritage Vesuvian Apricot Varieties
Lentiscosa Maracuoccio (Legumes)
Neapolitan Ancient Tomato Varieties
Neapolitan Papaccella (Vegetables)
Paternopoli Aprilatico Broccoli
Pertosa White Artichoke
Roman Conciato (Cheese)
Vairano Giant Lupin Bean

EMILIA ROMAGNA

Cervia Artisanal Sea Salt
Cocomerina Pear
Tosco-Romagnolo Apennine Raviggiolo
    (Cheese)

FRIULI VENEZIA GIULIA

Cavasso and Valcosa Onion
Çuç di Mont (Cheese)
Formadi Frant

Gorizia Rosa Radicchio
Latteria Turnaria Cheese
Pan di Sorc Venezia Giulia
Radic di Mont (Vegetables)
Resia Garlic

ITALY

Italian Extra-Virgin Olive Oil

LAZIO

Arsoli Bean
Marzolina (Cheese)
Palestrina Giglietto Biscuit
Priverno Chiacchietegli Broccoli
Rascino Lentil
Roman Countryside Caciofiore
Vallepietra Giant Bean

LIGURIA

Badalucco, Conio and Pigna Beans
Bitter Orange Flower Water
Brigasca Sheep (Cheese)
Cinque Terre Sciacchetrà (Wine)
Dried Calizzano and Murialdo Chestnut
Perinaldo Artichoke
Rose Syrup
Savona Chinotto (Fruit)
Valleggia Apricot
Vessalico Garlic

LOMBARDIA

Bagolino Bagòss (Cheese)
Calvenzano Melon
Felonica Tiròt (Bread)
High Mountain Honeys
Historic Rebel Cheese
Lodi Pannerone (Cheese)
Orobica Goat (Cheese)
Orobiche Valleys Traditional Stracchino
    (Cheese)
Saviore Valley Fatuli (Cheese)
Valtorta Agrì (Cheese)

MARCHE

Fig Lonzino
Montelupone Artichoke
Serra De' Conti Cicerchia (Legumes)
Sibillini Mountain Pecorino (Cheese)
Sibillini Mountains Pink Apples

PIEMONTE

Bagnario di Strevi Valley Moscato Passito
    (Wines)
Bormida Valley Terraces Dolcetto (Wines)
Bronda Valley Ramassin (Fruit)
Caprauna Turnip
Capriglio Pepper
Carema (Wines)
Carmagnola Ox-Horn Pepper
Coazze Cevrin (Cheese)
Cortereggio Canavese Piattella Bean

Cureggio and Fontaneto Blond Onion
Garbagna Bella Cherry
Heritage Caraglio Garlic
Heritage Piedomontese Apple Varieties
High Mountain Honeys
Langhe Sheep Tuma (Cheese)
Mondovì Cornmeal Biscuits
Montébore (Cheese)
Mountain Pasture Castelmagno (Cheese)
Nizza Monferrato Hunchback Cardoon
Orbassano Red Celery
Roccaverano Robiola (Cheese)
Saras del Fen (Cheese)
Tortona Strawberry
Tuma Macagn (Cheese)
Upper Elvo Raw Milk Butter

PUGLIA

Acquaviva Red Onion
Alta Murgia Traditional Bread
Bisceglie Sospiro
Carpino Broad Beans
Ceglie Biscuit
Gargano Citrus Fruits
Gargano Podolico Caciocavallo (Cheese)
Gravina Pallone (Cheese)
Murgia Carsica Black Chickpea
Polignano Carrots
San Michele Salentino Almond-Stuffed Figs
Toritto Almond
Torre Canne Regina Tomato
Torre Guaceto Fiaschetto Tomato

SARDEGNA

Casizolu (Cheese)
Osilo Pecorino (Cheese)
Pompia
San Gavino Monreale Saffron
Shepherds' Fiore Sardo (Cheese)

SICILIA

Aci Trunzu Kohlrabi
Belìce Vastedda (Cheese)
Bilìci Valley Siccagno Tomato
Bronte Pistachio
Castelvetrano Black Bread
Ciaculli Late-Winter Mandarino
Delia Cuddrireddra
Enna Piacentinu (Cheese)
Etna Heritage Apples
Giarratana Onion
Ispica Sesame
Leonforte Broad Bean
Madonie Manna
Madonie Provola (Cheese)
Maiorchino (Cheese)
Menfi Spiny Artichoke
Minuta Olive
Modica Cottoia Broad Bean
Monreale White Plums
Nebrodi Provola (Cheese)
Noto Almond
Nùbia Red Garlic
Paceco Cartucciaru Melon
Paglina Onion of Castrofilippo

Peach in a Bag
Polizzi Generosa Badda Bean
Polizzi Generosa Pepper
Rosolini Greens
Salina Caper
Sciacca and Ribera Wild Strawberry
Scicli Cosaruciaru Bean
Scillato Apricot
Sicilian Black Bee (Honey)
Trapani Sea Salt
Ustica Broad Bean
Ustica Lentil
Villalba Lentil

TRENTINO ALTO ADIGE

Aurina Valley Graukäse (Cheese)
Bleggiana Walnut
Lagorai Malga Cheese (Cheese)
Moena Puzzone (Cheese)
Mountain Trentingrana (Cheese)
Primiero Mountain Botiro (Cheese)
Sole, Rabbi and Pejo Valleys Raw Milk
    Casolét (Cheese)
Torbole Broccoli
Trentino Vin Santo (Wines)
Venosta Valley Ur-Paarl (Bread)
Vezzena (Cheese)

TOSCANA

Artisanal Pontremoli Testarolo (Bread)
Carmignano Dried Fig

Casola Marocca (Bread)
Certaldo Onion
Garfagnana Potato Bread
Goym Sfratto
Lucca Red Bean
Maremma Raw Milk Pecorino (Cheese)
Pistoia Mountain Pecorino (Cheese)
Roccalbegna Savory Biscuit
Sorana Bean

UMBRIA

Amerino Cottòra Broad Bean
Civita di Cascia Roveja
Lake Trasimeno Bean
Trevi Black Celery
Upper Tiber Valley Smoked Vinosanto
    (Wines)

VENETO

Aged Asiago (Cheese)
Ancient Bellun Valleys Barley Cereals and
    flour
Belfiore Decio Apple
Belluna Valley Giàlet Bean
Biancoperla Corn
Custoza Broccoletto
Grappa Mountain Morlacco (Cheese)
Grumolo delle Abbadesse
Lessinia Pear Misso
Malga Monte Veronese (Cheese)
Sant'Erasmo Violet Artichoke

SOUPS

Bazzoffia / SPRING VEGETABLE SOUP

Antica Osteria Fanti, Priverno (Latina), Lazio

Serves 4

4 ARTICHOKES, PREFERABLY
ROMANESCO ARTICHOKES

1 POUND CHARD, CHOPPED

1 CUP SHELLED PEAS

3 TO 4 OUNCES FAVA BEANS
IN THE SHELLS, SHELLED AND
PEELED (ABOUT ¼ CUP)

2 SPRING ONIONS, CHOPPED

EXTRA-VIRGIN OLIVE OIL FOR
COOKING AND DRIZZLING

SALT TO TASTE

THIN SLICES
COUNTRY-STYLE BREAD

4 LARGE EGGS

GRATED AGED SHEEP'S
CHEESE FOR FINISHING

Both the town of Sezze and the town of Priverno in the Pontine Marshes (the subject of Benito Mussolini's slogan, "Drain the swamp!") lay claim to this soup. The vegetables used are flexible, but a proper *bazzoffia* always contains artichokes, preferably the Romanesco variety and if at all possible those that grow on the upper portion of the plant. This is finished in a low, wide ceramic dish, and you will need enough bread to make two layers of it in the bottom of the dish—obviously, that will vary depending on the size of the dish.

Trim the artichokes, removing any hard outer leaves and sharp tips and removing and discarding the chokes. Cut into wedges and drop into a large pot of cold water. Add the chard, peas, fava beans, and onions to the water. Drizzle in some oil, season with salt, bring to a boil, then simmer over low heat until vegetables are very tender, about 1 hour.

Meanwhile, line the bottom of a deep ceramic dish with two layers of thinly sliced bread. As soon as the vegetables are done cooking, slip the eggs into the pot with the vegetables, where they should poach in the liquid. Transfer the contents of the pot to the dish on top of the bread, taking care not to break the egg yolks. Cover with a dish towel and set aside to allow the bread to soak up the liquid. Sprinkle with a generous amount of grated cheese, drizzle on a little more oil, and serve.

Menestra de fregoloti / TINY DUMPLINGS IN MILK

Ristorante Al Vò, Trento, Trentino

Serves 6

2½ CUPS UNBLEACHED
ALL-PURPOSE FLOUR

4 CUPS WHOLE MILK

2 TABLESPOONS UNSALTED
BUTTER

SALT TO TASTE

This is a complex soup for one with such basic ingredients. Garnish with grated cheese or black truffle if desired.

Place the flour in a bowl. In a thin stream, pour in half of the milk and 2 cups cold water. Mix by hand in the bowl to create a sandy mixture with clumps the size of corn kernels. Place the remaining milk in a saucepan with 2 cups water, bring to a boil, then very gradually drizzle the flour mixture into the milk mixture, whisking constantly. Simmer over low heat for 30 minutes, whisking very gently and frequently. Stir in the butter and a pinch of salt, cook for 2 additional minutes, and serve hot.

Minestrone / VEGETABLE STEW WITH SEMOLINA PASTA

Serafina Magro, Monterosso Calabro (Vibo Valentia), Calabria

In Calabria, this simple soup is traditionally made with semolina-and-water *latieddi* pasta, but you can use a high-quality store-bought semolina pasta if you like. A 500-gram package should do the trick. Traditionally, *latieddi*, which resemble fusilli, are shaped by being wrapped around a bamboo shoot sprout. A knitting needle, skewer, or thin dowel will also work. Similar vegetable soups are made all over Italy with regional and seasonal variations.

For the pasta, shape the flour into a well on a work surface. Gradually add lukewarm water to the center of the well, stopping between additions to incorporate the flour from the sides of the well, until you have a firm but malleable dough. This will take about 1 cup water total. Energetically knead the dough until elastic and well-combined, at least 15 minutes.

Roll the dough into ropes about ½-inch wide. Cut the ropes into pieces of pasta 4 inches long and shape each piece into a spiral (they will resemble fusilli) by wrapping it around a form (see note). Set aside to dry slightly.

Blanch the chard, zucchini, potatoes, and green beans in lightly salted water until tender (the potatoes may take a little longer than the rest). Drain and set aside.

In a large pot, sauté the onion and peas in olive oil until the onion begins to brown. Add the tomatoes and cook, covered, over low heat for 10 minutes. Add the chard, zucchini, potatoes, and green beans and cook, stirring occasionally, until the vegetables are well-combined. If the pot looks dry, add a small amount of water.

Meanwhile, bring a large pot of salted water to a boil and cook the pasta al dente. Drain and add to the pot with the vegetables. Stir to combine. Remove the pot from the heat and allow it to rest, covered, before serving. Serve with grated cheese.

Serves 4 to 6

2½ CUPS SEMOLINA FLOUR

2 POUNDS SWISS CHARD, CHOPPED

2 ZUCCHINI, DICED

3 POTATOES, PEELED AND DICED

10 OUNCES GREEN BEANS, TRIMMED AND CHOPPED

SALT TO TASTE

1 YELLOW ONION, THINLY SLICED

1 CUP SHELLED PEAS

EXTRA-VIRGIN OLIVE OIL FOR SAUTÉING

5 TO 6 CHERRY OR PLUM TOMATOES, CHOPPED

GRATED AGED SHEEP'S CHEESE OR PARMIGIANO REGGIANO TO TASTE

Minestrone alla Genovese / VEGETABLE SOUP WITH PESTO

Lorenza Costa, Camogli (Genova), Liguria

Serves 4 to 6

¾ CUP FRESH SHELLED
BORLOTTI BEANS OR DRIED
BORLOTTI BEANS, SOAKED
FOR AT LEAST 12 HOURS

1 MEDIUM YELLOW ONION,
DICED

2 RIBS CELERY, DICED

3 TO 4 CELERY LEAVES

2 CARROTS, DICED

EXTRA-VIRGIN OLIVE OIL FOR
SAUTEING AND DRIZZLING

2 ZUCCHINI, DICED

2 TOMATOES, DICED

½ CUP CHOPPED
GREEN BEANS

2 POTATOES,
PEELED AND DICED

1 PIECE PARMIGIANO
REGGIANO RIND

SALT TO TASTE

2½ CUPS SMALL DRIED
SEMOLINA PASTA

3 TO 4 TABLESPOONS PESTO

GRATED PARMIGIANO
REGGIANO OR FRESHLY
GROUND BLACK PEPPER
TO TASTE

The most common type of pasta for this soup is *bricchetti*, short narrow tubes. It is also served with *scucuzzo*, which is homemade pasta made with semolina and water (nowadays, many cooks add an egg for richness). The pasta is formed by pulling off little bits of dough that you then rub between your hands to make into tiny balls, each the size of a grain of rice. The soup may be served hot, warm, or cold.

If using dried beans, drain the beans of their soaking water.

In a large soup pot, sauté the onion, celery, celery leaves, and carrots until soft, about 5 minutes. Add the beans, zucchini, tomatoes, and green beans. Add enough water to cover by several inches, cover, and cook over low heat for 1 hour, adding water in small amounts if the pot begins to dry out.

Add the potatoes and the cheese rind and cook for at least 1 additional hour. Season with salt and pepper and add the pasta. Stir to combine, then cook until the pasta is al dente. Remove the pot from the heat, stir in the pesto, and allow to rest 10 to 15 minutes (the pasta will continue to cook) before serving.

Serve hot or warm with grated cheese on the side, or serve cold with a drizzle of extra-virgin olive oil and a generous grinding of black pepper.

Frittedda / STEWED FAVA BEANS, PEAS, ARTICHOKES, AND LETTUCE

Trattoria Da Salvatore, Petralia Soprana (Palermo), Sicilia

Serves 4

JUICE OF ½ LEMON

4 ARTICHOKES

1 CLOVE GARLIC, MINCED

1 MEDIUM YELLOW ONION, DICED

EXTRA-VIRGIN OLIVE OIL FOR SAUTÉING

4½ POUNDS YOUNG FAVA BEANS IN THE POD, SHELLED (ABOUT 2½ CUPS)

2 POUNDS PEAS IN THE POD, SHELLED (ABOUT 2½ CUPS)

1 SMALL HEAD LETTUCE, CUT INTO RIBBONS

1 BUNCH WILD FENNEL FRONDS, CHOPPED

SALT AND FRESHLY GROUND BLACK PEPPER TO TASTE

Frittedda is made with early spring vegetables, which in Sicilia begin to sprout in the Madonie Mountains in the month of May, but may appear as early as March on the plains. If your fava beans are young enough, they will not need to be peeled. This dish is delicious and versatile. It can be served as a first-course soup, as an entrée, or even over pasta. Salvatore Ruvutuso, owner of Trattoria Da Salvatore in Palermo, reports that sometimes very young and tender peapods, known locally as *rubbunedda*, are included as well. This benefits from resting before being served.

Squeeze the lemon juice into a large bowl of cold water. Trim the artichokes, removing any hard outer leaves and sharp tips and removing and discarding the chokes. Cut the artichokes into wedges and drop into the lemon water.

In a large pot, sauté the garlic and onion in olive oil over low heat until soft, about 5 minutes. Add the fava beans, peas, lettuce, and fennel. Add enough water just to cover the vegetables. Cook over low heat, adding water in small amounts to keep the vegetables moist, until the vegetables are tender, about 30 minutes total (but the time will depend on how fresh and young your vegetables are). Season with salt and pepper and allow to rest for at least 15 minutes before serving.

Mosa / ENRICHED MILK SOUP

Lidia Balzanelli, Rovereto, Trentino

Serves 6

4 CUPS WHOLE MILK

SALT TO TASTE

1⅔ CUPS CORNMEAL

¾ CUP UNBLEACHED ALL-PURPOSE FLOUR

MELTED UNSALTED BUTTER TO TASTE

Some people add a little bit of sugar to this creamy soup, especially when it is being served to children. For a more adult version, sprinkle with thin slices of white or black truffle.

Combine the milk with 2 cups water in a pot and place over medium heat. Season with a pinch of salt. Whisk the all-purpose flour with a small amount of water to make a smooth paste and set aside.

When the liquid begins to boil, stir in the cornmeal and then the all-purpose flour paste. Cook over low heat, stirring very frequently, until the mixture is creamy and no longer tastes raw, 20 to 30 minutes. Drizzle with melted butter and serve.

Spatatata / ENRICHED VEGETABLE SOUP

Trattoria La Tana dell'Orso, Bolsena (Viterbo), Lazio

In order to make a simple vegetable soup into a complete meal on its own, Italians often whisk in beaten egg or grated cheese or both. Be sure to whisk briskly and constantly after you add the egg in order to avoid curdling.

In a soup pot, sauté the onion in olive oil until it begins to brown. Add the tomatoes and sauté for 2 to 3 minutes, then add the potatoes and the calamint. Season with salt and black pepper or chili pepper and add enough warm water to cover. Simmer over medium heat until potatoes are tender, 30 to 45 minutes.

While the soup is cooking, toast or grill the bread and rub the toasted bread with garlic cloves.

When the soup is cooked, whisk in the eggs and cook, stirring constantly and briskly, until thickened, 3 to 4 minutes.

Arrange the toasted bread in four individual soup plates and top with the soup. Sprinkle on a generous amount of grated cheese and drizzle with a little more oil. Serve hot.

Serves 4

1 MEDIUM YELLOW ONION, THINLY SLICED

EXTRA-VIRGIN OLIVE OIL FOR SAUTÉING AND DRIZZLING

3 TOMATOES, PEELED, SEEDED, AND CRUSHED

4 MEDIUM POTATOES, PEELED AND SLICED ABOUT ¾-INCH THICK

3 TO 4 LEAVES CALAMINT

SALT AND FRESHLY GROUND BLACK PEPPER OR CHILI PEPPER TO TASTE

DAY-OLD BREAD, SLICED

2 TO 3 CLOVES GARLIC

4 LARGE EGGS, LIGHTLY BEATEN

GRATED PARMIGIANO REGGIANO TO TASTE

Skilà / LEEK AND ONION SOUP WITH RYE BREAD

Anna Marcoz, Aosta, Valle d'Aosta

This is a simple soup that is surprisingly complex in flavor. The cheese melts when you pour the hot soup over it. Toma is a cow's milk cheese that comes in both soft and hard versions. Use a dense-crumbed dark rye bread here for best results.

Bring a large pot of salted water (6 to 8 cups) to a boil and add the potatoes, celery, garlic, onion, and leek. Simmer until the vegetables are soft and have given up their flavor, about 45 minutes.

Place a slice of bread in the bottom of each of 4 individual bowls and sprinkle with the cheese. Ladle the hot soup over the bread and cheese, adjust seasoning, and serve hot.

Serves 4

SALT TO TASTE

4 MOUNTAIN POTATOES, PEELED AND DICED

1 RIB CELERY, SLICED

2 CLOVES GARLIC

1 MEDIUM YELLOW ONION, SLICED

1 LEEK, SLICED

4 SLICES RYE BREAD

¾ CUP DICED FONTINA CHEESE

¾ CUP DICED TOMA CHEESE

FRESHLY GROUND BLACK PEPPER TO TASTE

Ciambottella / VEGETABLE STEW

Trattoria La Pergola, Gesualdo (Avellino), Campania

Serves 4 to 6

10 TO 12 OUNCES
(1 LARGE OR 2 MEDIUM)
EGGPLANT, DICED

8 OUNCES (2 MEDIUM)
ZUCCHINI, DICED

7 OUNCES (1 TO 2 MEDIUM)
RED BELL PEPPER, SEEDED
AND DICED

EXTRA-VIRGIN OLIVE OIL FOR
PAN-FRYING AND SAUTÉING

1 MEDIUM YELLOW ONION ,
THINLY SLICED

11 OUNCES (1 PINT)
CHERRY TOMATOES

2 TO 2½ POUNDS
(6 TO 8 MEDIUM) POTATOES,
PEELED AND DICED

LEAVES OF 1 SPRIG BASIL

SALT TO TASTE

Browning some of the vegetables separately before adding them to the stew helps them preserve their flavors and gives the final dish added punch.

Line a baking sheet or large platter with paper towels or butcher's paper. Pan-fry the eggplant, zucchini, and bell pepper separately, each in a couple of inches of olive oil. (Wipe out the pan and use fresh oil if you are using the same pan.) As they are nicely browned, remove them from the oil with a skimmer or slotted spoon and spread the vegetables—still separate—on the prepared pan or platter to drain further.

In a soup pot, sauté the onion over low heat in a generous amount of olive oil. When the onion has browned, remove with a slotted spoon and discard. Add the cherry tomatoes and ½ cup water and cook over high heat, stirring frequently, for 5 minutes. Add the potatoes and enough water to cover and cook, stirring frequently, until the tomatoes and potatoes have broken down, about 30 minutes. Crush the potatoes with the back of a wooden spoon if necessary. Add the eggplant, zucchini, and bell pepper along with the basil leaves. Season to taste with salt and stir gently for a few minutes to combine the flavors. Remove from the heat and let the stew cool to room temperature before serving.

Prebugiun di patate e cavolo nero / POTATO PUREE WITH KALE

Trattoria La Brinca, Ne (Genova), Liguria

The Quarantina potato variety may be white or yellow and has a brief growing cycle of only forty days. These potatoes may be hard to locate, as they grow in the Ligurian Apennines, but any non-floury potatoes with dense flesh will work here. Use your best olive oil, preferably one that also hails from Liguria.

Bring a pot of water to a boil and cook the potatoes until easily pierced with a fork. Blanch the kale and drain. With a mortar and pestle, crush the garlic with a pinch of rock salt.

Drain the potatoes and peel them as soon as they are cool enough to handle. Crush them with a potato ricer fitted with the disk with the largest holes. Mix together the kale with the crushed garlic. Place the potatoes in a soup pot and place over low heat. Add the kale and garlic mixture a little at a time, stirring to combine between additions. Stir in a generous amount of olive oil to make a creamy puree. Serve warm drizzled with additional olive oil and garnished with the sliced onions, if using.

Serves 4

1 POUND QUARANTINA POTATOES

1 BUNCH TUSCAN KALE, ABOUT 1 POUND, CUT INTO RIBBONS

2 CLOVES GARLIC

ROCK SALT TO TASTE

EXTRA-VIRGIN OLIVE OIL FOR WHIPPING AND DRIZZLING

2 RED ONIONS OR A FEW SPRING ONIONS, SLICED, OPTIONAL

Acquacotta maremmana / BREAD SOUP WITH TOMATOES

Trattoria Da Ghigo, Campiglia Marittima (Livorno), Toscana

This kind of soup is highly flexible and is meant to use leftovers. The bread for this soup should be slightly stale, but not rock hard. If you don't have slightly stale bread on hand, slice fresh bread and let it sit out for an hour or two. If you prefer, use ½ cup to 1 cup canned tomato purée in place of the fresh tomatoes.

Slice the onions and sauté them in oil in a large soup pot until they give off all of their liquid but do not turn golden. Add the celery and any celery leaves to the onions. Tear the basil leaves by hand and drop them into the pot, and then add the chili pepper and cook for 2 to 3 minutes. Add 4 cups water, salt to taste, and the pureed tomatoes. Cook over low heat for 1 hour. Just before serving, add the eggs and let them poach in the soup. To serve, toast the bread lightly. Ladle a little soup into the bottom of an individual soup bowl and place 2 slices bread on top. Ladle some more soup over them, then gently place 1 poached egg on top. Repeat with remaining bread, soup, and eggs.

Serves 6

8 RED ONIONS

EXTRA-VIRGIN OLIVE OIL FOR SAUTÉING

1 RIB CELERY, STRINGS REMOVED, STALK DICED, AND LEAVES RESERVED

LEAVES OF 1 BUNCH BASIL

1 CHILI PEPPER, MINCED

SALT TO TASTE

5 TO 6 RIPE TOMATOES, PUREED THROUGH A FOOD MILL

6 LARGE EGGS

12 SLICES BREAD

Zuppa di cetrioli / COLD CUCUMBER SOUP

Christine Richter, Merano-Meran, Alto Adige

Serves 4 to 6

11 OUNCES (2 MEDIUM) CUCUMBERS

SALT TO TASTE

1 POUND (ABOUT 4 MEDIUM) RIPE TOMATOES

1 CLOVE GARLIC

1 LARGE EGG

WHITE WINE VINEGAR TO TASTE

EXTRA-VIRGIN OLIVE OIL FOR WHISKING AND DRIZZLING

FRESHLY GROUND WHITE PEPPER TO TASTE

There are many variations of this cold soup, which is quite refreshing on a summer day. You can omit the tomatoes amd puree the cucumbers with ½ cup or so of plain yogurt and some lemon juice. Garnishing this soup with something crisp to contrast its creamy texture is always a good idea: slices of cucumber or radish are a nice addition, as are chives and other herbs.

Peel the cucumbers, cut them into thin matchsticks, and place them in a strainer. Sprinkle with salt and toss to combine, then let the cucumbers sit for 1 hour so that they give off most of their liquid.

Meanwhile, peel the tomatoes and puree them with a food mill. Mince the garlic and place it in a small sieve, then press the garlic through the sieve with a rubber spatula to extract as much liquid as possible. Discard any solids that won't pass through the sieve.

Rinse the cucumbers, pat them dry, and puree them through a food mill as well, keeping them separate from the tomatoes.

In a bowl, whisk the egg with a generous amount of vinegar, a pinch of salt, and the garlic juice. Pour in olive oil in a thin stream while whisking vigorously until the mixture thickens into mayonnaise. In a large bowl, whisk together the cucumbers and tomato purées, then whisk in the egg mixture. Chill in the refrigerator for 15 minutes. Season to taste with salt and pepper and drizzle with a little more oil just before serving.

Pappa al pomodoro / TOMATO SOUP

Enoteca La Torre di Gnicche, Arezzo, Toscana

Serves 8 to 10

2 TO 3 CLOVES GARLIC

1 CUP TIGHTLY PACKED
BASIL LEAVES

1 CARROT

1 RIB CELERY

1 MEDIUM YELLOW ONION

2 RED ONIONS, THINLY SLICED

EXTRA-VIRGIN OLIVE OIL FOR
SAUTÉING AND DRIZZLING

SALT TO TASTE

GROUND CHILI PEPPER
TO TASTE

12 OUNCES VERY RIPE
PLUM TOMATOES

8 OUNCES DAY-OLD TUSCAN
BREAD, CUT INTO CUBES

Canned and jarred tomatoes are wonderful and have many uses, but this signature of Toscana is not one of them. Prepare this only in the heart of tomato season, as the flavor of the tomatoes is of paramount importance. another culinary signature of Toscana is its salt-free bread—that is the kind that you need to use here. It is sometimes called *pane sciocco*. If you are lucky enough to get your hands on some young green garlic shoots, slice them thinly and sprinkle them on top just before serving, or for a more muted flavor add them during the final phase of cooking.

In a soup pot, combine the garlic, basil, carrot, celery, and yellow onion. (Leave the carrot, celery, and onion whole.) Add about 12 cups water, bring to a boil, and simmer until the vegetables have given up their flavor. Remove the carrot, celery, and onion and reserve for another use.

In a pot at least 4 inches high, sauté the sliced red onions in olive oil with a pinch of salt and a pinch of chili pepper. When the onion is deeply browned, crush the tomatoes by hand and let them fall into the pot. (If you prefer you can peel and puree them with a food mill.) Cook until the tomatoes are quite thick and begin to grow darker in color, 7 to 8 minutes.

Add the bread, and about half of the reserved vegetable broth along with the garlic and basil. Stir until the bread absorbs the broth and breaks down. Add the remaining broth (it will look like a lot) and smooth the surface. The solids should be submerged under liquid. Cook without stirring until the first of the "seven veils" forms on the surface. When it does, stir with a wooden spoon to break it up, then again smooth surface so that the solids are submerged under liquid. Repeat this process 6 additional times, about 30 minutes total. Drizzle with additional olive oil and serve.

Crema di peperoni / BELL PEPPER SOUP

Osteria della Sciòa, Pelago (Firenze), Toscana

Serves 4 to 6

3 YELLOW BELL PEPPERS

1 MEDIUM YELLOW ONION, SLICED

1 CLOVE GARLIC

EXTRA-VIRGIN OLIVE OIL FOR SAUTÉING AND DRIZZLING

SALT AND FRESHLY GROUND BLACK PEPPER TO TASTE

2¾ CUPS WHOLE MILK

3 TABLESPOONS UNSALTED BUTTER

⅓ CUP UNBLEACHED ALL-PURPOSE FLOUR

2½ CUPS VEGETABLE BROTH

GRATED PARMIGIANO REGGIANO TO TASTE

2 TO 3 SLICES COUNTRY BREAD, TOASTED AND CUT INTO CROUTONS

Be sure to cook the flour and butter mixture just until it turns golden and to stir constantly as you do, as it can very quickly turn too dark and impart a bitter flavor to the finished soup.

Remove the seeds and any white ribs from the peppers and combine them with the onion and garlic in a soup pot along with a moderate amount of olive oil. Season with salt and pepper and sauté over medium-low heat, covered, until the peppers soften. Add enough water just to cover the vegetables, and stew until the peppers are very soft. Add a little of the milk and puree the mixture smooth. (An immersion blender is useful for this.)

In another pot, melt the butter over low heat, then sprinkle in the flour, stirring constantly. Cook until the mixture turns golden, then stir in the pepper puree and mix to combine. Add the remaining milk and the broth and stir to combine. Continue to cook, stirring constantly, until the mixture is well-combined and heated through, about 10 minutes. Remove from the heat. Top with a drizzle of oil and the grated cheese and add the croutons just before serving.

Minestra di vrughe / CHEESE CURD SOUP

Ristorante Gikappa, Oliena (Nuoro), Sardegna

Serves 8

SALT TO TASTE

1½ POUNDS (4 TO 5 MEDIUM) POTATOES, PEELED AND DICED

1½ CUPS SMALL DRIED SEMOLINA PASTA FOR SOUP, SUCH AS DITALINI OR TUBETTINI

1 CUP CHOPPED SALTED CHEESE CURDS

To make cheese, rennet is added to milk, which causes it to coagulate. The resulting mildly flavored white blocks of not-quite-cheese are then cut up into curds. On Sardegna, those blocks are known as *vrughe*. They can be made with any type of milk, but on Sardegna they are most often made with sheep's milk. *Vrughe* are also eaten in salads with fresh tomatoes and the local super-thin flatbread. You can vary this recipe by stirring in a few spoonfuls of tomato puree.

Place 8 cups water in a pot, salt lightly, and bring to a boil. Add the potatoes to the water and simmer until tender but still firm, about 15 minutes. Add the pasta and cook until al dente, then stir in the curds and simmer until just combined, 2 to 3 minutes. Serve warm.

Crema di rape di Caprauna con amaranto /
PUREE OF CAPRAUNA TURNIPS WITH POPPED AMARANTH

Nereo Pederzolli, Cavedine (Trento), Trentino

Caprauna turnips, which have a Slow Food Presidium, grow on the border between Piemonte and Liguria in the calcium rich soil of the Upper Tanaro Valley. They are exceptionally sweet and grow to a large size. Amaranth pops like popcorn when placed over heat. Don't bother covering the pan—the amaranth should pop so quickly that you won't have time. Just use a deep pot with high sides. While raw amaranth has a pungent scent, once popped it softens to a fragrant aroma similar to that of toasted hazelnuts.

To pop the amaranth, place a pot with high sides and a thick bottom (not a nonstick pan) over medium heat until quite hot. (There is no need to add oil.) Add the amaranth about 1 tablespoon at a time. Some of the amaranth should pop immediately and turn white. Shake the pan a little over the heat and when all the amaranth has popped, immediately spread it on a plate to cool.

For the puree, steam the turnips and potatoes until soft, about 20 minutes. Meanwhile, heat the vegetable broth in a small pot. Transfer the steamed vegetables to a soup pot and add the warm vegetable broth. It should cover the vegetables, but if it doesn't, add a little more water or broth until they are submerged. Add the butter and season with salt. Bring the soup to a boil, then simmer for a few minutes to combine the flavors. Puree with an immersion blender or food mill.

Taste and adjust seasoning and serve warm with popped amaranth sprinkled on top just before serving.

Serves 4 to 6

3 TABLESPOONS AMARANTH, PREFERABLY ORGANIC

1 POUND CAPRAUNA TURNIPS, PEELED AND CHOPPED

8 OUNCES (2 MEDIUM) POTATOES, PEELED AND CHOPPED

1¾ CUPS VEGETABLE BROTH

1 TABLESPOON UNSALTED BUTTER

SALT TO TASTE

Zuppa di funghi / MUSHROOM SOUP

Nereo Pederzolli, Cavedine (Trento), Trentino

Serves 4

1 POUND PORCINI OR
CHANTERELLE MUSHROOMS

EXTRA-VIRGIN OLIVE OIL
FOR SAUTÉING

2 POTATOES, PEELED
AND DICED

1 MEDIUM YELLOW ONION,
MINCED

1 CLOVE GARLIC, MINCED

1 RIB CELERY, MINCED

2 CARROTS, MINCED

SALT AND FRESHLY GROUND
BLACK PEPPER TO TASTE

1 TABLESPOON UNSALTED
BUTTER

2 TABLESPOONS UNBLEACHED
ALL-PURPOSE FLOUR

1 CUP WHOLE MILK

VEGETABLE BROTH TO TASTE

LEAVES OF 1 SPRIG
PARSLEY MINCED

GRATED TRENTINGRANA
CHEESE TO TASTE

Fresh mushrooms are best here, but if you can't locate porcini or chanterelles, you can use another variety of mushrooms or replace them with ¼ cup dried mushrooms that you have soaked in warm water for 30 minutes to soften. If you like, you can toast some cubes of firm bread in butter and add them to the finished soup, or whisk in 2 beaten eggs at the end of cooking to make the soup more substantial.

Gently brush any loose dirt off of the mushrooms, chop them, and soak them in cold salted water for 10 minutes, then drain.

In a large pot, heat olive oil for sautéing until very hot, then add the potatoes and the onion, garlic, celery, and carrots and sauté briefly. Add cold water in small amounts (watch for splattering) and continue cooking until the potatoes give off their starch. Add the mushrooms, season with salt and pepper, and cook over low heat, stirring frequently, until both potatoes and mushrooms are very soft, about 30 minutes.

Set aside a few pieces of diced mushroom for garnish and puree the remaining mushroom mixture.

In a large pot, melt the butter over low heat and sprinkle in the flour, stirring constantly. When the mixture turns golden, add the milk and ¼ cup water. Cook, stirring constantly, for 10 minutes, then stir in the pureed mushroom mixture. Cook, stirring constantly, for 10 additional minutes, adding vegetable broth in small amounts to bring the soup to the consistency you prefer, though it should not be overly thin.

Divide the soup among individual serving dishes and garnish with the reserved mushrooms, parsley, and grated cheese.

Minestra di riso e rape / RICE AND TURNIP SOUP

Enrica Berthod, Courmayeur, Valle d'Aosta

Serves 4

4 TABLESPOONS
UNSALTED BUTTER

3 TURNIPS, PEELED AND
THINLY SLICED

1½ CUPS RICE FOR SOUP

5 CUPS VEGETABLE BROTH

SALT TO TASTE

Rice appears in many dishes in the Valle d'Aosta region. Turnips are eaten year-round in the area and are sometimes sliced and dried for long-term storage in a wine cellar or other dark, cool, dry place.

In a soup pot with a heavy bottom, melt the butter over medium heat and sauté the turnips for 2 to 3 minutes, stirring frequently. Add the rice and stir to coat with the butter, then add the broth. Simmer, stirring frequently to keep the rice from sticking, until the rice is tender. Season with salt and serve hot.

Minestra di risi e tajadele / RICE AND EGG NOODLE SOUP ▷

Edmondo Fava, Treviso, Veneto

Serves 4

6 CUPS VEGETABLE BROTH

½ MEDIUM YELLOW ONION,
MINCED

EXTRA-VIRGIN OLIVE OIL
FOR SAUTÉING

¾ CUP RICE FOR SOUP

SALT TO TASTE

¾ CUP FRESH EGG
TAGLIATELLE

GRATED GRANA PADANO
TO TASTE

Rice is a star in the cuisine of the Veneto, where it appears in risotto (which tends to be soupier than the risotto found elsewhere in Italy) and brothy soups like this one. Rice goes well with just about anything—here it is paired with fresh egg pasta. See page 108 for a basic recipe for egg noodles. You should get just the right amount of noodles from a dough made with 1 large egg and ¾ cup flour. In Italy, rice labeled as being best for soup is usually *riso originario*, white rice with short, round grains, as opposed to the *carnaroli*, *vialone nano*, and *arborio* strains that are used for risotto.

Place the broth in a small pot and keep warm. In a soup pot, sauté the onion in a generous amount of olive oil. Add the broth, about ½ cup at a time, and wait for it to return to a boil before you add the next addition. Cook, stirring frequently to keep the rice from sticking, until the rice is tender. Season with salt, then bring the broth to a boil and add the tagliatelle. Stir and cook just until the noodles rise to the surface (1 minute or less). Serve with a generous amount of grated cheese.

Minestra di pane per la ribollita / BREAD SOUP FOR RIBOLLITA

Marilena Grosso, Colle di Val d'Elsa (Siena) Toscana

Serves 4 to 6

3 ½ CUPS DRIED
CANNELLINI BEANS,
SOAKED FOR 12 HOURS

2 SPRIGS PARSLEY

3 RIBS CELERY

2 CARROTS

EXTRA-VIRGIN OLIVE OIL FOR
SAUTÉING AND DRIZZLING

2 LARGE RED ONIONS, SLICED

1 LEEK, SLICED

1 CUP CANNED PEELED
TOMATOES

1 POUND (ABOUT 3 MEDIUM)
POTATOES, PEELED
AND DICED

1 BUNCH TUSCAN KALE,
CHOPPED

½ HEAD SAVOY CABBAGE,
CHOPPED

2 POUNDS CHARD, CHOPPED

SALT AND FRESHLY GROUND
BLACK PEPPER TO TASTE

1 LOAF STALE TUSCAN
(SALTLESS) BREAD, SLICED

2 CIPOLLINI ONIONS, MINCED

This bread soup is delicious the day it is made, but the next day it can be used to make *ribollita*, a classic economical dish of Toscana that has a completely different flavor—a kind of miracle of rebirth. The bread used here must be true Tuscan bread, meaning it is unsalted. The directions below are for baking *ribollita* in the oven, but it is also frequently made on the stovetop—just simmer gently in a wide pan and be sure the bottom doesn't scorch.

Soak the beans in cold water to cover by a couple of inches for at least 12 hours. Drain, rinse and boil in water to cover with 1 sprig parsley and 1 rib celery until tender. Remove and discard celery and parsley. Reserve the beans in their cooking water.

Mince the remaining 2 ribs celery, the carrots, and the leaves of the remaining sprig parsley. In a soup pot, heat a generous amount of oil and add the red onions and leek. As soon as they begin to brown, add the minced celery, carrots, parsley, and tomatoes and cook, stirring frequently, for 2 to 3 minutes. Add the potatoes, Tuscan kale, cabbage, and chard. Cook, stirring frequently, to combine, then add water to cover. Season with salt and pepper and cook over medium-low heat for 1½ hours.

Puree about half of the cooked cannellini beans through a food mill and add the pureed beans, the whole beans, and the cooking liquid to the pot. Stir to combine, bring to a boil, and cook over very low heat for an additional 30 minutes.

In a soup tureen or other large bowl, alternate layers of the bread slices with the soup, then set aside to rest. You can serve the bread soup now, but be sure to reserve at least some to make ribollita.

The following day, transfer the bread soup to a terracotta pot. Add a little water. Drizzle with oil, season with freshly ground pepper, and sprinkle on some of the minced onions. Bake in the oven without stirring until most of the liquid has evaporated and a crust has formed on top. Drizzle with additional oil and the remaining fresh onion and serve.

Zuppa alla fontina / FONTINA CHEESE SOUP

Lina Bionaz, Saint-Christophe, Valle d'Aosta

You can use either a rustic dark rye or whole wheat bread or white bread in this soup. The number of slices will depend on the size of the pot you are using, but you will want enough to cover the bottom twice. Feel free to adjust the amount of broth to make a more or less liquid soup as well. You can also make this in individual ovenproof crocks. Set them on a baking sheet to make it easier to get them in and out of the oven.

Preheat the oven to 350°F.

Arrange half of the bread slices in the base of an ovenproof pot. Arrange half of the slices of fontina on top of the bread in a single layer. Cover with another layer of the remaining bread and then another layer of the remaining fontina. Sprinkle on the Parmigiano Reggiano and season with a generous grinding of black pepper. Gently pour the broth down the side of the pot so that it doesn't dislodge the bread and cheese. Season with a little salt (depending on how salty the broth is) and bake in the preheated oven until the cheese has melted, about 10 minutes. Serve hot.

Serves 4

SLICED DAY-OLD BREAD, TO COVER THE BOTTOM OF THE POT TWICE

7 OUNCES FONTINA CHEESE, THINLY SLICED

1 CUP GRATED PARMIGIANO REGGIANO

FRESHLY GROUND BLACK PEPPER TO TASTE

8 CUPS VEGETABLE BROTH

SALT TO TASTE

Zuppa di cipolle / ONION SOUP WITH MELTED CHEESE

La Brasserie du Bon Bec, Cogne, Valle d'Aosta

Serves 4

7 TABLESPOONS
UNSALTED BUTTER

1 POUND (3 MEDIUM) YELLOW
ONIONS, THINLY SLICED

⅓ CUP UNBLEACHED
ALL-PURPOSE FLOUR

8 CUPS VEGETABLE BROTH

SALT TO TASTE

8 SLICES COUNTRY-STYLE
BREAD

½ CUP GRATED
PARMIGIANO REGGIANO

4 OUNCES GRUYÈRE,
THINLY SLICED

Similar soups topped with a golden crust of melted cheese are served all over the Alps—both in Italy and across its borders.

Preheat the oven to 400°F.

Melt 3 tablespoons of the butter in a large pot and sauté the onions until they are golden, about 5 minutes. Sprinkle in the flour and cook, stirring constantly, until it begins to color, about 3 minutes. Add the broth and simmer for 15 minutes. Season with salt.

Brown the bread slices in the remaining butter (bread absorbs a lot of fat as it cooks, so you may want to add a little butter to the pan at a time if you can't fit all the bread in a single layer and have to work in batches) and arrange the bread slices in a baking dish. Ladle the soup over the bread and sprinkle on the grated Parmigiano Reggiano. Arrange the slices of Gruyère in a single layer on top, overlapping slightly if necessary.

Bake in the preheated oven until a browned crust forms on top, about 15 minutes. Serve hot.

Spisuculöch / POTATO AND MILK SOUP WITH TORN PASTA

Rita Panelatti, Praso, Trentino

The word *spisuculöch* means "torn by hand," and the irregular size and shape of the pieces of pasta here is part of the dish's appeal. Spressa is a semi-hard alpine cheese made from partially skimmed cow's milk.

Melt the butter in a large pot. Sauté the onion and potatoes for a few minutes, then add 4 cups water, season with salt, and bring to a boil.

Meanwhile, combine the flour with the egg yolk and a pinch of salt to make a dough. With a rolling pin, roll out to a sheet of dough a little less than ¼ inch thick. Tear into small pieces.

When the potatoes are tender, add the pieces of pasta to the pot. Cook, stirring frequently, for an additional 5 minutes.

Stir in the milk and the grated cheese, then remove from the heat and serve piping hot.

Serves 4

1 TABLESPOON UNSALTED BUTTER

1 MEDIUM YELLOW ONION, DICED

2 POTATOES, PEELED AND DICED

SALT TO TASTE

1¼ CUPS UNBLEACHED ALL-PURPOSE FLOUR

1 EGG YOLK

2 CUPS WHOLE MILK

½ CUP GRATED SPRESSA CHEESE

Cucina / BEAN AND CABBAGE SOUP

Ristorante Il Passeggero, Massa, Toscana

Serves 4 to 6

2 CUPS DRIED BORLOTTI
BEANS, SOAKED OVERNIGHT

3⅓ POUNDS WILD GREENS
AND HERBS, SUCH AS
DANDELION, WILD FENNEL,
WILD LEEK, BORAGE,
MILK THISTLE, RAMPION,
PIMPINELLA, PRIMROSE,
DAISIES, VIOLETS, AND MORE

½ HEAD SAVOY CABBAGE,
CUT INTO RIBBONS

SALT TO TASTE

TOASTED SLICES OF
DAY-OLD BREAD

EXTRA-VIRGIN OLIVE OIL
FOR DRIZZLING

FRESHLY GROUND BLACK
PEPPER TO TASTE

This soup uses a mix of greens and herbs that is also called *cucina*. In the town of Massa, the market has stalls selling large bouquets of the mix. Always clean wild greens and herbs extremely carefully.

Drain the beans and boil them until soft. While the beans are cooking, prepare the greens and herbs: you will want to use the leaves of some and the bulbs of others.

Puree the cooked beans through a food mill and transfer to a soup pot. Thin the puree with water, then stir in the wild greens and herbs and the cabbage. Add more water to make a brothy mixture, bring to a boil, and simmer, stirring frequently, until thoroughly combined and thickened, about 1 hour. Taste and adjust salt.

Serve with the toasted bread, a generous drizzle of olive oil, and some black pepper.

Erbuzzu / WILD GREENS, BEANS, AND CHEESE CURD SOUP

Ristorante Santa Rughe, Gavoi (Nuoro), Sardegna

This soup is eaten widely on Sardegna. Leftovers improve with age and may be served at room temperature. A true *erbuzzu* will include at least 15 different types of wild herbs and greens, which grow in abundance on the banks of rivers on the island. Depending on the season, the mix may include wild garlic, brighteyes (a kind of dandelion), sorrel, wild fennel, wild sea beet, cress, wild chicory, wild carrot, black radish, sow thistle, cotton lavender, and bladder campion. Aim for a good balance of sweet and bitter herbs, and keep in mind that some are quite strong and may overwhelm the more meek choices. For the beans, choose a type of medium size, such as borlotti beans.

Place the beans in a bowl, add cold water to cover by a couple of inches, and soak for 10 to 12 hours.

When you are ready to make the soup, chop the wild herbs and greens. Place them in a large pot with 8 to 12 cups cold water and a pinch of salt. Bring to a boil, then turn down to a simmer and cook for 2 hours.

Drain the beans and add them to the pot. Cook until the beans are tender, about 45 additional minutes. Season with salt.

To serve, divide the soup among individual serving plates and top each serving with some of the cheese curds. Serve immediately.

Serves 6

1 CUP DRIED BEANS

4½ POUNDS WILD HERBS AND GREENS (SEE NOTE)

1 CUP CHOPPED SALTED CHEESE CURDS (SEE PAGE 30) OR GRATED AGED SHEEP'S CHEESE

SALT TO TASTE

Ceci e castagne / CHICK PEA AND CHESTNUT PUREE

Celestino Mariani, Castellafiume (L'Aquila), Abruzzo

Serves 4 to 6

2 CUPS DRIED CHICKPEAS

14 OUNCES (ABOUT 2⅓ CUPS)
DRIED CHESTNUTS

2 TO 3 CLOVES GARLIC

1 SPRIG ROSEMARY

1 BAY LEAF

3 TABLESPOONS
EXTRA-VIRGIN OLIVE OIL

SALT TO TASTE

This is the perfect autumn/winter soup and indeed is often served in the mountains of Abruzzo to celebrate Christmas Eve. Dried chestnuts are delicious and very handy to keep in your cupboard. They are best if soaked before cooking and pair especially well with legumes. Dried chestnuts are available in gourmet specialty stores. This is delicious with some toasted bread on the side.

The night before you plan to make the soup, soak the chickpeas in cold water to cover by a couple of inches. Soak the dried chestnuts in warm water for 8 to 10 hours as well.

Drain the chickpeas. Place the chickpeas in a soup pot, add enough water to cover by several inches, bring to a boil, and simmer until chickpeas are soft but not falling apart, about 2 hours. Drain and add the chestnuts, garlic, rosemary, bay leaf, oil, and a pinch of salt. Cook for 10 additional minutes, stirring frequently. Remove the rosemary and bay leaf and puree to the desired consistency with an immersion blender, holding back some whole chickpeas and chestnuts and a few rosemary leaves for garnish if you like.

Caulada vegetariana / FAVA, CABBAGE, FENNEL, AND BORAGE SOUP

Michele Ruzzu, Nulvi (Sassari), Sardegna

Serves 4

2 CUPS DRIED FAVA BEANS

3 STALKS WILD FENNEL

1 BUNCH BORAGE

1 POUND SAVOY CABBAGE,
CUT INTO RIBBONS

1 CHILI PEPPER, MINCED
(OPTIONAL)

SALT TO TASTE

4 SLICES DAY-OLD BREAD

Wild fennel has a stronger personality than the cultivated kind. To prepare fennel bulbs for cooking, remove and discard the outer "petals." The cooking time for dried fava beans can vary—if yours have been sitting on the shelf for a while, they may take longer than 1 hour total. Aim to add the fennel, borage, and cabbage to the pot about halfway through the cooking time.

Soak the beans in water to cover by several inches for at least 8 hours. Drain the beans and use a paring knife to cut off the small black dot on each one. Chop the fennel fronds and set aside. Trim the bulbs and cut them in half.

Place the fava beans in a large pot with a generous amount of water (8 to 10 cups) and bring to a boil. Turn down to a simmer and cook for about 30 minutes, then stir in the fennel, borage, Savoy cabbage, and chili pepper, if using. Season with salt and cook until beans are tender, about 30 additional minutes. To serve, place the bread slices in individual soup bowls and ladle the soup over them.

Zuppa di lenticchie / LENTIL SOUP

Trattoria Da Umberto, Ustica (Palermo), Sicilia

Ustica lentils are small, dark lentils that grow on the volcanic island of Ustica in the Tyrrhenian Sea, north of the island of Sicilia. They are planted and harvested almost entirely by hand and have their own Slow Food Presidium. This recipe includes summer vegetables, but the peppers, tomatoes, and zucchini can easily be replaced with winter vegetables, such as carrots, celery, and potatoes, when the seasons change, and celery leaves can stand in for the basil. Either serve this with slices of grilled or toasted bread, or break spaghetti into 2-inch lengths and cook it directly in the soup once the lentils are soft.

In a large pot combine the lentils, zucchini, bell peppers, tomatoes, onion, and basil with 4 cups water. Drizzle in some olive oil and bring to a boil, then turn down to a simmer and cook until the lentils have reached the desired consistency, about 45 minutes if you like them just tender, but closer to an hour if you prefer the lentils broken down into a creamier version. If the pot seems to be drying out before the lentils are cooked, add hot water in small amounts. When the lentils are cooked (and not before), season with salt.

Serves 4 to 6

2½ CUPS USTICA LENTILS

4 ZUCCHINI, CHOPPED

2 BELL PEPPERS, SEEDED AND CHOPPED

2 TOMATOES, PEELED, SEEDED, AND CHOPPED

1 LARGE YELLOW ONION, CHOPPED

LEAVES OF 1 SPRIG BASIL, TORN

EXTRA-VIRGIN OLIVE OIL FOR DRIZZLING

SALT TO TASTE

SALADS AND COMPOSED VEGETABLE DISHES

Insalata di sedano rapa e mele / APPLE AND CELERIAC SALAD

Baita Ermitage, Courmayeur, Valle d'Aosta

Serves 4

1 MEDIUM BULB CELERIAC,
ABOUT 12 OUNCES

1 TABLESPOON
WHITE VINEGAR

SALT TO TASTE

2 LARGE EGGS

JUICE OF ½ LEMON

EXTRA-VIRGIN OLIVE OIL,
FOR MAKING MAYONNAISE

2 DELIZIA
VALDOSTANA APPLES

½ CUP WALNUTS, CHOPPED

Celery root or celeriac is a round off-white root with a sweet flavor. It can be served cooked, as it is here, or raw. The vinegar in the cooking water keeps it from discoloring. *Delizia valdostana* apples are sweet and quite firm. Any crisp (not mealy) variety will work as a substitute.

Peel the celeriac, cut away and discard any woody core, and cut into julienne.

Bring a pot of water to a boil and add the vinegar and salt lightly. Boil the celery root until just tender but still crisp in the center. Set aside to cool for at least 1 hour.

In the meantime, to make a mayonnaise, in a medium bowl beat the eggs with a pinch of salt and the lemon juice, then add a generous amount of oil in a thin stream while whisking constantly until thickened.

Peel and core the apples and thinly slice them. In a bowl, toss the apple slices, the celery root, and the mayonnaise and stir to combine. Garnish the salad with chopped walnuts just before serving.

Insalata di barbabietole / BEET SALAD WITH YOGURT DRESSING

Lucia Bisiach, Monfalcone (Gorizia), Friuli Venezia Giulia

Serves 4 to 6

¾ CUP WHOLE
SHEEP'S MILK YOGURT

1 CLOVE GARLIC, CRUSHED

2 TABLESPOONS
WHITE WINE VINEGAR

SALT AND FRESHLY GROUND
WHITE PEPPER TO TASTE

4 SMALL BEETS,
STEAMED AND DICED

MESCLUN FOR SERVING

CUMIN SEEDS TO TASTE
(OPTIONAL)

If you purchase the vacuum-packed cooked beets available in most grocery stores these days, this salad can be ready in a matter of minutes, but even if you steam the beets yourself, it's not terribly time-consuming. It is a refreshing choice for a hot day, and the beautiful fuchsia color is always striking. In addition to or in place of the cumin seeds, you can also garnish this salad with some crumbled feta or other cheese.

In a large bowl, whisk together the yogurt, garlic, and vinegar. Season with salt and pepper. Add the beets and toss to combine. Arrange the mesclun in a bed on a serving platter or individual salad plates and arrange the beets on top of the mesclun. Garnish with cumin seeds, if using, and serve immediately.

Insalata Russa / MIXED VEGETABLE SALAD WITH MAYONNAISE

Ristorante La Salita, Monforte d'Alba (Cuneo), Piemonte

Don't let the name fool you: "Russian salad" is, confusingly, one of the signature dishes of Piemonte. There is a strong French influence in this region, and in the late 1800s and early 1900s, when many wealthy Russians were moving to Paris, deeming something "Russian" indicated that it was luxurious. That practice seems to have informed the curious name of this substantial dish.

Cook the potatoes, carrots, celery, bell peppers, and peas separately in lightly salted boiling water—just enough to cover the vegetables—until just tender and drain. Bring a fresh pot of water to a boil, add the cloves, the vinegar, and the sugar, and cook the zucchini and the green beans until tender as well. Drain vegetables well and set aside to cool.

To make a mayonnaise, in a large bowl beat the egg yolks with a pinch of salt and the lemon juice. Add the oil in a thin stream while whisking constantly. Fold the cooked and cooled vegetables into the mayonnaise and stir until evenly distributed. Transfer the mixture to a serving platter and garnish with olives and parsley.

Serves 4 to 6

8 POTATOES, PEELED AND DICED

4 CARROTS, DICED

4 RIBS CELERY, DICED

1 RED BELL PEPPER, DICED

1 YELLOW BELL PEPPER, DICED

¼ CUP SHELLED PEAS

SALT TO TASTE

3 TO 4 WHOLE CLOVES

2 TABLESPOONS WHITE WINE VINEGAR

2 TABLESPOONS SUGAR

4 ZUCCHINI, DICED

¼ CUP CHOPPED GREEN BEANS

3 EGG YOLKS

JUICE OF 1 LEMON

2 CUPS EXTRA-VIRGIN OLIVE OIL

⅔ CUP TUNA IN OLIVE OIL, DRAINED

¼ CUP TAGGIASCA OLIVES

¼ CUP MINCED PARSLEY

Insalata di crauti / SAUERKRAUT SALAD

Ristorante Martinelli, Ronzo-Chienis, Trentino

Serves 4 to 6

1 POUND SAUERKRAUT

SALT AND FRESHLY GROUND
BLACK PEPPER TO TASTE

GROUND CUMIN TO TASTE

1 GREEN APPLE

If you want to make your own sauerkraut (a common ingredient in the Trentino region, which was part of Austria-Hungary for many years), you will have to plan in advance: the fermentation process takes about four weeks. If not, look for organic sauerkraut fermented in a wooden barrel. The difference in taste and quality will be significant. The same is true of toasting and grinding your own cumin seeds.

Drain the sauerkraut of most of its liquid, but do not dry it out entirely. Place in a salad bowl and season with salt, pepper, and a pinch of cumin. Core, peel, and dice the apple and toss it with the sauerkraut. Serve immediately.

Insalata di cavolo cappuccio / GREEN CABBAGE SALAD

Ristorante Martinelli, Ronzo-Chienis, Trentino

Serves 4

1 POUND (2 MEDIUM HEADS)
GREEN CABBAGE

EXTRA-VIRGIN OLIVE OIL
FOR DRESSING AND FOR
CROUTONS

SALT AND FRESHLY GROUND
BLACK PEPPER TO TASTE

STALE BREAD FOR CROUTONS

Seek out an olive oil that hails from the shores of Lake Garda (the northern portion of the lake is located in Trentino) for this dish.

Remove the outer leaves from the cabbage and cut into quarters. Remove the hard cores and cut the leaves into thin ribbons. Arrange the cabbage in a salad bowl, dress with oil, salt, and a pinch of pepper.

Cut the bread into small cubes. In a pan over medium heat, toss the bread cubes in a small amount of olive oil until toasted. Sprinkle the bread over the salad and serve.

Insalata di verdure e fromadzo / SALAD WITH FROMADZO CHEESE

Ristorante Capanna Carla, Gressoney-la-Trinité, Valle d'Aosta

Back in the days when commerce was more complicated than it is now, obtaining olive oil in Valle d'Aosta was not simple—it had to be brought in from Liguria, from Provence, or from the shores of Lake Maggiore in Piemonte and Lombardia, and the journey was arduous. As a result, in this part of Italy there is a long tradition of using either walnut oil or cream to dress salads. Fromadzo is a cheese from the southern part of the Valle d'Aosta region made using partially skimmed cow's milk and sometimes flavored with herbs. It is lightly aged and dotted with small holes. You can use a different mild cow's milk cheese in its stead. Naturally, you can also vary this recipe by replacing the basil with a different aromatic herb or swapping in other vegetables of your choosing.

Cut the radishes into quarters or eighths, depending on their size. Cut the lettuce into ribbons and thinly slice the carrots and onions. Tear the basil leaves. Combine the vegetables and the basil in a salad bowl and toss to combine. Sprinkle the cheese on top, then either crumble the egg yolk by hand or force it through a sieve and add that as well.

To make the dressing, in a small bowl, whisk the cream and lemon juice. Season with salt and pepper and pour the dressing over the salad. Toss to combine and serve.

Serves 4

6 RADISHES

1 SMALL HEAD LETTUCE

4 CARROTS, THINLY SLICED

2 SPRING ONIONS OR YOUNG LEEKS

LEAVES OF 1 SPRIG BASIL

1¾ CUPS DICED OR CRUMBLED FROMADZO CHEESE

1 HARD-BOILED EGG YOLK

½ CUP HEAVY CREAM OR WHIPPING CREAM

JUICE OF 1 LEMON

SALT AND FRESHLY GROUND WHITE PEPPER TO TASTE

Insalata di bucce di piselli / PEA POD SALAD

Antonella Iadevaia, Cuneo, Piemonte

It should go without saying that you should use pea pods for this salad that have not been treated with pesticides. This is a fine example of Italy's longstanding tradition of zero-waste cooking.

Remove the strings from pea pods. Bring a large pot of salted water to a boil, add the peapods, and boil until tender, 3 to 4 minutes. Drain the pea pods in a colander. When they are cool enough to handle, pat them dry. Make a vinaigrette with extra-virgin olive oil, wine vinegar, and a pinch of salt. Stir in the garlic. Whisk to combine, then pour the vinaigrette over the pea pods and toss to combine.

Serves 6

1 POUND PEA PODS

EXTRA-VIRGIN OLIVE OIL FOR DRESSING

WINE VINEGAR FOR DRESSING

SALT TO TASTE

1 CLOVE GARLIC, MINCED

Insalata di cavolo rosso / RED CABBAGE SALAD

Adelaide Vaccaroni, Udine, Friuli Venezia Giulia

V

Serves 4 to 6

1 MEDIUM HEAD RED CABBAGE

SALT TO TASTE

1 ORANGE

EXTRA-VIRGIN OLIVE OIL,
FOR DRESSING

1 REINETTE APPLE

1 SMALL YELLOW ONION OR
SHALLOT, MINCED

RED WINE VINEGAR (OPTIONAL)

FRESHLY GROUND BLACK
PEPPER TO TASTE

Look for an organic orange with an unwaxed rind since you will be using the zest. You will want about 1 pound of cabbage once it is trimmed and cored, so plan accordingly.

Remove the outer leaves from the cabbage and cut into quarters. Remove the hard cores and cut the leaves into thin ribbons. Place in a bowl, salt lightly, toss, and set aside to rest.

Grate the orange zest and juice the orange. Whisk together zest, juice, and a small amount of olive oil to make a dressing. Peel and core the apple and grate it on the largest holes of a four-sided grater and combine with the dressing. Stir in the onion and a little red wine vinegar for extra acidity if you like, and season with a pinch of pepper. Lift the cabbage out of the bowl where it has been resting, leaving behind any liquid that has collected, and place it in a clean bowl. Dress, toss to combine, and serve.

Insalata di cavolfiore / SALAD OF CAULIFLOWER, CAPERS, AND OLIVES

Mario Carpentieri, Napoli, Campania

V

Serves 4

1 MEDIUM HEAD
CAULIFLOWER

SALT TO TASTE

1 TABLESPOON CAPERS

1 BELL PEPPER PRESERVED
IN VINEGAR

12 BLACK OLIVES, PITTED

EXTRA-VIRGIN OLIVE OIL
FOR DRESSING

WHITE WINE VINEGAR
FOR DRESSING

Clean cauliflower florets thoroughly—some grit can easily hide in the crevices. This salad can be served warm or at room temperature, but dress it right after the cauliflower is cooked, as warm cauliflower will blend with the other flavors and absorb the vinaigrette.

Divide the cauliflower into florets. Bring a large pot of salted water to a boil and cook the cauliflower until tender and easily pierced with a knife. Do not undercook. Meanwhile, rinse and drain the capers and drain the preserved bell pepper and cut it into strips. Place the olives (chopped if large), capers, and peppers in a large bowl. Prepare a vinaigrette with oil and vinegar. When the cauliflower is cooked, remove with a slotted spoon and add to the bowl. Dress with the prepared vinaigrette and toss gently to combine, then serve.

Toss the warm cauliflower with a dressing of oil and vinegar, the olives, the capers, the anchovies, and the pepper. Toss gently to combine and serve.

Tarassaco, mele ed erba cipollina /
SALAD OF DANDELION, APPLE, AND CHIVES
Osteria Bohemia, Soliera (Modena), Emilia-Romagna

Serves 4 to 6

1 BUNCH DANDELION

1 BUNCH CHIVES

3 APPLES

JUICE OF ½ LEMON

EXTRA-VIRGIN OLIVE OIL
FOR DRESSING

SALT TO TASTE

16 BORAGE FLOWERS

Choose young, tender dandelion for this salad. The greens are foraged in the wild in many parts of Italy.

Set aside a few whole dandelion leaves and chives for garnish, then cut the remaining dandelion leaves into ribbons and snip the chives. Peel, quarter, and core the apples and cut into thin slices. Arrange the apple slices in a salad bowl and drizzle the lemon juice over them to stop discoloration. Toss gently, then add the dandelion and the scallions.

Dress with oil and salt and toss gently. Divide the salad between individual salad plates and garnish with the reserved dandelion and chives and the borage flowers.

Insalata di arance / SLICED ORANGE SALAD
Trattoria U Locale, Buccheri (Siracusa), Sicilia

Serves 4 to 6

4 TO 6 ORANGES

1 SPRING ONION, VERY
THINLY SLICED

EXTRA-VIRGIN OLIVE OIL
FOR DRESSING

MINCED FRESH OREGANO
LEAVES TO TASTE

SALT AND FRESHLY GROUND
BLACK PEPPER TO TASTE

Citrus of all kinds grows on the island of Sicilia. For this salad, you can use blood oranges or any other variety. If you have a hard time obtaining fresh oregano, used chopped flat-leaf parsley in its place. This salad can also include thinly sliced fennel, chopped sun-dried tomatoes, or olives.

Peel the oranges and slice them thinly, discarding the membranes and any seeds. Cut the orange flesh into cubes. Place the orange cubes in a salad bowl and toss with the onion. Dress with a generous pour of olive oil. Add the oregano, season with salt and pepper, and toss to combine. Let the salad rest for 15 minutes at room temperature before serving.

Insalata di castraure / RAW ARTICHOKE SALAD

Trattoria Cortevecchia, Polesella (Rovigo), Veneto

The island of Sant'Erasmo in the Venice lagoon is home to a special variety of purple artichokes that develop a naturally saline flavor and have their own Slow Food Presidium. This salad uses the earliest baby artichokes, harvested at the start of the season. At that stage, they are so tender that you can even leave out the parsley and garlic and simply dress them with oil, salt, and pepper so that their flavor really takes center stage.

Trim the artichokes of any spiky tips, peel the stems, and cut them into julienne. Whisk together the lemon juice, a small amount of olive oil, the garlic, and about half of the minced parsley. Season with salt and pepper and toss with the artichokes until well-combined. Arrange the artichokes on a serving platter and garnish with the cheese shavings and remaining parsley.

Serves 4

8 SANT'ERASMO OR OTHER BABY ARTICHOKES

JUICE OF ¼ LEMON

EXTRA-VIRGIN OLIVE OIL FOR DRESSING

2 CLOVES GARLIC, MINCED

2 TABLESPOONS MINCED FLAT-LEAF PARSLEY

SALT AND FRESHLY GROUND BLACK PEPPER TO TASTE

GRANA PADANO CHEESE SHAVINGS TO TASTE

Insalata di cetrioli / CUCUMBER SALAD

Christine Richter, Merano-Meran, Alto Adige

Use the freshest cucumbers you can find in this summer salad—their crunch and delicate flavor are essential to its success. If you prefer, you can dress this salad with a combination of sour cream, pepper, and paprika, or a dressing of yogurt, mint, and minced garlic.

Peel the cucumbers and cut them into thin slices. Spread the cucumber slices in a single layer on a rack set over a bowl or in the sink and salt them. Let them sit until their bitter liquid has drained off, about 1 hour.

Rinse the cucumber slices, pat them dry, and transfer to a bowl. Make a vinaigrette by whisking oil, vinegar, and a little salt together. Dress the cucumbers with the vinaigrette. Season with paprika and white pepper and serve immediately.

Serves 4 to 6

4 TO 6 CUCUMBERS

SALT TO TASTE

EXTRA-VIRGIN OLIVE OIL FOR DRESSING

WHITE WINE VINEGAR FOR DRESSING

1 PINCH PAPRIKA

FRESHLY GROUND WHITE PEPPER TO TASTE

Insalata di fave cottoia / FAVA AND CELERY SALAD WITH WILD OREGANO

Trattoria La Rusticana, Modica (Ragusa), Sicilia

Serves 4 to 6

1 POUND DRIED
COTTOIA FAVA BEANS

SALT TO TASTE

1 RIB CELERY, DICED

1 PINCH GROUND
CHILI PEPPER

1 TEASPOON MINCED
WILD OREGANO LEAVES

EXTRA-VIRGIN OLIVE OIL
FOR DRESSING

RED WINE VINEGAR
FOR DRESSING

Not only do cottoia fava beans have their own Slow Food Presidium, but there is a confraternity devoted to them as well. The beans—harvested in May, but available in dried form year-round—were once rotated with grain crops in the fields around Modica, as they had the benefit of fixing nitrogen in the soil. Today this heirloom variety is being reintroduced in the area. You can use standard dried fava beans if the cottoia variety are not available near you.

Use the tip of a pairing knife to cut away the black spot on the tip of each bean, then soak the beans in water to cover by several inches for about 10 hours.

Drain the beans and rinse under running water. In a large pot, bring a generous amount of water to a boil, and cook the beans for 30 minutes. Drain the beans and add fresh warm water to the pot. Add the beans. Salt, bring to a boil, and cook the fava beans until some of their skins split and they are tender, about 30 minutes.

Drain the beans in a colander, then transfer them to a bowl. Add the celery, chili pepper, and oregano. Make a vinaigrette with olive oil and vinegar (not too heavy on the vinegar), stir to combine, and dress the beans with the vinaigrette. Allow to rest at room temperature for about 10 minutes before serving.

Insalata di zucchine e pinoli / ZUCCHINI AND PINE NUT SALAD

Trattoria Antica Cereria, Parma, Emilia-Romagna

Serves 4

1 POUND BABY ZUCCHINI,
THINLY SLICED INTO ROUNDS

¾ CUP PINE NUTS

1 CUP PARMIGIANO
REGGIANO SHAVINGS

2 TABLESPOONS
BALSAMIC VINEGAR

½ CUP EXTRA-VIRGIN OLIVE OIL

SALT TO TASTE

For a different version, the zucchini for this salad can also be steamed briefly until just al dente. Seek out true balsamic vinegar from Modena for this dish.

In a bowl, combine the zucchini, pine nuts, and Parmigiano Reggiano. Gently mix to combine.

With a fork whisk together the vinegar, olive oil, and a pinch of salt to make a dressing. Dress the salad, toss it gently, and then let it sit for about 15 minutes before serving.

Insalata di primavera / WILD GREENS SALAD

Rosina Idrame, San Damiano d'Asti (Asti), Piemonte

Look for the most tender wild greens you can find for this salad. Common choices in Italy include mâche, dandelion, rampion, watercress, arugula, and chervil, but anything you like will work. Always dress the salad just before serving, and go easy on the vinaigrette so that the disparate flavors of the greens you've chosen have a chance to shine.

Tear the lettuce and greens into a salad bowl. In a small bowl, combine oil and vinegar with a pinch of salt and whisk to make a vinaigrette. Add the vinaigrette to the salad, toss to coat the leaves, then snip the chives into the salad and toss again. Serve immediately.

Serves 6

4 SMALL HEADS LETTUCE

4 CUPS FORAGED GREENS

EXTRA-VIRGIN OLIVE OIL FOR DRESSING

RED WINE VINEGAR FOR DRESSING

SALT TO TASTE

1 BUNCH CHIVES

Insalata di cuscus / COUSCOUS SALAD

Marina Bendico, Capoterra (Cagliari), Sardegna

Couscous, a semolina pasta of fine pellets, is eaten widely on the west side of Sicily and the southwest side of Sardegna. The couscous we buy in the supermarket today is precooked couscous, meaning it has been steamed and dried. It therefore cooks very quickly when you add boiling liquid to it.

Heat a small amount of oil in a skillet and sauté the garlic until it turns golden, then remove and discard. Add the onions, carrots, and zucchini. Cook over low heat, stirring occasionally, for 5 minutes. Add the tomatoes and immediately remove from the heat.

Place the couscous in a heatproof bowl. Stir in 1 cup boiling water. Cover the bowl with plastic wrap and set aside to rest for 5 minutes. With a fork, break up any clumps of couscous, then cover again and set aside to rest for 5 additional minutes. The couscous should be tender and should have absorbed all of the liquid. Stir in the vegetables, add a drizzle of olive oil, a pinch of salt, and the basil leaves and serve at room temperature.

Serves 4 to 6

EXTRA-VIRGIN OLIVE OIL FOR SAUTÉING AND DRESSING

1 CLOVE GARLIC

2 SPRING ONIONS, THINLY SLICED

2 TO 3 CARROTS, CUT INTO JULIENNE

2 TO 3 ZUCCHINI, CUT INTO JULIENNE

4 TO 5 CHERRY TOMATOES, QUARTERED

1 CUP COUSCOUS

SALT TO TASTE

3 TO 4 LEAVES BASIL

Insalata di farro e verdure / VEGETABLE SALAD WITH FARRO

Locanda dell'Arte, Città Sant'Angelo (Pescara), Abruzzo

Serves 4 to 6

1 TABLESPOON WHITE
WINE VINEGAR

1 RED BELL PEPPER, SEEDED
AND CUT INTO JULIENNE

1 YELLOW BELL PEPPER,
SEEDED AND CUT INTO
JULIENNE

¼ CUP SHELLED PEAS

¼ CUP SLICED MUSHROOMS

2 CARROTS, CUT INTO
JULIENNE

3 SMALL ARTICHOKES,
TRIMMED AND CUT
INTO WEDGES

1 RIB CELERY,
CUT INTO JULIENNE

ABOUT 8 CUPS
VEGETABLE BROTH

1 MEDIUM YELLOW
ONION, MINCED

1 CLOVE GARLIC, MINCED

EXTRA-VIRGIN OLIVE OIL FOR
SAUTÉING AND DRESSING

1 CUP PEARLED FARRO

½ CUP WHITE WINE

½ CUP PITTED OLIVES

¼ CUP CAPERS,
RINSED AND DRAINED

2 TOMATOES,
CUT INTO WEDGES

1 CUCUMBER, PEELED
AND CUT INTO JULIENNE

LEAVES OF 1 SPRIG BASIL

SALT TO TASTE

This recipe is endlessly adaptable, so feel free to use what you have on hand. Farro is emmer wheat. It may be ground into flour, which is used to make pasta, bread, and other items, or eaten whole. Farro has existed since Etruscan times and has enjoyed a resurgence in popularity in Italy in recent years.

Bring a large pot of water to a boil. Add the vinegar. Cook separately (because each will have a different cooking time) until tender the peppers, peas, mushrooms, carrots, artichokes, and celery. Drain and set aside.

Place the broth in a small pot, bring to a boil, then turn down to a simmer. In a pot, cook the onion and garlic in olive oil over low heat. When they begin to color, add the farro and cook, stirring frequently, until it begins to toast. Add the wine and continue to cook until the liquid has evaporated. Begin to add the broth, about ½ cup at a time, stirring until incorporated between additions, until the farro is cooked al dente. You may not need all of the broth, or you may run low before the farro is cooked, in which case you can use hot water to finish cooking.

Allow the farro mixture to cool and when it has cooled, transfer it to a large bowl and combine with the cooked vegetables. Dress with additional olive oil. Toss with the olives and capers, then add the tomatoes and cucumber and tear and scatter on the basil leaves. Season with salt and serve.

Patate voiani e cucuzzedja /
BEANS, SQUASH, AND POTATOES WITH GARLICKY DRESSING

Luisa San le, Monterosso Calabro (Vibo Valentia), Calabria

Cucuzzedja is a long pale green squash (technically a gourd). Voiani beans are flat beans, meaning the outer pod is edible as well. Both vegetables are popular throughout Southern Italy.

Bring a large pot of salted water to a boil. Add the potatoes and cook until tender but still firm, then add the beans and cook until those are tender but still firm, and, finally, add the squash and cook until all three are completely tender. Drain the vegetables. Crush the potatoes and dice the squash while still warm, and in a bowl combine the potatoes and squash with the beans (left whole). For the dressing, combine the garlic with some olive oil and season with salt and chili pepper, if using. Pour the dressing over the warm vegetables. Toss gently to combine. Serve at room temperature.

Serves 4

SALT TO TASTE

3 TO 4 POTATOES, PEELED

2 POUNDS VOIANI FLAT BEANS OR OTHER FLAT BEANS, TRIMMED

2 POUNDS CUCUZZEDJA OR OTHER SQUASH, TRIMMED

2 CLOVES GARLIC, CRUSHED

EXTRA-VIRGIN OLIVE OIL FOR DRESSING

1 CHILI PEPPER, MINCED (OPTIONAL)

Panzanella / BREAD SALAD WITH RIPE TOMATOES

Ristorante Il Carlino d'Oro, Gaiole in Chianti (Siena), Toscana

V

Serves 4 to 6

2 POUNDS (1 LARGE LOAF OR
ABOUT 8 CUPS LARGE CUBES)
STALE BREAD

5 TOMATOES,
PEELED AND DICED

2 MEDIUM ONIONS, MINCED

LEAVES OF 1 SPRIG BASIL

EXTRA-VIRGIN OLIVE OIL
FOR DRESSING

WHITE WINE VINEGAR
FOR DRESSING

SALT TO TASTE

Stuffed zucchini blossoms are the perfect accompaniment to panzanella and are available in the same season. Clean the blossoms, pinch out their pistils, and place a cube of mozzarella in each one. Twist the ends closed. In a small bowl, combine 1 cup unbleached all-purpose flour, 1 large egg, and ⅓ cup crushed ice. Whisk in enough water to make a batter with the consistency of sour cream, then dredge the blossoms in that batter and fry them in hot oil.

Fill a large bowl with water and soak the bread for about 20 minutes. Squeeze very dry and tear it into pieces by hand, letting the pieces fall into a salad bowl. Add the tomatoes and the onion to the bowl, then tear the basil leaves into small pieces and add those as well. Make a dressing by whisking together olive oil, a restrained amount of vinegar, and salt and toss. Refrigerate for at least 1 hour before serving.

Barbabietole in agrodolce / SWEET AND SOUR BEETS

Lidia Balzanelli, Rovereto, Trentino

V

Serves 4

4 MEDIUM BEETS

SALT TO TASTE

½ CUP WHITE WINE VINEGAR

1 TABLESPOON SUGAR

3 TO 4 WHOLE BLACK
PEPPERCORNS

1 BAY LEAF

1 CLOVE GARLIC, UNPEELED

EXTRA-VIRGIN OLIVE OIL
FOR DRIZZLING

FRESHLY GROUND BLACK
PEPPER TO TASTE

Beets are eaten widely in the north of Italy. This recipe plays off of their natural sweetness.

Boil the beets in lightly salted water until tender. Drain, peel, and set aside to cool. (Be careful where you leave them, as they can stain.) Meanwhile, gently heat the vinegar and stir in the sugar until dissolved. Add the peppercorns, the bay leaf, and the garlic.

Slice the beets and transfer to a bowl or platter, then pour the vinegar mixture over them, passing it through a strainer. Remove and discard the peppercorns, bay leaf, and garlic. Season the beets with an additional drizzle of oliveoil, season with salt and freshly ground black pepper if they need more of either or both, and serve.

Cipolline in agrodolce / SWEET AND SOUR CIPOLLINI ONIONS

Giuliana Ascoli, Venezia, Veneto

Serves 4

⅓ CUP GOLDEN RAISINS

ABOUT ¼ CUP MARSALA

1 POUND CIPOLLINI ONIONS

EXTRA-VIRGIN OLIVE OIL
FOR SAUTÉING

SALT TO TASTE

2 TABLESPOONS SUGAR

1 TABLESPOON
RED WINE VINEGAR

Onions are so often the bridesmaid not just in Italian cuisine, but all over the world. Small, tender, squat cipollini onions are flavorful enough to work as a central ingredient, however, especially when left whole and tossed in a glaze like this one.

Soak the raisins in Marsala to cover. Meanwhile, sauté the cipollini onions in olive oil over medium heat, stirring occasionally. When the onions begin to color, season with salt. Add the sugar and vinegar and cook over low heat, stirring occasionally, for 30 minutes. Remove the raisins from the Marsala (reserve Marsala) and add to the onions. Stir together 2 tablespoons of the Marsala used to soak the raisins and 2 tablespoons water and add to the pan. Cook until the onions are golden and the liquid has caramelized to coat them, at least 30 additional minutes. Serve cold.

Tighe sott'aceto / GREEN PEPPERS PRESERVED IN VINEGAR

Rita Calzi, Ripalta Cremasca (Cremona), Lombardia

Serves 4 to 6

2 POUNDS *TIGHE* PEPPERS
OR OTHER SMALL GREEN
SWEET PEPPERS

ABOUT 8 CUPS WHITE
WINE VINEGAR

SALT TO TASTE

Tighe are small green horn-shaped peppers about 4 inches in length. In the area in and around Cremona they are often paired with *salva*, a kind of soft white local cow's milk cheese traditionally made with excess milk. (*Salva* means "save," and the cheese was made with leftover milk that was saved rather than being thrown away.) Always follow proper safety precautions when canning and preserving.

Seed and slice the peppers, spread them on a baking sheet, and let them dry in a cool, dry place for 48 hours. Transfer the peppers to glass jars and add the vinegar (it should fill the jars completely) and salt. Place a weight on top of the peppers to ensure that they remain submerged in the liquid. Place the lids on the jars and close tightly. For the following 2 days, keep an eye on the jars and add more vinegar if an air pocket forms at the top as the peppers decrease in volume. Let the peppers rest in the vinegar (store jars in a cool, dry place) for at least one month before serving.

Verdure agrodolci / PRESERVED SWEET AND SOUR VEGETABLES

Ristorante Il Basilisco, Treviso, Veneto

Serves 4 to 6

4 PLUM TOMATOES

1¼ CUPS WHITE WINE VINEGAR

1 CUP SUGAR

2 TABLESPOONS PLUS
1 TEASPOON SALT

6 WHOLE BLACK
PEPPERCORNS, CRUSHED

2 BAY LEAVES

1 POUND (ABOUT 1 BUNCH)
CELERY, CUT INTO ½-INCH DICE

12 OUNCES CELERIAC,
CUT INTO ½-INCH DICE

1 POUND (ABOUT
6 MEDIUM) CARROTS,
CUT INTO ½-INCH DICE

2 MEDIUM RED BELL
PEPPERS, SEEDED AND
CUT INTO ½-INCH DICE

2 MEDIUM YELLOW BELL
PEPPERS, SEEDED AND
CUT INTO ½-INCH DICE

1 POUND (ABOUT 3 MEDIUM)
YELLOW ONIONS,
CUT INTO ½-INCH DICE

14 OUNCES CIPOLLINI ONIONS,
CUT INTO ½-INCH DICE

1 POUND (ABOUT
3 MEDIUM) ZUCCHINI,
CUT INTO ½-INCH DICE

1 HEAD CAULIFLOWER,
CUT INTO ½-INCH DICE

2 HEADS BROCCOLI,
CUT INTO ½-INCH DICE

8 CUPS EXTRA-VIRGIN OLIVE OIL

You can adjust the ratio of water to vinegar in this recipe in order to make it more or less sour. Use a good olive oil here—its flavor matters.

Chop the tomatoes and puree them through a food mill to strain out the seeds and peels. In a large pot combine 8 cups water, the vinegar, the sugar, the salt, the peppercorns, the bay leaves, and the tomato puree and bring to a boil. When the liquid begins to boil, add the celery, celeriac, and carrots. When the mixture returns to a boil, add the bell peppers, onions, and zucchini. When the mixture returns to a boil again, add the cauliflower and broccoli. Cook for 10 additional minutes, then remove from the heat.

Taste and adjust seasoning, then drain off any excess liquid and transfer the vegetable mixture to glass jars. Fill the jars to the top with olive oil and either store in the refrigerator or process for longer storage and keep in a cool, dark place.

Giardiniera Rossa / RED GIARDINIERA WITH TOMATO SAUCE

Ristorante del Casot, Castell'Alfero (Asti), Piemonte

This colorful vegetable mixture can also be preserved in sterilized glass jars by processing for 40 minutes in a boiling water bath.

Chop the tomatoes and puree them through a food mill to strain out the seeds and peels. Place the tomato puree in a pot with the vinegar and olive oil. Add the salt and sugar and cook over medium heat for 20 minutes to reduce. Add the cauliflower and carrots and cook for 15 minutes. Add the celery, green beans, zucchini, onions, and bell peppers and cook until all the vegetables are tender but not too soft, about 10 additional minutes. Season with the nutmeg and stir in the olives. Allow to cool completely before serving.

Serves 4 to 6

4½ POUNDS TOMATOES

½ CUP WHITE WINE VINEGAR

1 CUP EXTRA-VIRGIN OLIVE OIL

3 TABLESPOONS ROCK SALT

1 TABLESPOON SUGAR

1 SMALL HEAD CAULIFLOWER, DIVIDED INTO FLORETS

4 MEDIUM CARROTS, DICED

1 BUNCH CELERY, DICED

10 OUNCES GREEN BEANS, TRIMMED AND CUT INTO THIRDS

2 ZUCCHINI, DICED

2 MEDIUM YELLOW ONIONS, DICED

2 RED BELL PEPPERS, SEEDED AND DICED

2 YELLOW BELL PEPPERS, SEEDED AND DICED

1 PINCH FRESHLY GRATED NUTMEG

¾ CUP PITTED GREEN OLIVES

Peperoni in agrodolce /
BELL PEPPERS PRESERVED IN SWEET AND SOUR SAUCE

Teotiste Griva, Cavoretto di Torino, Piemonte

*Makes about 6 pint jars
of peppers*

6 POUNDS RED
BELL PEPPERS

4 CUPS WHITE
WINE VINEGAR

½ CUP EXTRA-VIRGIN
OLIVE OIL

½ CUP SUGAR

SALT TO TASTE

Look for firm peppers with tight skin. In Piemonte there are two varieties of peppers with Slow Food Presidia: the ox-horn peppers from Carmagnola, in the Torino province, and the heart-shaped peppers from Capriglio, a village in the Monferrato Astigiano area. Both are meaty and thick, making them excellent candidates. The vinegar should preserve the peppers for the short term, but if you want to store these for longer, sterilize the jars once you have sealed them.

Wipe the peppers with a clean dishtowel one by one. Use the tip of a small paring knife to cut around the stem of one pepper and pull it out—most of the seeds will come out with it. Cut the pepper in half the long way and remove any remaining seeds and ribs. Chop, but not too finely. Pieces should be roughly 2 inches long. Repeat with remaining peppers.

Combine the vinegar, oil, and sugar in a pot and add just a pinch of salt. Bring the liquid to a boil and as soon as it begins to boil, add the peppers and cook for 2 to 3 minutes after the liquid returns to a boil. If you prefer your peppers crisp, cook them for 2 minutes, but if you prefer them softer, let them cook for 3 minutes.

With a slotted spoon or skimmer, transfer the peppers from the pot to glass jars with wide enough mouths that the pieces of pepper will fit through them and won't get squashed. Let the vinegar mixture cool in the pot. When the vinegar mixture in the pot has cooled, pour it into the jars, filling them to the top. Seal and let the peppers rest at least 1 month before eating them.

Peperoncini sott'olio / HOT PEPPERS PRESERVED IN OIL

Marta Piazzolla, Civitella del Tronto (Teramo), Abruzzo

Makes about 6 pint jars of peppers

2 POUNDS CHILI PEPPERS

⅓ CUP SALT

EXTRA-VIRGIN OLIVE OIL FOR PRESERVING

Chili peppers are eaten throughout the Abruzzo region—both in the interior and on the coast—and they are believed to aid in digestion. Preserving them makes them available year-round.

Slice the peppers into thin rounds, remove the seeds, and toss with the salt. Set aside for 24 hours. Transfer the salted pepper slices to a strainer and let the liquid drain out of them for 2 hours. Transfer the sliced pepper to glass jars and add olive oil to fill to the top. Seal the jars. Let the peppers rest for at least 2 weeks before eating. Store in a cool, dry place for up to 1 year.

Involtini di melanzane sott'olio / EGGPLANT ROLLS IN OLIVE OIL

Ristorante Liviù, Dipignano (Cosenza), Calabria

Serves 6

2 LONG EGGPLANT

¼ CUP BREADCRUMBS

1 HEAPING TABLESPOON SALTED CAPERS, RINSED, DRAINED, AND CHOPPED

1 TEASPOON MINCED OREGANO LEAVES

LEAVES OF 1 SPRIG CALAMINT, MINCED

LEAVES OF 1 SPRIG WILD FENNEL, MINCED

WHITE WINE VINEGAR FOR MOISTENING

EXTRA-VIRGIN OLIVE OIL FOR MOISTENING AND FILLING CONTAINER

SALT TO TASTE

Herbaceous eggplant rolls like these make a nice appetizer and can also be served as part of a cheese board. You can vary the herbs to fit your taste.

Slice the eggplant the long way about ¼-inch thick. Grill slices on both sides. In a bowl combine the breadcrumbs, capers, oregano, calamint, and fennel. Moisten with a little vinegar and a generous amount of extra-virgin olive oil. Season the breadcrumb mixture with salt. Spread the grilled eggplant slices on a work surface and spread a layer of the breadcrumb mixture on each.

Roll up the slices and arrange them packed snugly together and seams on the bottom in a glass container with a tight-fitting lid. Add enough olive oil to fill the container to the top and close it. The eggplant will keep in the refrigerator for 1 week. For longer storage, hermetically seal in sterilized jars.

Zolle sott'olio / GARLIC SCAPES IN OLIVE OIL

Taverna de li Caldora, Pacentro (L'Aquila), Abruzzo

Garlic scapes are the stems of garlic plants, in this area almost always of the Sulmona red garlic variety (part of the Slow Food Ark of Taste). They are harvested in May, usually early in the morning, when the soil is damp.

Bring a pot of vinegar to a boil. Add the scapes and boil for 5 minutes. Drain and spread on clean dishtowels to dry. When the scapes are dry, transfer them to sterile jars and add enough oil to fill the jars to the top. Seal tightly.

Serves 4

10 OUNCES GARLIC SCAPES

WHITE WINE VINEGAR FOR BOILING

EXTRA-VIRGIN OLIVE OIL FOR PRESERVING

SALT TO TASTE

Cicoriette sott'olio / BABY CHICORY PRESERVED IN OIL

Ristorante La Mangiatoia, Rotondella (Matera), Basilicata

Chicory is a family of bitter greens that includes radicchio, dandelion, and—in its cultivated form—endive. For this recipe, select small heads of green chicory with spiky leaves that are still attached. This makes a delicious addition to all kinds of sandwiches.

Bring a large pot of salted water to a boil and cook the chicory until tender but not overly soft, about 15 minutes. Meanwhile, prepare an ice water bath in a large bowl. Place the vinegar in a second large bowl. Drain the chicory and transfer to the ice water bath. Drain the chicory again and transfer to the bowl with the vinegar. Let the chicory marinate in the vinegar for 1 hour.

Remove the chicory from the vinegar, squeeze dry, and transfer to sterilized glass jars, interspersing the chicory heads with garlic, chili peppers, and calamint leaves. Fill the jars to the top with olive oil and let the chicory marinate for several days before serving.

Makes about 4 pint jars of chicory

SALT TO TASTE

1 POUND SMALL HEADS CHICORY, TRIMMED BUT NOT DETACHED

2½ CUPS WHITE WINE VINEGAR

5 CLOVES GARLIC, HALVED

2 CHILI PEPPERS

5 CALAMINT LEAVES

EXTRA-VIRGIN OLIVE OIL FOR PRESERVING

Alivi cunzati / OLIVES WITH MINT AND GARLIC

Pippo Privitera, Misterbianco (Catania), Sicilia

FRESH GREEN OLIVES

COARSE SALT TO TASTE

GARLIC

LEMONS

CELERY LEAVES

BAY LEAVES

MINT LEAVES TO TASTE

CHILI PEPPERS

WILD FENNEL

RED WINE VINEGAR
FOR PRESERVING

OREGANO TO TASTE

EXTRA-VIRGIN OLIVE OIL
FOR PRESERVING

The best olives to use here are the Nocellara Etnea, Ogliarola Messinese, and Tonda Iblea varieties. You want fresh olives to start—in other words, olives that have not been cured yet. If you cannot find fresh olives, you can purchase brined green olives and start with the second step of the process. These should keep in tightly sealed glass jars for several months. Vary the proportions here to suit your taste. Be sure to make enough brine to submerge the olives completely.

Crush the olives and salt them with coarse salt, then arrange them in a terracotta or glass container with water, garlic, lemon wedges (preferably the Interdonato variety) and celery leaves. Change the water every day for 5 days. Next, to the container add a brine made with 1½ teaspoons of coarse rock salt for every 4 cups water, along with lemon wedges, lightly crushed garlic cloves, bay leaves, mint leaves, and whole chili peppers. Finally, roll up a dry sprig of wild fennel and place it in the container so that it presses down on the ingredients and keeps them submerged in the brine. Hermetically seal the container and keep in a cool, dry place for at least 15 days before using.

Bring equal parts water and red wine vinegar to a boil and add the olives. Cook for 5 minutes, then drain. Transfer the olives to a large bowl. Add minced garlic, mint leaves, a sprinkling of oregano, and toss to combine. Transfer to glass jars and add extra-virgin olive oil to cover.

Chiodini e funghi di muschio sott'olio /
CHIODINO AND STRAW MUSHROOMS PRESERVED IN OIL

Margherita Festa, Matera, Basilicata

Makes about 8 cups

EXTRA-VIRGIN OLIVE OIL FOR
COOKING AND PRESERVING

1 PINCH GROUND
CHILI PEPPER

2 CUPS WHITE WINE VINEGAR

¾ TEASPOON SALT

1 WHOLE CLOVE

2 POUNDS CHIODINO AND STRAW
MUSHROOMS, TRIMMED

Chiodino and straw mushrooms are small and are preserved whole. Look for firm mushrooms for this recipe. Do not let them get too soft while cooking.

In a pot combine a small amount of oil and the chili pepper. Stir in the vinegar and 2 cups water, the salt, and the clove. Bring to a boil, then add the mushrooms. Cook the mushrooms for 1 minutes after the liquid returns to a boil. Drain the mushrooms and transfer to sterilized jars. When the mushrooms are cool, add enough extra-virgin olive oil to cover them completely. Hermetically seal for longer storage.

Bagné 'nt l'Euli / VEGETABLES DIPPED IN OLIVE OIL

Anna Maria Montersino, Lequio Tanaro (Cuneo), Piemonte

Serves 6

2 TOMATOES

1 YELLOW BELL PEPPER

1 RED BELL PEPPER

1 GREEN BELL PEPPER

2 BUNCHES YOUNG CARROTS

2 RIBS CELERY

6 SPRING ONIONS,
ROOTS TRIMMED

6 STALKS GREEN GARLIC,
ROOTS TRIMMED

EXTRA-VIRGIN OLIVE OIL
FOR DIPPING

SALT TO TASTE

This dish (the name is Piemonte dialect for "dip in oil") is all about the quality of the ingredients, so look for *olio novello* (preferably made from Ligurian olives) and the most tender vegetables you can find. This was originally served as breakfast, but now appears on the table at any time of day.

Cut the tomatoes into eighths. Seed the peppers and cut into strips. Cut the carrots into julienne or cut them in half the long way if they are small. Cut the celery into julienne. Arrange the cut vegetables and the other vegetables on a serving platter and place it in the center of the table.

Provide each diner a small bowl of oil and a small dish of salt and allow everyone to serve themselves, dip in the oil, season with salt, and enjoy.

Melanzane in saor / MARINATED ROASTED EGGPLANT

Trattoria al Forno, Refrontolo (Treviso), Veneto

Serves 4

2 MEDIUM ROUND EGGPLANT

SALT TO TASTE

EXTRA-VIRGIN OLIVE OIL FOR
DRIZZLING AND SAUTÉING

4 MEDIUM YELLOW ONIONS,
CUT INTO JULIENNE

¼ CUP WHITE WINE VINEGAR

2 BAY LEAVES

2 WHOLE CLOVES

FRESHLY GROUND BLACK
PEPPER TO TASTE

¼ CUP PLUS 1 TABLESPOON
BLACK RAISINS

⅓ CUP PINE NUTS

Saor is an ancient Veneto method that used vinegar to preserve foods in the days before refrigeration. As the eggplant rests it soaks up the marinade and becomes increasingly flavorful.

Preheat the oven to 350°F. Slice the eggplant about ½-inch thick. Arrange the slices in a single layer on a baking sheet, salt lightly, and drizzle with a little olive oil. Bake in the preheated oven until soft, about 20 minutes. Set aside to cool.

For the marinade, in a large skillet, sauté the onions in a generous amount of olive oil. Add the vinegar, the bay leaves, and the cloves. Season with salt and pepper and cook over medium heat until wilted, about 20 minutes. Remove from the heat and stir in the raisins and pine nuts. Remove and discard bay leaves and cloves.

Arrange a layer of eggplant slices in a glass container with a tight-fitting lid. Drizzle on some of the marinade and a drizzle of oil. Continue alternating layers until you have used up all of the eggplant and marinade, ending with a layer of marinade on top. Cover and refrigerate at least 24 hours before serving.

Coste di sedano con cipollata / CELERY WITH ONION SPREAD

Emanuela Busà, Firenze, Toscana

This creamy onion spread can also be served on toasted bread.

Bring a pot of salted water to a boil, blanch the pepper for 10 minutes, then drain and allow to cool. Peel the pepper and remove and discard the seeds and ribs from the interior, then chop it and chop the onions and place both in a food processor fitted with the metal blade or with an immersion blender, puree them until well-combined and soft. Transfer the puree to a bowl, season with salt and pepper, and gradually fold in the robiola until well-combined. Fold in lemon juice (you may not want to use all of it) and enough oil so that the mixture has a creamy consistency. Serve with the celery for dipping.

Serves 4

1 RED BELL PEPPER

2 SPRING ONIONS

SALT AND FRESHLY GROUND BLACK PEPPER TO TASTE

6 OUNCES ROBIOLA CHEESE

JUICE OF 1 LEMON

1 TO 2 TABLESPOONS EXTRA-VIRGIN OLIVE OIL

8 TO 12 RIBS CELERY, CUT INTO JULIENNE

Verdurine all'aceto balsamico / VEGETABLES IN BALSAMIC VINEGAR

Trattoria Cattivelli, Monticelli d'Ongina (Piacenza), Emilia-Romagna

True balsamic vinegar from Modena is a delicacy: rich and layered. Serve just the broccoli florets here and reserve the stalks for another use.

Bring a pot of salted water to a boil and cook the carrots, then the fennel, then the broccoli florets separately, removing them with a slotted spoon and running cold water over them when they are cooked. Set aside to drain and cool. Just before serving, whisk together the vinegar, oil, and a pinch of salt and pour the dressing over the vegetables. Toss to combine and serve

Serves 4

SALT TO TASTE

1 LARGE CARROT, CUT INTO JULIENNE

1 BULB FENNEL, THINLY SLICED

2 HEADS BROCCOLI, FLORETS DIVIDED

1 TEASPOON BALSAMIC VINEGAR

1 TO 2 TABLESPOONS EXTRA-VIRGIN OLIVE OIL

Zucchine e pomodori con ricotta /
ZUCCHINI AND TOMATOES STUFFED WITH RICOTTA

Sora Maria e Arcangelo, Olevano Romano (Roma), Lazio

Serves 4

8 BABY ZUCCHINI

4 ROUND TOMATOES

EXTRA-VIRGIN OLIVE OIL
FOR SAUTÉING

½ MEDIUM YELLOW ONION,
THINLY SLICED

⅔ CUP (ABOUT 6 OUNCES)
RICOTTA

SALT TO TASTE

AROMATIC HERBS TO TASTE

Use tender baby zucchini with their blossoms still attached and round tomatoes for this recipe (not plum tomatoes of other long varieties). You can use any herbs you like: parsley, basil, chives, mint, and marjoram all work well.

Steam the zucchini until tender. Blanch the tomatoes and peel them, then sauté briefly in a little olive oil with the onion until softened. In a small bowl, whisk the ricotta with a pinch of salt and enough water to loosen to the consistency of sour cream. Force through a sieve to make it completely smooth, if necessary.

To serve, place 2 zucchini and 1 tomato on each individual serving plate. Drizzle the ricotta over the zucchini and garnish the tomatoes with the aromatic herbs.

Caciofiore con carote di Viterbo /
CACIOFIORE CHEESE WITH VITERBO CARROTS

Vittorio Rossi, Tarquinia (Viterbo), Lazio

Serves 8 to 10

11 POUNDS CARROTS,
PREFERABLY VITERBO
CARROTS

1 GALLON PLUS 4 CUPS
RED WINE VINEGAR

10 POUNDS
(ABOUT 20 CUPS) SUGAR

3 TABLESPOONS
WHOLE CLOVES

3 WHOLE NUTMEG

3 CINNAMON STICKS

1 TO 2 POUNDS
ROMAN COUNTRYSIDE
CACIOFIORE CHEESE

This is a long and complex process. If you like you can include raisins, chopped candied fruit, pine nuts, or anise seeds with the carrots. Some people even include chocolate to heighten the sweetness. Viterbo carrots are purple on the outside (though they have an orange interior) and exceptionally flavorful. Roman countryside caciofiore cheese has its own Slow Food Presidium and is a sheep's cheese made with rennet from artichokes or cardoons. Its slight bitterness marries perfectly with the sweetness of the carrots.

Bring a large pot of water to a boil and cook the carrots, whole, until just tender enough to pierce with a fork. Drain and cut the long way into thin slices. Spread the carrot slices out on a sheet pan and set in the sun until completely dried. Transfer the carrot slices to a terracotta container and add the vinegar, which should cover them completely. Set aside to rest for 2 to 3 days.

Remove the carrots from the vinegar and combine the vinegar with about a third of the sugar, 1 tablespoon cloves, 1 nutmeg, and 1 cinnamon stick. Bring the mixture to a boil and boil for 15 minutes, then add the carrots and cook for 5 minutes. Remove the carrots and preserve the vinegar mixture. The next day, add about half of the remaining sugar, 1 nutmeg, and 1 cinnamon stick to the reserved vinegar mixture, bring to a boil, cook for 15 minutes, then add the carrots and cook for 5 minutes. Remove the carrots and preserve the vinegar mixture. On the third day, add the remaining sugar, the remaining nutmeg, and the remaining cinnamon stick to the liquid, boil for 15 minutes, then add the carrots and cook for 5 minutes or a little less if the carrots seem very soft. The liquid should be syrupy at this point. If it is not, remove the carrots and reduce it until it is.

If you plan to serve the carrots within the next couple of days, store them in a terracotta container and cover with a dishtowel. For longer storage, transfer to sterilized jars and fill the jars with their cooking liquid, then seal hermetically. To serve, pair the carrots with caciofiore cheese.

Cardi acidi / TART CARDOONS

Luisa Gargiulo, Marino (Roma), Lazio

Serves 4

4 LEMONS

2 POUNDS CARDOONS

ABOUT 1 CUP
EXTRA-VIRGIN OLIVE OIL

SALT TO TASTE

This is a traditional Jewish dish from the area in and around Rome. It is served cold. Cardoons are a thistle with a flavor somewhat similar to that of artichokes. To clean them, peel off any fibrous ribs, strings, and leaves.

Fill a large bowl with cold water and squeeze in the juice of 1 lemon. Chop the cardoons into 1-inch pieces and drop the pieces into the prepared bowl. Let the cardoon pieces sit in the water, preferably overnight. Drain the cardoon pieces and transfer to a pot. Add 1 cup olive oil and 1 cup water. If the liquid doesn't cover the vegetables, continue to add equal amounts of oil and water until they are fully submerged. Place the pot over low heat and cook until all the water has evaporated and only oil and the cardoon pieces remain, about 2 hours.

Juice the remaining 3 lemons. Season the cardoons with salt and add the lemon juice. Cook over low heat for 10 minutes, then remove from heat and allow the cardoons to cool. By the time they have cooled, they should have absorbed the lemon juice.

Montasio con composta di frutta / MONTASIO CHEESE WITH FRUIT COMPOTE

Maurizio Depari, Grado (Gorizia), Friuli Venezia Giulia

Select fruit that is not overly ripe for this dish, as you don't want it to disintegrate completely while cooking. You can also add liqueur, grated lemon or orange zest, and other spices to the compote. For long-terms storage of the compote, transfer to sterile glass jars and hermetically seal. Montasio is a slightly tangy ḌOP (Protected Designation of Origin) cow's milk cheese from northeastern Italy.

Peel and core the apples and cut them into wedges. In a pot with a heavy bottom, combine the sugar with ½ cup water to dissolve, then place over low heat and cook, stirring frequently, until it begins to color. Add the apples, plums, and apricots and the cinnamon stick. Cook over high heat, stirring constantly, for 2 minutes, then turn down to a low simmer and cook for 30 minutes. Keep an eye on the pot to be sure the fruit does not overcook—you want it to retain its shape.

To serve, remove and discard the pieces of cinnamon stick. Place some of the cheese—sliced or cut into cubes—on each individual serving plate and arrange a portion of the fruit compote alongside it.

Serves 4 to 6

3 TO 4 APPLES

12 OUNCES (5 TO 6) PLUMS, HALVED AND PITTED

12 OUNCES (ABOUT 10) APRICOTS, HALVED AND PITTED

1½ CUPS SUGAR OR HONEY

1 CINNAMON STICK, ROUGHLY CHOPPED

12 TO 14 OUNCES MONTASIO CHEESE

Radicchio marinato / MARINATED RADICCHIO

Osteria alla Pasina, Casier (Treviso), Veneto

Serves 4

1½ CUPS WHITE
WINE VINEGAR

5 TO 6 JUNIPER BERRIES

2 TEASPOONS WHOLE
BLACK PEPPERCORNS

2 TABLESPOONS SUGAR

4 HEADS TREVISO
RADICCHIO, TRIMMED
BUT LEFT ATTACHED

½ CUP EXTRA-VIRGIN
OLIVE OIL

SALT TO TASTE

Radicchio is more than just a salad green in Italy—it is often served cooked, which softens its bitter flavor. Treviso radicchio has long leaves.

Combine 2 quarts of water and the vinegar in a large pot and bring to a boil. Add half the juniper berries, 1 teaspoon black peppercorns, and the sugar. Stir to combine, then add the radicchio and cook at a brisk simmer for 10 minutes.

Drain the radicchio in a colander and as soon as the heads are cool enough to handle, cut them in half the long way and arrange them in a glass container. Coarsely grind the remaining 1 teaspoon black peppercorns, crush the remaining juniper berries, and combine both with the oil and salt to taste. Pour this mixture over the radicchio and marinate in a cool place for about 10 hours.

Patate e fagiolini con pesto / POTATOES AND GREEN BEANS IN PESTO

Lucia Parodi, Latte di Ventimiglia (Imperia), Liguria

Serves 4

4 MEDIUM YELLOW POTATOES

14 OUNCES GREEN BEANS

¼ CUP PESTO

In Liguria, the birthplace of pesto, it is frequently paired with green beans and potatoes. You can, of course, leave the green beans whole after trimming their ends, but we think chopping them makes for a more attractive presentation, and it only takes a moment.

Bring a pot of water to a boil, boil the potatoes, then remove with a slotted spoon and drain. As soon as the potatoes are cool enough to handle, peel them, cut them into slices about ½-inch thick, and arrange them decoratively around the border of a platter. Meanwhile, blanch the green beans until just tender, then drain and when they are cool enough to handle, cut them into pieces a little less than ½ inch long. Toss the green beans with the pesto and place them in the center of the platter. Serve immediately.

CROSTINI AND TOASTS

Crostini al Salignon / SALIGNON CHEESE CROSTINI

Ristorante Capanna Carla, Gressoney-la-Trinité, Valle d'Aosta

Serves 4

½ CUP RICOTTA

2 TABLESPOONS FENNEL
SEEDS, LIGHTLY CRUSHED

1 TABLESPOON CRUSHED
RED CHILI PEPPER

1 TABLESPOON EXTRA-VIRGIN
OLIVE OIL

8 SLICES DAY-OLD RYE BREAD

3 TABLESPOONS UNSALTED
BUTTER

Use day-old rye bread for these crostini, or if you have very soft fresh bread, cut it into slices and let them air-dry for an hour or so. *Salignon* is a spicy dairy product made from whey. It is heated and then pressed, drained, and mixed with salt, pepper, chili pepper, and aromatic herbs. You can spice plain ricotta to create something very similar at home, though of course, if you can find *salignon* you should use it.

In a bowl, thoroughly combine the cheese with the fennel seeds, chili pepper, and olive oil. Spread the mixture on the sliced bread. Shave the butter into thin curls and dot the crostini with butter.

Crostini con salsa allo scalogno / CROSTINI WITH SHALLOTS

Grazia Bussola, Negrar (Verona), Veneto

Serves 4

4 SHALLOTS

SALT AND FRESHLY GROUND
BLACK PEPPER TO TASTE

2 EGG YOLKS

1½ CUPS EXTRA-VIRGIN
OLIVE OIL

1 TABLESPOON LEMON JUICE

8 SLICES BREAD, TOASTED

The flavor of the shallots is softened by steaming, resulting in a sophisticated and subtle taste rather than one that bowls you over. This is as good on thin slices of fine-crumbed bread as it is on thicker slices of a country-style loaf.

Peel and halve the shallots and steam them until soft, about 5 minutes. Place the shallots in a blender or a food processor fitted with the metal blade. Season with salt and pepper and add the egg yolks. Puree, then begin to add the olive oil in a thin stream. When you have added about half of the oil and the sauce begins to thicken, add the lemon juice and puree to combine, then add the remaining olive oil in a thin stream, stopping every once in a while to be sure the sauce doesn't overheat. Spread the resulting mixture on the toasted bread and serve.

Crostini con gambi di carciofi / CROSTINI WITH ARTICHOKES

Osteria di Montecodruzzo, Roncofreddo (Forlì-Cesena), Emilia-Romagna

Raviggiolo cheese is a mild soft cheese that plays off the bitterness of artichokes. Make sure to purchase artichokes with their stems, which are meaty and flavorful.

Fill a bowl with cold water and add the lemon juice. Trim the artichokes, dropping the hearts and stems into the prepared bowl, then drain and dice. Sauté the artichoke dice in a little olive oil with the shallot until tender. Season with salt and pepper and tear in the mint and basil leaves. Toast the bread slices and top each slice with cubes of raviggiolo and cooked artichokes.

Serves 4

JUICE OF 1 LEMON

8 ARTICHOKES WITH STEMS

EXTRA-VIRGIN OLIVE OIL FOR SAUTÉING

1 SHALLOT, SLICED

SALT AND FRESHLY GROUND PEPPER TO TASTE

3 TO 4 MINT LEAVES

3 TO 4 BASIL LEAVES

8 SLICES BREAD

½ CUP DICED RAVIGGIOLO CHEESE

Crostini con cavolfiori / CROSTINI WITH CAULIFLOWER

Paola Braccioni, Urbania (Pesaro e Urbino), Marche

Toast the bread and rub it with the garlic cloves. Set aside.

Cook the cauliflower in boiling salted water until tender but still crisp in the center, about 8 minutes. Remove cauliflower with a slotted spoon or skimmer, reserving cooking water. Chop the cauliflower finely, leaving some whole small florets. Place the chopped cauliflower in a bowl, season with salt, and toss gently to combine.

Dip the toasted bread in the cauliflower cooking water briefly to soften, then arrange in a single layer on a serving platter. Scatter the diced cauliflower and florets on top. Drizzle with a generous amount of oil and vinegar, season with black pepper, and serve immediately.

Serves 4

8 THICK SLICES COUNTRY-STYLE BREAD

4 CLOVES GARLIC

2 POUNDS CAULIFLOWER

SALT TO TASTE

EXTRA-VIRGIN OLIVE OIL FOR DRIZZLING

WHITE WINE VINEGAR FOR DRIZZLING

FRESHLY GROUND BLACK PEPPER TO TASTE

Crostini con salsa al tartufo / TRUFFLE CROSTINI

Cesaria Gioia, Terni, Umbria

Serves 4

4 TABLESPOONS
UNSALTED BUTTER

1 CLOVE GARLIC

1 SMALL BLACK TRUFFLE,
ABOUT ⅓ OUNCE, MINCED

JUICE OF ½ LEMON

SALT AND FRESHLY GROUND
BLACK PEPPER TO TASTE

4 SLICES DAY-OLD
BREAD, TOASTED

White truffle is always used cold, but black truffle gives off a lovely aroma when heated gently. Any leftover truffle butter will keep in the refrigerator for several days.

In a small pot, melt the butter. Sauté the garlic until golden, then remove and discard and set the butter aside to cool. When the butter has cooled, stir in the truffle and lemon juice and season with salt and pepper. Return to low heat and cook just until butter begins to sizzle. Brush onto the toasted bread and serve immediately.

Ajòli / AIOLI FOR CROSTINI

Adriano Ravera, Boves (Cuneo), Piemonte

Serves 4 to 6

2 CLOVES GARLIC

1 EGG YOLK

EXTRA-VIRGIN OLIVE OIL
FOR THICKENING

SALT TO TASTE

8 SLICES TOASTED BREAD

Ajòli, a garlicky mayonnaise, makes a wonderful topping for toasted bread and is also served with plain boiled potatoes in Piemonte.

In a mortar and pestle, crush the garlic to a puree. Add the egg yolk and a pinch of salt and process to combine. Add olive oil drop by drop while continuing to stir in the same direction until the sauce is dense and shiny. Spread on the toasted bread and serve.

Acquasala / BREAD SLICES RUBBED WITH RIPE TOMATOES

Giovanna Tarantino, Carapelle (Foggia), Puglia

Pugliese bread has a crumb with large holes and a dark crust. Bread baked in a wood-burning oven will work best here, as it rehydrates without getting too soft or crumbly. Do be sure to prepare this dish in advance so that it can rest, as the flavor develops as it sits. This is a very ancient dish long eaten by people who made their living fishing or farming. Sometimes it incorporates basil leaves, a little minced chili pepper, a handful of capers, or some garlic rubbed on the bread along with the tomatoes.

Slice the bread and sprinkle the slices with water to soften slightly. Cut the tomatoes in half and rub the cut sides against the bread until only the skins remain behind. Combine the onion, oregano, and a generous amount of oil, season with salt, and spoon this mixture over the tomato-rubbed bread. Let the bread rest for 2 hours before serving.

Serves 4 to 6

1 LARGE DAY-OLD LOAF PUGLIESE BREAD

3 TO 4 RIPE TOMATOES

1 MEDIUM YELLOW ONION, MINCED

OREGANO TO TASTE

EXTRA-VIRGIN OLIVE OIL FOR MOISTENING

SALT TO TASTE

Pani cunzatu / SEMOLINA BREAD WITH TOMATOES AND SHEEP'S CHEESE

Agriturismo Vultaggio, Trapani, Sicilia

This simple sandwich has long been eaten as a snack on the island of Sicilia. Semolina bread is made with hard wheat that makes it particularly absorbent.

Cut the loaf of bread in half horizontally and with a paring knife cut slits all over both sides of the cut side of the bread. Pour the oil over the bottom half of the loaf, place the top half on top, cut side down, and press the two halves together to distribute the oil evenly. Remove the top half of the loaf again. Spared out the slices of tomato and sprinkle on the grated cheese, Season with salt and pepper. Replace the top half of the loaf again, press lightly to adhere, and cut the loaf into thick slices.

Serves 4 to 6

1 LOAF SEMOLINA BREAD

½ CUP EXTRA-VIRGIN OLIVE OIL

2 TOMATOES, SLICED

1 CUP GRATED SEMI-AGED SICILIAN SHEEP'S CHEESE

SALT AND FRESHLY GROUND BLACK PEPPER TO TASTE

Pane guttiau / THIN FLATBREADS WITH HERBS AND CHEESE ▷

Gesuino Mura, Sassari, Sardegna

Serves 4

¾ CUP DICED FRESH
SHEEP'S CHEESE

½ TEASPOON MINCED
FRESH OREGANO

4 PIECES PANE CARASAU,
ABOUT 20 INCHES IN
DIAMETER

EXTRA-VIRGIN OLIVE OIL
FOR DRIZZLING

SALT TO TASTE

1 SPRIG FENNEL OR
OTHER AROMATIC HERBS,
CHOPPED OR TORN

Pane carasau is Sardegna's famous brittle flatbread, also known as *carta da musica*. It comes in large thin sheets and generally has one smooth side and one rough side. Here it is treated in two different ways: crisp and moist.

Toss the cheese with the oregano, Brush the porous side of 2 pieces of the bread lightly with water until it is flexible. Cut each bread into 4 to 6 pieces. divide the cheese mixture among the flexible pieces of bread, and fold each up into a packet. Break up the remaining the bread into small pieces and heat them briefly (a toaster oven is best) just until warm, about 3 minutes. Spread on a serving platter and drizzle with oil, season with salt, and scatter the fennel over the bread. Serve immediately.

Cecamariti / FRIED BREAD WITH PEAS AND BROCCOLI RABE

Ristorante Masseria San Pietro, Vernole (Lecce), Puglia

Serves 4 to 6

2½ CUPS PEAS

EXTRA-VIRGIN OLIVE OIL FOR
SAUTÉING AND DRIZZLING

2 CLOVES GARLIC, MINCED

GROUND CHILI PEPPER
TO TASTE

1 POUND BROCCOLI RABE,
ROUGHLY CHOPPED

4 TO 5 CUPS CUBED DAY-OLD
SEMOLINA BREAD

The strange name of this dish means that it renders husbands blind. It is soupy enough that it should be eaten with a spoon.

Place the peas in a pot with water just to cover, salt lightly, and simmer until tender. Meanwhile, in a skillet, heat a small amount of olive oil and add the garlic and ground chili pepper. Sauté for 1 to 2 minutes, then add the broccoli rabe and cook, stirring frequently, until wilted. In a separate skillet, brown the cubes of bread in oil until crisp. Toss the peas (remove with a slotted spoon and leave any excess liquid behind), broccoli rabe, and toasted bread cubes. Drizzle with additional olive oil, season with additional ground chili pepper, and serve.

Fetta con cavolo nero / KALE TOAST

Osteria L'Acquolina, Terranuova Bracciolini (Arezzo), Toscana

Serves 4

SALT TO TASTE

EXTRA-VIRGIN OLIVE OIL
FOR COOKING WATER
AND DRIZZLING

FRESHLY GROUND BLACK
PEPPER TO TASTE

1 BUNCH TUSCAN KALE,
TOUGH CORES DISCARDED

4 SLICES TUSCAN
(UNSALTED) BREAD

Tuscan bread is always made without salt. This is traditionally made with *olio novello*, olive oil from a fresh pressing, and Tuscan kale (sometimes labeled black kale or lacinato kale) that has survived the frost and is therefore extra-sweet.

Bring a pot of salted water to a boil, salt it lightly and add some oil and a handful of black pepper. Add the kale. Meanwhile, arrange the bread on a platter and drizzle a little of the cooking water over it. Drizzle on olive oil. Remove the cooked kale with a slotted spoon or skimmer and set it on top of the bread. Drizzle on additional oil, a sprinkling of pepper, and a little more salt, if needed, and serve.

Fettunta / TOASTED GARLIC BREAD

Pia Lippi, Pisa, Toscana

Serves 4 to 6

1 LOAF TUSCAN
(UNSALTED) BREAD

4 TO 5 CLOVES GARLIC

SALT TO TASTE

EXTRA-VIRGIN OLIVE OIL
FOR DRIZZLING

Warm fettunta makes a perfect starter before almost any meal. Though the ingredients are simple, they are specific: use Tuscan bead, which is unsalted, and grassy, freshly pressed olive oil. For a heartier meal, ladle cooked cannellini beans (or almost anything else you like) over the fettunta.

Cut the loaf into 1-inch slices and toast on each side so that the interior remains soft but the outside is crisp. Rub a peeled garlic clove on one side of the bread and place garlic-side up on a platter. Season with salt and drizzle with a generous amount of olive oil. Serve warm.

Frega di pomodoro / TOASTED BREAD WITH CHOPPED TOMATOES

Luciano Bezzini, Castagneto Carducci (Livorno), Toscana

The tomatoes are key: they must be just-picked and perfectly ripe, but not overripe, and they should be the round, smooth-skinned variety. This is the perfect summertime snack.

Combine the tomatoes, olive oil, and salt. Toast the bread. Rub the bread with the garlic. Arrange the toasted bread on a platter and spoon the tomato mixture on top of it.

Serves 4

10 OUNCES (ABOUT 2 MEDIUM) PERFECTLY RIPE TOMATOES, CHOPPED

½ CUP EXTRA-VIRGIN OLIVE OIL

SALT TO TASTE

16 SLICES DAY-OLD TUSCAN (UNSALTED) BREAD

5 CLOVES GARLIC

PASTA

Spaghetti aglio olio e peperoncino / SPICY GARLIC SPAGHETTI

Trattoria L'Oste della Bon'Ora, Grottaferrata (Roma), Lazio

Serves 4

3 CLOVES GARLIC (SEE NOTE)

1 CHILI PEPPER, CHOPPED

EXTRA-VIRGIN OLIVE OIL
FOR SAUTÉING

SALT TO TASTE

11 OUNCES SPAGHETTI

LEAVES OF 1 SPRIG
PARSLEY, MINCED

For this dish, you can leave the garlic cloves whole, cut them into halves or thirds, mince them, or crush them—each will lend a slightly different level of garlicky flavor to this punchy favorite. If you prefer less spice, pour the hot oil mixture over the drained spaghetti in the serving bowl rather than tossing it in the skillet.

Brown the garlic and chili pepper in a large skillet in a generous amount of oil. When the garlic has browned, remove and discard both garlic and hot pepper. Bring a large pot of salted water to a boil and cook spaghetti, stirring frequently, until al dente. Drain the pasta, add it to the skillet with the oil and toss over medium heat until coated. Garnish with minced parsley.

Spaghetti con le nocciole / TOASTED HAZELNUT SPAGHETTI

Ristorante Il Brigante, Giffoni Sei Casali (Salerno), Campania

Giffoni hazelnuts have thin peels that come off very easily, but most hazelnuts are not terribly difficult to skin. Simply toast them until they are aromatic, then place them in a clean flat-weave dishtowel and rub vigorously. The skins will flake right off.

Bring a pot of salted water to a boil for cooking the pasta. Meanwhile, toast the hazelnuts lightly, then skin them and chop them. Mince the garlic and chili pepper and sauté in a generous amount of olive oil in a skillet large enough to hold the pasta once it is cooked. Add the hazelnuts to the skillet and sauté briefly, then add a few spoonfuls of the pasta cooking water. Sprinkle in minced parsley and adjust salt to taste. When the spaghetti is cooked al dente, drain it and add it to the skillet and toss briefly over medium heat to combine.

Serves 4

SALT TO TASTE

14 OUNCES SPAGHETTI

⅔ CUP GIFFONI HAZELNUTS

1 CLOVE GARLIC

1 PIECE CHILI PEPPER

EXTRA-VIRGIN OLIVE OIL FOR SAUTÉING

LEAVES OF 1 SPRIG PARSLEY, MINCED

Linguine allo scammaro / LINGUINE WITH CAPERS AND OLIVES

Osteria-Gastronomia Timpani e Tempura, Napoli, Campania

Serves 4

1 POUND GRAGNANO
LINGUINE OR OTHER
LONG PASTA

2 CLOVES GARLIC

EXTRA-VIRGIN OLIVE OIL
FOR SAUTÉING

1½ CUPS GREEN OLIVES,
PITTED

¾ CUP CAPERS, RINSED
AND DRAINED

LEAVES OF 1 SPRIG PARSLEY,
MINCED

1½ CUPS GAETA OLIVES,
PITTED

1½ CUPS GRATED
PECORINO ROMANO

SALT TO TASTE

Scammaro is a dialect word for the meatless days prescribed by the Church.

Bring a large pot of salted water to a boil for cooking the pasta. While the linguine are cooking, sauté the garlic in olive oil in a skillet until golden, then remove and discard. Add the green olives and sauté for a minute or two, then add the capers. Sauté for 1 additional minute and add about ¼ cup of the pasta cooking water. Cook, stirring, for 2 minutes, then add the parsley and Gaeta olives. Toss to combine. When the pasta is cooked al dente, drain and add to the skillet. Toss over medium heat, sprinkle on the grated cheese, toss again, and serve hot.

Busiate al pesto trapanese / BUSIATE WITH ALMOND AND TOMATO PESTO

Osteria Cantina Siciliana, Trapani, Sicilia

The Italian word *pesto* simply means paste, and while the basil-rich pesto of Genova is the most famous, other areas of Italy have their own. The pesto in Trapani is intensely garlicky. Busiate are a long spiral pasta. If you can't find them, use bucatini instead.

With a mortar and pestle, crush the almonds with the garlic and basil. Continue to process the paste while drizzling in a thin stream of olive oil. Transfer to a bowl and stir in the grated cheese. In the mortar (don't bother to clean it) crush the tomatoes (work in batches if your mortar isn't large enough to hold them all), then stir those into the mixture as well. Season to taste with salt and pepper. Bring a large pot of water to a boil and cook the pasta. Once the pasta is cooked al dente, drain it and toss it with the pesto. Serve immediately.

Serves 4 to 6

¼ CUP BLANCHED ALMONDS

6 CLOVES GARLIC

8 LEAVES BASIL

EXTRA-VIRGIN OLIVE OIL FOR DRIZZLING

1 CUP GRATED AGED SHEEP'S CHEESE

1 POUND PLUM TOMATOES, PEELED, SEEDED, AND CHOPPED

SALT AND FRESHLY GROUND BLACK PEPPER TO TASTE

1 POUND 5 OUNCES BUSIATE

Trenette al pesto / TRENETTE WITH PESTO

Lorenza Costa, Camogli (Genova), Liguria

Serves 4

4 BUNCHES
GENOVESE BASIL

1 TO 2 CLOVES GARLIC

1 PINCH ROCK SALT

¼ CUP PINE NUTS

¼ CUP GRATED
GRANA PADANO

2 TABLESPOONS GRATED
AGED SHEEP'S CHEESE

1 TABLESPOON
UNSALTED BUTTER

SALT TO TASTE

EXTRA-VIRGIN OLIVE OIL
FOR THINNING

14 OUNCES TRENETTE

You can't make a true pesto without Genovese basil, but it is hard to find outside of Liguria, so be sure to select the smallest, most tender basil leaves possible.

Remove the basil leaves from the steams, rinse them, and very gently dry them without crushing them. Place the garlic in a mortar with a pinch of rock salt and grind with the pestle. Gradually add the basil leaves, grinding between additions. Gradually add the pine nuts, both types of cheese, and the butter, grinding to combine between additions. When the mixture has turned into a paste, taste and add a little fine salt if necessary, then transfer the mixture to a bowl and gently stir in extra-virgin olive oil in a thin stream, stirring constantly, until you are pleased with the consistency of the pesto.

Bring a pot of salted water to a boil for the pasta and cook until al dente. Reserve 1 tablespoon of the pasta cooking water, then drain the pasta and transfer to a serving bowl. Thin the pesto with the pasta cooking water, then toss with the pasta and serve immediately.

Vermicelli cu' 'o pesce fujuto /
VERMICELLI WITH TOMATO SAUCE THAT TASTES OF THE SEA

Antonio Rizzo, Napoli, Campania

Serves 4

SALT TO TASTE

14 OUNCES VERMICELLI

8 PIÉNNOLO TOMATOES

3 CLOVES GARLIC

EXTRA-VIRGIN OLIVE OIL
FOR SAUTÉING

LEAVES OF 1 SPRIG BASIL

Piénnolo tomatoes grow along the shore and are impregnated with the saline flavor of the ocean.

Bring a large pot of salted water to a boil for cooking the pasta. Crush the tomatoes lightly and crush the garlic cloves. In a skillet, sauté the garlic in extra-virgin olive oil until golden. Add the tomatoes and a pinch of salt and cook for a few minutes. When the pasta is cooked al dente, drain it and toss with the tomato sauce over medium heat to combine. Tear the basil leaves over the pasta (or leave whole if they are small) and serve hot.

Pasta allo scarpariello / QUICK PASTA WITH TOMATOES

Ristorante Arcara, Cava de' Tirreni (Salerno), Campania

The name of this very popular dish, literally "cobbler's pasta," hints at its origins: apparently the many cobblers in the Quartieri Spagnoli neighborhood used to whip it up as a quick lunch at midday. This is traditionally made with the small, teardrop-shaped tomatoes known as *spunzilli*, which are extra sweet. Be sure you have some bread on hand to wipe up every bit of the delicious sauce.

Seed and chop the tomatoes. In a skillet large enough to hold the pasta, sauté the garlic, chili pepper, and 4 basil leaves in the olive oil over low heat. Add the tomatoes, season with salt, and cook until tomatoes are soft and have given up their liquid, 12 to 15 minutes.

Meanwhile, bring a large pot of salted water to a boil and cook the pasta al dente. Drain and add to the skillet with the tomatoes. Gradually sprinkle on the cheese and toss over the heat to combine. Garnish with the remaining basil leaves and serve.

Serves 4

1½ PINTS CHERRY TOMATOES

2 CLOVES GARLIC

1 PIECE CHILI PEPPER

LEAVES OF 1 SPRIG BASIL

¼ CUP EXTRA-VIRGIN OLIVE OIL

SALT TO TASTE

14 OUNCES SHORT GRAGNANO PASTA

½ CUP GRATED AGED SHEEP'S CHEESE

¾ CUP GRATED PARMIGIANO REGGIANO

Pasta 'ncaciata con broccoletti / PASTA WITH BROCCOLI RABE AND CHEESE

Trattoria Fratelli Borrello, Sinagra (Messina), Sicilia

Serves 4 to 6

1 POUND BROCCOLI RABE

EXTRA-VIRGIN OLIVE OIL FOR SAUTÉING

SALT TO TASTE

1 POUND PENNETTE RIGATE

1 CUP GRATED MAIORCHINO CHEESE OR OTHER AGED SHEEP'S CHEESE

4 OUNCES PROVOLONE, SLICED

There are dozens of variations on this dish, the name of which simply indicates that it is topped with a generous amount of *cacio*, or cheese. In summer, you can use eggplant in place of the broccoli rabe, or fresh shelled peas. Sometimes the dish incorporates slices of hard-boiled egg. Maiorchino cheese is made mostly from sheep's milk with a little goat or cow's milk included, all from animals that graze in the Nebrodi Mountains. The curds are poked with a thin stick to help them drain. Maiorchino has a dedicated Slow Food Presidium. During Carnival celebrations, shepherds stage a race to see who can roll a large wheel of this cheese fastest.

Preheat oven to 350°F. Chop the broccoli rabe. Sauté in a large skillet in olive oil until tender, adding 1 to 2 tablespoons of water at a time to keep it from sticking to the pan. Meanwhile, bring a large pot of salted water to a boil and cook the pasta al dente. Drain and transfer to a bowl. Toss with the cooked broccoli rabe, then transfer the pasta to a baking dish. Sprinkle the grated maiorchino cheese on top, then arrange the sliced provolone on top. Bake in the preheated oven until the cheese has melted and browned, about 10 minutes. Serve hot.

Pasta con i talli / PASTA WITH TENERUMI LEAVES

Sabina Zuccaro, Siracusa, Sicilia

Tenerumi are the leaves and tendrils of the cucuzza squash plant. They are eaten widely throughout Sicilia. If you aren't lucky enough to have cucuzza growing in your backyard, you can replace them with spinach of chard.

Soak the tomatoes in lukewarm water until soft. Drain, mince, and set aside. Bring a large pot of salted water to a boil and cook the tenerumi leaves for 20 minutes. Remove with a slotted spoon or skimmer and drain, then squeeze dry and chop. Bring the cooking water back to a boil for cooking the pasta.

Meanwhile, in a large skillet sauté the chili pepper and garlic in the olive oil. Add the chopped greens and the sun-dried tomatoes and cook, stirring frequently, for 10 minutes. Cook the pasta until al dente, then drain (reserve about ½ cup cooking water) and add to the skillet. Cook over medium heat, tossing, for 2 minutes. If the pan looks dry, stir in a little of the cooking water. Sprinkle on the cheese, stir to combine, and serve hot.

Serves 4 to 6

2 CUPS SUN-DRIED TOMATOES

SALT TO TASTE

3 BUNCHES (2 TO 2½ POUNDS) TENERUMI LEAVES

1 DRIED RED CHILI PEPPER, MINCED

2 CLOVES GARLIC, MINCED

¾ CUP EXTRA-VIRGIN OLIVE OIL

12 OUNCES SHORT PASTA

1 CUP GRATED CACIOCAVALLO OR AGED SHEEP'S CHEESE

'O sicchio d'a munnezza / SPAGHETTI WITH NUTS AND DRIED FRUIT ➤

Osteria 'E Curti, Sant'Anastasia (Napoli), Campania

Serves 8

SALT TO TASTE

10 RAISINS

½ CUP HAZELNUTS

¾ CUP WALNUTS

8 BLACK OLIVES

1 CLOVE GARLIC,
LIGHTLY CRUSHED

EXTRA-VIRGIN OLIVE OIL
FOR SAUTÉING

16 PINE NUTS

18 CAPERS, RINSED
AND DRAINED

9 OUNCES (ABOUT 20)
PIÉNNOLO CHERRY
TOMATOES, SEEDED AND
CHOPPED

1 PINCH DRIED OREGANO

LEAVES OF 1 SPRIG
PARSLEY, MINCED

1¾ POUNDS SPAGHETTI

This is a waste-not-want-not sauce typical of Italy—it is made from a little bit of this and a little bit of that.

Bring a large pot of salted water to a boil for the pasta. Soak the raisins in water to cover to soften, then drain and squeeze dry. Skin the hazelnuts and chop the hazelnuts and walnuts. Pit the olives. In a skillet quickly sauté the garlic in olive oil until golden. Add the nuts, raisins, and capers and sauté for 2 minutes. Add the tomatoes to the pan, season with a little salt (keep in mind the olives and capers are salty) and cook over medium heat until tomatoes soften, 4 to 5 minutes. Add the olives, a pinch of oregano, and the parsley. Cook, stirring, to combine, then cover, and set aside off the heat. Cook the pasta in the boiling water until al dente, then drain and toss with the prepared sauce over medium heat to combine.

Pasta con salsa Calabra / PASTA WITH THICK TOMATO SAUCE

Rosa Lazzaro, Sant'Andrea Apostolo dello Ionio (Catanzaro), Calabria

Serves 4

3½ POUNDS TOMATOES

1 MEDIUM YELLOW ONION

1 CLOVE GARLIC

3 TABLESPOONS UNSALTED BUTTER

SALT TO TASTE

LEAVES OF 1 SPRIG BAIL

1 RED CHILI PEPPER, MINCED

12 OUNCES FUSILLI

The easiest way to peel fresh tomatoes is to cut an X into the base of each, then dip them briefly in boiling water. The skin should pull away easily.

Peel and seed the tomatoes, then crush them by hand, squeezing out as much liquid as possible. Thinly slice the onion. Mince the garlic. Melt the butter in a large skillet and sauté the onion and the garlic until golden. Add the tomatoes, season with salt, and cook over the lowest possible heat until the tomatoes have collapsed.

When the tomatoes have collapsed, force the mixture through a sieve and place it in a clean pot. Cook over the lowest possible heat until very thick. Tear in the basil and add the chili pepper, stir a few times, then remove from the heat. Bring a large pot of salted water to a boil and cook the pasta al dente. Drain and transfer to a serving bowl. Top with the tomato sauce, toss to combine, and serve.

Norma / PASTA WITH EGGPLANT AND RICOTTA SALATA

Aldo Bacciulli, Catania, Sicilia

Sicilia has no shortage of delicious dishes, but this is one of the best known. Though the etymology of its name has never been firmly established, what is known is that composer Vincenzo Bellini—a native of Catania—wrote a famous opera titled *Norma* in 1831. The work was so successful that to call something a "Norma" in the area was to pay it the highest compliment.

Line a baking sheet with paper towels. Peel the eggplants, slice them and soak them in salted water for at least 1 hour to purge them of their bitter liquid. Peel the tomatoes, then chop them. In an earthenware pot, combine the tomatoes and garlic and cook over very low heat until thickened. Remove from the heat, then drizzle in olive oil and tear in most of the basil leaves, reserving 4 to 6 for garnish. Pan fry the eggplant in several inches of oil until golden brown and drain on the prepared pan.

Bring a large pot of salted water to a boil and cook the pasta al dente. Transfer to a serving bowl. Add the tomato sauce and mix. Divide the pasta among individual serving bowls and top each with some of the eggplant, a sprinkling of grated cheese, and one of the reserved basil leaves. Serve hot.

Serves 4 to 6

2 EGGPLANT

SALT TO TASTE

3½ POUNDS PLUM TOMATOES, PEELED AND CHOPPED

2 CLOVES GARLIC

EXTRA-VIRGIN OLIVE OIL FOR DRIZZLING AND PAN-FRYING

LEAVES OF 1 SPRIG BASIL

1 POUND RIGATONI

2 CUPS GRATED RICOTTA SALATA

Curzul olio e pangrattato /
EGG NOODLES WITH OLIVE OIL AND BREADCRUMBS

Antica Trattoria del Teatro, Lugo (Ravenna), Emilia-Romagna

Serves 4

3⅓ CUPS UNBLEACHED
ALL-PURPOSE FLOUR

4 LARGE EGGS

SALT TO TASTE

EXTRA-VIRGIN OLIVE OIL
FOR SAUTÉING

½ CUP BREADCRUMBS

Curzul are long egg noodles that are square if viewed from the end (in other words, the noodles are as wide as the sheet of pasta is thick). Their name refers to leather shoelaces, which are the same shape.

Form the flour into a well on the work surface. Place the eggs in the center and stir lightly with a fork to break yolks. Begin to pull in the flour from the sides of the well and combine it with the flour. Once you have a crumbly dough, knead until it is smooth and compact. Shape the dough into a ball, cover (an overturned bowl works well), and set aside to rest for 15 minutes.

On a clean work surface, roll out the dough to a sheet about ¹⁄₁₀ inch. Let the sheet of dough dry for a few minutes, then roll it into a loose cylinder. With a sharp knife, cut the cylinder into noodles ¹⁄₁₀ inch wide. Separate the noodles by shaking them gently with your hands and spread them on a baking sheet.

Bring a large pot of salted water to a boil for cooking the pasta. Once you have added the pasta to the pot, in a large skillet, heat a little olive oil, then add the breadcrumbs. Scoop out the pasta with a slotted spoon or skimmer as soon as it rises to the surface (egg pasta cooks quickly) and transfer it to the skillet. Toss over medium heat until the breadcrumbs are toasted and coat the past, 1 to 2 minutes. Serve hot.

Chitarrina allo zafferano / THIN EGG NOODLES WITH SAFFRON SAUCE

Ristorante Santa Chiara, Guardiagrele (Chieti), Abruzzo

A *chitarra* is Italian for guitar but also refers to a special tool for making pasta: It is a box with wires strung at regular intervals (like its namesake) so that when you rest a sheet of pasta dough on top of it and roll over it with a rolling pin, the sheet presses along the wires and divides into noodles that are square rather than flat. (If you don't have one, use the thinnest noodle segment of a crank pasta machine.) The town of Navelli in Abruzzo is famed for its bright red saffron, which is said to be less bitter than standard saffron. It is included in the Slow Food Ark of Taste.

Form the flour into a well on the work surface. Place the eggs in the center and stir lightly with a fork to break yolks. Begin to pull in the flour from the sides of the well and combine it with the flour. Once you have a crumbly dough, knead briskly until it is smooth and compact, about 10 minutes. Shape the dough into a ball, wrap in plastic wrap, and set aside to rest for 30 minutes.

Divide the pasta dough into two equal parts and roll each out each portion into a thin sheet. Let the sheets of pasta dough dry briefly on a dish towel or wooden surface. cut the sheets into the size of your chitarra (see Note). Place two pieces on top of each other on the chitarra and roll lightly with a rolling pin. Repeat with remaining sheets of dough.

To make the broth, in a large pot combine the carrot, onion, celery, and tomato with 6 cups water and a pinch of salt. Bring to a boil, then simmer briskly until the liquid has reduced by about half. Drain and reserve.

Warm about ¼ cup of the reserved broth and combine with the saffron threads and powdered saffron. Stir to dissolve and set aside. Peel and slice the potatoes. Thinly slice the shallot. Melt the butter in a large skillet and add the shallot. Sauté until golden. Add the sliced potatoes and enough broth to cover and braise until potatoes are tender, adding more broth in small amounts if needed. (The potatoes should be just covered—not boiling in a large amount of broth.) When the potatoes are cooked, puree them with any cooking liquid left in the skillet. Stir in the cream. Taste and adjust salt.

Serves 4

2½ CUPS UNBLEACHED ALL-PURPOSE FLOUR

3 LARGE EGGS

1 CARROT

1 MEDIUM YELLOW ONION

1 RIB CELERY

1 MEDIUM TOMATO

SALT TO TASTE

1 PINCH SAFFRON THREADS

1 TABLESPOON PLUS 1 TEASPOON NAVELLI SAFFRON POWDER

11 OUNCES (2 MEDIUM) POTATOES

1 SHALLOT

4 TABLESPOONS UNSALTED BUTTER

3 TABLESPOONS HEAVY CREAM OR WHIPPING CREAM

¾ CUP GRATED AGED COW'S MILK CHEESE

Chitarrina allo zafferano / THIN EGG NOODLES WITH SAFFRON SAUCE
continued

Bring a large pot of salted water to a boil for cooking the pasta. Place the potato mixture in a clean skillet and stir in the reserved broth and saffron mixture. Cook, stirring frequently, until combined, 3 to 4 minutes. Meanwhile, cook the pasta until al dente (egg pasta cooks quickly), then drain and add to the skillet. Cook, tossing, until combined, about 2 additional minutes, then sprinkle on about half of the cheese. Stir to combine and serve immediately with the remaining cheese passed on the side.

Tagliatelle con aspraggine e Prugnoli /
NOODLES WITH OXTONGUE GREENS AND PRUGNOLO MUSHROOMS
Ristorante L'Elfo, Capracotta (Isernia), Molise

Serves 4 to 6

10 OUNCES PRUGNOLO
MUSHROOMS

SALT TO TASTE

1 BUNCH OXTONGUE GREENS

1 CLOVE GARLIC

EXTRA-VIRGIN OLIVE OIL
FOR SAUTÉING

2 TABLESPOONS DRY
WHITE WINE

14 OUNCES EGGLESS
TAGLIATELLE

Oxtongue (*Helminthotheca echioides*) looks like dandelion, and like dandelion, it is considered a weed in most places, and while it is edible, it can be overly bitter for some tastes when raw, so it is typically cooked. Oxtongue grows wild in California, as well as in Europe and Africa. Prugnolo mushrooms are foraged throughout central Italy.

Slice the mushrooms. Bring a pot of salted water to a boil and cook the oxtongue greens until tender. Remove with a slotted spoon or skimmer and set aside, reserving the cooking water. In a skillet, sauté the garlic in olive oil until golden, then add the mushrooms and cook, stirring occasionally, until they give up their liquid. Add the cooked oxtongue greens to the skillet and cook, stirring, for 2 minutes, then add the white wine and cook until evaporated. Cook, stirring frequently, for 10 additional minutes, adding the cooking water from the greens in small amounts so that the skillet stays moist. Meanwhile, bring a large pot of salted water to a boil for cooking the pasta. Cook the pasta al dente, drain, toss with the mushroom mixture, and serve hot.

Pici all'aglione / GARLICKY EGG PASTA

Trattoria Le Panzanelle, Radda in Chianti (Siena), Toscana

This is an intentionally garlicky sauce—you can use fewer cloves of garlic if you like. You can also make the pici with just 1 egg or, as is more traditional, just water and no egg at all.

Shape the 6⅔ cups flour into a well on the work surface. Place the eggs in the center with a pinch of salt and stir lightly with a fork to break yolks. Begin to pull in the flour from the sides of the well and combine it with the flour. As you do, gradually add warm water, 1 to 2 tablespoons at a time. Continue adding water and incorporating flour until you have a soft dough. Knead until compact. Shape into a ball, cover with a linen kitchen towel, and set aside to rest for 30 minutes.

With a rolling pin, roll out the dough to a thin sheet (but not paper-thin), then cut the sheet of dough into thin strips. Lightly brush the work surface with a little oil, then roll the strips of dough on the surface into thin strings about as thick as spaghetti. Flour them lightly as you finish them to keep them from sticking.

Bring a large pot of salted water to a boil and cook the pasta. While the pasta is cooking, mince the garlic and in a skillet sauté it over very low heat in the butter and 2 tablespoons oil. When the garlic just begins to color, add about ¼ cup of the pasta cooking water to stop it from cooking.

Drain the pasta, leaving it a little more moist than usual, and add it to the skillet. Sprinkle on the grated cheese and toss over medium heat until the cheese is evenly distributed and melted. Sprinkle with black pepper and serve immediately.

Serves 4 to 6

6⅔ CUPS UNBLEACHED ALL-PURPOSE FLOUR, PLUS MORE FOR FLOURING NOODLES

2 LARGE EGGS

SALT TO TASTE

2 TABLESPOONS EXTRA-VIRGIN OLIVE OIL, PLUS MORE FOR OILING THE SURFACE

10 CLOVES GARLIC

1 TABLESPOON UNSALTED BUTTER

2 CUPS GRATED AGED SHEEP'S CHEESE

FRESHLY GROUND BLACK PEPPER TO TASTE

Orecchiette con cime di rapa / ORECCHIETTE WITH BROCCOLI RABE

L'Antica Locanda, Noci (Bari), Puglia

Serves 4 to 6

½ CUP FRESH BREADCRUMBS

EXTRA-VIRGIN OLIVE OIL
FOR SAUTÉING

2 CLOVES GARLIC

12 TO 14 OUNCES
BROCCOLI RABE

SALT TO TASTE

12 OUNCES ORECCHIETTE

GROUND CHILI PEPPER TO
TASTE (OPTIONAL)

This is probably the most famous dish from the Puglia region. You can purchase orecchiette already made, but if you would like to try your hand at crafting these "little ears" made of semolina flour and all-purpose flour, see page 126.

In a small skillet, toast the breadcrumbs in oil until golden and crisp. Set aside. Mince the garlic. Chop the broccoli rabe. Bring a large pot of salted water to a boil and add the orecchiette. Cook for 10 minutes, stirring frequently, then add the broccoli rabe.

In a large skillet, brown the garlic in a generous amount of oil. When the pasta is cooked al dente, drain pasta and broccoli rabe and add to the skillet with the garlic. Toss over medium heat until well-combined. Sprinkle on the reserved breadcrumbs and the chili pepper, if using, and toss for 1 to 2 additional minutes, then serve hot.

Paglia e fieno allo scalogno di Romagna /
GREEN AND YELLOW NOODLES WITH ROMAGNA SHALLOTS

Osteria La Campanara, Galeata (Forlì-Cesena), Emilia-Romagna

Serves 4

7 OUNCES SPINACH

SALT TO TASTE

2½ CUPS UNBLEACHED
ALL-PURPOSE FLOUR

3 LARGE EGGS

6 RIPE TOMATOES

14 OUNCES ROMAGNA
SHALLOTS

¼ CUP PLUS 1 TABLESPOON
EXTRA-VIRGIN OLIVE OIL

FRESHLY GROUND BLACK
PEPPER TO TASTE

Sweet teardrop-shaped Romagna shallots, an IGP (Protected Geographic Origin) product, have grown in and around Ravenna, Forlì, and Bologna for more than a century. They are eaten either fresh or dried. You can substitute standard shallots if that's all that's available in your area.

Blanch the spinach in salted water, drain, squeeze dry, and mince very finely. On the work surface, shape the flour into a well. Place the eggs in the center with a pinch of salt. Use fork to beat the eggs and then gradually to pull in flour from the sides of the well. Knead by hand into a soft and well combined dough. Divide the dough in half and knead the minced spinach into one piece until the color is uniform. Shape each piece of dough into a ball, cover (an overturned bowl works well), and set aside to rest for 1 hour.

While the dough is resting, make the sauce. Peel, seed, and dice the tomatoes and set aside in a sieve to drain. Thinly slice the shallots. Place the oil in a skillet and set over the lowest possible heat. Add the shallots, toss to combine, cover the skillet, and cook for 30 minutes, adding about 1 tablespoon of water at a time to keep the skillet moist and to keep the shallots from browning. Once cooked, the mixture should be soft, but not brown. Add the tomatoes and cook, uncovered, stirring occasionally, for 15 minutes. Season with salt and pepper.

Roll out the two pieces of pasta dough separately into thin sheets. Place one on top of the other and without pressing too hard (you don't want to seal them, so sprinkle a small amount of flour in between if necessary to keep them from sticking), roll them into a cylinder. Cut them into thin noodles, about 1/10 inch wide or a little wider. Shake the noodles gently to separate them. Bring a large pot of salted water to a boil and cook the pasta until it rises to the surface (egg pasta cooks quickly). Drain and transfer to the skillet with the shallots. Toss over low heat to combine and serve hot.

Umbricelli al tartufo nero /
THICK HANDMADE SPAGHETTI WITH BLACK TRUFFLE

Trattoria La Palomba, Orvieto (Terni), Umbria

Umbricelli are like very thick spaghetti. Because each strand is made by hand, they have a rough and slightly irregular texture. Black summer truffles have a bumpy black exterior, but the interior is more of a grayish brown color.

On a work surface, shape the flour into a well. Place the egg whites and a pinch of salt in the center and begin to knead, incorporating enough water to make a compact and elastic dough. Knead until firm, shape into a ball, place in a bowl, cover with a kitchen towel, and set aside to rest for about 20 minutes.

Meanwhile, peel and crush the garlic. Chop the mushrooms. In a skillet, sauté the garlic. Add the mushrooms and cook until they have given up their liquid and it has evaporated. Remove from the heat. Finely grate a little of the truffle on top. Mince the parsley and stir in, then adjust salt to taste and allow to cool.

Divide the pasta dough into 2 or 3 equal parts and roll each one into a sheet a little less than ½ inch thick. Cut into strips about ⅒ inch wide. Roll a strip under your palms on the work surface until it is round. Repeat with remaining strips

Bring a large pot of salted water to a boil, add the pasta, and cook until al dente, 7 to 8 minutes. While the pasta is cooking, puree the mushroom mixture to a creamy consistency. Wipe out the skillet and return the mushroom puree to the skillet. Toss to combine, then remove from the heat and shave the remaining truffle over the top. Serve immediately.

Serves 4

3⅓ CUPS UNBLEACHED ALL-PURPOSE FLOUR

4 EGG WHITES

SALT TO TASTE

2 CLOVES GARLIC

5 TO 6 PORCINI MUSHROOMS OR OTHER FIRM, FLAVORFUL MUSHROOMS

EXTRA-VIRGIN OLIVE OIL FOR SAUTÉING

3 OUNCES BLACK SUMMER TRUFFLE

LEAVES OF 1 SPRIG PARSLEY

Maccheroni dolci / HANDMADE COCOA POWDER PASTA

Osteria Perbacco, Cannara (Perugia), Umbria

Serves 4

3 CUPS UNBLEACHED
ALL-PURPOSE FLOUR

1 EGG WHITE

2¾ CUP WALNUTS

⅔ CUP BREADCRUMBS

¾ CUP SUGAR

½ TEASPOON GROUND
CINNAMON

GRATED ZEST OF 1 LEMON

¼ CUP PLUS 3 TABLESPOONS
UNSWEETENED COCOA
POWDER

SALT TO TASTE

Sweet pasta may sound like a modern bit of gimmickry, but it actually has a long history in Italy and was a must at fancy banquets. Cocoa powder, of course, only became known to Italians after the exploration of the Americas, as it is native to that part of the world. Locally, this used to be eaten as a first course on Christmas and New Year's, but these days many people in the area serve it as a dessert. It pairs well with Vernaccia di Cannara.

On a work surface, knead together the flour, the egg white, and enough water to make a soft, elastic dough. Shape into a ball, cover (an overturned bowl works well), and set aside to rest for 15 to 20 minutes. Roll the dough into a sheet. Let the sheet dry for a few minutes, roll into a loose cylinder, and cut into strips a little less than ¼ inch wide.

Finely chop the walnuts. In a bowl combine the breadcrumbs, walnuts, sugar, cinnamon, lemon zest, and cocoa powder. Stir to combine and set aside.

Bring a lightly salted pot of water to a boil for the pasta and cook the pasta until it rises to the surface. Briefly drain the pasta, leaving it a little more moist than usual, then transfer to a serving bowl, alternate layers of the pasta with the prepared breadcrumb mixture, ending with the breadcrumb mixture on top. Allow to cool completely before serving.

Pencianelle al pomodoro / YEASTED NOODLES IN TOMATO SAUCE

Ristorante Giardino degli Ulivi, Castelraimondo (Macerata), Marche

The incorporation of yeast gives pasta dough a pleasantly chewy texture. Each noodle will be a slightly different thickness because you shape them by hand. That irregularity is part of their charm.

Dissolve the yeast in 1 cup warm (not hot water) until foamy. Beat the egg whites and a pinch of salt with the yeast mixture. Shape the flour into a well on the work surface and pour the yeast and egg mixture into the center of the well. Begin drawing in flour from the sides of the well, and when you have a crumbly mixture knead until you have a soft, elastic, compact dough, about 15 minutes. If the dough feels too dry, add a little water. Shape into a ball and set aside to rest in a cool, dry place.

When you are ready to shape the pasta, heavily dust a baking sheet with 1 to 2 cups flour. Pinch off a piece of dough and hold it over the floured baking sheet. Rub it between your palms to elongate it and let it drop onto the floured baking sheet. Repeat with remaining dough.

Let the pasta rest while you make the sauce. Thinly slice the onion. In a skillet, sauté the onion in ¼ cup olive oil until golden, then add the chili pepper, if using, and the tomato puree. Simmer to thicken, then taste and adjust salt.

Bring a large pot of salted water to a boil for the pasta. Stir in the remaining 2 tablespoons olive oil. Lift the pasta from the baking sheet and shake off excess flour (a sieve is helpful for this), then drop in the boiling water and cook al dente. (The pasta will cook very quickly.) Remove the pasta with a skimmer, reserving cooking water, and transfer to the pot with the sauce. Toss over medium heat to combine, stirring in the grated cheese as you do. If the dish looks dry, add a tablespoon or two of the pasta cooking water. Serve hot.

Serves 4 to 6

½ CAKE COMPRESSED YEAST OR 1½ TEASPOONS ACTIVE DRY YEAST

2 EGG WHITES, LIGHTLY BEATEN

SALT TO TASTE

8 CUPS UNBLEACHED ALL-PURPOSE FLOUR, PLUS 1 TO 2 CUPS FOR DUSTING

1 MEDIUM YELLOW ONION

¼ CUP PLUS 2 TABLESPOONS EXTRA-VIRGIN OLIVE OIL

GROUND CHILI PEPPER TO TASTE (OPTIONAL)

3 CUPS CANNED PEELED TOMATOES AND THEIR JUICES

½ CUP GRATED AGED SHEEP'S CHEESE

Lolli con le fave / HANDMADE SEMOLINA PASTA WITH FAVA BEANS

Trattoria La Rusticana, Modica (Ragusa), Sicilia

Serves 4 to 6

1 POUND FRESH FAVA BEANS

1 RIB CELERY

1 MEDIUM YELLOW ONION

SALT TO TASTE

3 CUPS SEMOLINA FLOUR

EXTRA-VIRGIN OLIVE OIL
FOR DRIZZLING

GROUND CHILI PEPPER
TO TASTE

FRESH THYME TO TASTE

Lolli pasta is similar to cavatelli. You can also make this dish with dried fava beans. Soak 2 to 3 cups of the dried beans for about 10 hours, then cook them in boiling water for 30 minutes before proceeding with the recipe. If fresh fava beans are very young, they will not need to be peeled (though they do need to be shelled, i.e., removed from their pods). If the skin around each individual bean has developed, though, it needs to be removed. The task is a bit tedious, but the rewards are worth it.

Shell and peel the fava beans. Remove any black spots with the tip of a sharp paring knife. Place the fava beans in a pot with a generous amount of water. Mince the celery and onion and add to the pot, along with a pinch of salt. Bring to a boil and simmer, stirring occasionally, until fava beans are very soft, about 1 hour.

While the beans are cooking, shape the flour into a well on the work surface. Add salted warm water to the center of the well and begin to pull in flour from the sides of the well. Continue adding water and combining it with the flour until you have a firm dough. Knead until smooth and elastic. Pull off a piece of pasta and roll into a thin rope about the size of a thin breadstick. Cut the rope into 2- to 2¼-inch lengths. Place one piece of on the work surface in front of you. Pressing gently in the center with your fingers, push the piece of pasta dough away from you. It should thin in the center and roll up at the sides so that it resembles a hot dog bun. Set aside on a baking sheet or tray and repeat with remaining dough. Let the shaped pasta dry for about 30 minutes.

When the beans are cooked, the mixture should still be fairly brothy. If it seems dry, stir in water to thin the mixture. Bring to a boil and add the pasta. Taste and add a little salt if necessary, then cook the pasta with the beans until the pasta is al dente, about 5 minutes. Divide among individual serving bowls, drizzle with olive oil, sprinkle with chili pepper and fresh thyme leaves, and serve hot.

Strangozzi con zucchine, ricotta e tartufo /
EGG SEMOLINA PASTA WITH ZUCCHINI AND TRUFFLE

Ristorante L'UmbriaCo, Acquasparta (Perugia), Umbria

Serves 4

2½ CUPS SEMOLINA FLOUR,
PLUS MORE FOR DUSTING

1 LARGE EGG

2 TEASPOONS SALT,
PLUS MORE TO TASTE

2 ZUCCHINI, SEEDED AND
CUT INTO JULIENNE

½ CUP WHITE WINE

1 SHALLOT

EXTRA-VIRGIN OLIVE OIL
FOR SAUTÉING

½ CUP VEGETABLE BROTH

MINCED CHILI PEPPER
TO TASTE

12 SQUASH BLOSSOMS

1 CUP GRATED
GRANA PADANO

AGED NORCIA RICOTTA
SHAVINGS FOR GARNISH

1½ OUNCES BLACK
SUMMER TRUFFLE

In Norcia, sheep's milk ricotta is drained, then coated in wheat bran and aged. A finished form looks like a large speckled egg. If you cannot find Norcia ricotta in your area, substitute any other ricotta salata. Semolina flour, made from durum wheat, is used in many kinds of pasta.

For the pasta, knead together the 2½ cups semolina flour, about ¼ cup water, the egg, and 2 teaspoons salt until you have a compact but elastic dough. Divide into 2 or 3 equal portions and on a work surface roll each into a very thin sheet, then roll each into a loose cylinder and with a sharp knife cut into noodles a little more than ¹⁄₁₀ inch wide. Spread the noodles out on the work surface, dust with semolina flour, and set aside to dry for a couple of hours.

Cut any seeds out of the zucchini, then cut them into julienne. Place the wine in a small saucepan and bring to a boil, then (very carefully) light the surface to burn off the alcohol. Mince the shallot. In a skillet, sauté the shallot in a small amount of oil until it just begins to sizzle, then add the wine and cook until evaporated. Add the vegetable broth, the zucchini, and the chili pepper. Season with salt and cook until zucchini are tender but still a little crisp, about 5 minutes. Pinch off the pistils from the squash blossoms and discard. Trim the stems.

Bring a large pot of salted water to a boil and cook the pasta until tender, 4 to 5 minutes, then drain and add to the skillet with the zucchini. Toss over medium heat while stirring in the grated cheese. Tear the zucchini blossoms in and stir to combine, then cook for just a few seconds more. Transfer to a serving bowl, garnish with the Norcia ricotta shavings, grate the black truffle on top, and serve immediately.

Cannerozzi allo zafarano /
EGG SEMOLINA PASTA WITH GROUND PEPPER POWDER

Federico Valicenti, Terranova di Pollino (Potenza), Basilicata

Finely ground semolina flour is sometimes labeled as durum flour. Sun-dried sweet Senise peppers are also known as *peperoni cruschi.*

Combine the 2¾ cups flour, eggs, and a pinch of salt to make a dough. Knead until smooth and elastic. Spread out dishtowels and flour generously. Roll the dough into a thin sheet and cut into small squares, then shape the squares into tubes by wrapping them one by one around a knitting needle or skewer (or the special tool made for this purpose if you have one). Set aside to rest on the floured towels.

When you are ready to serve the dish, bring a large pot of salted water to a boil, add the pasta, and cook until al dente, stirring frequently. Meanwhile, heat a little extra-virgin olive oil in a skillet. Add the ground pepper powder and stir until dissolved. Add the ricotta and stir to loosen and combine. If the ricotta is stiff, add a few tablespoons of the pasta cooking water to thin it to a creamy consistency. When the pasta is cooked, drain it and add it to the skillet. Season with a generous amount of freshly ground black pepper, and serve immediately.

Serves 4

2¾ CUPS FINELY GROUND SEMOLINA FLOUR, PLUS MORE FOR DUSTING

3 LARGE EGGS

SALT TO TASTE

EXTRA-VIRGIN OLIVE OIL FOR SAUTÉING

1 TEASPOON FINELY GROUND SUN-DRIED SENISE PEPPERS

1¼ CUPS RICOTTA

FRESHLY GROUND BLACK PEPPER TO TASTE

Maccaruni con i cacocciuli /
EGG SEMOLINA PASTA WITH WILD CARDOON BUDS
Osteria Da Giglio, Caulonia (Reggio di Calabria), Calabria

Serves 4 to 6

4 CUPS SEMOLINA FLOUR

4 LARGE EGGS

SALT TO TASTE

14 OUNCES WILD
CARDOON BUDS

EXTRA-VIRGIN OLIVE OIL
FOR DRIZZLING

2 CLOVES GARLIC

GROUND CHILI PEPPER TO
TASTE (OPTIONAL)

Wild cardoons—members of the thistle family—grow to large size and sprout fluffy purple flowers atop buds that resemble artichokes. They can be fried or preserved in oil. In Sicilia, boiled wild cardoons were once a popular street food. People would stroll around while plucking the leaves one by one.

Knead together the semolina flour and eggs with a pinch of salt until you have a smooth and elastic dough. (This will take some time and energy.) With a rolling pin, roll into a thin sheet. Cut the sheet into small squares. Set one square in the center of the work surface. Place a round metal skewer or knitting needle on top of it. Roll the needle with the palms of your hands so that the piece of dough forms a tube around it. Slide off the tube, set aside, and repeat with remaining pieces of dough.

Gently open the cardoon buds and place them in a pot. Drizzle with oil, season with salt, and add water to cover. Cover the pot with a tight-fitting lid and cook over low heat until all the water has evaporated, about 15 minutes. Add the garlic and a little more olive oil to the pot and continue to cook until golden and tender. Adjust salt to taste and stir in the chili pepper, if using.

Bring a large pot of salted water to a boil and cook the pasta. When the pasta is al dente, drain it and transfer to the pot with the cardoon buds. Stir to combine, drizzle with a little more oil, and serve immediately.

Tonnacchioli con le sparacogne /
EGG YOLK SEMOLINA PASTA WITH BRYONY SHOOTS

Trattoria San Giorgio e il Drago, Randazzo (Catania), Sicilia

Bryony shoots look like scraggly asparagus. This fast-growing plant is foraged in the woods in several different areas of Italy. While the shoots are edible, the other parts of the plants may have undesired effects and can even be toxic. Always consult with an experienced botanist or other expert before consuming anything you find in the wild. Pencil-thin wild asparagus make a good substitute for bryony.

Combine the semolina flour, the egg yolks, and a pinch of salt to make a crumbly dough, then add as much water as necessary to make a firm, elastic dough. Knead until well-combined, then wrap in a dishtowel and set aside to rest for 30 minutes.

Meanwhile, blanch the bryony in salted boiling water until just tender, 3 to 4 minutes. Drain, chop, and sauté in a small amount of oil in a skillet for 2 minutes. Add the wine and cook until evaporated. Season and adjust salt.

Divide the pasta dough into 4 equal pieces and roll out each to ¹⁄₁₀ inch thick. Cut into strips. Bring a large pot of salted water to a boil and cook the pasta al dente. Drain and add to the skillet with the bryony. Toss over medium heat to combine, then sprinkle with grated cheese and serve immediately.

Serves 4 to 6

4 CUPS SEMOLINA FLOUR

2 EGG YOLKS

SALT TO TASTE

1 POUND BRYONY SHOOTS

EXTRA-VIRGIN OLIVE OIL FOR SAUTÉING

½ CUP DRY WHITE WINE

GRATED AGED SHEEP'S CHEESE TO TASTE

Pizzoccheri / BUCKWHEAT NOODLES WITH CHEESE

Trattoria Altavilla, Bianzone (Sondrio), Lombardia

Serves 4 to 6

3⅓ CUPS BUCKWHEAT FLOUR

1 CUP UNBLEACHED
ALL-PURPOSE FLOUR

SALT TO TASTE

1 LARGE OR 2 SMALL
POTATOES

2 CUPS (ABOUT ¼ HEAD)
FINELY CHOPPED
SAVOY CABBAGE

1 CUP GRATED
PARMIGIANO REGGIANO

9 OUNCES CASERA CHEESE

14 TABLESPOONS (1 STICK
PLUS 6 TABLESPOONS)
UNSALTED BUTTER

2 TABLESPOONS
MINCED ONION

FRESHLY GROUND
BLACK PEPPER TO TASTE

Hearty *pizzoccheri* are prepared in a variety of ways, but they are most often matched with greens, such as cabbage or chard. Cow's milk casera and other alpine cheeses are frequently found in the mix as well.

On a work surface, combine the two types of flour with a pinch of salt and shape into a well. Add some water to the center of the well and begin to pull in flour from the sides of the well, adding water as needed, until you have a crumbly dough. Knead until firm and well-combined. With a rolling pin, roll the dough into a sheet about ¹⁄₁₀ inch thick and cut into strips 2¾ inches wide. Stack the strips together and cut them into rectangular noodles a little less than ½ inch wide and 2¾ inches long.

Peel and dice the potatoes. Bring a large pot of salted water to a boil and add the potatoes and the cabbage. When the water returns to a boil, gradually add the noodles, a handful at a time. Stir frequently to ward off sticking. Cook until pasta is cooked al dente and potatoes are tender, about 10 minutes.

When the pasta is cooked, remove some with a skimmer or slotted spoon and transfer to a warm serving platter. Top the pasta with some of the grated Parmigiano and shave on the casera. Continue to alternate layers of noodles and cheese until you have used up both.

Melt the butter in a skillet and brown the onion in the butter, then drizzle the butter and onions on top of the pasta. Do not mix. Season with freshly ground black pepper and serve immediately.

Orecchiette mollicate /
ORECCHIETTE WITH BREADCRUMBS AND DRIED PEPPERS

Ristorante Le Lucanerie, Matera, Basilicata

Serves 4

1½ CUPS SEMOLINA FLOUR

¾ CUP UNBLEACHED
ALL-PURPOSE FLOUR

SALT TO TASTE

4 SUN-DRIED SENISE PEPPERS

EXTRA-VIRGIN OLIVE OIL
FOR BLANCHING PEPPERS
AND SAUTÉING

10 TO 12 CHERRY TOMATOES

2 CUPS FRESH BREADCRUMBS

1 CUP GRATED AGED
CACIORICOTTA CHEESE

Cacioricotta is a mild aged cheese. Dried Senise peppers are sweet, not spicy, so they don't compete with the taste of the cheese.

Combine the two types of flour and a pinch of salt with enough warm water to make a smooth and elastic dough. Knead until well-combined, then cover (an overturned bowl is useful for this) and set aside to rest for at least 30 minutes.

Meanwhile, seed and stem the peppers. Heat some oil in a small pot and dip the peppers in the hot oil for a few seconds to crisp. Drain on paper towels, then cool in the refrigerator. Seed and chop the tomatoes.

Cut off a piece of the pasta dough about the size of an egg and roll it into a rope about ¾ inch wide. Slice the rope into disks about 1 inch wide. Place a disk on the work surface and press your thumb against it, dragging it across the work surface slightly in the direction away from you. The disk should form a cup shape. Repeat with remaining disks and then remaining dough. Let the orecchiette rest at room temperature.

In a skillet, toast the breadcrumbs in a little olive oil until golden. Break the peppers into the skillet by hand. Cook, stirring frequently, for 2 additional minutes. Taste and adjust salt.

Bring a large pot of salted water to a boil and cook the pasta al dente. Drain and add to the skillet with the breadcrumbs. Cook, tossing to combine, over medium heat for 2 to 3 minutes. Add the grated cheese and stir to combine, then stir in the tomatoes and serve hot.

Fregola con carciofi e cardi selvatici /
FREGOLA PASTA WITH ARTICHOKES AND WILD CARDOONS

Ristorante La Rosella, Giba (Carbonia-Iglesias), Sardegna

Fregola, the signature pasta of Sardegna, resembles couscous. It is often cooked like risotto through the incorporation of small amounts of broth or other liquid.

To make the fregola, place the semolina flour in a large earthenware bowl with a flat bottom. (If you don't have a large bowl, work in batches—the semolina flour should be spread thinly enough that you see the bottom of the bowl.) Fill a small bowl with lukewarm water and olive oil. Moisten your fingertips in the oil mixture and move them in a circular motion through the semolina flour, spiraling from the outside to the center, and dipping your fingers frequently so that they remain damp. The flour should clump into small balls. Spread the fregola out in a single layer on a baking sheet and let it rest until it is dry to the touch. Preheat the oven to 350°F and toast the fregola until golden, about 10 minutes. Set aside to cool.

Add the lemon juice to a large bowl of cold water. Trim the artichokes, cut out their chokes, and drop them into the prepared bowl of lemon water. Trim the cardoons and add them to the water as well. Bring a pot of salted water to a boil and blanch the cardoons, then drain and chop them. Thinly slice the onion. Mince the sun-dried tomatoes. Thinly slice the artichokes. Chop the cardoons. Place the broth in a small pot and keep warm.

Sauté the onion and garlic in oil in a skillet until golden. Remove and discard the garlic. Add the sun-dried tomatoes, artichokes, and cardoons and cook over medium heat, stirring frequently, for 15 minutes. Add the fregola and stir to coat, then begin adding the warm broth, about ¼ cup at a time, waiting for the last addition to be incorporated before adding the next, until fregola is cooked, 10 to 15 minutes. Sprinkle with a pinch of chili pepper and serve warm.

Serves 4

2⅓ CUPS SEMOLINA FLOUR

EXTRA-VIRGIN OLIVE OIL FOR FREGOLA DOUGH AND SAUTÉING

JUICE OF 1 LEMON

8 ARTICHOKES

7 OUNCES WILD CARDOONS

SALT TO TASTE

1 LARGE YELLOW ONION

3 SUN-DRIED TOMATOES

ABOUT 4 CUPS VEGETABLE BROTH

1 CLOVE GARLIC

GROUND CHILI PEPPER TO TASTE

Macarrones de ortu /
HANDMADE SEMOLINA PASTA WITH POTATOES AND TOMATOES

Ristorante Gikappa, Oliena (Nuoro), Sardegna

Serves 4

2¾ CUPS SEMOLINA FLOUR

SALT TO TASTE

3 RIPE TOMATOES

1 POUND (ABOUT 3 MEDIUM) POTATOES

1 CLOVE GARLIC

1 MEDIUM YELLOW ONION

EXTRA-VIRGIN OLIVE OIL FOR SAUTÉING

½ CUP GRATED SMOKED AGED RICOTTA

These long, thin pieces of macaroni resemble bucatini. The fresh tomatoes here can be replaced with about ½ cup tomato puree or chopped canned peeled tomatoes and their juices.

Shape the flour into a well on the work surface. Add a pinch of salt and some water to the center of the well and begin to pull in flour from the sides of the well. Continue adding water and combining it with the flour until you have a soft dough. Knead until smooth and elastic. Shape the dough into a ball, wrap in a dishtowel, and set aside to rest for 30 minutes. Then roll out the dough into a thin sheet and cut the sheet into strips. Wrap each strip around a thin skewer to form a long thin tube. Spread out the pasta in a single layer and allow to dry.

Meanwhile, seed and chop the tomaoes. Peel the potatoes and slice them. Bring a large pot of salted water to a boil. Add the potato slices and cook for 5 minutes, then add the pasta and cook until al dente, about 15 additional minutes.

While the pasta is cooking, mince the garlic and the onion and then brown in a skillet in a generous amount of oil. Add the tomatoes, season with salt, and cook over medium heat for 15 minutes. When the pasta and potatoes are cooked, drain and transfer to a serving bowl. Toss with the prepared sauce, then sprinkle on the grated cheese and serve.

Sagne 'ncannulate con pomodoro /
TWISTED HANDMADE SEMOLINA PASTA WITH TOMATOES
Trattoria Cucina Casareccia Le Zie, Lecce, Puglia

Sagne 'ncannulate noodles are like long fusilli. Some people use a knitting needle or round skewer for spiraling them, but the technique for shaping them by hand without a tool provided below isn't difficult. After a couple of tries, you should get the hang of it fairly quickly.

Shape the flour into a well on the work surface. Add a pinch of salt and some water to the center of the well and begin to pull in flour from the sides of the well. Continue adding water and combining it with the flour until you have a soft dough. Knead until smooth and elastic. Cover (an overturned bowl is useful for this) and set aside to rest, then roll out into a thin (but not paper-thin) sheet. Cut the sheet into strips a little less than ½ inch wide. Gently hold one end of the strip against the work surface with one hand and with your other hand roll the other end at an angle so the strip twists but does not overlap itself. After you roll it slowly a couple of turns, you should be able to quickly roll it against the work surface to finish the noodle. Shape into a loose horseshoe and set aside on a baking sheet or tray. Repeat with remaining strips. Set aside to rest until dry, 2 to 3 hours.

Thinly slice the onion. Halve the tomatoes. In a skillet, sauté the onion in olive oil. Add the tomatoes, season with salt, and tear in the basil leaves. Cook, stirring frequently, for 15 minutes.

Bring a large pot of salted water to a boil and cook the pasta. When the pasta is cooked, drain it and transfer to a serving bowl. Toss with the tomato sauce and top with grated or crumbled cheese and serve immediately.

Serves 4 to 6

4⅔ CUPS SEMOLINA FLOUR

SALT TO TASTE

4½ POUNDS (ABOUT 7 PINTS) CHERRY TOMATOES

1 MEDIUM YELLOW ONION

4 BASIL LEAVES

GRATED OR CRUMBLED CACIORICOTTA, AGED SHEEP'S CHEESE, OR AGED RICOTTA TO TASTE

EXTRA-VIRGIN OLIVE OIL FOR SAUTÉING

Bigoli con cardoncino e cardoncelli /
BIGOLI WITH WILD THISTLE AND OYSTER MUSHROOMS

Ristorante La Bottega dell'Allegria, Corato (Bari), Puglia

Serves 4 to 6

11 OUNCES WILD THISTLE

5 OUNCES (ABOUT ½ PINT)
CHERRY TOMATOES

¼ CUP EXTRA-VIRGIN
OLIVE OIL

2 CLOVES GARLIC

2⅔ CUPS (ABOUT
7 OUNCES) CHOPPED
OYSTER MUSHROOMS

SALT TO TASTE

11 OUNCES BIGOLI

¼ CUP GRATED OR CRUMBLED
RICOTTA MARZOTICA

¼ CUP MINCED PARSLEY

Wild thistles are foraged throughout the Murge area of Puglia. The thistle family includes artichokes and cardoons. If you can't find wild thistle in your area, the best substitute is either cardoons or artichoke stems, trimmed of any stringy fibers. Ricotta marzotica is lightly aged and wrapped in grass, which gives it its distinctively "green" taste. Bigoli are rustic thick spaghetti often made with whole wheat flour.

Trim the wild thistle of any tough fibers and dice. Halve the cherry tomatoes and set aside. Heat the oil in a skillet and brown the garlic. Add the mushrooms and cook, stirring frequently, until they have begun to brown. Add the tomatoes and cook, stirring frequently, until both mushrooms and tomatoes have given up their liquid, 5 to 10 minutes.

Meanwhile, bring a large pot of salted water to a boil and cook the thistle for 5 minutes. Add the bigoli and cook until pasta is cooked al dente.

Drain thistle and pasta and add to the skillet with the mushrooms and tomatoes. Toss over medium heat for a few minutes, then stir in the cheese and parsley and serve hot.

Fregnacce con verdure / BUCKWHEAT PASTA WITH AROMATIC HERBS

Ristorante Enoteca Il Bistrot, Rieti, Lazio

This dish pairs buckwheat noodles with aromatic herbs and spring vegetables. Fresh rosemary, parsley, marjoram, basil, chives, and oregano are all good options for the herbs. Small leaves can be left whole; larger leaves should be chopped or torn by hand. For the vegetables, the most common choices are asparagus tips, trimmed and thinly sliced baby artichokes, tiny chiodini mushrooms, shelled peas, shelled and peeled fava beans, and puntarelle (a type of chicory). If using puntarelle, slice the long, slender leaves into strips and let them soak in ice water while you prepare the dish—they will curl up into spirals. This pasta can also be served in a tomato sauce with black olives.

Combine the three types of flour and knead with 1 pinch salt, a drizzle of olive oil, and enough water to make a compact but elastic dough. Roll the dough into a thin sheet and cut into irregular pieces.

In a skillet, heat the 2 tablespoons olive oil and add the aromatic herbs (minced and/or torn if necessary) and the garlic. Cook over low heat until garlic browns, then remove and discard garlic. Season with salt and pepper. Add the vegetables. Cook until tender, adding the broth in small amounts to keep the mixture from sticking to the pan, about 10 minutes. Stir in grated ricotta salata.

Bring a large pot of salted water to a boil and cook the pasta al dente. Drain and toss over low heat in the skillet with the vegetables to combine, then serve hot.

Serves 4

2½ CUPS UNBLEACHED ALL-PURPOSE FLOUR

⅓ CUP SEMOLINA FLOUR

⅓ CUP BUCKWHEAT FLOUR

SALT TO TASTE

2 TABLESPOONS EXTRA-VIRGIN OLIVE OIL, PLUS A DRIZZLE FOR PASTA DOUGH

MINCED AROMATIC HERBS TO TASTE (SEE NOTE)

1 CLOVE GARLIC

FRESHLY GROUND BLACK PEPPER TO TASTE

2 TO 3 CUPS SPRING VEGETABLES (SEE NOTE)

ABOUT ½ CUP VEGETABLE BROTH

GRATED RICOTTA SALATA TO TASTE

Agnolotti verdi / GREEN AGNOLOTTI

Ristorante del Mercato da Maurizio, Cravanzana (Cuneo), Piemonte

Serves 4 to 6

SALT TO TASTE

1 CUP RICE

½ CUP GRATED PARMIGIANO
REGGIANO, PLUS MORE
FOR SERVING

4 TABLESPOONS UNSALTED
BUTTER, PLUS MORE
FOR SERVING

1 POUND (ABOUT
1½ BUNCHES) CHARD

¼ HEAD SAVOY CABBAGE

1 HEAD ESCAROLE

¼ CUP TIGHTLY PACKED
BORAGE LEAVES

2 LEEKS

4 CUPS UNBLEACHED
ALL-PURPOSE FLOUR

3 LARGE EGGS

1 TABLESPOON EXTRA-VIRGIN
OLIVE OIL

LEAVES OF 1 SPRIG SAGE

Bring a pot of salted water to a boil and cook the rice as you would pasta, stirring frequently, until tender. Drain and mix with the ½ cup grated Parmigiano and 4 tablespoons butter until well-combined. Bring a pot of salted water to a boil and cook the chard until just tender. Remove to a colander with a slotted spoon or skimmer. Set aside a little less than half the chard for making the pasta dough. Cook the cabbage, escarole, borage, and leeks in the pot until just tender, then drain. Combine the larger portion of the chard with the remaining greens and mince as finely as possible. Stir the minced greens into the rice mixture and set aside.

Mince the remaining portion of chard very finely. Combine the flour and the minced chard and form into a well on the work surface. Place the eggs and olive oil in the center with a pinch of salt and stir lightly with a fork to break yolks. Begin to pull in the flour from the sides of the well and combine it with the flour. Once you have a crumbly dough, knead briskly until it is smooth and compact and an even green color throughout. Roll the dough into thin sheets.

Arrange small portions of the rice filling along the edge of the dough, leaving a ½-inch margin from the edge and about ½ inch between each portion. Fold the sheet of dough over to cover the portions of dough. Press with your fingers to seal and cut along the edge with a wheel cutter. You should now have a long tube of dough with evenly spaced portions of filling. Pinch between the portions of filling with your fingertips to seal. Use the wheel cutter to cut the pieces apart, starting from the side where the fold is and moving the cutter quickly. The pieces of pasta should fold over slightly to create the characteristic shape. Repeat with remaining dough and filling. Let the pasta rest for a couple of hours. When you are ready to cook the pasta, melt some butter for serving with a few sage leaves to flavor the butter. Meanwhile, bring a large pot of salted water to a boil and cook the pasta just until it rises to the top, which will take only a couple of minutes. Remove the pasta with a slotted spoon or skimmer and transfer to a serving bowl. Pour the melted butter on top, sprinkle with additional grated Parmigiano, and serve hot.

Cresc' tajat ai carciofi / CORNMEAL PASTA WITH SPICY ARTICHOKES

Ristorante La Baita, Arcevia (Ancona), Marche

Serves 4

SALT TO TASTE

2⅓ CUPS POLENTA

1 LARGE EGG

2½ CUPS UNBLEACHED
ALL-PURPOSE FLOUR

½ CUP GRATED AGED
SHEEP'S CHEESE

FRESHLY GROUND BLACK
PEPPER TO TASTE

JUICE OF ½ LEMON

3 ARTICHOKES

4 RIPE TOMATOES

½ MEDIUM YELLOW ONION,
MINCED

EXTRA-VIRGIN OLIVE OIL FOR
SAUTÉING AND DRIZZLING

1 CHILI PEPPER

½ CUP VERDICCHIO DEI
CASTELLI DI JESI WHITE WINE

LEAVES OF 1 SPRIG PARSLEY,
MINCED

This unusual pasta is made using leftover polenta, so if you have some already cooked, don't bother to make more. The pasta is also good when topped with cannellini beans and tomatoes.

First, make polenta: bring a large pot of salted water to a boil and drizzle in the polenta, stirring to avoid creating lumps. Cook over low heat, stirring constantly, until thickened and no longer raw tasting, about 40 minutes. Remove the polenta from the heat and allow to cool, then transfer to a bowl. Beat in the egg, the flour, and the grated cheese. Knead (as the polenta cools it will get stiffer) until well combined. Season with salt and pepper. Spread the mixture about ⅒ inch thick and use a smooth wheel cutter to cut into medium-size lozenges or diamonds.

For the sauce, in a large bowl combine the lemon juice with cold water. Trim any hard leaves from the artichokes, remove the chokes, and cut into julienne, then drop into the prepared water. Peel and seed the tomatoes and dice them. Mince the onion and sauté it in a large pot in oil with the chili pepper. Add the wine and cook until evaporated. Add the artichokes and cook until tender, 5 to 6 minutes. Add the tomatoes and cook until well combined and soft. Season with salt.

Bring a large pot of salted water to a boil and cook the pasta al dente, 2 to 3 minutes. Drain and add to the pot with the artichokes. Cook, stirring, to combine, then drizzle with a little olive, sprinkle on parsley, and serve.

Tagliatelle piccanti di castagne /
CHESTNUT NOODLES WITH PORCINI MUSHROOMS

Trattoria La Pergola, Gesualdo (Avellino), Campania

You can leave the garlic and chili pepper whole and discard them before serving, or mince and incorporate them if you like extra heat.

Combine the flours with a pinch of salt and shape into a well on the work surface. Add some water to the center of the well and begin to pull in flour from the sides of the well, adding water as needed, until you have a crumbly dough. Knead until firm and well-combined, adding enough water to make a smooth and elastic dough. Wrap the dough in plastic wrap and set aside to rest for 30 minutes. With a rolling pin, roll out the dough into a thin sheet and cut into noodles a little less than ¼ inch wide. Spread out and allow to dry slightly.

Bring a large pot of salted water to a boil and cook the pasta. While the pasta is cooking, slice the mushrooms. In a skillet, brown the garlic, chili pepper, and mushrooms in oil until the mushrooms have given up all of their liquid. Add the cherry tomatoes, season with salt, and cook until well combined, about 10 minutes, incorporating small amounts of pasta cooking water (¼ to ½ cup) to keep the pan moist. When the pasta is cooked al dente, drain and add to the skillet. Toss over medium heat to combine, then sprinkle with the minced parsley and serve.

Serves 4

1⅔ CUPS CHESTNUT FLOUR

1 CUP SEMOLINA FLOUR

SALT TO TASTE

4 OUNCES PORCINI MUSHROOMS

1 CLOVE GARLIC

1 CHILI PEPPER

EXTRA-VIRGIN OLIVE OIL FOR SAUTÉING

6 CHERRY TOMATOES

LEAVES OF 1 SPRIG PARSLEY, MINCED

Tagliolini di castagne con noci e cacao /
CHESTNUT NOODLES WITH WALNUTS AND COCOA

Ristorante Il Vecchio Castagno, Serrastretta (Catanzaro), Calabria

Serves 4

1 CUP WALNUTS

1¾ CUPS SEMOLINA FLOUR

2¼ CUPS CHESTNUT FLOUR

2 LARGE EGGS

¼ CUP UNSWEETENED
COCOA POWDER

SALT TO TASTE

1 CUP (9 OUNCES) SHEEP'S
MILK RICOTTA

¼ CUP WHOLE MILK

EXTRA-VIRGIN OLIVE OIL
FOR SAUTÉING

FRESHLY GRATED NUTMEG
TO TASTE

GRATED SMOKED RICOTTA
TO TASTE (OPTIONAL)

Cocoa powder is naturally bitter, but because most of the time it is eaten in sweet desserts with plenty of sugar, that side of its character frequently is hidden. Here, it gets a chance to shine.

Grind the walnuts finely, but don't let them turn into a paste. Set aside. Combine the semolina flour and chestnut flour and shape into a well on the work surface. Place the eggs in the center of the well and beat lightly with a fork. Begin to pull in flour from the side of the well until you have a crumbly dough. Sprinkle on the cocoa powder and salt and continue kneading, adding water in small amounts, until you have a compact but soft dough. Roll into a sheet of medium thickness for pasta (meaning not paper-thin), dust lightly with flour, then roll up and cut into thin noodles with a knife. Gently shake the noodles to separate, then set them aside to rest on the work surface.

In a skillet, whisk the ricotta with the milk to loosen it to the consistency of sour cream. Drizzle in a little oil, season with grated nutmeg, and cook, stirring frequently, over low heat for 10 minutes.

Bring a large pot of salted water to a boil and cook the pasta al dente. When the pasta is cooked, drain and add to the skillet. Toss to combine for a minute or two, then sprinkle on the walnuts and the smoked ricotta, if using. Serve hot.

Pasta di carrube al sugo di pistacchi / CAROB PASTA WITH PISTACHIOS

Trattoria U Sulicc'enti, Rosolini (Siracusa), Sicilia

Bronte pistachios from Sicilia are extremely flavorful. Carob powder—made by grinding the pods of the carob tree—looks like cocoa powder but has its own particular flavor.

Combine the semolina flour and carob powder with a pinch of salt and shape into a well on the work surface. Place the eggs in the center of the well and beat lightly with a fork. Begin to pull in flour from the side of the well until you have a crumbly dough, then knead until you have a smooth and elastic dough. Allow the dough to rest (covered with an overturned bowl) for 30 minutes.

Meanwhile, coarsely chop the pistachios. Thinly slice the leek and sauté the leek in oil in a skillet until golden. Add the pistachios and season with salt and pepper. Toss just until toasted, then remove from the heat.

With a rolling pin, roll out the pasta dough into a very thin sheet less than ¹⁄₁₀ inch thick. Let the sheet of dough dry briefly, then roll into a loose cylinder and with a sharp knife cut into ¾ inch wide noodles. Gently shake the noodles to separate them and spread them out on the work surface to dry briefly.

Bring a large pot of salted water to a boil and cook the pasta until al dente. It should cook in just a few minutes. Add a little of the pasta cooking water to the skillet with the pistachios, then drain the pasta and add it to the skillet as well. Toss over medium heat until combined, then serve hot.

Serves 4 to 6

1½ CUPS SEMOLINA FLOUR

½ CUP CAROB POWDER

SALT TO TASTE

2 LARGE EGGS

2 CUPS BRONTE PISTACHIOS

1 SMALL LEEK

EXTRA-VIRGIN OLIVE OIL FOR SAUTÉING

FRESHLY GROUND BLACK PEPPER TO TASTE

Cavatelli a mischiglio /
CAVATELLI WITH SEMOLINA, BARLEY, CHICKPEA, AND FAVA FLOURS

Ristorante Luna Rossa, Terranova di Pollino (Potenza), Basilicata

Serves 6

⅔ CUP SEMOLINA FLOUR

⅔ CUP BARLEY FLOUR

¾ CUP CHICKPEA FLOUR

¾ CUP FAVA BEAN FLOUR

SALT TO TASTE

1 POUND 5 OUNCES (ABOUT
2 PINTS) RIPE CHERRY OR
GRAPE TOMATOES

2 BAY LEAVES

¼ CUP EXTRA-VIRGIN
OLIVE OIL

Satisfying legumes and grains have long fed the people of Basilicata and are often ground into flour, though this is a fairly new interpretation. Typically in the past, flours like these were cooked into a kind of porridge similar to polenta.

Combine the four flours with a pinch of salt and shape into a well on the work surface. Add some warm water to the center of the well and begin to pull in flour from the sides of the well, adding water as needed, until you have a crumbly dough. Knead until soft and no longer sticky. Set the dough aside (cover with an overturned bowl) to rest for at least 30 minutes.

While the dough is resting, chop the tomatoes. Heat 1 tablespoon oil in a skillet and sauté the tomatoes just until softened. Season with salt, then add ½ cup water. Cook over low heat for 15 minutes.

Pinch off a piece of the pasta dough and roll into a rope about ½ inch wide. Cut into 1-inch pieces. Place one of the pieces of pasta dough on the work surface and press in the center with your index finger and middle finger, rocking slightly, so that the center thins and the edges curl up. The piece of pasta should look like a hot dog bun. Repeat with remaining dough.

Bring a large pot of salted water to a boil and cook the pasta until al dente, 5 to 7 minutes. Meanwhile, in a small skillet, heat the remaining 3 tablespoons oil with the bay leaves until they begin to give off their aroma. Remove and discard the bay leaves and add the flavored oil to the skillet with the tomatoes and cook, stirring, for 1 minute. When the pasta is cooked, drain it and transfer to a serving bowl, then top with the tomato sauce and serve hot.

Ravioli di erbe selvatiche al burro /
RAVIOLI WITH RAMSON, NETTLES, AND WILD SPINACH IN BUTTER SAUCE

Ristorante Lanzenschuster, San Genesio Atesino-Jenesien, Alto Adige

Lambsquarters, or wild spinach, is more flavorful and has a little more body than typical supermarket spinach, but you can always swap in standard spinach if you have trouble tracking it down. Nettles are covered in little prickly hairs that become harmless once cooked but can be irritating, so always wear gloves when you are dealing with them. Ramson is wild garlic and is very similar to the ramps (wild leeks) that are foraged in some parts of North America in the spring.

Combine the flours and form them into a well on the work surface. Place the eggs, egg yolks, and olive oil in the center with a pinch of salt and stir lightly with a fork to break yolks. Begin to pull in the flour from the sides of the well and combine it with the flour, adding water as needed to keep the dough soft. Once you have a crumbly dough, knead briskly until it is smooth and elastic. Set aside to rest (cover with an overturned bowl) for 30 minutes.

While the dough is resting, prepare the filling. Bring a pot of water to a boil and cook the nettle leaves (discard hard stems), ramps, and lambsquarters until tender, about 2 minutes. Drain and squeeze as dry as possible, then puree through a sieve. Thinly slice the onion and sauté it with the garlic in olive oil. When the garlic has browned, remove and discard it. Add the cooked greens and season with salt, pepper, and nutmeg.

Roll out the pasta dough into a thin sheet and cut it into disks. Place about 1 teaspoon of the filling (depending on the size of the disks) in the center of half of the disks. Cover with the remaining disks and seal around the perimeter of each by pressing with your fingertips.

Bring a large pot of salted water to a boil and cook the pasta just until it rises to the surface, 2 to 3 minutes. Drizzle with the melted butter, sprinkle with the parsley, and serve hot.

Serves 4 to 6

1¼ CUPS SEMOLINA FLOUR

2 CUPS UNBLEACHED ALL-PURPOSE FLOUR

3 LARGE EGGS

3 EGG YOLKS

2 TABLESPOONS EXTRA-VIRGIN OLIVE OIL

14 OUNCES NETTLES

7 OUNCES RAMSON

7 OUNCES LAMBSQUARTERS

1 MEDIUM YELLOW ONION

1 CLOVE GARLIC

EXTRA-VIRGIN OLIVE OIL FOR SAUTÉING

SALT AND FRESHLY GROUND BLACK PEPPER TO TASTE

FRESHLY GRATED NUTMEG TO TASTE

3 TO 4 TABLESPOONS UNSALTED BUTTER, MELTED

LEAVES OF 1 SPRIG PARSLEY, MINCED

Ravioli di patate con erbette /
POTATO DOUGH RAVIOLI WITH WILD GREENS AND HERBS

Signaterhof, Renon-Ritten, Alto Adige

Serves 4 to 6

SALT TO TASTE

1½ POUNDS WILD GREENS
AND HERBS

1¼ CUPS RICOTTA

FRESHLY GRATED NUTMEG
TO TASTE

2 POUNDS (ABOUT 6 MEDIUM)
POTATOES

ABOUT 2 CUPS UNBLEACHED
ALL-PURPOSE FLOUR

6 EGG YOLKS

½ CUP GRATED
PARMIGIANO REGGIANO

MELTED BUTTER TO TASTE

There are many wild herbs and greens to choose among in the mountainous region of Alto Adige. When you cook them, don't use a tremendous amount of water—that will help preserve their flavor. Ramson (wild garlic) or ramps (wild leeks) are an excellent option. The amount of flour the potatoes can absorb varies depending on the type of potatoes you use, the stage when they were picked, and how they were stored. The dough should be soft and dry enough to roll, but still ever so slightly sticky (like a gnocchi dough). Add flour gradually in small amounts until you reach that stage. For a pretty presentation, reserve a few tender leaves of wild herbs and a few tablespoons of the greens for the filling and use them for garnish.

Fill a pot with a few inches of water, season with salt, bring to a boil, and cook the greens and herbs until tender. Drain, squeeze out as much liquid as possible, and mince. Combine the cooked greens with the ricotta and a sprinkling of nutmeg and set aside.

Boil the potatoes until tender enough to pierce with a fork, then peel and crush with a potato ricer. Combine the potatoes and 1¾ cups flour on a work surface. Beat the egg yolks with a pinch of salt and knead the flour and potato mixture, adding the egg yolks a little at a time to distribute evenly. If the dough is so sticky that it is hard to knead, incorporate additional flour a little at a time. (It can also help to flour your hands.) When you have a soft dough, roll it out into a thin sheet. Cut into strips twice as wide as you would like your ravioli to be and arrange small portions of the filling on one side, leaving a margin near the edge. Fold the empty side of the strip of dough over the filling, press lightly with your fingertips all around the filling to seal, then cut into squares with a serrated wheel cutter. Repeat with remaining dough and filling.

To cook, bring a large pot of salted water to a boil. Add the ravioli and cook until they float to the top, about 5 minutes. Remove with a slotted spoon or skimmer and transfer to a serving bowl. Top with the grated Parmigiano and melted butter, toss to combine, and serve immediately.

Klotznnudln / RAVIOLI WITH DRIED PEARS AND RICOTTA

Antica Trattoria da Giusi, Malborghetto-Valbruna (Udine), Friuli Venezia Giulia

Serves 4

1 POUND DRIED PEARS

SALT TO TASTE

1 CUP UNBLEACHED
ALL-PURPOSE FLOUR

1 LARGE EGG

½ MEDIUM YELLOW
ONION, MINCED

1 TABLESPOON
UNSALTED BUTTER

¾ CUP RICOTTA

MELTED BUTTER FOR SERVING

The dried pears in this dish are evidence of the influence that Austrian cuisine has wielded on neighboring Friuli Venezia Giulia, where certain areas were once part of the Austro-Hungarian Empire. Round pasta of this type always results in a certain amount of scraps of dough. You can reroll the scraps to make a few more ravioli, or chop them into small random shapes like confetti and use those in soup. Chopped small egg pasta can be frozen, and there's no need to thaw it—just drop it into soup and let it cook until tender.

Place the pears in a small pot, add water to cover by several inches, bring to a boil, and simmer until very soft, about 1 hour.

While the pears are cooking, prepare the pasta dough. Dissolve a pinch of salt in about ¼ cup warm water. Shape the flour into a well on the work surface and add the egg and the salted water to the center of the well. With a fork, gently beat to break the yolk. Begin pulling in flour from the sides of the well until you have a crumbly dough, adding more water as necessary. Knead the dough (again, adding water if necessary) until it is smooth and compact.

Drain the softened pears and mince them. Mince the onion, and in a skillet, sauté the onion in 1 tablespoon butter. In a bowl, stir together the ricotta, sautéed onion, and minced pears. Taste and adjust salt.

With a rolling pin, roll out the pasta dough into a very thin sheet and cut it into disks 2¾ inches to 3 inches in diameter. Place a small spoonful of the ricotta mixture in the center of one disk. Fold the pasta in half to make a half-moon and seal the edges firmly by pressing with your fingertips. (Moisten your fingertips if necessary.) Repeat with remaining dough and filling. Bring a large pot of salted water to a boil and cook the pasta until it rises to the surface. Remove with a slotted spoon or skimmer and transfer to a serving bowl. Drizzle with melted butter, toss, and serve immediately.

Culurzones di patate e menta / POTATO AND MINT STUFFED PASTA

Ristorante Pisturri, Magomadas (Oristano), Sardegna

Use as much or as little cheese in the filling as you like. If you err on the side of caution with the cheese, you may need to incorporate a second egg in order for it to have the correct consistency. The filling should be smooth but dense—neither runny nor stiff and crumbly.

Shape the flour into a well on the work surface and add 1 egg, a pinch of salt, and a little warm water to the center of the well. With a fork, gently beat to break up the egg. Begin pulling in flour from the sides of the well until you have a crumbly dough. Knead the dough until it is smooth and compact, adding as much additional warm water as necessary. Wrap in a dishtowel and set aside to rest in a cool place for 1 hour.

Bring a large pot of water to a boil and cook the potatoes until easily pierced with a fork. Once the potatoes are cool enough to handle, peel them, crush them, and combine them with 1 egg, mint, and sheep's cheese. If the mixture is very dry and stiff, incorporate another egg.

Roll the pasta into a thin sheet and cut into rectangles 1 inch wide and 2 inches long. Place a portion of the potato mixture off-center on a rectangle, then fold the empty half of the rectangle over the filling and press with your fingertips to seal the edges. Repeat with remaining dough and filling.

Bring a large pot of salted water to a boil and cook the pasta until it rises to the surface. Gently remove with a slotted spoon or skimmer, drain, and transfer to a serving bowl, then top with the tomato sauce and serve immediately.

Serves 4

2½ CUPS SEMOLINA FLOUR

ABOUT 2 LARGE EGGS

SALT TO TASTE

1 POUND 5 OUNCES (ABOUT 4 MEDIUM) POTATOES

LEAVES OF 1 SPRIG MINT, MINCED

GRATED AGED SPICY SHEEP'S CHEESE TO TASTE

TOMATO SAUCE FOR SERVING, WARM

Pansotti con salsa di noci / CHEESE-STUFFED PASTA IN WALNUT SAUCE

Osteria Panzallegra, Sarzana (La Spezia), Liguria

Serves 6

3⅓ CUPS UNBLEACHED
ALL-PURPOSE FLOUR

4 LARGE EGGS

SALT TO TASTE

2 CUPS GRATED YOUNG
SHEEP'S CHEESE

1¼ CUPS RICOTTA

1½ CUPS GRATED
PARMIGIANO REGGIANO

2 EGG YOLKS

FRESHLY GROUND
BLACK PEPPER TO TASTE

3¾ CUPS WALNUTS

2 TABLESPOONS PINE NUTS
(OPTIONAL)

1 CLOVE GARLIC

3 TABLESPOONS
UNSALTED BUTTER

ABOUT 2 TABLESPOONS
WHOLE MILK

In Liguria, the filling for triangular pansotti may also incorporate minced wild greens and herbs or borage and chard.

Shape the flour into a well on the work surface and add the eggs, a pinch of salt, and a couple tablespoons of water to the center of the well. With a fork, gently beat to break up the eggs. Begin pulling in flour from the sides of the well until you have a crumbly dough. Knead the dough until it is smooth and compact, adding more water as necessary. Roll out the dough into a thin sheet and cut into squares with 4-inch sides.

In a bowl combine the sheep's cheese, ricotta, and Parmigiano. Stir in the egg yolks and season with salt and pepper. Place a portion of the filling (about 1 tablespoon) in the center of one of the squares and fold in half with the edges meeting to form a right triangle. Press around the edges to seal. Repeat with remaining squares and filling.

Grind the walnuts (with the pine nuts, if using) to a fine powder but not a paste. Mince the garlic. In a large skillet, melt the butter, then cook the garlic in the butter until golden. Add the ground nuts and cook, stirring frequently. When the nuts are nicely toasted, add the milk and cook, stirring frequently, until it has reduced and the mixture is well-combined and creamy. Taste and adjust salt.

Bring a large pot of salted water to a boil and cook the pasta until it rises to the surface, 2 to 3 minutes. Remove with a skimmer, transfer to the skillet, toss briefly over medium heat to combine, and serve immediately.

Cancì / TORTELLI WITH SPINACH AND CHEESE

Trattoria Garsun, Marebbe-Enneberg, Alto Adige

These round ravioli may also be served fried in the Alto Adige region. They reflect the influence of the Ladin ethnic and linguistic group in this area. These were once topped with grated *ziger*, a curd cheese scented with black pepper and chives, but these days that cheese is difficult to track down even in its native area. It is included in the Slow Food Ark of Taste.

Shape the flour into a well on the work surface and add the eggs, a pinch of salt, and the olive oil to the center of the well. With a fork, gently beat to break up the eggs. Begin pulling in flour from the sides of the well until you have a crumbly dough. Knead the dough until it is smooth and compact. Wrap in a dishtowel and set aside to rest for at least 15 minutes.

Blanch the spinach in lightly salted boiling water, then squeeze dry and mince. Mince the onion. Melt 1 tablespoon butter in a skillet and sauté the onion and spinach until any remaining liquid has evaporated. Grind very finely, preferably with a food processor fitted with the metal blade. In a bowl, combine the spinach with the ricotta. Season with salt, pepper, and nutmeg. If the mixture is runny, add breadcrumbs in small amounts until it feels stiff enough to work as a filling for the pasta.

Roll out the pasta dough very thin, about ⅟20 inch thick. With a cutter or the rim of a drinking glass, cut the sheet into circles about 2 ¼ to 2 ½ inches in diameter. Place 1 teaspoon of the spinach mixture in the center of one disk. Fold in half and press the edges to seal into a half-moon. Repeat with remaining disks and filling.

Bring a large pot of water to a boil and cook the pasta. While the pasta is cooking, melt the remaining 3 tablespoons butter in a large skillet over low heat. When the pasta rises to the surface, gently remove it with a slotted spoon or skimmer and add it to the skillet. Toss over low heat to combine, then sprinkle with grated Grana Padano and serve immediately.

Serves 4 to 6

1⅔ CUPS UNBLEACHED ALL-PURPOSE FLOUR

2 LARGE EGGS

SALT TO TASTE

1 TABLESPOON EXTRA-VIRGIN OLIVE OIL

1 POUND SPINACH

½ YELLOW ONION

4 TABLESPOONS UNSALTED BUTTER

¾ CUP RICOTTA

FRESHLY GROUND BLACK PEPPER TO TASTE

FRESHLY GRATED NUTMEG TO TASTE

ABOUT ¼ CUP BREADCRUMBS

GRATED GRANA PADANO FOR SERVING

Tortelli con la coda / "TAIL" TORTELLI

Ristorante Antica Locanda del Falco, Gazzola (Piacenza), Emilia-Romagna

Serves 4

4 CUPS UNBLEACHED
ALL-PURPOSE FLOUR
OR 00 FLOUR

7 LARGE EGGS

4 OUNCES SPINACH

SALT TO TASTE

1¼ CUPS RICOTTA

2 CUPS GRATED
PARMIGIANO REGGIANO,
PLUS MORE FOR SERVING

FRESHLY GRATED NUTMEG
TO TASTE

BUTTER FOR SERVING

SAGE LEAVES FOR SERVING

This pasta is a little fussy to produce (though the process isn't difficult—once you've made a few, you'll pick up speed quickly), but they are beautiful and always make an impression. Butter and sage is a classic topping for this type of pasta, but it also pairs beautifully with chopped porcini mushrooms.

Shape the flour into a well on the work surface and add 5 eggs to the center of the well. With a fork, gently beat to break up the eggs. Begin pulling in flour from the sides of the well until you have a crumbly dough. Knead the dough until it is smooth and compact. Let the dough rest (covered with an overturned bowl) for 30 minutes.

Blanch the spinach in lightly salted boiling water, then squeeze dry and mince. In a bowl, combine the spinach with the ricotta, the 2 cups grated Parmigiano, and the 2 remaining eggs. Season with salt and nutmeg. Whisk very smooth.

Roll out the pasta dough into a very thin sheet, then cut into squares with 2-inch sides. Place about 1 teaspoon of the filling slightly off center on a square. Place the square in the palm of one hand and with the other hand pinch over alternating sides of the dough (right-left-right-left) to form a braid down the center and a little tail at the end. Pinch to seal. Repeat with remaining squares of dough and filling.

Bring a large pot of water to a boil and cook the pasta. While the pasta is cooking, melt butter in a large skillet with the sage leaves. When the pasta rises to the surface, gently remove it with a slotted spoon or skimmer and add it to the skillet. Toss over low heat to combine, then sprinkle with grated Parmigiano and serve immediately.

Tortelli di zucca / SQUASH TORTELLI

Hostaria Viola, Castiglione delle Stiviere (Mantova), Lombardia

Mantova squash has a particularly dry flesh that makes it great for this filling. Kobucha squash shares many of the same qualities. Mostarda is a zesty chutney that balances the sweetness of the squash and the amaretto cookies.

Preheat oven to 400°F. Peel, seed, and chop the squash. Mince the shallot. Scatter on a baking pan and roast in the preheated oven until squash is tender, about 30 minutes.

Shape the flour into a well on the work surface and add the eggs to the center of the well. With a fork, gently beat to break up the eggs. Begin pulling in flour from the sides of the well until you have a crumbly dough. Knead the dough until it is soft and compact. Let the dough rest (covered with an overturned bowl) for at least 30 minutes.

Crush the cooked squash through a potato ricer and place in a medium pot. Beat in the butter. Crumble the amaretto cookies and stir into the mixture. Mince any large chunks of apple in the mostarda and stir that in as well, along with the grated Parmigiano. If the mixture seems runny, stir in breadcrumbs until it is firm. Season with nutmeg, salt, and pepper, and stir in the zest or ginger, if using. Cook, stirring, over medium heat until the mixture is compact and firm and feels like a soft dough.

Use a crank pasta machine to roll out the pasta dough into a thin sheet, then cut into 2-inch squares with a wheel cutter. Place a small amount of the squash mixture on a square than fold in half, pressing firmly with your fingertips around the edge to seal.

Bring a large pot of water to a boil and cook the pasta. While the pasta is cooking, melt butter for serving in a skillet with the sage leaves. When the pasta rises to the surface, gently remove it with a slotted spoon or skimmer and transfer to a serving bowl. Pour the butter and sage over the pasta, toss gently to combine, and serve immediately.

Serves 6 to 8

1 MANTOVA SQUASH OR OTHER WINTER SQUASH, ABOUT 4½ POUNDS, PEELED, SEEDED, AND CHOPPED

1 SHALLOT

5 CUPS UNBLEACHED ALL-PURPOSE FLOUR

6 LARGE EGGS

1 TABLESPOON UNSALTED BUTTER, PLUS MORE FOR SERVING

5 AMARETTO COOKIES, CRUMBLED

⅓ CUP APPLE MOSTARDA, MINCED

2 CUPS GRATED PARMIGIANO REGGIANO

ABOUT ¼ CUP BREADCRUMBS

FRESHLY GRATED NUTMEG TO TASTE

SALT AND FRESHLY GROUND BLACK PEPPER TO TASTE

GRATED ORANGE OR LEMON ZEST OR GRATED GINGER (OPTIONAL)

3 TO 4 SAGE LEAVES

Ravioli di ricotta con zucchero e cannella /
RICOTTA RAVIOLI WITH SUGAR AND CINNAMON

Ristorante Zenobi, Colonnella (Teramo), Abruzzo

Serves 10

2 CUPS SHEEP'S MILK RICOTTA

1 CUP SUGAR, PLUS MORE
FOR SERVING

1 TABLESPOON PLUS
1 TEASPOON GROUND
CINNAMON, PLUS MORE
FOR SERVING

ABOUT ¼ CUP FRESH
BREADCRUMBS

3 CUPS UNBLEACHED
ALL-PURPOSE FLOUR

2 LARGE EGGS

4 EGG YOLKS

The filling for these unusual ravioli (served as a first course, though they are fairly sweet) should be the right consistency for piping, neither too stiff nor too loose. You may not need the breadcrumbs at all if your ricotta is thick enough, and if your ricotta seems very liquid, you may want to drain it in a sieve before using. The cinnamon flavor of the filling should be quite pronounced and the filling sweet. For an intriguing savory/sweet combination, top these with tomato sauce instead of the sprinkling of cinnamon and sugar.

In a bowl, combine the ricotta, 1 cup sugar, and 1 tablespoon plus 1 teaspoon cinnamon. The mixture should be the correct consistency to be piped with a pastry bag. If it feels too liquid, stir in some breadcrumbs, about a tablespoon at a time, until it feels stiff enough to pipe but not overly dry.

Shape the flour into a well on the work surface and add the eggs, egg yolks, and a scant ½ cup water to the center of the well. With a fork, gently beat to break up the eggs. Begin pulling in flour from the sides of the well until you have a crumbly dough. Knead the dough until it is smooth and compact. Set aside to rest (covered with an overturned bowl) for 30 minutes.

Roll out the dough into a thin sheet. Transfer the ricotta mixture to a pastry big fitted with a plain tip and pipe portions of the ricotta mixture in evenly spaced rows on one half of the dough, leaving a margin along the edge. Fold the empty half of the sheet over the filling, press between the portions of filling and along the edges with your fingertips to seal, then cut into ravioli with a serrated wheel cutter. Bring a large pot of unsalted water to a boil and cook the ravioli until they rise to the surface. Remove to a colander and drain completely dry. Transfer to a serving bowl. Combine additional cinnamon and sugar in a small bowl, sprinkle the mixture over the ravioli, and serve.

Cajoncìe di Moena / RYE RAVIOLI WITH WILD SPINACH

Ristorante Tyrol, Moena, Trentino

Serves 6

½ MEDIUM YELLOW ONION

1 TABLESPOON
UNSALTED BUTTER, PLUS
MORE FOR SERVING

1 POUND WILD SPINACH

⅔ CUP MASCARPONE
OR OTHER FRESH, CREAMY
CHEESE

SALT TO TASTE

FRESHLY GROUND BLACK
PEPPER TO TASTE

FRESHLY GRATED NUTMEG
TO TASTE

3½ CUPS RYE FLOUR

2 CUPS UNBLEACHED
ALL-PURPOSE FLOUR, PLUS
MORE FOR DUSTING

4 LARGE EGGS

4 EGG YOLKS

2 TABLESPOONS
EXTRA-VIRGIN OLIVE OIL
(OPTIONAL)

POPPY SEEDS FOR SERVING

GRATED SMOKED RICOTTA
FOR SERVING

Lots of different names exist for these hearty ravioli made with rye flour. The filling can include all kinds of greens—feel free to substitute cultivated spinach or chard if you can't get wild spinach. Like the tortelli on page 145, this recipe reflects the Ladin heritage in northern Italy. Some people like to include a spoonful or two of olive oil in the dough. It makes it easier to handle, but it also changes the texture slightly.

Mince the onion and in a skillet sauté it in the 1 tablespoon butter until soft and light golden. Add the wild spinach and cook until softened, about 3 minutes. Mince and set aside. When the spinach is cool, combine it with the mascarpone, season with salt, pepper, and nutmeg, and refrigerate.

Shape the flour into a well on the work surface and add the eggs and yolks to the center of the well, along with the olive oil, if using. With a fork, gently beat to break up the eggs. Begin pulling in flour from the sides of the well until you have a crumbly dough. Knead the dough until it is soft and compact. Roll out into a very thin sheet and dust very lightly with flour, then with a wheel cutter cut into squares with 2 ½-inch sides.

Remove the filling from the refrigerator and knead for a few seconds, then use the tip of a teaspoon to place a little bit of the filling in the center of one square of pasta. Fold the square into a triangle, taking care not to trap any air in the pocket with the filling. Press to seal. Repeat with remaining squares and filling.

Bring a large pot of salted water to a boil and cook until the past rises to the surface, a few minutes at most. Remove with a slotted spoon or skimmer and toss with melted butter, grated smoked ricotta, and poppy seeds.

Bring a large pot of water to a boil and cook the pasta. While the pasta is cooking, melt butter for serving in a skillet with the poppy seeds. When the pasta rises to the surface, gently remove it with a slotted spoon or skimmer and transfer to a serving bowl. Pour the butter and poppy seeds over the pasta, toss gently to combine, sprinkle with the grated ricotta, and serve immediately.

Schlutzkrapfen / RYE SPINACH TORTELLI

Ristorante Krone, Aldino-Aldein, Alto Adige

The rye flour in the dough for this pasta gives it a nice resistance and a little more heft. If you are new to working with pasta dough, try working with small pieces of the dough (about the size of an egg) at a time rather than rolling out the entire amount of dough into a thin sheet at once. Keep any remaining pieces covered so they don't dry out.

Shape the two types of flour into a well on the work surface. In a small bowl beat the egg with the olive oil, about ¼ cup warm water, and a pinch of salt. Pour the liquid into the center of the well. Begin pulling in flour from the sides of the well until you have a crumbly dough. Knead the dough until it is soft and compact, adding more water if necessary. Wrap the dough in a dishtowel and set aside to rest for 30 minutes.

Blanch the spinach in lightly salted boiling water, then squeeze dry and mince. Mince the garlic. Melt 1 tablespoon butter in a skillet and sauté the onion and garlic over medium heat until golden. Turn down to low heat and stir in the spinach and ricotta, 1 tablespoon Parmigiano, and 1 tablespoon minced chives. Season with nutmeg, salt, and pepper and stir to combine thoroughly.

Working quickly to keep it from drying out, roll out the pasta dough into a very thin sheet. With a cutter, cut into disks 2¾ inches in diameter. Place 1 teaspoon of the filling on one disk. Moisten the edges of the disk with water, then fold the disk in half to make a half moon. Press gently to seal. Repeat with remaining disks and filling.

Bring a large pot of water to a boil and cook the pasta. While the pasta is cooking, brown butter for serving in a skillet. When the pasta rises to the surface, gently remove it with a slotted spoon or skimmer and transfer to a serving bowl. Pour the browned butter over the pasta, toss gently to combine, sprinkle with grated Parmigiano and minced chives and serve immediately.

Serves 4 to 6

1½ CUPS RYE FLOUR

¾ CUP UNBLEACHED ALL-PURPOSE FLOUR

1 LARGE EGG

1 TABLESPOON EXTRA-VIRGIN OLIVE OIL

SALT TO TASTE

14 OUNCES (ABOUT 2 CUPS) SPINACH

1 CLOVE GARLIC

⅓ CUP MINCED ONION

1 TABLESPOON UNSALTED BUTTER, PLUS MORE FOR SERVING

½ CUP RICOTTA

1 TABLESPOON GRATED PARMIGIANO REGGIANO, PLUS MORE FOR SERVING

1 TABLESPOON MINCED CHIVES, PLUS MORE FOR SERVING

FRESHLY GRATED NUTMEG TO TASTE

FRESHLY GROUND BLACK PEPPER TO TASTE

Tultei / LEEK RAVIOLI COOKED ON A GRIDDLE

Trattoria Il Borgo, Ormea (Cuneo), Piemonte

Serves 4

8 CUPS UNBLEACHED
ALL-PURPOSE FLOUR

¾ CUP HEAVY CREAM OR
WHIPPING CREAM

1 TABLESPOON EXTRA-VIRGIN
OLIVE OIL, PLUS MORE FOR
SAUTÉING

SALT TO TASTE

1 LEEK

4 CUPS WHOLE MILK

FRESHLY GROUND BLACK
PEPPER TO TASTE

2 POUNDS (ABOUT 6)
POTATOES, PEELED

7 OUNCES WILD GREENS
AND HERBS, SUCH AS NETTLES
AND LAMBSQUARTERS

BRUZZU CHEESE FOR SERVING

Wild greens are traditional here, but feel free to substitute cultivated spinach, chard, kale, mustard greens, or any other type you like. Bruzzu, which is part of the Slow Food Ark of Taste, is creamy, slightly sour fermented ricotta.

Shape the flour into a well on the work surface. Place ¼ cup cream, 1 tablespoon olive oil, and a pinch of salt in the center of the well. Begin pulling in flour from the sides of the well until you have a crumbly dough. Knead the dough until it is soft and compact,. Wrap the dough in a dishtowel and set aside to rest.

Mince the leek and sauté in a small pot in a little oil. Add the milk and cook over low heat, stirring occasionally, for 1 hour. Stir in the remaining ½ cup cream and season with salt and pepper. Peel the potatoes and boil them until soft enough to pierce with a fork, about 1 hour. Puree with a potato ricer or food mill. Blanch the greens, drain, squeeze dry, and mince. In a bowl combine the potatoes, the greens, and the leek mixture and stir until smooth and combined.

Use a crank pasta machine to roll the dough into thin strips. Dot half of the pasta strips with small amounts of the filling, then top with the remaining strips of pasta. Press gently to seal around the filling and cut into large ravioli. Cook the ravioli on a griddle, turning once to brown both sides, and serve warm.

Lasagna verde / VEGETABLE LASAGNA

Barbara Torresan, Milano, Lombardia

Like many baked dishes, this is even tastier the day after it is prepared, as the flavors meld together as it sits. It's a great dish for entertaining as you can make it entirely in advance and simply reheat it when your guests arrive.

Shape 5¼ cups flour into a well on the work surface. Add the eggs and a pinch of salt to the center of the well. With a fork, gently beat to break up the eggs. Begin pulling in flour from the sides of the well until you have a crumbly dough. Knead the dough until it is smooth and compact. Roll out into a very thin sheet and cut into large rectangular noodles. Bring a large pot of salted water to a boil and cook the pasta until it rises to the surface. Remove with a slotted spoon or skimmer and drain, then blot dry.

Soak the raisins in warm water to cover to soften, then drain. Blanch the spinach in lightly salted water, then drain and squeeze dry. Melt 1 tablespoon butter in a small pot and sauté the spinach, raisins, and pine nuts. Mince the spinach mixture and set aside. Thinly slice the fontina cheese.

Prepare the béchamel: combine the remaining ¾ cup flour with 1½ cups of the milk and whisk until there are no lumps. (You can use the mini-chop attachment of an immersion blender to do this quickly and easily.) In a small pot, melt the remaining 7 tablespoons butter. Add the curry powder and a pinch of salt. Whisk in the milk and flour mixture, then add the remaining 2 ½ cups milk in a thin stream, whisking constantly. Whisk over medium heat until thickened.

Preheat oven to 400°F. Spread about ¼ cup of the béchamel on the bottom of a baking pan. Cover with a layer of noodles. Spread some of the spinach mixture on top. Spread on a little more of the béchamel and arrange a few slices of fontina cheese on top. Continue making layers in this order until you have used all of the ingredients, ending with a layer of béchamel. Sprinkle the grated Parmigiano on top. Bake in the preheated oven until browned and crisp on top, about 20 minutes. Let the lasagna settle for a few minutes before serving.

Serves 4 to 6

6 CUPS UNBLEACHED ALL-PURPOSE FLOUR

4 LARGE EGGS

SALT TO TASTE

1 TABLESPOON GOLDEN RAISINS

1½ POUNDS SPINACH

8 TABLESPOONS (1 STICK) UNSALTED BUTTER

1 TABLESPOON PINE NUTS

7 OUNCES FONTINA

4 CUPS WHOLE MILK

1 TABLESPOON CURRY POWDER

GRATED PARMIGIANO REGGIANO TO TASTE

Cannelloni di cardi / CARDOON CANNELLONI

Livia Borgata, Montegrosso d'Asti (Asti), Piemonte

Serves 4 to 6

2½ CUPS UNBLEACHED
ALL-PURPOSE FLOUR

3 LARGE EGGS

SALT TO TASTE

JUICE OF ½ LEMON

2 POUNDS CARDOONS

2 TABLESPOONS
UNSALTED BUTTER

1½ CUPS GRATED
PARMIGIANO REGGIANO

1 CUP RICOTTA

FRESHLY GROUND
BLACK PEPPER TO TASTE

FRESHLY GRATED NUTMEG
TO TASTE

EXTRA-VIRGIN OLIVE OIL
FOR DRIZZLING

2 TO 3 CLOVES GARLIC

Cardoons lend an unusual flavor to this classic dish. These tasty thistles look a bit like celery but taste more like artichokes.

Shape the flour into a well on the work surface. Add the eggs and a pinch of salt to the center of the well. With a fork, gently beat to break up the eggs. Begin pulling in flour from the sides of the well until you have a crumbly dough. Knead the dough until it is smooth and compact, adding water in small amounts. Roll out into a very thin sheet and cut into large rectangular noodles 4¾ by 4 inches. Fill a bowl with ice water. Bring a large, low, wide pot of salted water to a boil and cook the noodles until tender, about 5 minutes. Remove with a slotted spoon or skimmer and transfer to the ice water, then blot dry on dishtowels.

Fill a bowl with cold water and add the lemon juice. Trim and chop the cardoons, letting them drop into the lemon water as you do. (It will stop them from turning brown.) Cook the cardoons in boiling water until tender, then drain and mince. In a skillet, melt the butter, then sauté the minced cardoons. Stir in 1 cup of the grated Parmigiano. Let the cardoon mixture cool, then combine with ¾ cup of the ricotta and season with salt, pepper, and nutmeg.

In a small skillet, heat some oil with the garlic and cook until the garlic is very dark brown. Remove and discard garlic and whisk the flavored oil with the remaining ¼ cup ricotta and the remaining ½ cup Parmigiano. Top one of the cooked noodles with some of the cardoon mixture and roll up. Place seam-side down in a baking dish. Repeat with remaining noodles and filling, arranging the rolls in a single layer, though they can be tucked together fairly tightly. Top with the ricotta mixture and bake in the preheated oven until heated through and browned on top, about 20 minutes.

Gnocchi di patate alla bava / POTATO GNOCCHI WITH CHEESE AND BUTTER
Lina Bionaz, Saint-Christophe, Valle d'Aosta

Gnocchi dough is easy to make, but it's hard to give an exact measurement for the amount of flour you'll need—there are too many variables. Just add flour slowly, and keep your hands and your work surface dusted lightly with flour as well. You can also layer the cooked gnocchi with fontina and butter, put them in a baking pan, dot the top with a little more butter, and bake at 375°F or 400°F until the top is browned.

Boil the potatoes until tender. Peel and crush with a potato ricer or through a sieve, letting it drop onto the work surface. When the potato puree is cool enough to handle, sprinkle on the flour a little at a time, kneading it between additions, until you have a soft dough. Add flour just until the dough is no longer sticky; you may not need all of the flour.

Pull off a piece of dough and shape it into a rope about ½-inch wide. Cut the rope into pieces no longer than 1 ¼ inches long. Lightly flour a large dishtowel. With your thumb, press one piece of the dough against the back of the tines of a fork (or a gnocchi board, a little wooden board with ridges) and let it drop onto the prepared dishtowel. Repeat with remaining dough. Let the gnocchi dry for about 2 hours.

Meanwhile, cut the cheese into thin slices. Combine it with the milk in a small pot and melt over low heat, stirring frequently. Season with pepper and nutmeg.

Bring a large pot of salted water to a boil and cook the gnocchi. When they rise to the surface, remove them with a slotted spoon or skimmer and transfer to a large bowl. Pour most of the prepared milk mixture over the pasta and toss to combine. Divide among individual serving dishes and top with the remaining milk mixture.

Serves 4

1 POUND STARCHY POTATOES

1 CUP
UNBLEACHED ALL-PURPOSE FLOUR

11 OUNCES FONTINA

½ CUP WHOLE MILK

FRESHLY GROUND BLACK PEPPER TO TASTE

FRESHLY GRATED NUTMEG TO TASTE

SALT TO TASTE

4 TABLESPOONS UNSALTED BUTTER

Agnolotti con formadi frant / CHEESE AND WALNUT STUFFED AGNOLOTTI

Ristorante Al Castello, Fagagna (Udine), Friuli Venezia Giulia

Serves 4 to 6

1¼ CUPS RICE FLOUR

2 LARGE EGGS

1 EGG YOLK

SALT TO TASTE

1 TEASPOON XANTHAN GUM
(OPTIONAL)

4 OUNCES (1 SMALL) POTATO

7 OUNCES FORMADI
FRANT CHEESE OR OTHER
SEMI-AGED CHEESE

¾ CUP WALNUTS

FRESHLY GRATED NUTMEG
TO TASTE

GROUND CINNAMON TO TASTE

1 STICK (8 TABLESPOONS)
UNSALTED BUTTER

If you don't have a small fluted cutter for making the pasta, cut out disks about 2¾ inches in diameter. Place about 1 teaspoon of the potato mixture in the center of each disk, and fold them into half-moons, then press along the edges to seal. Formadi frant, which has a Slow Food Presidium, is made by combining bits and pieces of cheeses made in the mountains around Udine that, in true Italian fashion, are recycled rather than being discarded because a rind has broken or some other mishap has kept them from completing the aging process. More aged cheese is grated, while cheese at the younger end of the spectrum is simply sliced. They are then combined with milk, cream, and seasonings and the mixture is packed in wooden molds and aged for about forty days. The resulting cheese has a lovely balance of sweet and savory flavors. There is really no substitute for formadi frant (and the real thing is very varied, as it has no fixed "ingredients"), so replace with any semi-aged cheese you like.

Shape the rice flour into a well on the work surface and add the eggs and yolk, a pinch of salt, and the xanthan gum, if using, to the center of the well. With a fork, gently beat to break up the eggs. Begin pulling in flour from the sides of the well until you have a crumbly dough. Knead the dough until it is smooth and compact. Wrap in a dishtowel and set aside to rest in a cool place for 30 minutes.

Meanwhile, cook the potato in boiling water until easily pierced with a fork. Peel and crush through the smallest holes of a potato ricer. Finely grate the cheese and combine with the potatoes. Finely chop ¼ cup of the walnuts and mix into the potato mixture. Season with nutmeg and cinnamon (a pinch of each) and mix until well-combined.

Roll out the pasta dough into a thin sheet and place portions of the filling, about 1 teaspoon each, in rows on half of the dough. Fold over the other half of the dough, press in between each portion with your fingertips to seal, then use a 1½-inch fluted cutter to cut disks stuffed with the filling.

Agnolotti con formadi frant / CHEESE AND WALNUT STUFFED AGNOLOTTI

continued

Chop the remaining ½ cup walnuts, reserving a few whole walnuts for garnish. In a skillet, melt the butter and toast the chopped walnuts until fragrant. Meanwhile, bring a large pot of salted water to a boil and cook the pasta until it rises to the surface. Remove with a slotted spoon or skimmer and transfer to a serving bowl. Pour on the melted butter and chopped walnuts and toss, then garnish with the reserved whole walnuts and serve immediately.

Cojëtte al Seirass / POTATO DUMPLINGS IN GARLIC BUTTER

Adriano Ravera, Boves (Cuneo), Piemonte

Serves 6

2¼ POUNDS POTATOES

SALT TO TASTE

1 TABLESPOON
EXTRA-VIRGIN OLIVE OIL

3⅓ CUPS UNBLEACHED
ALL-PURPOSE FLOUR

4 TABLESPOONS
UNSALTED BUTTER

2 CLOVES GARLIC

⅔ CUP SEIRASS OR
OTHER RICOTTA

FRESHLY GROUND
BLACK PEPPER TO TASTE

Seirass is Piemonte's answer to ricotta. It's a little creamier and richer than ricotta made elsewhere, and it is formed into little cones. Seirass del fen, which is wrapped in hay, has a Slow Food Presidium. Pressing gnocchi against the tines of a fork is more than just a pretty decorative touch—it creates little ridges that do a wonderful job of trapping sauce.

Boil the potatoes until tender. Peel and crush with a potato ricer or through a sieve, letting it drop onto the work surface. When the potato puree is cool enough to handle, sprinkle on a pinch of salt and 1 tablespoon olive oil. Begin adding the flour a little at a time, kneading it between additions, until you have a soft dough. Add flour just until the dough is no longer sticky; you may not need all of the flour.

Pull off a piece of the dough and roll it into a rope about the size of a finger. Cut into ¾-inch lengths. Press each piece against the tines of a fork to imprint with lines.

Bring a large pot of salted water to a boil and cook the gnocchi. While the gnocchi are cooking, in a small pot melt the butter and sauté the garlic until the garlic is browned and the butter is foamy. Remove and discard garlic. As the gnocchi rise to the surface (they cook quickly), remove with a slotted spoon or skimmer and transfer to a bowl. Toss with the seirass to combine. Drizzle on the garlic butter, season with a generous grinding of pepper, stir to combine, and serve.

Ravioles / RICH POTATO DUMPLINGS

Locanda Codirosso, Stroppo (Cuneo), Piemonte

Toma di montagna, as its name implies, is a cheese made in the mountains. It encompasses a wide category of cheeses aged to different degrees. You can use a cheese such as fontina in its stead.

Boil the potatoes until tender, peel, and while they are still warm crush them with a potato ricer. Stir the cheese into the warm potatoes—it should melt. Transfer the mixture to a work surface, knead in the egg yolk, and then begin kneading in the flour gradually until you have a smooth dough. (You may not need all of the flour.)

Pull off a piece of the dough and roll into a long rope ¾ inch in diameter. Cut into small dumplings. Repeat with remaining dough. Pick up a dumpling and roll it between the palms of your hands to shape it elongate and thin the ends. It should have a round "belly" in the center. Repeat with remaining dough.

Bring a large pot of salted water to a boil. Melt the butter in a pot large enough to hold the dumplings. Cook the dumplings in the boiling water until they rise to the surface, then remove them with a slotted spoon or skimmer and transfer them to the pot with the melted butter. Drizzle on the cream, toss gently to combine, and serve immediately.

Serves 6

2¼ POUNDS POTATOES

1 CUP DICED TOMA DI MONTAGNA

1 EGG YOLK

2½ CUPS UNBLEACHED ALL-PURPOSE FLOUR

SALT TO TASTE

6 TABLESPOONS UNSALTED BUTTER

2 TABLESPOONS HEAVY CREAM OR WHIPPING CREAM

Struki lessi / STUFFED POTATO DUMPLINGS

Trattoria Sale e Pepe, Stregna (Udine), Friuli Venezia Giulia

Serves 10 to 12

2¼ POUNDS POTATOES

2½ TO 3½ CUPS UNBLEACHED
ALL-PURPOSE FLOUR

1 LARGE EGG

SALT TO TASTE

FRESHLY GRATED NUTMEG
TO TASTE

¼ CUP GOLDEN RAISINS

5 TABLESPOONS
UNSALTED BUTTER

¼ CUP PINE NUTS

3 CUPS WALNUTS

1 TABLESPOON GRAPPA

¼ TEASPOON GROUND
CINNAMON

¼ CUP SUGAR

These are even better if you make the dough a day in advance and let it rest. This is an ancient recipe and reflects the fact that sugar was once used frequently in savory dishes. These are served warm or cool.

Cook the potatoes in boiling water until tender, peel, and crush with a potato ricer, letting them fall onto the work surface. Combine with the egg, salt, and a little nutmeg. Knead in the flour a little at a time until you have a soft dough. You may not need all the flour. Set aside to rest in a cool place.

Soak the raisins in warm water to soften, then drain and squeeze dry. Melt 1 tablespoon butter in a skillet and toast the pine nuts. Grind the walnuts very finely, but do not let them turn into a paste. Combine the pine nuts, walnuts, raisins, and grappa and toss to combine thoroughly. Stir in a pinch of cinnamon and 2 tablespoons sugar.

Pinch off a piece of the dough and shape into a large-diameter rope. Cut into pieces the size of a large dumpling. Roll out one piece of dough to a disk, place some of the filling in the center, and fold in half to make a half-moon. Pinch the border together to seal, then set the dumpling with the pinched border facing upward and use an index finger to press down on the top in the center to indent it. The ends will curve upward a little. Repeat with remaining dough and filling.

Bring a large pot of salted water to a boil for cooking the dumplings. Melt the remaining 4 tablespoons butter. Cook the dumplings until they rise to the surface. Remove with a slotted spoon or skimmer and transfer to a serving dish. Drizzle with the melted butter, sprinkle with the remaining 2 tablespoons sugar and remaining pinch cinnamon, and serve either warm or cold.

Gnocchi di susine / POTATO PLUM DUMPLINGS

Antica Trattoria da Giusi, Malborghetto-Valbruna (Udine), Friuli Venezia Giulia

This may sound like a dessert, but it is a first course with roots in Austria, just to the north of Friuli Venezia Giulia. You can use apricots in place of the plums if you like.

Boil the potatoes until easily pierced with a fork. Peel, crush with a potato ricer letting them drop onto the work surface, and allow to cool. Add the eggs and a pinch of salt to the potato mixture and gradually knead in the flour until you have a soft dough. You may not need all of the flour. Roll a piece of the dough into a rope about 3 inches in diameter and cut into slices ½ to ⅔ inch thick.

Pit a plum, leaving the two halves attached as best as possible. Place the plum in the center of a piece of dough. Gently stretch the dough around the plum so that it is a little less than ½-inch thick all around. Eliminate any excess dough. Repeat with remaining plums and dough. Knead the dough scraps together and reuse them.

Place the butter in a pot and cook over medium heat until lightly browned, then stir in the sugar and keep warm. Bring a large pot of salted water to a boil and cook the dumplings for a few minutes. Remove with a skimmer or slotted spoon to individual serving plates, drizzle with the sweetened butter, sprinkle with ground cinnamon, and serve warm.

Serves 4

2¼ POUNDS POTATOES

2 LARGE EGGS

SALT TO TASTE

1¾ CUPS UNBLEACHED
ALL-PURPOSE FLOUR

30 SMALL PLUMS

16 TABLESPOONS (2 STICKS)
UNSALTED BUTTER

SUGAR TO TASTE

GROUND CINNAMON TO TASTE

Strangolapreti / SPINACH DUMPLINGS

Romana Bertolini, Levico Terme, Trentino

Serves 6

5 TO 6 CUPS STALE
BREAD CUBES

ABOUT 1 CUP WHOLE MILK

1 POUND 5 OUNCES
WILD SPINACH

2 LARGE EGGS

ABOUT ¼ CUP UNBLEACHED
ALL-PURPOSE FLOUR

SALT TO TASTE

1 MEDIUM YELLOW ONION

3 TO 4 TABLESPOONS BUTTER

GRATED AGED CHEESE
FOR SERVING

These are a cult favorite in Trentino. Legends abound about the name, which means "priest stranglers." One recounts that in the mid-1800s a priest who was a dedicated hunter spent the day in the woods but neglected to bring enough food with him. When he returned home, ravenous, his housekeeper made him a dish of these green dumplings, one of which got stuck in his throat as he gobbled them down.

Soak the bread in milk to cover until soft. Blanch the wild spinach in lightly salted water, drain, squeeze dry, and puree with a food mill or by forcing through a sieve. Lift the bread out of the milk and crumble into a clean bowl. Add the eggs and cooked spinach and stir to combine. Stir in ¼ cup flour. The mixture should be soft and elastic, not quite as stiff as a dough, but not runny. If it is too stiff, add a little of the soaking milk. If it is too loose, add flour in small amounts.

Bring a large pot of salted water to a boil. Mince the onion. Melt the butter in a skillet and sauté the onion until golden. Dip a metal spoon in water, then use it to scoop out about 1 tablespoon of the bread mixture. Use your hand to shape the dough into a round or oval dumpling while it is still on the spoon. Slide it off the spoon and into the water. Repeat with remaining dough, dipping the spoon in water each time. (This helps the dumplings slide off easily.) Cook the dumplings until they float to the surface, then remove them with a slotted spoon or skimmer and transfer to a serving bowl. Drizzle on the melted butter and onion, sprinkle on the grated cheese, and serve immediately.

Chicchere di spinaci e patate / SPINACH AND POTATO DUMPLINGS

Ristorante Gavarini, Villafranca in Lunigiana (Massa-Carrara), Toscana

The amount of cheese you use in these dumplings is up to you. You can also increase the amount of spinach if you'd like them to have an especially intense green color. These are tasty when served with a tomato and basil sauce reduced with a little cream.

Blanch the spinach. Squeeze dry and mince. Cook the potatoes in boiling water until tender. Let them cool, then peel them and crush them with a potato ricer, letting them fall onto the work surface. Combine with the egg, minced spinach, and Parmigiano. Knead in the flour a little at a time until you have a soft dough. You may not need all the flour.

Pull off a piece of the dough and shape it into a thin rope. Cut into pieces about ½ inch long. Repeat with remaining dough.

Bring a large pot of salted water to a boil and cook the dumplings until they rise to the surface. Remove with a slotted spoon or skimmer and transfer to a serving bowl. Drizzle with a little melted butter and serve immediately.

Serves 4

7 OUNCES (ABOUT 1 CUP) SPINACH

5 LARGE POTATOES

1 LARGE EGG

GRATED PARMIGIANO REGGIANO TO TASTE

ABOUT 3⅓ CUPS UNBLEACHED ALL-PURPOSE FLOUR

SALT TO TASTE

MELTED BUTTER FOR SERVING

Cappellacci di magro / CHEESE CAPPELLACCI

Giuliana D'Este, Ferrara, Emilia-Romagna

Serves 4

3⅓ CUPS UNBLEACHED
ALL-PURPOSE FLOUR

6 LARGE EGGS

1½ CUPS GRATED
GRANA PADANO,
PLUS MORE FOR SERVING

SALT TO TASTE

FRESHLY GRATED NUTMEG
TO TASTE

BUTTER FOR SERVING

SAGE LEAVES FOR SERVING

Cappellacci are like large tortellini. Like all fresh egg pasta, they cook in a flash, so keep an eye on the pot and scoop them out as soon as they float to the surface.

Shape the flour into a well on the work surface and add 4 eggs to the center of the well. With a fork, gently beat to break up the eggs. Begin pulling in flour from the sides of the well until you have a crumbly dough. Knead the dough until it is smooth and compact. Let the dough rest (covered with an overturned bowl) for 30 minutes.

In a bowl combine the 1½ cups grated cheese and the remaining 2 eggs. Season with salt and nutmeg.

Roll out the dough into a sheet less than ¹⁄₁₀ inch thick. Cut into disks 2½ inches in diameter. Place about 1 teaspoon of the cheese mixture in the center of one square and fold it into a half moon. Seal the edges with your fingertips. Pinch the two corners of the half-moon together. Repeat with remaining disks and filling.

Bring a large pot of water to a boil and cook the pasta. While the pasta is cooking, melt butter in a large skillet with the sage leaves. When the pasta rises to the surface, gently remove it with a slotted spoon or skimmer and add it to the skillet. Toss over low heat to combine, then sprinkle with grated Grana Padano and serve immediately.

Strangulaprievete verdi / BREAD AND SPINACH DUMPLINGS

Federico Valicenti, Terranova di Pollino (Potenza), Basilicata

Serves 4

1 POUND SPINACH

½ MEDIUM YELLOW ONION

EXTRA-VIRGIN OLIVE OIL
FOR SAUTÉING

ABOUT 3 CUPS CRUMBLED
STALE BREAD, CRUSTS
REMOVED

1 LARGE EGG

2 TABLESPOONS GRATED
PARMIGIANO REGGIANO OR
GRANA PADANO

¼ CUP UNBLEACHED
ALL-PURPOSE FLOUR

SALT AND FRESHLY GROUND
BLACK PEPPER TO TASTE

3 TO 4 TABLESPOONS
UNSALTED BUTTER

LEAVES OF 1 SPRIG SAGE

Many different sauces are good with these dumplings: try them with a spicy sauce of cherry tomatoes and mushrooms, or sautéed asparagus.

Blanch the spinach, then squeeze dry. Mince the onion. Heat a little oil in a large, low skillet and sauté the onion until golden. Add the spinach and cook, stirring frequently, for 5 minutes. Mince very fine (a food processor fitted with the metal blade is useful) and transfer to a bowl. Stir in the crumbled stale bread, then lightly beat the egg and add that as well. Stir in the grated cheese and the flour. If the mixture seems runny, add more crumbled bread a little at a time until it is firm. Season with salt and pepper.

Roll the dough into thin ropes and cut into pieces about ¾ inch long. Bring a large pot of salted water to a boil and cook the dumplings. While the dumplings are cooking, melt the butter in a skillet with the sage leaves over medium heat. As soon as the dumplings rise to the surface, remove with a slotted spoon or skimmer and transfer to a serving bowl. Drizzle on the melted butter and sage and serve immediately.

Malfatti di bagòss di alpeggio / SPINACH AND CHEESE DUMPLINGS

Trattoria La Madia, Brione (Brescia), Lombardia

Malfatti means "misshapen." In the Lombardia region, this refers to large torpedo-shaped oval dumplings. Bagòss is a raw cow's milk cheese with a touch of saffron incorporated. It is made in large wheels that can weigh up to 48 pounds. The rind is rubbed with flaxseed oil, giving it a brownish tint.

Blanch the spinach, then squeeze dry and mince. Set aside about one quarter of the spinach. Mince the cheese very finely. Set aside about 2 cups of the cheese. Combine the remaining cheese with the flour and the larger portion of the spinach and form into a well on the work surface. Place the eggs in the center of the well, beat the eggs gently with a fork, then begin pulling in dry ingredients form the sides of the well. When you have a crumbly dough, knead until soft and well-combined. Pull off a piece of dough and cut into large pieces. Shape each piece into an oval. Repeat with remaining dough. Spread the dumplings out in a single layer and allow to rest.

Place the reserved spinach in a large skillet and add enough broth to make a fairly liquid mixture. Cook over medium heat, stirring frequently, until it has reached a creamy consistency. Bring a large pot of salted water to a boil and cook the dumplings until they rise to the surface. Remove with a slotted spoon or skimmer and add to the skillet with the spinach. Sprinkle in the reserved cheese and cook, stirring, until the cheese has melted and the dumplings are coated with the spinach. Transfer to individual serving dishes. Thinly slice the celery, if using, and scatter it on top. Serve immediately.

Serves 10

1¾ POUNDS SPINACH

3½ POUNDS Bagòss
di Alpeggio CHEESE OR
OTHER SEMI-AGED COW'S
MILK CHEESE

3 CUPS UNBLEACHED
ALL-PURPOSE FLOUR

6 LARGE EGGS

ABOUT ½ CUP
VEGETABLE BROTH

SALT TO TASTE

2 TO 3 RIBS CELERY
(OPTIONAL)

Gnocc de la Cua / GREEN GNOCCHI WITH AGED CHEESE

Ristorante da Giusy, Ponte di Legno (Brescia), Lombardia

Serves 4

7 OUNCES WILD GREENS OR
SPINACH OR CHARD

3 MEDIUM POTATOES

SALT TO TASTE

4 CUPS UNBLEACHED
ALL-PURPOSE FLOUR

1 TABLESPOON EXTRA-VIRGIN
OLIVE OIL

½ MEDIUM YELLOW ONION

2 TO 3 TABLESPOONS
UNSALTED BUTTER

GRATED AGED MALGA
CHEESE TO TASTE

In Lombardia these little dumplings are made with foraged wild greens, but spinach or chard will work just as well. Malga cheese is an Alpine cow's milk cheese. You can use grated Parmigiano in its place. Whichever cheese you use, include a generous amount.

Blanch the greens, then drain, squeeze dry, and mince. Separately, boil 1 potato until tender. Peel the 2 remaining potatoes and chop roughly (the pieces needn't be the same size). Bring a large pot of salted water to a boil and cook the chopped potatoes for 5 minutes. Reserve the potatoes and their cooking liquid. Peel the whole boiled potato and pass it through a potato ricer, letting it fall onto the work surface. On the work surface, knead together the pureed potato, the flour, the blanched greens, and the oil. Incorporate some of the potato cooking water a little at a time to make a soft, smooth dough. You will probably need ½ cup to ¾ cup total.

Bring the pot with the chopped potato back to a boil. Mince the onion and in a small skillet brown it in the butter. Use a spoon to shape small dumplings from the greens mixture. Add the dumplings to the pot with the chopped potato and cook for 3 minutes after they rise to the surface. Remove dumplings and potatoes with a skimmer or slotted spoon and transfer to a serving bowl, alternating layers of dumplings and potatoes with layers of grated cheese. Top with the onion and butter and serve immediately.

Fregoloz alle erbe / GREEN FLOUR DUMPLINGS

Ristorante Borgo Poscolle, Cavazzo Carnico (Udine), Friuli Venezia Giulia

Never add baking soda to a pot after the water has come to a boil—it will bubble up and come over the sides of the pot. These dumplings are purposely irregular in shape. It's part of their rustic charm.

Fill a large bowl with ice water. Fill a pot with water, add salt and a pinch of baking soda, and bring to a boil. Blanch the greens, then drain and place in the ice water. Remove the greens from the ice water, squeeze dry, and chop. Mince the shallot. Melt 1 tablespoon butter in a skillet and sauté the shallot, then add the chopped greens. Transfer the puree to a blender or a food processor fitted with the metal blade and puree, adding milk in a thin stream until the mixture has reached a creamy consistency. Transfer to a bowl and stir in the flour and egg and season with salt, pepper, and nutmeg. Knead into a dense and well combined dough. If it seems too stiff, add a little more milk.

Bring a large pot of salted water to a boil, lower the heat so that it simmers, and drop in spoonfuls of the dough. (Don't worry about making them all the same size.) As they rise to the surface, remove with a slotted spoon or skimmer to a colander to drain. When all the dumplings are cooked, in a large skillet, melt the remaining 7 tablespoons butter. Add the dumplings and gently toss over medium heat to combine. Top with the grated cheese and serve.

Serves 4

SALT TO TASTE

1 PINCH BAKING SODA

12 OUNCES FORAGED GREENS, SUCH AS NETTLES, DANDELION, BLADDER CAMPION, AND AMARANTH

1 SHALLOT

8 TABLESPOONS (1 STICK) UNSALTED BUTTER

¼ CUP TO 1 CUP WHOLE MILK

2 CUPS UNBLEACHED ALL-PURPOSE FLOUR

1 LARGE EGG

FRESHLY GROUND BLACK PEPPER TO TASTE

FRESHLY GRATED NUTMEG TO TASTE

1 CUP GRATED SMOKED RICOTTA

Gnocchi di zucca con ricotta affumicata /
SQUASH GNOCCHI WITH SMOKED RICOTTA

Trattoria dalla Marianna, Valdobbiadene (Treviso), Veneto

Serves 5

1 BUTTERNUT SQUASH,
ABOUT 3½ POUNDS

1 LARGE EGG

ABOUT 2½ CUPS
UNBLEACHED
ALL-PURPOSE FLOUR

SALT TO TASTE

GRATED SMOKED
RICOTTA TO TASTE

BROWNED BUTTER
FOR SERVING

Squash appears in many guises on the tables of the Veneto. These gnocchi can also be served with a spoonful of cinnamon and sugar in place of the cheese. These are quenelles—formed with two spoons—so the mixture should be fairly soft, as they are dropped into boiling water and firm up while cooking.

Peel, seed, and chop the squash. Steam until tender, then puree. Combine the squash with the egg and season with salt. Gradually knead in the flour until you have a smooth, soft mixture.

Bring a large pot of salted water to a boil. With a spoon, scoop up a bit of the squash mixture, about the size of a walnut, and use another spoon to shape it into an oval. Drop it into the boiling water and repeat until you have used up the squash mixture. Cook the dumplings for about 2 minutes, then drain and transfer to a serving bowl. Sprinkle the grated smoked ricotta over the dumplings. Drizzle on a generous amount of brown butter.

Gnudi dell'orto / VEGETABLE DUMPLINGS

Emanuela Busà, Firenze, Toscana

Like the Squash Gnocchi with Smoked Ricotta, these are quenelles. To shape a quenelle use two spoons and form it gently into an oval.

Trim the zucchini, peel the carrots, and peel the onion. Bring a large pot of water to a boil and cook the zucchini, carrots, and onion for 20 minutes. Remove with a slotted spoon or skimmer (reserve cooking water), drain, and set aside to cool. When the vegetables are cool, puree them together. Beat the egg in a bowl, then stir in the vegetable puree. Season with salt, pepper, and nutmeg. Add the flour and beat into a smooth and elastic mixture.

Chop the herbs. In a pot, melt the butter and add the herbs. Cook until aromatic, then set aside. Bring the vegetable cooking water back to a boil. With a spoon, scoop up a bit of the vegetable mixture and use a second spoon to shape it into an oval. Drop it into the boiling water and repeat until you have used up the mixture. Cook the dumplings until they rise to the surface. Remove with a slotted spoon or skimmer and add to the pot with the butter and herbs. Toss gently to combine over medium heat. If the dumplings look dry, add a tablespoon or two of the cooking water. Sprinkle with grated cheese and serve immediately.

Serves 4 to 6

10 OUNCES (ABOUT 2 MEDIUM) ZUCCHINI

5 OUNCES (ABOUT 2 LARGE) CARROTS

1 MEDIUM YELLOW ONION

1 LARGE EGG

SALT AND FRESHLY GROUND BLACK PEPPER TO TASTE

FRESHLY GRATED NUTMEG TO TASTE

2½ CUPS UNBLEACHED ALL-PURPOSE FLOUR

AROMATIC HERBS, SUCH AS CHIVES, SAGE, PARSLEY, AND OREGANO, TO TASTE

4 TABLESPOONS UNSALTED BUTTER

½ CUP GRATED PARMIGIANO REGGIANO

Gnocchetti di ortiche con salsa di funghi /
NETTLE DUMPLINGS WITH MUSHROOM SAUCE

Ristorante La Clusaz, Gignod, Valle d'Aosta

Serves 4

SALT TO TASTE

7 OUNCES (ABOUT 2 SMALL) POTATOES

1 CUP NETTLE LEAVES

1 EGG YOLK

ABOUT ⅓ CUP UNBLEACHED ALL-PURPOSE FLOUR

14 OUNCES PORCINI MUSHROOMS

1 CLOVE GARLIC

UNSALTED BUTTER FOR SAUTÉING

ABOUT ½ CUP VEGETABLE BROTH

FRESHLY GROUND BLACK PEPPER TO TASTE

CHEESE SHAVINGS FOR FINISHING

Nettles—sometimes called stinging nettles—are covered in little fibers that are quite painful to touch. Be sure to wear gloves when dealing with them. Once the nettles are cooked, the fibers are harmless. It's worth the challenge of dealing with them to enjoy these delicious, slightly astringent greens.

Bring a large pot of salted water to a boil and cook the potatoes until tender enough to pierce with a fork. Drain the potatoes, and when they are cool enough to handle, peel them and crush them with a potato ricer. Meanwhile, blanch the nettles, drain them, and once they are cool enough to handle, squeeze them dry and mince them. Combine the potato and minced nettles on the work surface and knead in the egg yolk and a little salt. Begin kneading in the flour a little at a time until you have a soft, smooth, and well-combined dough. You may not need all of the flour.

Pull off a piece of the dough and roll into a rope with a diameter a little less than ¼ inch. Cut into dumplings slightly longer than ½ inch. Repeat with remaining dough.

Slice the mushrooms. Halve the garlic clove and rub the cut sides all over a pot. Melt the butter in the pot, then add the sliced mushrooms. Season with salt and pepper and add a little broth just to cover. Simmer over low heat until mushrooms are crisp-tender. Bring a large pot of salted water to a boil and cook the dumplings just until they rise to the surface. Remove with a slotted spoon or skimmer and transfer to the pot with the mushrooms. Toss over medium heat to combine, top with cheese shavings, and serve hot.

Gnocchi di castagne in cialda / CHESTNUT GNOCCHI IN CHEESE CUPS

Anna Marcoz, Aosta, Valle d'Aosta

Serves 8

7 OUNCES SHELLED
CHESTNUTS

SALT TO TASTE

1 TABLESPOON
UNSALTED BUTTER

¼ CUP HONEY

1½ POUNDS (4 TO 5 MEDIUM)
POTATOES

¾ CUP UNBLEACHED
ALL-PURPOSE FLOUR

1 LARGE EGG

2 CUPS GRATED
PARMIGIANO REGGIANO

¼ CUP FONDUTA

FRESHLY GRATED NUTMEG
TO TASTE

WHITE ALBA TRUFFLE
FOR SERVING

Glazed chestnuts like those incorporated into this gnocchi dough are frequently served with cheese and slices of buttered whole wheat bread as an antipasto in Valle d'Aosta. Fonduta is a creamy cheese sauce. See the recipe on page 206 to make your own.

Cook the chestnuts in lightly salted water until tender. Drain and transfer to a skillet with the butter and honey and cook over medium heat, tossing, until the chestnuts are coated in a glaze. Puree through a food mill or by forcing through a sieve.

Boil the potatoes until tender enough to pierce with a fork. Drain them, peel them, and crush them with a potato ricer or food mill. On a work surface, knead together the chestnut puree, the potato puree, the flour, and the egg until soft and well combined. Pull off a piece of the dough, roll into a rope, and cut into dumplings. Repeat with remaining dough.

Heat a skillet and sprinkle in ¼ cup Parmigiano in a thin disk. When the cheese begins to darken, remove it with a spatula and gently fit it into a ramekin to shape it into a cup. Repeat with remaining cheese and let the cups cool, then very gently remove them from the ramekins and set aside.

Bring a large pot of salted water to a boil and cook the dumplings. Place the fonduta in a skillet and warm over low heat. When the dumplings are cooked, remove with a slotted spoon or skimmer and transfer to the skillet. Sprinkle on a little nutmeg and toss to combine. To serve, place the cheese cups on individual serving plates. Divide the dumplings between them. Shave white truffle on top and serve immediately.

Gnocchetti di polenta con porcini /
POLENTA GNOCCHI WITH PORCINI MUSHROOMS

Trattoria Il Poeta Contadino, Casalbuttano ed Uniti (Cremona), Lombardia

Leftover polenta can be used to make these small dumplings, but if you need to start from scratch, cook 1 cup dry polenta in 2 cups of water, following the instructions in the recipe on page 204. Cooled polenta will be very firm, but you can break it up easily with a food processor.

Slice the mushrooms. In a skillet, heat the olive oil and add the mushrooms, garlic, and a pinch of salt and cook until mushrooms have softened and given up their liquid. Remove and discard garlic and set mushrooms aside.

In a food processor fitted with the metal blade, process the polenta and eggs until smooth. Transfer the mixture to a work surface and sprinkle on 1 cup of the grated Grana Padano and the flour. Season with salt and pepper and knead into a soft dough.

Preheat oven to 350°F. Butter 4 individual earthenware baking dishes with 1 tablespoon of the butter and set aside. Pinch off a piece of the dough, roll it into a thin rope, and cut into small dumplings. Repeat with remaining dough. Bring a large pot of salted water to a boil and cook the dumplings. Place the remaining 5 tablespoons of the butter in a skillet with the sage and melt over medium heat. When the dumplings are cooked, remove with a slotted spoon or skimmer and transfer to the skillet. Toss to combine, then divide among the 4 individual baking dishes. Divide the mushrooms among the servings as well, then sprinkle with a generous amount of grated Grana Padano and season with black pepper. Bake in the preheated oven until browned on top, about 10 minutes, and serve piping hot.

Serves 4

14 OUNCES PORCINI MUSHROOMS

1 TABLESPOON EXTRA-VIRGIN OLIVE OIL

1 CLOVE GARLIC (UNPEELED)

SALT TO TASTE

4 CUPS COOKED POLENTA

2 LARGE EGGS

1 CUP GRATED GRANA PADANO, PLUS MORE FOR SERVING

2 CUPS UNBLEACHED ALL-PURPOSE FLOUR

FRESHLY GROUND BLACK PEPPER TO TASTE

6 TABLESPOONS UNSALTED BUTTER

LEAVES OF 1 SPRIG SAGE

Canederli di Puzzone di Moena /
BUCKWHEAT DUMPLINGS WITH PUZZONE DI MOENA CHEESE

Oberraindlhof, Senales-Schnals, Alto Adige

Serves 4 to 6

¼ CUP SLICED LEEKS

EXTRA-VIRGIN OLIVE OIL
FOR SAUTÉING

7 CUPS BUCKWHEAT
BREAD CUBES

1¼ CUPS WHOLE MILK

2 LARGE EGGS

¼ CUP BUCKWHEAT FLOUR

½ CUP DICED MOENA CHEESE

4 OUNCES (ABOUT 1 SMALL)
POTATO

2 TABLESPOONS
MINCED ONION

ABOUT ¼ CUP
VEGETABLE BROTH

2 TABLESPOONS GROPPELLO
DI REVÒ RED WINE

SALT TO TASTE

Canederli are large bread dumplings, often the size of a golf ball or even a little larger. These offer the delicious surprise of a piece of cheese in the center. Puzzone di Moena cheese is a cow's milk cheese made from June to September. The surface of the cheese is rinsed with water frequently during aging to encourage fermentation, and as a result the rind is brick-red. There is a Slow Food Presidium dedicated to it. *Puzzone* means "big stinker" and refers to the cheese's strong aroma.

Sauté the leeks in a small skillet in a small amount of oil, then add 2 tablespoons water and simmer until leeks are soft and liquid has evaporated. Place the bread in a bowl and add milk. Toss to combine and let the bread sit until it is soft (tossing occasionally to be sure all the bread gets moist), then crumble it and work in the eggs, the flour, and the leek mixture. Pull off a piece of the mixture and shape it into a large dumpling (about the size of a golf ball or larger) with a piece of the cheese in the center. Repeat with remaining mixture and cheese. Let the dumplings rest.

Peel and slice the potato. Brown the onion in a skillet in a small amount of olive oil. Add the potato, 3 tablespoons vegetable broth, and 1 tablespoon of the wine. Season with salt and cook, stirring frequently, until the potatoes are tender. Add the remaining 1 tablespoon wine and cook for 1 to 2 minutes, then remove from the heat. Puree in a blender or food mill and taste. Adjust seasoning, and if the mixture seems overly thick, thin it with a little more broth.

Bring a large pot of salted water to a boil and cook the dumplings for 15 minutes. Remove with a slotted spoon or skimmer and transfer to a serving bowl. Top with the potato mixture and serve immediately.

Gnocchi alla romana / BAKED SEMOLINA DUMPLINGS

Osteria del Velodromo Vecchio, Roma, Lazio

Including the egg yolks makes this an even richer dish. This is a great choice for entertaining, as you can prepare it in advance.

Place the milk in a pot and bring to a boil, then slowly drizzle in the semolina flour, stirring constantly with a wooden spoon to avoid lumps. Season with salt and nutmeg and cook over low heat, stirring constantly, until it has formed a thick porridge, about 30 minutes. Remove the semolina from the heat and whisk in 1 tablespoon grated Parmigiano and the egg yolks, if using. Brush a marble work surface with water. Pour the mixture onto the surface. Working quickly (it will stiffen as it cools) with a spatula, smooth the top and make it an even thickness a little less than ½ inch. Allow to cool.

Place a shelf on the second level from the top of the oven and preheat the broiler, if necessary. With a cookie cutter or the rim of a drinking glass, cut out disks from the cooled semolina. Try to cut the disks next to each other to get as many as possible, but reserve any scraps. Thickly butter a baking pan with about 2 tablespoons of the butter, then melt the remaining butter. Arrange a layer of disks in the prepared pan, then fill in any gaps with the scraps. Sprinkle with some of the grated cheese and drizzle with a little of the melted butter. Continue to alternate layers of the disks with the cheese and butter until you have used up both, ending with a drizzle of butter and a sprinkling of cheese on top. Broil until a golden crust forms on top, about 10 minutes, then allow to rest briefly before serving.

Serves 4

4 CUPS WHOLE MILK

2½ CUPS SEMOLINA FLOUR

SALT TO TASTE

FRESHLY GRATED NUTMEG TO TASTE

ABOUT 1 CUP GRATED PARMIGIANO REGGIANO

2 EGG YOLKS (OPTIONAL)

10 TABLESPOONS (1 STICK PLUS 2 TABLESPOONS) UNSALTED BUTTER

Gnocchi di colla / BREAD DUMPLINGS WITH POTATOES

Renata Nonis, Rovetta (Bergamo), Lombardia

Serves 4 to 6

½ STALE ROLL

½ CUP WHOLE MILK

SALT TO TASTE

2 MEDIUM WHITE POTATOES

1 LARGE EGG

3⅓ CUPS UNBLEACHED
ALL-PURPOSE FLOUR

4 TABLESPOONS
UNSALTED BUTTER

LEAVES OF 1 SPRIG SAGE

GRATED AGED CHEESE
FOR SERVING

Italians have made an art of turning humble ingredients into a feast, and this recipe is a prime example of that skill. A bit of stale bread is combined with ingredients found in almost every kitchen to make something that tastes fantastic.

In a bowl, soak the ½ roll in the milk to soften. Meanwhile, peel and dice the potatoes. Bring a large pot of salted water to a boil. Cook the potatoes until tender. Reserve potatoes in cooking water.

Crumble the soaked roll. Lightly beat the egg and add to the bread mixture. Stir in the flour. The mixture should be fairly dry and stiff. Gradually add water until the mixture is medium density and holds together when you squeeze some in your palm. Bring the cooking water with the potatoes in it back to a boil.

With a table spoon, scoop up a bit of the bread mixture to form a dumpling. Dip the spoon into the boiling water and the dumpling should slide off. Repeat, working quickly, until you have used up the bread mixture. Cook the dumplings for about 15 minutes. Melt the butter in a skillet with the sage leaves. Remove the dumplings and diced potato with a slotted spoon or skimmer and transfer them to a serving dish. Drizzle with the melted butter and sage leaves and sprinkle on grated cheese. Serve immediately.

Canederli ai formaggi / WHOLE WHEAT BREAD DUMPLINGS WITH CHEESE

Oberraindlhof, Senales-Schnals, Alto Adige

There are several different types of cow's milk malga cheese made in the Val di Fassa. You can choose one type, or combine several aged to different stages. Canederli can also be served in broth.

Set aside a small piece of cheese for grating on the finished dish, then cut the rolls and the cheese into ½-inch cubes. In a bowl, combine the cheese, the rolls, and the flour. Beat the eggs with the milk (if your rolls are on the stale side, you may want to add a few additional tablespoons of milk) and season with a pinch of salt. Pour this liquid over the bread and cheese cubes and toss to combine. Shape the mixture into balls about 1 ½ inches in diameter.

Bring a large pot of salted water to a boil and cook the dumplings for 15 minutes.

Remove the dumplings with a slotted spoon or skimmer and divide among individual serving bowls. Drizzle with melted butter and grate the reserved cheese on top. Sprinkle with chives and serve immediately.

Serves 4 to 6

7 OUNCES MALGA CHEESE FROM VAL DI FASSA

8 TO 10 WHOLE WHEAT ROLLS

¾ CUP WHOLE WHEAT FLOUR

2 LARGE EGGS

½ CUP WHOLE MILK

SALT TO TASTE

MELTED BUTTER FOR SERVING

1 TABLESPOON MINCED CHIVES

Gnocchi verdi / GREEN BREAD DUMPLINGS

Maso Cantanghel Trattoria da Lucia, Civezzano, Trentino

Serves 4

4 STALE SOURDOUGH ROLLS

11 OUNCES (ABOUT 1 BUNCH) CHARD OR SPINACH

4 CUPS MIXED HERB LEAVES, SUCH AS MINT, LEMON BALM, LEAF CELERY, CHIVES, AND WILD FENNEL

3 CUPS WHOLE MILK

5 LARGE EGGS

6 CUPS FRESH BREADCRUMBS

SALT TO TASTE

ABOUT ¼ CUP UNBLEACHED ALL-PURPOSE FLOUR

14 TABLESPOONS (1 STICK PLUS 6 TABLESPOONS) UNSALTED BUTTER

2 CUPS GRATED AGED MALGA CHEESE

Traditionally these are made with spaccatine, small sourdough rolls with deep slashes cut into the top before baking. If you are lucky enough to have your own kitchen garden, use whichever herbs you have on hand.

Soak the sourdough rolls in water for about 8 hours. They should be very soft.

Pull off the stems of the chard and reserve for another use. With a blender, puree the mixed herbs and the chard leaves with about ½ cup of the milk. Reserve a few tablespoons of the puree, and transfer the rest into a bowl. Lightly beat the eggs and add them to the bowl. Squeeze the sourdough rolls dry and crumble those into the bowl. Stir in the breadcrumbs and the remaining 2½ cups milk and season with salt.

Bring a large pot of salted water to a boil. If the mixture seems too loose to hold together, add flour a little at a time until it is a little stiffer, but keep in mind that it will firm up while cooking. With a table spoon, scoop up a bit of the bread mixture to form a dumpling and slide it into the water. Repeat with remaining mixture until you have used it up. After the dumplings have risen to the surface, cook them for 5 additional minutes.

While the dumplings are cooking, combine the reserved puree and the butter and melt in a small pot over low heat. Thin with a little water if necessary and season with salt. When the dumplings are cooked, remove them with a slotted spoon or skimmer and transfer to a serving bowl. Pour on the butter sauce, stir to combine, then sprinkle with grated cheese and serve immediately.

Gratini / GRATED BREAD DUMPLINGS

Franca Simeoni, Trento, Trentino

These are tiny dumplings made using a grater, each one only slightly larger than a grain of rice. They are so small that they don't need to be cooked on the stove—just pour hot broth over them and let them sit for a few minutes so that they are tender.

In a bowl combine the breadcrumbs, the eggs, and the cheese. Season with salt and nutmeg. Knead by hand into a compact dough. If it feels too stiff, knead in water in small amounts to soften. Grate the dough to make tiny dumplings. Place the dumplings in a soup tureen or other serving bowl. Place the broth in a pot and bring to a rolling boil, then pour it over the dumplings and let them sit in the hot broth until softened, about 5 minutes. Serve immediately.

Serves 4

2¼ CUPS BREADCRUMBS

2 LARGE EGGS

2 TO 3 TABLESPOONS GRATED AGED CHEESE

SALT TO TASTE

FRESHLY GRATED NUTMEG TO TASTE

8 CUPS VEGETABLE BROTH

RICE AND OTHER GRAINS

Risotto al Barolo / BAROLO RISOTTO

Locanda dell'Arco, Cissone (Cuneo), Piemonte

Serves 4

½ CUP MINCED SHALLOT

1 CLOVE GARLIC, MINCED

EXTRA-VIRGIN OLIVE OIL
FOR SAUTÉING

1⅔ CUPS VIALONE NANO RICE

2 CUPS BAROLO

1 MEDIUM TOMATO, PEELED,
SEEDED, AND CHOPPED,
OR ½ CUP CANNED PEELED
TOMATOES, CHOPPED

2 TO 3 SAGE LEAVES

LEAVES OF 2 SPRIGS
ROSEMARY

4 CUPS VEGETABLE BROTH

SALT AND FRESHLY GROUND
BLACK PEPPER TO TASTE

3 TABLESPOONS UNSALTED
BUTTER

GRATED PARMIGIANO
REGGIANO TO TASTE

This risotto recipe has a rest period after the wine has been added and before the broth is added. This helps to deepen the flavor of the finished dish. Just be sure to allow yourself enough time.

In a large skillet, sauté the shallot and garlic in a little olive oil, then add the rice. Cook, stirring constantly, over high heat until the rice is coated and translucent. Add the wine and cook over high heat until the alcohol has evaporated. Remove from heat and allow the rice to rest in the skillet for 30 minutes. Meanwhile, peel, seed and chop the tomato (or chop canned tomatoes, if using). Mince the sage and rosemary together and set aside.

After 30 minutes, place the broth in a small pot and keep warm. Place the skillet over medium-low heat. Stir in the tomato, season with salt and pepper, then begin adding the broth in small amounts, stirring constantly and waiting until the last addition has been absorbed before adding the next. With each addition, this will take a little longer. Stir constantly with a wooden spoon and cook until rice is just tender with a tiny bit of crunch still in the center. Stir in the minced sage and rosemary and cook until rice is al dente, then remove from the heat and stir in the butter and grated Parmigiano until melted.

Risotto coi fenoci / FENNEL RISOTTO

Dora Vittorini, Venezia, Veneto

Make this with the youngest, most tender fennel you can find. While fennel tastes assertively of licorice when raw, cooking mellows its flavor considerably.

Place the broth in a small pot and keep warm. Thinly slice the onion. In a large skillet, melt the butter and sauté the onion. Add the fennel strips. Season with salt, add a little water, and cook until soft, about 10 minutes. Stir in the rice and cook, stirring, until rice is translucent and coated with the butter. Begin adding the hot broth in small amounts, stirring constantly and waiting until the last addition has been absorbed before adding the next. With each addition, this will take a little longer. Stir constantly with a wooden spoon and cook until rice is al dente, then remove from the heat, stir in the grated Parmigiano, and serve.

Serves 4

4 CUPS VEGETABLE BROTH

1 MEDIUM YELLOW ONION

5 TO 6 BULBS FENNEL

4 TABLESPOONS BUTTER

SALT TO TASTE

1½ CUPS VIALONE NANO OR ARBORIO RICE

½ CUP GRATED PARMIGIANO REGGIANO

Risotto piccante / SPICY RISOTTO

Rosaria Salvatore, Tropea (Vibo Valentia), Calabria

Risotto is a northern dish originally, but it is now made all over Italy. Calabria is home to a large number of varieties of chili peppers in all shapes and sizes.

Cut the peppers into strips and set aside. Place the broth in a small pot and keep warm. In a skillet brown the garlic in a generous amount of extra-virgin olive oil, then remove the garlic and add the chili peppers. Immediately add the rice. Cook, stirring, for a few minutes, then add the wine. When the wine has evaporated, begin adding hot broth in small amounts, stirring constantly and waiting for liquid to be absorbed before the next addition. When the rice has been cooking for 30 to 35 minutes, add the tomatoes and crush with the back of the spoon once they soften. Continue cooking, adding broth, until rice is al dente, about 10 additional minutes. Remove from the heat, taste and adjust salt, then stir in the Parmigiano and pine nuts. Tear 5 to 6 basil leaves over the risotto and serve.

Serves 4

2 GREEN CHILI PEPPERS

2 RED CHILI PEPPERS

ABOUT 4 CUPS VEGETABLE BROTH

1 CLOVE GARLIC

EXTRA-VIRGIN OLIVE OIL FOR SAUTÉING

1¾ CUPS SHORT-GRAIN RISOTTO RICE

½ CUP DRY WHITE WINE

8 TO 12 CHERRY TOMATOES

SALT TO TASTE

½ CUP GRATED PARMIGIANO REGGIANO

¼ CUP PINE NUTS

5 TO 6 BASIL LEAVES

Risotto con i carletti / RISOTTO WITH MAIDENSTEARS

Ristorante Pironetomosca, Treville di Castelfranco Veneto (Treviso), Veneto

Serves 6

1 MEDIUM YELLOW ONION

1 CARROT

1 RIB CELERY

1 LEEK, HALVED

SALT TO TASTE

9 OUNCES MAIDENSTEARS
SHOOTS AND LEAVES

1 SPRING ONION, MINCED

EXTRA-VIRGIN OLIVE OIL FOR
SAUTÉING AND DRIZZLING

2⅓ CUPS CARNAROLI RICE

½ CUP DRY WHITE WINE

4 TABLESPOONS UNSALTED
BUTTER, CUT INTO PIECES

½ CUP GRATED
GRANA PADANO CHEESE

FRESHLY GROUND BLACK
PEPPER TO TASTE

Maidenstears, or *Silene vulgaris*, are foraged in Italy. They have a grassy flavor similar to other wild greens, but are less bitter. This recipe includes instructions for preparing a vegetable stock, but if you already have your own on hand feel free to use it.

In a large pot, combine 12 cups cold water, the yellow onion, the carrot, the celery, and ½ leek. Add a pinch of salt, bring to a boil, and cook for about 1 hour to extract all the flavor from the vegetables. Strain, place broth in a small pot, and keep warm. Meanwhile, bring a large pot of water to a boil and blanch the maidenstears for 1 minute, then drain and mince.

Mince the remaining leek and set aside. In a large skillet, sauté the spring onion in oil, then add the maidenstears and cook, stirring frequently, for 5 minutes. In a separate large skillet, sauté the minced leek in oil until golden, then add the rice and cook, stirring, until coated and transparent. Add the wine and cook, stirring constantly, until the liquid has evaporated. Begin adding the broth in small amounts, stirring constantly and waiting for the broth to be absorbed before the next addition. Cook for about 20 minutes, then add the maidenstears and cook until rice is tender, about 20 additional minutes, continuing to stir in broth so that the skillet never dries out completely. Stir in the butter and cheese, taste and adjust salt, drizzle with oil, season with pepper, stir to combine, and serve.

Risotto carmasciano pere e mosto cotto /
RISOTTO WITH PEARS AND CARMASCIANO CHEESE

Oasis Sapori Antichi, Vallesaccarda (Avellino), Campania

The combination of pears and cheese always works beautifully, whether on a cheese plate, in a salad, or in this risotto. Carmasciano cheese, which is part of the Slow Food Ark of Taste, is a sheep's cheese with a lot of small holes in it and a bit of a bite that grows more pronounced as it ages. Mosto cotto is a syrupy condiment made by boiling grape juice to reduce it. It's available in gourmet specialty stores, but you can also make your own. Mastantuono pears, which come from Avellino, are small and round and particularly sweet.

Peel and core the pears and cut half into dice and slice the other half. Place the diced pears in a bowl with sparkling mineral water to cover and lemon juice and set aside to rest for 10 minutes. Meanwhile, toss the pear slices with the sugar and cook in a skillet over medium heat, stirring frequently, until just beginning to caramelize. Set both aside. Grate about half of the cheese and leave the rest whole. Place the broth in a small pot and keep warm.

Sauté the spring onion in a large skillet in a little olive oil. Add the rice to the skillet and cook, stirring, until coated and transparent. Add the wine and cook, stirring constantly, until the liquid has evaporated. Begin adding the broth in small amounts, stirring constantly and waiting for the broth to be absorbed before the next addition. Cook for about 10 minutes, then drain the diced pears and add them to the skillet. Cook until rice is al dente, continuing to stir in broth so that the skillet never dries out completely. Off the heat, stir in the butter and the grated cheese. Season to taste with salt and pepper. Transfer to a serving platter and shave the remaining cheese over the rice, then drizzle on the mosto cotto and garnish with the caramelized pears and chives.

Serves 4 to 6

2 TO 3 MASTANTUONO PEARS OR BARTLETT PEARS

SPARKLING MINERAL WATER FOR SOAKING

¼ TEASPOON LEMON JUICE

2 TABLESPOONS SUGAR

6 OUNCES CARMASCIANO CHEESE OR OTHER AGED SHEEP'S CHEESE

4 CUPS VEGETABLE BROTH

½ CUP THINLY SLICED SPRING ONION

EXTRA-VIRGIN OLIVE OIL FOR SAUTÉING

1½ CUPS CARNAROLI RICE

¼ CUP DRY WHITE WINE

7 TABLESPOONS UNSALTED BUTTER

SALT TO TASTE

FRESHLY GROUND BLACK PEPPER TO TASTE

¼ CUP MOSTO COTTO

¼ CUP SNIPPED CHIVES

Risi e bisi / RICE WITH PEAS

Rita Zambon, Castelfranco Veneto (Treviso), Veneto

Serves 4

4 SPRIGS PARSLEY

1 MEDIUM YELLOW ONION

1 CARROT

1 RIB CELERY

2 TO 3 CELERY LEAVES

SALT TO TASTE

1¼ TO 1½ POUNDS ORGANIC
PEAS IN THEIR PODS

1 SPRING ONION

18 TABLESPOONS (2 STICKS
PLUS 2 TABLESPOONS)
UNSALTED BUTTER

1½ CUPS CARNAROLI RICE

½ CUP DRY WHITE WINE

1 CUP GRATED
GRANA PADANO CHEESE

FRESHLY GROUND
BLACK PEPPER TO TASTE

Spring wouldn't be spring in the Veneto without rice with fresh peas, served to mark the feast of Saint Mark on April 25. This dish is always served *all'onda*, meaning that it is loose enough to create ripples (*onda* means "wave") in the pan.

Mince the parsley leaves and set aside. Make a broth: combine the yellow onion, carrot, celery, celery leaves, parsley stems, and a little salt. Add cold water to cover and simmer until vegetables have given up their flavor. Strain, transfer to a small pot, and keep warm. Shell the peas. Set the peas aside and simmer the pods in a small amount of salted water until very soft, then puree with a food mill. Mince the spring onion.

In a large skillet, melt 7 tablespoons of butter and sauté the spring onion until softened. Add the rice and cook, stirring, until it begins to sizzle, then add the wine and cook until evaporated. Add the peas about ½ cup at a time, stirring to absorb between additions. Add the pea pod puree, also working gradually. When all the pea pod puree has been added, begin adding the vegetable broth in small amounts, stirring constantly and waiting until the last addition has been absorbed somewhat before adding the next. After about 20 minutes, sprinkle in the minced parsley, then continue adding broth until the rice is cooked al dente and the dish is very moist, about 20 additional minutes. Season with salt and pepper. Remove from heat. Cut up the remaining 11 tablespoons butter and sprinkle into the skillet. Sprinkle on the grated Grana Padano as well. Stir until the butter and cheese have melted and serve.

Riso con asparagi e uova / RICE WITH ASPARAGUS AND EGGS

Natalina Favaro, Peschiera del Garda (Verona), Veneto

Basmati rice is not native to Italy, obviously, but it has become quite popular there in recent years, where it has been adopted for traditional Italian dishes such as this rice salad.

Bring a pot of water to a boil and cook the asparagus until tender but still crisp. Drain and chop. Heat olive oil in a pot and add the rice. Cook, stirring, until coated and translucent. Add 4 cups water, season with salt, and bring to a boil. Lower the heat to a simmer, cover with a tight-fitting lid, and cook until the rice has absorbed the liquid and is tender, about 18 minutes. Allow to cool to room temperature.

While the rice is cooking, place the eggs in a small pot, add water to cover, and bring to a boil. Turn down to a simmer and cook to the hard-boiled stage, 10 to 12 minutes. Remove the eggs with a slotted spoon and transfer to ice water. Peel the hard-boiled eggs and separate yolks from whites. Cut the whites into strips and crumble the yolks.

In a large bowl, gently toss the rice with the hard-boiled eggs and asparagus. Drizzle with a little olive oil, taste and adjust salt, and serve at room temperature.

Serves 4

9 OUNCES ASPARAGUS

EXTRA-VIRGIN OLIVE OIL FOR SAUTÉING AND DRESSING

2 CUPS BASMATI RICE

SALT TO TASTE

2 TO 3 LARGE EGGS

Riso asparagi e spinacini /
RICE WITH BABY ASPARAGUS AND TENDER SPINACH

Barbara Torresan, Milano, Lombardia

Serves 4 to 6

14 OUNCES ASPARAGUS

SALT TO TASTE

3 CUPS VEGETABLE BROTH

⅓ CUP FRESH SHELLED
PETITE PEAS

1 MEDIUM WHITE ONION

4 TABLESPOONS
UNSALTED BUTTER

2 CUPS CARNAROLI OR
VIALONE NANO RICE

½ CUP DRY WHITE WINE,
BLONDE BEER, OR HARD CIDER

½ CUP BABY SPINACH

FRESHLY GROUND BLACK
PEPPER TO TASTE

LEAVES OF 1 SPRIG THYME

COARSELY GRATED ZEST
OF ½ LEMON

Spotlight the flavor of young spring vegetables in this tasty rice dish. Pencil-thin wild asparagus work well here. If you like, you can top each portion with a tablespoon of stracciatella di bufala, a soft and creamy curd cheese.

Peel the stalks of the asparagus if necessary and arrange vertically in an asparagus pot or other pot. Fill the pot about halfway up the height of the asparagus with water, add a pinch of salt, and cook over medium heat just until the stalks are tender and tips are still crisp. Remove, reserving cooking water, and shock in ice water. Chop stalks but leave tips whole. Strain the asparagus cooking water, combine it with the vegetable broth, and place in a small pot. Keep warm. Steam or simmer the peas in salted water until soft.

Thinly slice the onion. In a skillet, melt 3 tablespoons of the butter and sauté the onion until browned, then add the rice and cook until translucent and coated. Add the wine and cook until evaporated. Stir in the chopped asparagus stalks. Begin adding the broth in small amounts, stirring frequently and waiting for the broth to be absorbed before the next addition. When the rice is almost cooked, still just slightly brittle in the center, season with salt, and stir in the baby spinach and the peas. Reserve a few asparagus tips for garnish and stir in the rest. Season with pepper. Mix to combine and taste. Stir in the remaining 1 tablespoon butter until melted, then remove from heat. Garnish with the thyme, lemon zest, and reserved asparagus tips and serve.

Soufflé di riso / RICE SOUFFLÉS

Luigina Favario, Donato (Biella), Piemonte

Serves 4

2 TABLESPOONS UNSALTED
BUTTER, PLUS MORE FOR
BUTTERING RAMEKINS

SALT TO TASTE

¼ CUP RICE

2 TABLESPOONS UNBLEACHED
ALL-PURPOSE FLOUR

1 CUP WHOLE MILK, SCALDED

FRESHLY GROUND
WHITE PEPPER

FRESHLY GRATED NUTMEG

4 LARGE EGGS, SEPARATED

1 CUP GRATED
PARMIGIANO REGGIANO

Individual soufflés always seem to put a smile on everyone's face. These make a nice light lunch when accompanied by a salad and perhaps a selection of cheeses.

Preheat oven to 350°F. Butter 4 ramekins and set aside. Bring a large pot of salted water to a boil and cook the rice as if it were pasta, stirring frequently, until al dente. Drain and set aside to cool. While the rice is cooling, prepare a béchamel. Melt 2 tablespoons butter in a small skillet. Whisk in the flour and cook, stirring constantly, until golden. Whisk in the milk and cook, whisking constantly, until the mixture begins to boil and thickens to the consistency of sour cream. Season with salt, pepper, and nutmeg. Set aside to cool. Beat the egg whites to stiff peaks. In a separate bowl, beat the egg yolks, rice, and grated Parmigiano together. Fold the egg whites and the béchamel into the egg yolk mixture. Divide among the prepared ramekins and bake in the preheated oven until puffed and golden, about 40 minutes.

Gnocchi di riso / RICE DUMPLINGS

Giuseppina Steffanoni, Milano, Lombardia

Serves 4

8 CUPS VEGETABLE BROTH

1½ CUPS RICE

SALT TO TASTE

4 LARGE EGGS

BREADCRUMBS FOR BINDING

GRATED CHEESE, SUCH AS
PARMIGIANO REGGIANO,
TO TASTE

MELTED UNSALTED BUTTER
TO TASTE

Use a starchy short-grain rice for these dumplings, and be sure to drain it well before adding it to the eggs. The dough should form a clump when you pinch off a piece of it.

Place the broth in a large pot, bring to a boil, then cook the rice like pasta, stirring frequently, until al dente. Taste and adjust salt. With a skimmer, remove the rice to a sieve to drain, reserving the broth in the pot. In a bowl, beat the eggs and then stir in the cooked rice. Add enough breadcrumbs to make a fairly dense, dry dough. Roll out the dough into ropes and cut the ropes into small dumplings. Bring the broth back to a boil and cook the dumplings in the broth until tender, about 5 minutes. Remove with a skimmer and transfer to individual serving dishes. Top with melted butter and grated cheese and serve immediately.

Riso selvatico e cavolfiore / WILD RICE WITH CAULIFLOWER

Clarissa Monnati, Roma, Lazio

Wild rice is actually a type of grass in the Zizania family. When it is fully cooked, many of the grains will have burst open, revealing their white interiors.

Break down the cauliflower into florets. Bring 4 cups of salted water to a boil and cook the cauliflower until soft, then drain, reserving cooking water. Add the rice to the cooking water, turn down to a simmer, cover, and cook until the rice has absorbed all of the liquid and is tender, about 45 minutes.

Thinly slice the onion and sauté in a skillet in olive oil. Add the cooked cauliflower florets and crush with a fork. Add the rosemary and cook, stirring frequently, for 10 minutes. Divide the wild rice among individual serving dishes and top with the cauliflower mixture. Garnish with olives and serve.

Serves 4 to 6

14 OUNCES (1 MEDIUM HEAD) CAULIFLOWER

SALT TO TASTE

2½ CUPS WILD RICE

1 MEDIUM YELLOW ONION

EXTRA-VIRGIN OLIVE OIL FOR SAUTÉING

LEAVES OF 1 SPRIG ROSEMARY, MINCED

¼ CUP PITTED OLIVES

Orzotto al Teroldego / RISOTTO-STYLE BARLEY WITH TEROLDEGO WINE

Nando Ferrari, Trento, Trentino

Serves 4

2½ CUPS PEARLED BARLEY

4 CUPS VEGETABLE BROTH

1 MEDIUM YELLOW ONION

2 CLOVES GARLIC

EXTRA-VIRGIN OLIVE OIL
FOR SAUTÉING

2 CUPS TEROLDEGO
ROTALIANO WINE

GRATED AGED CHEESE
TO TASTE

2 TABLESPOONS UNSALTED
BUTTER (OPTIONAL)

SALT TO TASTE

Barley can be treated like rice and slowly cooked with the addition of liquid, but it tends to take longer than rice, so it should be soaked for a few hours before using. Barley has been eaten in the mountainous areas of Italy for centuries, most often in soups. Teroldego Rotaliano is a dark red wine with an intense flavor. It should be alternated with the broth for best results and will turn the barley a deep red. Use an olive oil from the Trentino shore of Lake Garda if at all possible.

Place the barley in a large bowl and add cold water to cover by several inches. Soak for 2 hours, then drain. Place the broth in a small pot and keep warm. Thinly slice the onion and brown the onion and garlic in a copper pot with a handle in extra-virgin olive oil. Add the barley and cook, stirring, for a few minutes, until the barley is coated with the oil. Add about 1 cup of the hot broth and stir briskly and continuously. Continue cooking and adding liquid, alternating between the hot broth and the wine, and waiting for liquid to be absorbed before the next addition. When the barley has been cooking for 15 minutes, begin to taste occasionally. When it is al dente, stir in the grated cheese and the butter, if using. Adjust salt and cook, stirring constantly, until barley is tender. Remove from heat and stir in a little more olive oil.

Orzotto alle verdure / RISOTTO-STYLE BARLEY WITH VEGETABLES

Taverna Kus, San Zeno di Montagna (Verona), Veneto

Barley is cooked risotto-style here, but it is given a head start with a preliminary boiling. Feel free to swap in any vegetables that are in season in your area.

Place the beans in a bowl with cold water to cover by several inches and soak for 8 to 10 hours. Drain and cook in lightly salted water until tender, about 40 minutes, then drain again. Meanwhile, bring another large pot of salted water to a boil and add the barley. Cook, stirring frequently, until al dente, about 20 minutes. Drain and set aside.

Mince the onion. Dice the zucchini. Place the broth in a small pot and keep warm. In a skillet, sauté the onion in olive oil until golden. Add the zucchini and 2 tablespoons of the broth and cook for 10 minutes, stirring frequently.

Transfer the drained barley to a pot with enough broth just to cover and simmer for 5 minutes. Add the zucchini and the beans and cook, stirring constantly and adding broth in small amounts, until barley is tender, about 10 additional minutes. Each time, wait for the last addition of liquid to be absorbed before adding the next. Off the heat, stir in the butter, the grated cheese, the tomatoes, the basil, and the chives. Serve immediately.

Serves 4 to 6

½ CUP DRIED BORLOTTI BEANS

SALT TO TASTE

1½ CUPS PEARLED BARLEY

½ MEDIUM YELLOW ONION

3 ZUCCHINI

3 CUPS VEGETABLE BROTH

EXTRA-VIRGIN OLIVE OIL FOR SAUTÉING

2 TABLESPOONS UNSALTED BUTTER.

GRATED PARMIGIANO REGGIANO TO TASTE

3 CHERRY TOMATOES, SEEDED AND CHOPPED

3 LEAVES BASIL

¼ CUP MINCED CHIVES

Orzotto con pere e asìno /
RISOTTO-STYLE BARLEY WITH PEARS AND ASÌNO CHEESE

Trattoria da Neto, Udine, Friuli Venezia Giulia

Serves 4

3 CUPS VEGETABLE BROTH

2 SHALLOTS

4 BOSC PEARS

4 TABLESPOONS
UNSALTED BUTTER

1 CUP PEARLED BARLEY

SALT TO TASTE

4 OUNCES FRESH ASÌNO
CHEESE

1 TABLESPOON MINCED
CHIVES (OPTIONAL)

The pears are cut and grated at the last minute here to keep them from browning, but if you prefer to do that work in advance, toss them with a little lemon juice to stop discoloration. Do use Bosc pears, which will remain a little firm rather than disintegrating completely. Asìno cheese has been made in the Carnia area since the seventeenth century. It is a cow's milk cheese that is very creamy and soft. The fresh version is quite mild.

Place the broth in a small pot and keep warm. Mince the shallots. Melt the butter in a skillet and brown the shallots. While the shallots are cooking, peel and core 2 of the pears and cut into small dice. Add the diced pear to the skillet immediately. Add the barley and cook, stirring, for a few minutes until barley is coated with the butter. Add about ½ cup of the hot broth and cook, stirring constantly, until absorbed. Continue to add broth in small amounts, stirring contently and waiting for the last addition to be absorbed before you add the next, until barley is tender, about 40 minutes. Season with salt. Quickly core the remaining 2 pears and grate them on the large holes of a box grater. (Do not grate the peels.) Add the grated pears to the skillet immediately. Remove skillet from the heat, drop in the cheese by the spoonful, and stir to combine. Garnish with chives, if using.

Farrotto con porcini / FARRO WITH PORCINI

Osteria Giocondo, Rivisondoli (L'Aquila), Abruzzo

Farro is a kind of wheat that has been grown in Italy since the Etruscan era. Whole grains of farro make a delicious change from rice, and here they are cooked in the style of risotto. Cooking time for farro can vary widely, so use the 40 minutes here as a guide, but taste early and often.

Place the broth in a small pot and keep warm. Thinly slice the onion. Slice or dice the mushrooms and set aside. In a skillet, melt about half the butter and sauté the onion until golden. Add the farro and cook, stirring constantly, until coated with the butter and fragrant, about 2 minutes. Add the wine and cook, stirring constantly, until evaporated. Begin adding the broth in small amounts, stirring constantly and waiting until the last addition of liquid has been absorbed before adding the next.

In a separate skillet, sauté the garlic and chili pepper until the garlic browns, then add the mushrooms. Season with salt and cook, stirring frequently, until softened and browned. When the farro seems about halfway cooked—soft on the outside but still brittle in the center, probably after about 20 minutes—add the mushrooms to the skillet with the farro. Continue to cook, adding broth, until tender, about 20 additional minutes. Remove from the heat, stir in the remaining 2 tablespoons butter until melted, and serve.

Serves 4

4 CUPS VEGETABLE BROTH

1 MEDIUM YELLOW ONION

1 POUND PORCINI MUSHROOMS

4 TABLESPOONS UNSALTED BUTTER

1 CUP PEARLED FARRO

2 CLOVES GARLIC

1 PIECE CHILI PEPPER

EXTRA-VIRGIN OLIVE OIL FOR SAUTÉING

½ CUP DRY WHITE WINE

SALT TO TASTE

Crocchette di quinoa e miglio / QUINOA AND MILLET CROQUETTES

Camilla Forti, Milano, Lombardia

Serves 4

1 MEDIUM CARROT

1 MEDIUM YELLOW ONION

1 RIB CELERY

EXTRA-VIRGIN OLIVE OIL FOR
SAUTÉING AND BRUSHING

½ CUP QUINOA

½ CUP MILLET

1⅔ CUPS VEGETABLE BROTH

SALT TO TASTE

CURRY POWDER TO TASTE

1 BUNCH CHIVES, SNIPPED

1 LARGE EGG

GRATED PARMIGIANO
REGGIANO TO TASTE

FINELY GROUND CORNMEAL
OR RICE FLOUR
FOR WORK SURFACE

FRESHLY GROUND BLACK
PEPPER TO TASTE

Both quinoa and millet should be rinsed well before using. Simply place them in a sieve, rest the sieve in a bowl, and run cold water through the sieve until the bowl is full. Swish the grains around in the sieve, then lift the sieve, empty the bowl, and repeat. Do this until the water runs clear, usually three to four rinses. (This is especially crucial for quinoa, as it has a natural coating that can taste unpleasant.) These croquettes can also be fried in several inches of olive oil rather than baked. Any scraps will be tasty, though they won't look as pretty. You can also cut these into squares or diamonds to avoid waste.

Cut the carrot, onion, and celery into small dice. In a pot, sauté the carrot, onion, and celery in oil until softened. Add the quinoa and the millet and cook, stirring, until grains are coated, then add the vegetable broth and season with salt. Bring to a boil, then turn down to a simmer and cook, stirring occasionally, until millet is tender and quinoa is cooked and broth has been absorbed, about 20 minutes. Set aside to cool.

Preheat oven to 425°F. Line a baking sheet with parchment paper, brush with oil, and set aside. When the mixture is cool, season with a pinch of curry and stir in the chives. Lightly beat the egg and add. Stir in the grated cheese. Cover a work surface with parchment and sprinkle it generously with cornmeal. With a damp rolling pin, roll out the mixture to an even thickness. With a ring mold or cookie cutter, cut the rolled mixture into disks. Transfer to the prepared pan, brush with oil, and bake in the preheated oven, turning once, until browned and crisp, 15 to 20 minutes. You may want to run the croquettes under the broiler to finish them.

Pomodori ripieni di quinoa / QUINOA-STUFFED TOMATOES

Barbara Torresan, Milano, Lombardia

Always rinse quinoa well before using to eliminate the layer of saponin that coats it. Pair these light tomatoes with a green salad for a perfect summer meal.

Place the quinoa in a pot and add the broth or water and a pinch of salt. Bring to a boil, then simmer until the liquid has been absorbed and the quinoa is transparent and tender, about 20 minutes. Set aside to cool.

While the quinoa is cooking, use a paring knife to cut off the stem ends of the tomatoes. (Reserve them for serving if you like.) Core the tomatoes, leaving shells intact. Salt their interiors and set them upside down in a sieve to drain for 10 minutes.

When the quinoa is warm but no longer piping hot, toss it with oil, salt, pepper, and the basil. Mince the carrot. Peel and seed the cucumber and mince that as well. Remove any seeds and ribs from the pepper and mince. Stir the minced vegetables, capers, and olives into the quinoa mixture. Stir in the lemon juice, then taste and adjust seasonings. When you are happy with the flavor, stuff the tomatoes with the quinoa mixture. Drizzle with a little more oil and chill in the refrigerator for 30 minutes before serving.

Serves 4 to 6

2 CUPS QUINOA

2 CUPS VEGETABLE BROTH OR WATER

8 RIPE TOMATOES

SALT TO TASTE

EXTRA-VIRGIN OLIVE OIL FOR DRESSING AND DRIZZLING

FRESHLY GROUND WHITE PEPPER TO TASTE

LEAVES OF 1 SPRIG BASIL, MINCED

1 MEDIUM CARROT

1 MEDIUM CUCUMBER

1 YELLOW BELL PEPPER

1 TABLESPOON CAPERS, RINSED AND DRAINED

1 TABLESPOON MINCED OLIVES

JUICE OF ½ LEMON

POLENTA AND OTHER PORRIDGES

Polenta grassa / POLENTA WITH CHEESE AND MILK

Letizia Palesi, Champorcher, Valle d'Aosta

Serves 4

4 CUPS WHOLE MILK

SALT TO TASTE

3 CUPS COARSELY
GROUND POLENTA

CLARIFIED BUTTER TO TASTE

DICED TOMA CHEESE
TO TASTE

GRATED PARMIGIANO
REGGIANO TO TASTE

Clarified butter has had all the solids removed. If you do not have clarified butter on hand, soften some standard butter over low heat and use that in its stead. Toma cheese is produced in the north of Italy in both the mountains and on the plains. Polenta is prepared with various types of cheese all over this area of the country.

Combine the milk with 4 cups water in a pot. Season with salt and bring to a boil. As soon as the liquid begins to boil, drizzle in the polenta in a thin stream while stirring constantly to be sure no lumps form. Turn down the heat until the polenta is simmering, stir in clarified butter, and continue cooking, stirring constantly, until polenta no longer tastes raw and is dense and pulling away from the sides of the pot, about 45 minutes. Stir in the toma and cook for a few additional minutes, then transfer to a serving platter, sprinkle on the grated Parmigiano, and serve.

Polenta con Fonduta / POLENTA WITH FONDUTA SAUCE

Ristorante La Clusaz, Gignod, Valle d'Aosta

Serves 4

1 POUND FONTINA CHEESE

½ CUP PASTRY FLOUR

4 CUPS WHOLE MILK

SALT TO TASTE

3 CUPS POLENTA

1 EGG YOLK

Fonduta is a classic white sauce made with fontina, a semi-soft cow's milk cheese.

Cut the fontina into cubes and toss with the pastry flour. Place in a bowl, add the milk (which should cover the cheese) and refrigerate for 4 hours.

Bring 8 cups of salted water to a boil and as soon as it begins to boil, drizzle in the polenta in a thin stream while stirring constantly with a wooden spoon or spatula to be sure no lumps form. Cook over medium heat, stirring very frequently, until polenta no longer tastes raw and is dense and pulling away from the sides of the pot, about 2 hours.

When the polenta is almost cooked, transfer the cheese and milk to a pot and place over low heat. When the cheese melts, whisk in the egg yolk, working energetically to avoid curdling. Simmer until the sauce is dense, about 30 minutes total. Serve the polenta with the sauce on top.

Polenta con stracchino e tartufo nero /
POLENTA WITH STRACCHINO CHEESE AND BLACK TRUFFLE

Trattoria Dentella, Bracca (Bergamo), Lombardia

Polenta, surely one of the most humble foods in the world, is elevated by being paired with black truffle and with the excellent traditional stracchino produced in the Orobiche Valleys, which has its own Slow Food Presidium. The word *stracchino* comes from a local dialect word for "tired," as it was made from the milk of cows during transhumance, the period when cattle are moved from one pasture area to another as the seasons change. Because it was prepared on the road, it was not processed at length. The result is a very loose spreadable cheese with a tangy edge. Though the traditional type of stracchino may be difficult to locate outside of this area, other versions of this creamy dairy product are often available in Italian specialty stores.

Bring 4 cups salted water to a boil and drizzle in the polenta in a thin stream while stirring constantly and briskly with a whisk to be sure no lumps form. Cook, continuing to stir constantly, until the polenta no longer tastes raw and is dense and pulling away from the sides of the pot, about 50 minutes.

When the polenta is almost cooked, place the stracchino and the milk in the top of a double boiler and whisk over low heat until melted and creamy. Separately, melt the butter.

To serve, scoop portions of polenta into individual bowls. Make an indentation in the center of each portion and divide the stracchino mixture evenly, pouring it into these indentations. Drizzle with melted butter and shave a generous amount of black truffle over each serving.

Serves 4 to 6

SALT TO TASTE

1¼ CUPS POLENTA

11 OUNCES STRACCHINO

¼ CUP WHOLE MILK

7 TABLESPOONS UNSALTED BUTTER

1 SMALL BLACK TRUFFLE

Toc' in Braide / EXTRA-CREAMY POLENTA WITH MONTASIO CHEESE

Walter Dri, Udine, Friuli Venezia Giulia

Serves 6

2 STICKS PLUS 5 TABLESPOONS
UNSALTED BUTTER

½ CUP FINELY GROUND
POLENTA

2¾ CUPS WHOLE MILK

ROCK SALT TO TASTE

1¾ CUPS COARSELY
GROUND POLENTA

11 OUNCES MONTASIO
CHEESE OR LATTERIA
CHEESE, GRATED

This dish has three parts: the polenta itself, a cheesy fonduta sauce, and a buttery mixture known as a *morchia* made with finely ground polenta. The fonduta sauce should be pourable but thick. If it seems too thin, brown a few tablespoons of flour in a few tablespoons of butter to make a roux and whisk that into the mixture. Depending on the season, this dish may also incorporate white asparagus or porcini or chanterelle mushrooms. Though these are gourmet adaptations, in its original version this dish was intended as an inexpensive and filling food that farmers in Friuli Venezia Giulia could bring with them to the fields. In the Como area, eating polenta was a communal exercise: diners, each armed with his or her own wooden spoon, gathered around to scoop polenta directly from the large copper pot where it was cooked.

For the morchia, melt the butter in a copper pot and drizzle in the finely ground polenta in a very thin stream, whisking constantly. Cook over medium heat, whisking constantly, until the polenta no longer tastes raw and the mixture is a rich golden color.

For the polenta, combine ¾ cup milk with 2¼ cups water in a pot and bring to a boil. Salt, and then drizzle in the coarsely ground polenta in a thin stream while stirring constantly with a whisk to be sure no lumps form. Cover the pot with a tight-fitting lid and let the polenta cook in its own steam—do not stir or disturb the crust that forms on top—until it no longer tastes raw and is creamy, about 45 minutes.

For the fonduta sauce, place the remaining 2 cups milk in a pot and bring to a boil, then remove from the heat and stir in the grated cheese. If any lumps form, smooth the mixture with an immersion blender.

To serve, scoop portions of polenta into the center of individual bowls. Make an indentation in the center of each portion with the back of a spoon and pour 2 to 3 tablespoons of the fonduta into each indentation. Form a ring around the perimeter of each portion with the morchia and serve hot.

Polenta Macafana / POLENTA WITH CHICORY AND CHEESE

Maria Girardini, Cimego, Trentino

The stoneground polenta from Storo, a town in the province of Trento with fewer than 5,000 residents, is famously fragrant and is made from a special variety of corn that is a dark, reddish color. This classic dish using that polenta seems to hail from Cimego, a tiny village near Storo that at last count had 413 inhabitants. Rest assured, this dish will still be tasty if made with standard corn polenta. Trentingrana cheese is an aged cheese similar to Parmigiano Reggiano that is grated over pasta and other first courses in the Trentino region. Spressa is a cow's milk cheese that may be aged to various stages. Young spressa will be quite soft, while aged spressa is firmer.

Bring a large pot of salted water to a boil, add the chicory, and cook until just tender, no longer than 5 minutes. Drizzle in the polenta in a thin stream while stirring constantly to be sure no lumps form. Continue cooking, stirring constantly, until the polenta no longer tastes raw and is dense and beginning to pull away from the sides of the pot. Scatter in the diced spressa cheeses and cook, continuing to stir constantly, for 10 additional minutes. The cheese should melt into the polenta completely.

Mince the onion. Melt the butter in a skillet and brown the minced onion in the butter. Transfer the cooked polenta to a soup tureen or other large serving bowl. Sprinkle on the grated trentingrana cheese, season with pepper, and pour the browned onion and butter over the polenta. Serve hot.

Serves 8

SALT TO TASTE

3 POUNDS WILD CHICORY, CUT INTO RIBBONS

6 CUPS STORO POLENTA

7 OUNCES YOUNG SPRESSA CHEESE, DICED

1⅓ POUNDS AGED SPRESSA CHEESE, DICED

1 MEDIUM YELLOW ONION

1 STICK PLUS 6 TABLESPOONS (14 TABLESPOONS) UNSALTED BUTTER

11 OUNCES AGED TRENTINGRANA CHEESE, GRATED

FRESHLY GROUND BLACK PEPPER TO TASTE

Roascht / POLENTA WITH POTATOES AND ONIONS

Kürbishof, Antervo-Altrei, Alto Adige

Serves 4 to 6

¼ TEASPOON SALT

2⅓ CUPS POLENTA

14 OUNCES (3 SMALL) POTATOES

½ YELLOW ONION

EXTRA-VIRGIN OLIVE OIL FOR SAUTÉING

Polenta traditionally is made with specific equipment, including a large copper pot (usually a cauldron that could be suspended in a fireplace) and a wooden paddle with a long, thick handle used for stirring. In many parts of Italy, cooked polenta is poured onto a wooden board that is then placed in the center of the table.

Place 6 cups of water in a pot—preferably a copper polenta pot—and bring to a boil. Add the salt and then drizzle in the polenta in a thin stream while stirring constantly with a wooden paddle to be sure no lumps form. Continue cooking, stirring constantly, until the polenta no longer tastes raw and is very dense. Pour the warm polenta onto a wooden board and let it cool. It will firm up.

Meanwhile, bring a pot of water to a boil and cook the potatoes until tender. Drain and peel as soon as they are cool enough to handle, then let them cool completely. Grate both the firm polenta and the cooked potatoes on the largest holes of a four-sided grater. Thinly slice the onion and sauté in olive oil in a large skillet until browned. Add the grated polenta and potatoes and cook over medium heat, stirring constantly, until browned, about 20 minutes.

Polenta con caurigli / GREEN POLENTA

Matteo Iannacone, Venafro (Isernia), Molise

You can also make this dish with a mix of broccoli and broccoli rabe or kale. Once the vegetables break down after cooking, the polenta will be tinted green. This dish actually improves with age—warm through any leftovers in the oven before serving.

Place 8 cups water in a large pot—preferably a copper polenta pot—and bring to a boil. Add salt and then add the broccoli. Cook the broccoli for a few minutes after the water returns to a boil, then drizzle in the polenta in a thin stream while stirring constantly to be sure no lumps form. Continue cooking, stirring constantly, until the polenta no longer tastes raw and is dense and beginning to pull away from the sides of the pot, about 45 minutes.

Thinly slice the garlic (remove any green shoots) and sauté in a generous amount of extra-virgin olive oil with the chili pepper until browned, then stir the garlic mixture into the polenta until combined.

Serves 6

SALT TO TASTE

2 POUNDS BROCCOLI, CHOPPED

4½ CUPS POLENTA

4 TO 5 CLOVES GARLIC

EXTRA-VIRGIN OLIVE OIL FOR SAUTÉING

1 CHILI PEPPER, MINCED

Zuf / POLENTA WITH SQUASH

Dorina Treppo, Tarcento (Udine), Friuli Venezia Giulia

You can use any type of winter squash you like in this dish, a specialty in the Carnia area. One small squash will yield about 3 cups once it is peeled, seeded, and cut into cubes, but this is not a recipe that requires great exactitude.

Melt the butter in a large pot, preferably a copper polenta pot. Add the squash and a few tablespoons of water and cook over medium heat until very soft, adding a little more water at a time if necessary to keep the squash from sticking. Mash the squash against the side of the pot to break it down, then add the milk and season with salt. Bring to a boil and as soon as the liquid begins to boil, drizzle in the polenta and cook, stirring constantly, until polenta no longer tastes raw and the mixture is creamy, about 30 minutes. If the polenta seems very dense but still tastes raw, add water in small amounts to thin it.

Serves 4

3 TABLESPOONS UNSALTED BUTTER

3 CUPS CUBED WINTER SQUASH

2 CUPS WHOLE MILK

SALT TO TASTE

⅔ CUP POLENTA

Polenta di castagne con taleggio e verza /
CHESTNUT POLENTA WITH TALEGGIO CHEESE AND CABBAGE

Andrea Montagnosi, Bergamo, Lombardia

Serves 4 to 6

1 SMALL HEAD
SAVOY CABBAGE

2 CUPS CHESTNUT FLOUR

1¼ CUPS POLENTA

4 CUPS WHOLE MILK

SALT TO TASTE

1 CUP CUBED
TALEGGIO CHEESE

Chestnut flour lends this polenta a nutty flavor. Both taleggio cheese and cabbage are frequently used in the northern reaches of Italy. You can cut the cabbage into ribbons rather than serving whole leaves. Roast the cabbage instead for a slightly different flavor.

Pull the cabbage leaves off of the head of cabbage. Discard core. Bring a pot of water to a boil and blanch the cabbage leaves. Drain and set aside. In a bowl, combine the chestnut flour and polenta. Combine 3½ cups milk with 3⅓ cups water in a large pot and bring to a boil. As soon as it boils, salt and drizzle in the chestnut flour and polenta mixture in a thin stream, whisking briskly to avoid letting lumps form. Cook, stirring very frequently, for 45 minutes until the polenta no longer tastes raw and is pulling away from the sides of the pot. If the mixture begins to get very dense before it is cooked, add water in small amounts to thin it.

Combine the remaining ½ cup milk and the taleggio in the top of a double boiler and cook, whisking, until the cheese has melted. Divide the taleggio mixture among individual serving bowls. Place a few spoonfuls of polenta in the center of each and top with the cabbage. Serve hot.

Fagottini di verza con polenta / STUFFED CABBAGE WITH POLENTA

Letizia Palesi, Champorcher, Valle d'Aosta

As delicious as fresh polenta is when piping hot and creamy, leftover polenta is a treat in its own right. As polenta cools it firms up. Firm polenta can be cut into slices and pan-fried or layered with other ingredients and baked, as it is here. Sant'Andrea is a medium-grain rice with plenty of starch. Use any variety of Italian rice as a substitute, if needed.

Preheat oven to 400°F. Bring a pot of water to a boil and blanch the cabbage leaves. Drain and pat dry. Bring a large pot of salted water to a boil and cook the rice as you would pasta, stirring frequently, until it is halfway cooked—tender on the outside but still a little brittle in the center. Drain and set aside. Mince the onion and sauté it in the 2 tablespoons oil in a large skillet. Toss the drained rice in the skillet over medium heat for a few minutes to combine.

Gently spread the cabbage leaves on a work surface and divide the rice mixture among them. Roll up the leaves into packets. With a toothpick, attach a bay leaf to each cabbage packet. Place the polenta slices in a single layer in a baking pan and set one stuffed cabbage leaf on top of each slice. Drizzle with a little olive oil and bake in the preheated oven until warmed through, 7 to 8 minutes. Remove bay leaves and toothpicks before serving.

Serves 4

8 SAVOY CABBAGE LEAVES

SALT TO TASTE

1½ CUPS SANT' ANDREA RICE

1 MEDIUM YELLOW ONION

2 TABLESPOONS EXTRA-VIRGIN OLIVE OIL, PLUS MORE FOR DRIZZLING

8 BAY LEAVES

8 THICK SLICES LEFTOVER POLENTA

Polenta di roveja con cipolla e pecorino /
WILD PEA POLENTA WITH ONIONS AND SHEEP'S CHEESE

Osteria Il Picciolo di Rame, Caldarola (Macerata), Marche

Serves 4 to 6

SALT TO TASTE

4 CUPS ROVEJA FLOUR

1 TABLESPOON EXTRA-VIRGIN
OLIVE OIL, PLUS MORE FOR
DRIZZLING

⅓ CUP CHOPPED ONION

GRATED AGED SHEEP'S
CHEESE TO TASTE

The *roveja* is a type of wild pea that is dark green and brown. Native to the Umbria-Marche border, it tastes similar to fava beans and chickpeas. It is available whole in dried form and also ground into flour that is used to make soup and polenta. A Slow Food Presidium is dedicated to this ancient legume. The consistency of this polenta is very similar to that of a corn polenta, but roveja polenta cooks much more quickly.

In a pot, bring 4 cups salted water to a boil. As soon as it boils, drizzle in the roveja flour in a thin stream, stirring constantly with a whisk to keep lumps from forming. Cook, stirring constantly, until the mixture no longer tastes raw and is pulling away from the sides of the pot, about 15 minutes.

Transfer the cooked mixture to a platter and spread no more than ¾ inch thick. Allow to cool and when the mixture has cooled completely and firmed up, cut it into strips about 1 inch long.

Heat 1 tablespoon olive oil in a skillet with 3 tablespoon water and cook the onion in it until soft. When the liquid has completely evaporated, add the polenta strips and stir over medium heat until strips are heated through. Sprinkle on the grated cheese, drizzle with a little more olive oil, and serve immediately.

Viandon / RYE BREAD POLENTA

Franca Gallo, Aosta, Valle d'Aosta

Serves 4

7 TABLESPOONS
UNSALTED BUTTER

1 CUP CUBES DAY-OLD
RYE BREAD

2½ TO 3 CUPS WHOLE MILK

SALT TO TASTE

2 CUPS POLENTA

5 OUNCES FONTINA
CHEESE, DICED

On holidays in the town of Valtournenche in the Valle d'Aosta region, this dish often takes a place of honor at the table. This type of polenta enriched with cheese is quite common in the area. Another similar version, *panicha*, calls for stirring the fontina into the polenta about halfway through the cooking time, resulting in a different but equally tasty flavor.

In a skillet, melt 3 tablespoons butter. Add the rye bread cubes and toast until browned on all sides. In a copper pot, combine the milk with an equal amount of water and bring to a boil. Salt and drizzle in the polenta in a thin stream, mixing with a whisk so that no lumps form. Cook the polenta, stirring constantly, until it no longer tastes raw, at least 1 hour. about 10 minutes before the polenta is fully cooked, stir in cubes of stale rye bread toasted in a generous amount of melted butter, fontina cheese, and the remaining 4 tablespoons butter. To serve, divide among individual serving bowls and serve piping hot.

Pappa sciansca / WHEAT PORRIDGE WITH WINE

Giovanna Barzan, San Donà di Piave (Venezia), Veneto

Serves 6

3 CUPS UNBLEACHED
ALL-PURPOSE FLOUR

ABOUT 2 CUPS DRY
WHITE WINE

2 CUPS WHOLE MILK

3 TABLESPOONS SUGAR

SALT TO TASTE

GROUND CINNAMON TO TASTE

This porridge mixes savory and sweet flavors. Spices such as cinnamon have been used in both savory and sweet preparations in the Veneto for centuries, because the Venetian Republic was a major player in the spice trade.

Place the flour in a bowl. Whisk in about the wine, a spoonful at a time, to make a smooth paste. You may not need all of the wine, or you may need a little more. Stir in the milk to make a very soupy mixture. Stir in the sugar, a pinch of salt, and a pinch of ground cinnamon, then cook over low heat, stirring constantly, until thickened, about 20 minutes.

Peilà d'orzo / BARLEY PORRIDGE

Ristorante Hostellerie de l'Atelier, Cogne, Valle d'Aosta

Peilà is Valle d'Aosta dialect for a kind of porridge made with rye flour, buckwheat flour, cooked whole barley, or barley flour with plenty of butter and regional cheeses. Traditionally, it is prepared on a wood-burning stove, so if you are lucky enough to have one, don't hesitate to use it. In the years before refrigerators were commonplace in this area, locals would clarify butter made from the milk of local cows (this is more of a butter region than an olive oil region) and keep it in jars so that it would not go bad. Since we don't have the same concerns in modern times, you can substitute about 7 tablespoons of fresh butter melted in the top of a double boiler for the clarified butter.

Peel the potatoes. Bring a large pot of salted water to a boil and cook the potatoes until tender. Remove potatoes, reserving cooking liquid in the pot. Crush the potatoes with a potato ricer and let them fall back into the pot. Place over medium heat. Drizzle in the flours and cook, stirring constantly, over low heat for 20 minutes. Stir in the cheese and cook until melted, then remove from heat and stir in the clarified butter.

Serves 4

1¾ POUNDS (5 TO 6 MEDIUM) STARCHY POTATOES

SALT TO TASTE

1¼ CUPS UNBLEACHED ALL-PURPOSE FLOUR

1 CUP BARLEY FLOUR

6 OUNCES FONTINA CHEESE, DICED

6 OUNCES TOMA CHEESE, DICED

4 TABLESPOONS CLARIFIED BUTTER, WARM

Paparotta / SEMOLINA PORRIDGE

Trattoria La Pergola, Gesualdo (Avellino), Campania

In Italy, both tomatoes and peppers are dried for purposes of preservation and used to flavor numerous dishes. Sun-dried peppers, known as *peperoni cruschi*, add flavor to this simple dish.

In a pot, sauté the onion in the olive oil. Remove the onion with a slotted spoon or skimmer and set aside. Sauté the peppers in the oil, then remove and set aside. Add 2 cups of water to the pot with the oil. Combine the pepper into the pot, and return the onion to the same pot. Bring to a boil, then drizzle in the semolina in a very thin stream, whisking to keep lumps from forming. Cook over medium heat until the mixture is dense and no longer tastes raw, about 15 minutes, adding hot water if it seems overly dense before it is fully cooked. Season with salt, divide among individual serving dishes, and allow to rest for a few minutes before serving.

Serves 4

1 MEDIUM YELLOW ONION, THINLY SLICED

¼ CUP EXTRA-VIRGIN OLIVE OIL

4 SUN-DRIED RED PEPPERS, SEEDED AND SLICED INTO ROUNDS

1 CUP FINELY MILLED SEMOLINA FLOUR

SALT TO TASTE

LEGUMES

Purè di cicerchie di Castelvecchio / PUREED CICERCHIA BEANS
Trattoria La Conca alla Vecchia Posta, L'Aquila, Abruzzo

Serves 4

¾ CUP DRIED
CICERCHIA BEANS

SALT TO TASTE

LEAVES OF 1 SPRIG
ROSEMARY

1 BAY LEAF

1 CLOVE GARLIC,
UNPEELED

EXTRA-VIRGIN OLIVE OIL
FOR DRIZZLING

Cicerchia are pale yellow or white beans that have a bumpy surface rather than the usual smooth skin of dried beans. They make an excellent canvas for all sorts of flavors. When cooking, you can add thyme, marjoram, oregano, and either black pepper or chili pepper to the pot.

Soak the beans in cold water for 8 to 12 hours. Drain the beans of their soaking water and place them in a pot with fresh water to cover by a couple of inches. Season with salt. Add the rosemary, bay leaf, and garlic. Cover the pot and cook over low heat until the beans are easily crushed, about 2 1/2 hours.

Remove and discard the bay leaf and garlic. With a slotted spoon or skimmer, remove the beans to a blender and puree, adding small amounts of their cooking water until the puree is smooth and creamy, but not too liquid. Drizzle with extra-virgin olive oil before serving.

Crauti e fagioli / BROWNED BORLOTTI BEANS AND SAUERKRAUT
Adele Moretti, Bolzano-Bozen, Alto Adige

Serves 4 to 6

1 CUP DRIED BORLOTTI BEANS

1 TABLESPOON
UNSALTED BUTTER

5⅓ CUPS SAUERKRAUT

SALT AND FRESHLY GROUND
BLACK PEPPER TO TASTE

Cooking times for dried beans can be hard to guess. Though they are dried, beans can still be more or less fresh. Try to shop in a store with good turnover, and if the beans have been in your cupboard for quite a while, try to give them a good long soak and plan on cooking them for a long period as well. And always taste a few beans when checking for doneness—even in the same batch, their cooking times can vary.

Soak the beans in cold water to cover by several inches for at least 8 hours. Drain, rinse, and transfer to a pot. Add fresh water to cover, bring to a boil, then simmer until soft. Drain and set aside.

In a large skillet, melt the butter. Add the sauerkraut and sauté for 5 minutes, then add the drained beans and continue cooking, stirring occasionally, until the beans and the sauerkraut are nicely browned. Season with salt and pepper and serve.

Fasoi in salsa / SPICED BORLOTTI BEANS

Maria Rigodanza, Lonigo (Vicenza), Veneto

If you are lucky enough to find fresh borlotti beans in their pods, snatch them up and skip the soaking. You'll need about 2 pounds of beans in their pods to get 3 cups once shelled. They will also have a much shorter cooking time.

Soak the beans for at least 8 hours in water to cover by several inches. Drain and transfer to a pot with fresh water to cover. Add the carrot, celery, and onion. Season with salt and pepper. Bring to a boil, then simmer until soft and creamy, about 3 hours.

Meanwhile, mince the garlic and sauté it in a skillet in the extra-virgin olive oil. When the garlic begins to color, add the herbs and sauté until wilted. Add the vinegar and simmer gently for 10 minutes. Season with cinnamon and pepper.

When the beans are cooked, drain them and discard the carrot, celery, and onion. Pour the warm sauce over the warm beans. Stir to combine, cover, and allow to rest at room temperature for at least 2 hours before serving.

Serves 4

3 CUPS DRIED
BORLOTTI BEANS

1 MEDIUM CARROT

1 RIB CELERY

1 MEDIUM YELLOW ONION

2 CLOVES GARLIC

¼ CUP EXTRA-VIRGIN
OLIVE OIL

MINCED FLAT-LEAF
PARSLEY, BASIL, CALAMINT,
SAGE, AND ROSEMARY

¼ CUP RED WINE VINEGAR

GROUND CINNAMON TO TASTE

FRESHLY GROUND
BLACK PEPPER TO TASTE

Crauti rostidi / BEANS WITH SAUERKRAUT

Angelo Taninelli, Rovereto, Trentino

Serve this rustic dish with bread fresh from the oven. In the Trentino region, this was a very common snack. It is delicious paired with a classic sparkling wine from the area.

Boil the beans until tender, about 40 minutes for fresh beans and 2 hours for soaked dried beans. When soft, drain them.

Place the olive oil in a large cast-iron skillet and sauté the sauerkraut over high heat, stirring, for 5 minutes. Add the beans and cook until the mixture is browned and crusty and beginning to char in spots. Season with salt and pepper and serve.

Serves 4

¼ CUP SHELLED FRESH
BORLOTTI BEANS OR DRIED
BORLOTTI BEANS SOAKED
IN WATER TO COVER FOR AT
LEAST 12 HOURS

1 TABLESPOON
EXTRA-VIRGIN OLIVE OIL

5⅓ CUPS SAUERKRAUT

SALT AND FRESHLY GROUND
BLACK PEPPER TO TASTE

Fagiolane alla Barbera / FAGIOLANE BEANS IN BARBERA WINE

Ristorante Stevano, Cantalupo Ligure (Alessandria), Piemonte

Serves 4

1¼ CUPS DRIED VAL BORBERA
FAGIOLANE BEANS

1 MEDIUM YELLOW ONION

LEAVES OF 1 SPRIG ROSEMARY

2 FRESH BAY LEAVES

1 TABLESPOON UNSALTED
BUTTER, ROOM TEMPERATURE

1 TABLESPOON EXTRA-VIRGIN
OLIVE OIL

SALT AND FRESHLY GROUND
BLACK PEPPER TO TASTE

½ CUP BARBERA WINE

Val Borbera fagiolane beans are harvested by hand. They are large white beans (hence their long soaking time) and are part of the Slow Food Ark of Taste. They marry beautifully with the deep, rich Barbera wine from the region.

Soak the beans for 18 to 24 hours in water to cover by several inches. Drain and cook in fresh water until tender, then let the beans cool in the cooking water.

Meanwhile, mince together the onion, rosemary, and bay leaves and combine with the butter and olive oil. Season with salt and pepper. Place the mixture in a large pot and sauté, stirring frequently, over low heat until onion softens, about 5 minutes. Don't let the mixture brown excessively. Add the wine to the pot, raise the heat to medium, and simmer until the wine has evaporated. When the wine has evaporated, begin adding about ¼ cup water at a time to keep the mixture moist and cook for an additional 30 minutes. When the beans have cooled, remove them with a slotted spoon or skimmer and combine them with the sauce.

Pasta e fagioli / PASTA AND LAMON BEANS

Osteria da Paeto, Pianigia (Venezia), Veneto

Serves 4 to 6

Lamon beans (there are several varieties) are an IGP (Protected Geographic Origin) product in Italy. If you cannot track them down, substitute regular borlotti beans. Tagliatelle are fresh egg noodles. You can also use maltagliati (egg pasta chopped into random shapes) or about 1 cup small dried semolina pasta, such as ditalini, in this dish. You may want to chop the tagliatelle roughly or break them into pieces by hand to make them easier to eat. If you can locate fresh borlotti beans, use them and skip the soaking in the recipe below. You will need about 1 pound of beans in their pods to obtain 1½ cups of shelled beans.

Soak the beans in cold water to cover by several inches for 12 hours. Mince the onion, carrot, and celery and sauté them in a large pot in a small amount of olive oil. Drain and rinse the soaked beans, then add them to the pot. Add cold water to cover and cook until the beans are tender, about 1½ hours. When the beans are cooked, remove about half of them and puree. Return the pureed beans to the pot with the whole beans. (You can use an immersion blender and do this right in the pot.)

In a small skillet, sauté the rosemary and garlic until fragrant and browned, then remove the rosemary and garlic and add the flavored oil to the pot with the beans. Season with salt and pepper and bring to a boil, then cook the pasta in the pot with the beans.

1½ CUPS DRIED LAMON BEANS

1 MEDIUM YELLOW ONION

1 MEDIUM CARROT

2 RIBS CELERY

EXTRA-VIRGIN OLIVE OIL FOR SAUTÉING

1 SPRIG ROSEMARY

2 CLOVES GARLIC

SALT AND FRESHLY GROUND BLACK PEPPER TO TASTE

3 OUNCES TAGLIATELLE

Pendolon / POTATO AND BORLOTTI BEAN WEDGES

Ristorante La Segheria, San Martino di Castrozza, Trentino

Serves 6 to 8

1½ CUPS FRESH SHELLED
BORLOTTI BEANS

2 POUNDS (ABOUT 6)
POTATOES

2 WHITE ONIONS

7 TABLESPOONS
UNSALTED BUTTER

SALT AND FRESHLY GROUND
BLACK PEPPER TO TASTE

This dish is made in a copper *paiolo*, the pot traditionally used in this area for cooking polenta. The cooking in mountainous areas of Italy is quite hearty. Potatoes are often used as a base.

Cook the beans in abundant water until tender. In a separate pot, boil the potatoes until tender enough to be pierced easily. Drain the beans. Drain the potatoes and peel them once they are cool enough to handle

Thinly slice the onions and place a copper pot over medium heat. Melt 5 tablespoons butter and add the onions. Cook, stirring frequently, until golden, about 7 minutes. Add the potatoes and with a wooden spatula crush them forcefully into a fairly smooth puree. Add the cooked beans and crush about one quarter of them, leaving the rest whole. Season with salt and pepper. Cook over low heat, stirring constantly, for 3 additional minutes, adding in the remaining 2 tablespoons butter in small pieces. Pour the mixture onto a wooden cutting board, spread it into a circle about 1-inch thick, and let it cool. Cut into wedges and serve lukewarm or cold.

Secra e suriata / BEAN, BREAD, AND CHARD CAKE

Luisa San le, Monterosso Calabro (Vibo Valentia), Calabria

Choose any type of beans you like for this satisfying savory cake.

Soak the beans in cold water to cover by several inches overnight. The next day, drain them and add them to a large pot with a generous amount of water, a pinch of salt, the chili pepper, and the onion, if using. Bring to a boil, then turn down to a simmer and cook until tender. Drain.

Meanwhile, separate the green leaves from the stalks of the chard. Chop the stems into ¾-inch lengths and tear the leaves into small pieces by hand. Bring a large pot of salted water to a boil, add the stems, and cook for 5 minutes. Add the green leaves and cook until both are tender. Drain and squeeze dry.

In a large skillet, heat a generous amount of olive oil and add the bread cubes and garlic. toss over high heat until the bread is toasted, then add the chard and cook for 5 minutes, stirring frequently. Lastly, stir in the beans. Sprinkle on the cheese and season with a little salt. With a wooden spoon, press the ingredients against the bottom of the skillet and cook over medium heat until a crust forms on the bottom, about 15 minutes. Use a lid to turn the cake and brown the other side. Allow to cool to room temperature before serving.

Serves 4

1¼ CUPS DRIED BEANS

SALT TO TASTE

1 CHILI PEPPER

1 CLOVE GARLIC

1 MEDIUM YELLOW ONION (OPTIONAL)

2 POUNDS (2 TO 3 BUNCHES) CHARD

ABOUT 2 CUPS CUBES OF DAY-OLD BREAD

EXTRA-VIRGIN OLIVE OIL FOR TOASTING BREAD AND BROWNING CAKE

¼ CUP GRATED AGED SHEEP'S CHEESE

Millecosedde / "THOUSAND THINGS" BEAN SOUP

Antonina De Marco, Castrovillari (Cosenza), Calabria

Serves 4

¼ CUP DRIED
CANNELLINI BEANS

¼ CUP DRIED CHICKPEAS

¼ CUP CICERCHIA BEANS

¼ CUP DRIED FAVA BEANS

¼ CUP LENTILS

3 CUPS SAVOY CABBAGE
CUT INTO RIBBONS

1 RIB CELERY, THINLY SLICED

2 MEDIUM YELLOW ONIONS,
THINLY SLICED

1¼ CUPS SLICED FRESH
PORCINI MUSHROOMS

1½ CUPS SHORT
DRIED SEMOLINA PASTA,
SUCH AS DITALINI

SALT TO TASTE

½ CUP GRATED AGED
SHEEP'S CHEESE

FRESHLY GROUND BLACK
PEPPER TO TASTE

EXTRA-VIRGIN OLIVE OIL
FOR DRIZZLING

If you cannot obtain porcini mushrooms, use dried porcini. Soak them in lukewarm water for about 20 minutes to soften, then carefully lift them out of the soaking water, leaving behind any grit, and squeeze them dry. Roughly chop and continue. Their flavor is intensified by the drying process, so you won't need as many.

Soak all of the legumes in cold water to cover by several inches for 12 hours. Drain them and rinse.

Place the legumes, the cabbage, the celery, the onions, and the mushrooms in a large pot with 8 cups water. Bring to a boil, then turn down to a simmer and cook for 2 hours. Stir in the pasta, season with salt, and cook until pasta is tender, about 10 additional minutes.

To serve, ladle into individual soup bowls and top each serving with grated cheese and a generous grinding of pepper, as well as a drizzle of olive oil.

Fagioli all'uccelletto / CANNELLINI BEANS WITH SAGE

Osteria Il Vignaccio, Camaiore (Lucca), Toscana

If you are lucky enough to find Bigliolo beans, which are sweet and tender with a very thin skin, use them in this recipe, where their flavor really shines. If not, go with standard fresh cannellini beans, or even dried beans that you have soaked overnight in water to cover by several inches.

Shell the beans. Bring a large pot of salted water to a boil and add the shelled beans, 2 garlic cloves, and 4 sage leaves. Cook at a simmer until the beans are soft. Transfer to a colander or sieve to drain, but reserve cooking water.

Mince the remaining 2 garlic cloves and 4 sage laves and sauté briefly in oil. Add the beans, tomatoes, and basil leaves. Season with salt and pepper, add enough of the cooking water to cover, and cover the pan with a tight-fitting lid. Simmer until most of the liquid has evaporated and the beans are extremely soft, adding additional cooking water if needed to keep them moist.

Serves 6

1 ¾ POUNDS FRESH CANNELLINI BEANS, PREFERABLY THE BIGLIOLO VARIETY

SALT TO TASTE

4 CLOVES GARLIC

8 SAGE LEAVES

EXTRA-VIRGIN OLIVE OIL FOR SAUTÉING

14 OUNCES PLUM TOMATOES, CHOPPED

2 BASIL LEAVES

FRESHLY GROUND BLACK PEPPER TO TASTE

Cotolette di lupini / LUPINI BEAN "CUTLETS"

Federico Valicenti, Terranova di Pollino (Potenza), Basilicata

Serves 4

3 CUPS BRINED LUPINI BEANS, RINSED AND DRAINED

2 TABLESPOONS EXTRA-VIRGIN OLIVE OIL, PLUS MORE FOR PAN-FRYING

ABOUT ¼ CUP UNBLEACHED ALL-PURPOSE FLOUR, PLUS MORE FOR DREDGING

1 TABLESPOON MINCED TARRAGON, CHIVES, PARSLEY, OR A COMBINATION (OPTIONAL)

SALT TO TASTE

2 TO 3 SPRIGS ROSEMARY

1 LEMON, CUT INTO WEDGES

Lupini beans sold in brine and are often eaten as a snack in Italy. They have a rather thick outer coat that is almost always removed.

Steam the lupini or simmer in boiling water until their coats are soft. Peel and then bring fresh water to a boil and simmer the beans again until tender but still firm, at least 1 additional hour.

Remove the beans with a skimmer or slotted spoon, reserving cooking water. Puree the beans with some of their cooking water and the 2 tablespoons olive oil in a blender until soft and smooth. Add a little more cooking water if needed. Add flour, about 1 tablespoon at a time, until the mixture is dense enough to form a patty. (You may not need the full ¼ cup of flour, or you may need a little more.) Mix in the herbs, if using, and season with salt.

Place some flour for dredging in a soup plate. Place several inches of olive oil in a pot with high sides and the rosemary sprigs. Bring the oil to temperature for frying, and meanwhile shape the bean mixture into flat oval patties. Dredge the patties in the flour and fry in the oil, turning once, until golden on both sides, about 5 minutes. Work in batches if necessary to keep from crowding the pot. Drain briefly, then serve hot with lemon wedges.

Zimino di fagioli / CANNELLINI BEANS AND CHARD

Ristorante La Cinquantina, Cecina (Livorno), Toscana

These stewed beans—which are first cooked on their own and then simmer gently with tomatoes and chard—benefit from being prepared in advance, so be sure to plan ahead. As they cool, their flavor will improve further.

Soak the beans in cold water to cover by several inches for 8 to 12 hours. Place the beans in a pot and add cold water just to cover. Bring to a boil, then turn down to a simmer and cook until just tender. While the beans are cooking, strip away any thick stems from the chard and reserve for another use. Bring another large pot of lightly salted water to a boil and blanch the greens. Drain, squeeze dry, and mince.

When the beans are tender, drain them. In a clean pot large enough to hold the beans, heat a small amount of olive oil and sauté the garlic until it begins to turn golden. Add the minced chard and turn the heat to high. Stir in the tomato paste and cook, stirring frequently, for a few minutes. Add the canned tomatoes and break them up, then add the beans with their cooking liquid. Season with salt and pepper, turn the heat as low as possible, and let the beans simmer gently until the liquid is reduced by half. Allow the beans to cool completely and then reheat them just before serving and serve hot.

Serves 4 to 6

1½ CUPS DRIED CANNELLINI BEANS

1 BUNCH CHARD

SALT TO TASTE

EXTRA-VIRGIN OLIVE OIL FOR SAUTÉING

3 CLOVES GARLIC, MINCED

2 TABLESPOONS TOMATO PASTE

¼ CUP CANNED TOMATOES

FRESHLY GROUND BLACK PEPPER TO TASTE

Purè di ceci / CHICKPEA PURÉE

Trattoria Martin Pescatore, Milano, Lombardia

Serve slices of rustic toasted bread rubbed with the cut side of a garlic clove with this purée. Cooked chicory also makes a nice addition.

Soak the chick peas for 12 hours in cold water to cover by several inches and the baking soda. Drain and rinse the beans and place in a pot with the onion, sage, and bay leaf. Add water just to cover, bring to a boil, then simmer until the beans are soft.

When the beans are soft, remove and discard bay leaf and puree the beans with an immersion blender while drizzling in the oil until you have a creamy puree. Season with salt and freshly ground black pepper.

Serves 4

2½ CUPS DRIED CHICKPEAS

1 PINCH BAKING SODA

1 SPRING ONION

2 TO 3 SAGE LEAVES

1 BAY LEAF

½ CUP EXTRA-VIRGIN OLIVE OIL

SALT AND FRESHLY GROUND BLACK PEPPER TO TASTE

Ciceri e tria / CHICKPEAS WITH FRIED AND BOILED NOODLES

Trattoria Cucina Casareccia Le Zie, Lecce, Puglia

Serves 4 to 6

2 CUPS DRIED CHICKPEAS

½ TEASPOON BAKING SODA

1 CLOVE GARLIC

1 RIB CELERY

2 BAY LEAVES

SALT TO TASTE

3⅓ CUPS SEMOLINA FLOUR

EXTRA-VIRGIN OLIVE OIL
FOR SAUTÉING

FRESHLY GROUND
BLACK PEPPER TO TASTE

Tria are noodles similar in size to tagliatelle. This classic of Puglia is always served to celebrate Saint Joseph on March 19, usually with garlicky broccoli added to the mix.

Place the chickpeas in cold water to cover by several inches and add the baking soda. Soak for 12 hours. Rinse and drain the chickpeas and place them in a pot with water to cover. Bring to a boil and skim off any foam, then add the garlic, celery, and bay leaves. Season with salt, turn down to a simmer, and cook until tender, about 2 hours.

Meanwhile, make the pasta. Shape the flour into a well on a work surface and add a pinch of salt, then place enough warm water in the well to make a soft dough as you gradually pull in flour from the sides of the well. Knead until combined, then set aside to rest for at least 10 minutes. With a rolling pin, on a lightly floured surface roll into a thin sheet, then roll into a loose cylinder and cut into strips 1 to 1½ inches wide. Spread pasta in a single layer on a clean kitchen towel and set aside to dry.

When the chickpeas are almost cooked, bring a large pot of salted water to a boil and cook about three quarters of the pasta until al dente. Drain the cooked pasta and add to the chickpeas. In a skillet, brown the reserved (uncooked) pieces of pasta in some oil. Remove and discard bay leaves. If you prefer a soupier dish, ladle out the chickpeas and pasta and their cooking water into individual soup plates. If you prefer a drier dish, use a slotted spoon or skimmer and allow much of the cooking liquid to drain back into the pot. In either case, scatter some of the browned pasta on each serving, season with pepper, drizzle with olive oil, and serve hot.

Lagane e ceci / CHICKPEAS WITH EGGLESS LAGANE NOODLES

Osteria Nunzia, Benevento, Campania

Serves 6

2 CUPS DRIED CHICKPEAS

1 PINCH BAKING SODA

SALT TO TASTE

1 CLOVE GARLIC, MINCED

LEAVES OF 1 SPRIG
ROSEMARY, MINCED

7 TO 8 CHERRY TOMATOES,
CHOPPED

EXTRA-VIRGIN OLIVE OIL
FOR SAUTÉING

14 OUNCES LAGANE OR
OTHER EGGLESS NOODLES

LEAVES OF 1 SPRIG PARSLEY,
CHOPPED

GROUND CHILI PEPPER
(OPTIONAL)

Lagane are rectangular noodles that resemble lasagna noodles, though they are made with semolina pasta and water—never eggs. Their sturdy texture makes them a great match for all kinds of legumes.

Soak the chickpeas in water to cover by several inches for 12 hours. Drain the chickpeas and sprinkle them with the baking soda. Bring a large pot of salted water to a boil, rinse the chickpeas, then add them to the pot and cook for 30 minutes.

Meanwhile, sauté the garlic, rosemary, and tomatoes in oil. When the tomatoes have broken down and the chickpeas are tender but not completely soft, add both the tomato mixture and the pasta to the chickpeas. Cook, stirring occasionally, until pasta is cooked and chickpeas are soft. Stir in the parsley and the chili pepper, if using.

Fave 'ngrecce / SPICY FAVA BEANS

Osteria de le Cornacchie, Petritoli (Ascoli Piceno), Marche

Serves 4

2½ POUNDS FRESH FAVA
BEANS IN THEIR PODS

SALT TO TASTE

1 CLOVE GARLIC

3 TO 4 LEAVES SVELTO MINT
OR SPEARMINT

GROUND CHILI PEPPER
TO TASTE

EXTRA-VIRGIN OLIVE OIL
FOR DRESSING

Dressing the beans while they are still hot means they absorb the flavors better. Svelto mint, which grows in the Petritoli area of the Marche region, grows in the spring and has a very strong flavor.

Shell and peel the fava beans. Bring a large pot of salted water to a boil and cook the beans until soft, at least 20 minutes. When the beans are soft, drain them and transfer them to a bowl. Mince the garlic and mint together and make a dressing for the beans of the garlic mixture, a pinch of chili pepper, salt, and extra-virgin olive oil. Pour this dressing over the beans and toss to combine.

Bagiana / STEWED FAVA BEANS

Ilda Cardinali, Passignano sul Trasimeno (Perugia), Umbria

Central Italy offers a wide choice of similar fava dishes; in this area fresh fava beans are also eaten raw, usually accompanied by sheep's cheese. Fava beans must be removed from their pods, and then, unless they are very young and tender, the tough outer covering of each been must be removed as well. Use a paring knife to handle this quickly.

Shell and peel the fava beans and bring a large pot of salted water to a boil. Cook the beans for 30 minutes, then drain and set aside.

While the beans are cooking, mince together the onions and basil or wild fennel. Heat a small amount of olive oil in a large skillet with high sides and sauté the onion mixture until golden. Add the tomato puree and the fava beans and cook, stirring with a wooden spoon, until combined. Add the vegetable broth, season with salt, and cook, uncovered, for 30 minutes, stirring occasionally. Top with a generous grinding of black pepper and serve piping hot.

Serves 6

2¼ POUNDS FRESH FAVA BEANS IN THEIR PODS

SALT TO TASTE

2 MEDIUM YELLOW ONIONS

LEAVES OF 1 SPRIG BASIL OR WILD FENNEL

EXTRA-VIRGIN OLIVE OIL FOR SAUTÉING

¼ CUP TOMATO PUREE

6 CUPS VEGETABLE BROTH OR WATER

FRESHLY GROUND BLACK PEPPER TO TASTE

Biete e fave / FAVA BEANS WITH CHARD

Adriana Mastrodicasa, Francavilla al Mare (Chieti), Abruzzo

This delicious and versatile springtime dish works as a side dish, an appetizer, or a main course.

Bring a large pot of water to a boil and cook the chard and the fava beans together for 30 minutes. Meanwhile, in a large skillet, sauté the garlic in a generous amount of extra-virgin olive oil. Remove the beans and greens from their cooking water with a skimmer or slotted spoon and add to the skillet. Add the chili pepper and salt to taste. Cook, stirring, for 5 minutes, then serve.

Serves 4 to 6

2 POUNDS CHARD, ROUGHLY CHOPPED

2 CUPS FRESH SHELLED AND PEELED FAVA BEANS (ABOUT 2½ POUNDS IN THEIR PODS)

3 CLOVES GARLIC

EXTRA-VIRGIN OLIVE OIL FOR SAUTÉING

1 CHILI PEPPER, MINCED

SALT TO TASTE

Incapriata di fave con cicorielle selvatiche /
FAVA PURÉE WITH WILD CHICORY

Ristorante Cibus, Ceglie Messapica (Brindisi), Puglia

Serves 4 to 6

2 CUPS SMALL DRIED
FAVA BEANS

7 OUNCES (1 TO 2 MEDIUM)
POTATO

SALT TO TASTE

EXTRA-VIRGIN OLIVE OIL
FOR DRIZZLING

14 OUNCES WILD CHICORY

Long, slow cooking really brings out the best in beans. The fava beans for this dish should be light in color, not the larger brown ones. The puree and the greens are served separately so that the diner can combine them to reach the desired balance of bitter (the chicory) and sweet (the fava beans). Sometimes this is served with slices of raw red onion or with fried peppers, and it may also be found with a scattering of browned breadcrumbs on top.

Place the beans in an earthenware pot, add water to cover by several inches, and soak for 2 hours. While the beans are soaking, make a fire in a wood-burning oven or preheat a home oven to 250°F. When the beans have soaked for 2 hours, peel the potato and add it to the pot with the beans. Cover the pot and bake for 3 hours. Uncover, season with salt, and continue cooking until very soft.

When the beans are soft, with a wooden spoon, crush the beans and potato against the sides of the pot until the mixture is broken down into a puree. Drizzle on a generous amount of olive oil. Bring a pot of salted water to a boil and blanch the chicory. Squeeze the blanched chicory dry drizzle with oil. Serve the two parts of the dish separately and allow diners to help themselves.

Lenticchie di Onano stufate / STEWED LENTILS

Elvira Alfonsi, Onano (Viterbo), Lazio

Serves 4

1¾ CUPS ONANO LENTILS

1 RIB CELERY, CHOPPED

1 MEDIUM YELLOW ONION,
CHOPPED

1 MEDIUM CARROT, CHOPPED

1 CLOVE GARLIC

1 SPRIG ROSEMARY,
OR 2 BAY LEAVES

SALT TO TASTE

Thin-skinned Onano lentils are part of the Slow Food Ark of Taste and have a flavor redolent of hay or chamomile.

Place the lentils in a pot with cold water to cover, along with the celery, onion, carrot, garlic, and rosemary. Salt to taste. Place the pot over medium heat and simmer uncovered until soft, about 20 minutes after it reaches a boil. If the lentils appear dry as they are cooking, add boiling water to the pot in small amounts. Remove rosemary or bay leaves before serving.

Pancotto contadino / FAVA BEANS OVER BREAD CUBES

Ristorante Medioevo, Monte Sant'Angelo (Foggia), Puglia

Serves 4 to 6

1 CUP DRIED FAVA BEANS, PEELED OR UNPEELED

SALT TO TASTE

¼ CUP EXTRA-VIRGIN OLIVE OIL, PLUS MORE FOR DRIZZLING

4 MEDIUM YELLOW ONIONS, THINLY SLICED

1 POUND (ABOUT 3 MEDIUM) POTATOES, PEELED AND CUBED

1 POUND (ABOUT ½ MEDIUM HEAD) SAVOY CABBAGE, CORED AND CHOPPED

6 TOMATOES, CHOPPED

¼ TEASPOON DRIED FENNEL POLLEN

6 SLICES DAY-OLD PUGLIESE BREAD, CUT INTO 1-INCH CUBES

For this dish you want whole dried fava beans, not the split type. Fennel pollen is removed by hand from wild fennel blossoms, a painstaking process accounting for its steep price. If you have access to wild fennel, dry 2 heads of the flowers, then place them top-down in a plastic bag and shake them vigorously to dislodge the pollen. Pugliese bread has a dark crust and large holes in the crumb. Look for a loaf baked in a wood-burning oven. This is traditionally served with brined black olives as an accompaniment.

If using unpeeled beans, remove the black dot from each bean with a paring knife. Soak the beans in cold water to cover by several inches for 12 hours. Drain and bring a pot of lightly salted water to a boil. If using unpeeled beans, remove the peel with a paring knife. Add the beans and cook until soft, 50 to 60 minutes, adding water to the pot if necessary to keep the beans covered.

Meanwhile, place the ¼ cup oil in a pot and sauté the onion over medium heat, uncovered, until golden. Add the potatoes, the cabbage, the tomatoes, and the fennel pollen. Cook, covered, for 10 minutes, then add water to cover, adjust salt, and cook for an additional 20 minutes. When the fava beans are soft, drain them and add them to the pot with the vegetables. Cook for an additional 10 minutes.

Place the cubes of bread in a soup tureen, then ladle the soup over them and set aside to rest until the bread has softened and absorbed the cooking liquid but has not broken down, 2 to 3 minutes. Serve drizzled with additional olive oil.

Lenticchie di Castelluccio in umido / SIMMERED CASTELLUCCIO LENTILS

Taverna Castelluccio, Norcia (Perugia), Umbria

Castelluccio, which sits more than 4,500 feet above sea level, is known for producing some of the world's tastiest lentils. They are small in size and exceedingly tender when cooked due to their thin skins.

In an earthenware pot that is not too large but has high sides, combine 4 cups water, the lentils, the garlic, and the celery. Cook over low heat until the lentils are soft, adding boiling water in small amounts if needed to keep the lentils moist. Cooking time will depend on how hard the water is in your area, but it should take about 45 minutes from the time the lentils come to a boil. Season with salt and drizzle with oil, then serve.

Serves 4

2 CUPS CASTELLUCCIO LENTILS

1 CLOVE GARLIC

1 RIB CELERY, CHOPPED

SALT TO TASTE

EXTRA-VIRGIN OLIVE OIL FOR DRIZZLING

Purè di lenticchie / LENTIL PURÉE

Graziano Spaziani, Bevagna (Perugia), Umbria

Most lentils do not need to be soaked before cooking, but if you think yours are on the dry side or have thick skins, soak them in cold water to cover, then drain and rinse them before staring.

Bring a pot of lightly salted water to a boil, add the lentils, and simmer until soft. Drain the lentils. Separately, simmer the celery, carrot, onion, potato, tomato, and parsley in water to cover until the vegetables are soft and have given up their flavor. Add the drained lentils, bring to a boil, and simmer for 10 minutes. Puree the entire mixture. Stir in the olive oil and the Parmigiano Reggiano, if using. Serve with the toasted bread and a generous grinding of black pepper.

Serves 4

SALT TO TASTE

2½ CUPS LENTILS

1 RIB CELERY, CHOPPED

1 MEDIUM CARROT, CHOPPED

1 MEDIUM YELLOW ONION, CHOPPED

1 POTATO, PEELED

1 TOMATO

LEAVES OF 1 SPRIG PARSLEY

1 TABLESPOON EXTRA-VIRGIN OLIVE OIL

¼ CUP GRATED PARMIGIANO REGGIANO (OPTIONAL)

8 SLICES DAY-OLD BREAD, TOASTED

FRESHLY GROUND BLACK PEPPER TO TASTE

FRITTATE, CUSTARDS, AND OTHER EGG DISHES

Frittata di peperoni / YELLOW PEPPER FRITTATA

Rosanna Dotta, La Morra (Cuneo), Piemonte

Serves 4

1 POUND 5 OUNCES
(ABOUT 3 MEDIUM)
YELLOW BELL PEPPERS

EXTRA-VIRGIN OLIVE OIL
FOR SAUTÉING

1 MEDIUM YELLOW ONION,
THINLY SLICED

SALT AND FRESHLY GROUND
BLACK PEPPER TO TASTE

4 LARGE EGGS

There is no better last-minute meal than a vegetable frittata. Even one made only with onions is delicious. Adding bell peppers, as in this version, elevates it further.

Seed the peppers, remove any white ribs, and cut into thin strips. Place a small amount of olive oil in a skillet and place over low heat. Sauté the onion until golden. Add the peppers, season with salt and pepper, and add a few tablespoons of water to keep the peppers from sticking as you cook them, stirring frequently, until soft, about 10 minutes.

Beat the eggs with a pinch of salt. When the peppers are soft, pour the egg mixture into the skillet. With a spatula, push the cooked eggs from the edge into the center. At the same time, tilt the pan toward the edge that you are pushing in so that still-liquid egg mixture runs down and fills the now-empty space. Repeat several times. When the bottom of the frittata is firm but the top is still soft, cook over medium heat without moving until the bottom is browned and set, 2 to 3 minutes. Using the spatula, slide the frittata out of the pan, then flip it back into the pan so that the browned side is facing up. Cook until the bottom is browned and set, 2 to 3 additional minutes.

Frittata di patate e mele / POTATO AND APPLE FRITTATA

Letizia Palesi, Champorcher (Aosta), Valle d'Aosta

Serves 4

4 TABLESPOONS
CLARIFIED BUTTER

4 LARGE POTATOES, PEELED
AND THINLY SLICED

2 REINETTE APPLES,
CORED, SEEDED, PEELED,
AND THINLY SLICED

4 LARGE EGGS

SALT TO TASTE

Reinette apples are firm and not too sweet—an interesting addition to this frittata. Clarified butter has had all its water and solids removed so that it doesn't burn.

Line a baking sheet with paper towels and set aside. Place the butter in a skillet and heat over low heat. Add the potatoes and cook, shaking the pan frequently, for 30 minutes. Add the apples and cook for 20 additional minutes.

In a medium bowl, beat the eggs with a pinch of salt. Pour the eggs into the skillet and turn the heat to medium. With a spatula, push the cooked eggs from the edge into the center. At the same time, tilt the pan toward the edge that you are pushing in so that still-liquid egg mixture runs down and fills the now-empty space. Repeat several times. When the bottom of the frittata is firm but the top is still soft, cook over medium heat without moving until the bottom is browned and set, 2 to 3 minutes. Using the spatula, slide the frittata out of the pan, then flip it back into the pan so that the browned side is facing up. Cook until the bottom is browned and set, 2 to 3 additional minutes. Drain on the prepared baking sheet for a couple of minutes, then serve hot.

Frittata con bruscandoli / HOP SHOOT FRITTATA

Trattoria Da Procida, San Biagio di Callalta (Treviso), Veneto

Hop shoots emerge from the soil in early spring. Their taste and texture are similar to those of asparagus.

Trim any hard stems from the hop shoots and chop them. In a 14-inch skillet, melt the butter with the olive oil. Add the shoots and sauté over low heat until softened. Meanwhile, in a bowl beat the eggs with the grated cheese and season with salt and pepper. Pour the egg mixture into the skillet. With a spatula, push the cooked eggs from the edge into the center. At the same time, tilt the pan toward the edge that you are pushing in so that still-liquid egg mixture runs down and fills the now-empty space. Repeat several times. When the bottom of the frittata is firm but the top is still soft, cook over medium heat, gently shaking the pan occasionally, until the bottom is browned and set, 2 to 3 minutes. Using the spatula, slide the frittata out of the pan, then flip it back into the pan so that the browned side is facing up. Cook until the bottom is browned and set, 2 to 3 additional minutes. Cut into wedges and serve.

Serves 4

8 LARGE EGGS

6 OUNCES HOP SHOOTS (SEE NOTE)

2 TABLESPOONS GRATED GRANA PADANO

2 TABLESPOONS UNSALTED BUTTER

2 TABLESPOONS EXTRA-VIRGIN OLIVE OIL

SALT AND FRESHLY GROUND BLACK PEPPER TO TASTE

Froscia di ricotta / RICOTTA FRITTATA

Ristorante Acquarius, Santo Stefano Quisquina (Agrigento), Sicilia

Sheep's milk ricotta tends to be a little lighter tasting than cow's milk ricotta. Excellent ricotta is produced all over Sicilia, but the quality of the ricotta made in the Sicani Mountains is unmatched and it is recommended here.

Place the ricotta in a cheesecloth-lined strainer set over a bowl and drain for 24 hours. The next day, in a bowl beat the eggs with salt and pepper. Heat a large skillet over medium heat with a small amount of olive oil and break up the ricotta (it will be fairly solid) and add it to the skillet. Sauté briefly. Pour in the egg mixture. At first, every few seconds tilt the pan while pushing the more solid eggs from the edge into the center so that the still-uncooked egg mixture fills the space around the perimeter. When the bottom is firm but the top is soft, let cook undisturbed until the bottom is browned. This should take about 5 minutes total. Flip the frittata, return to the pan, and cook until both sides are browned, an additional 2 to 3 minutes. Garnish with calamint leaves and serve.

Serves 4 to 6

1¼ CUP SHEEP'S MILK RICOTTA

6 LARGE EGGS

SALT AND FRESHLY GROUND BLACK PEPPER TO TASTE

EXTRA-VIRGIN OLIVE OIL FOR SAUTÉING

LEAVES OF 1 SPRIG CALAMINT, TORN

Frittata con le vitabbie / WILD VITALBA FRITTATA

Orazio Falchi, Foligno (Perugia), Umbria

Serves 4

1 BUNCH VITALBA SPROUTS

2 TABLESPOONS
EXTRA-VIRGIN OLIVE OIL

4 LARGE EGGS

SALT TO TASTE

Vitalba is a wild vine that grows on other shrubs. The young sprouts are tender and edible, but the rest of the plant is slightly toxic, so be sure to forage with someone knowledgeable and don't pick anything more than the very tops. Vitalba is also known as Old Man's Beard and Traveler's Joy.

Mince the sprouts. Heat about half of the olive oil in a large skillet. In a bowl, beat the eggs with a pinch of salt. Sauté the sprouts until tender, then beat them into the egg mixture. Add the remaining olive oil to the skillet. Pour the egg mixture into the skillet. With a spatula, push the cooked eggs from the edge into the center. At the same time, tilt the pan toward the edge that you are pushing in so that still-liquid egg mixture runs down and fills the now-empty space. Repeat several times. When the bottom of the frittata is firm but the top is still soft, cook over medium heat until the bottom is browned and set, 2 to 3 minutes. Using the spatula, slide the frittata out of the pan, then flip it back into the pan so that the browned side is facing up. Cook until the bottom is browned and set, 2 to 3 additional minutes.

Sformato di bucce di piselli / PEA POD CUSTARD

Giuliana D'Este, Ferrara, Emilia-Romagna

Serves 4 to 6

SALT TO TASTE

1 POUND PEA PODS

EXTRA-VIRGIN OLIVE OIL FOR
SAUTÉING AND OILING PAN

2 SPRING ONIONS,
THINLY SLICED

2 LARGE EGGS,
LIGHTLY BEATEN

1 CUP GRATED
PARMIGIANO REGGIANO

FRESHLY GRATED NUTMEG
TO TASTE

2 TO 3 SLICES DAY-OLD
BREAD, TOASTED

This unusual custard makes good use of pea pods—a prime example of Italy's waste-not-want-not culinary style.

Preheat the oven to 325°F. Bring a large pot of salted water to a boil and blanch the pea pods. Drain, dry, and sauté in a small amount of oil with the onions. Process this mixture through a food mill to make a smooth puree. Whisk the puree with the eggs, the Parmigiano, and a pinch of nutmeg.

In a food processor fitted with the metal blade, grind the toasted bread into breadcrumbs. Lightly oil a ring pan and coat the pan with the breadcrumbs. Pour in the pea pod mixture and then set the ring pan in a baking pan. Pour hot water into the dish to create a water bath. Bake in the preheated oven until set. Allow to cool for about 10 minutes, then unmold to a serving platter.

Frittata con aglio rosso / FRITTATA WITH RED GARLIC

Taverna de li Caldora, Pacentro (L'Aquila), Abruzzo

Garlic scapes—the stems of the plants—are in season in the spring. They are a little too tough to eat raw, but are delicious cooked. Serve this frittata hot or cold. See page 69 for instructions on preserving garlic scapes so you can enjoy them year-round.

Bring a large pot of salted water to a boil and blanch the scapes. In a medium bowl beat the eggs with a pinch of salt. Stir in the scapes. Place a small amount of olive oil in a skillet and place over low heat. Pour in the egg mixture. With a spatula, push the cooked eggs from the edge into the center. At the same time, tilt the pan toward the edge that you are pushing in so that still-liquid egg mixture runs down and fills the now-empty space. Repeat several times. When the bottom of the frittata is firm but the top is still soft, cook over medium heat without moving until the bottom is browned and set, 2 to 3 minutes. Using the spatula, slide the frittata out of the pan, then flip it back into the pan so that the browned side is facing up. Cook until the bottom is browned and set, 2 to 3 additional minutes. Serve hot, room-temperature, or cold.

Serves 4 to 6

SALT TO TASTE

10 OUNCES SULMONA RED GARLIC SCAPES

4 LARGE EGGS

EXTRA-VIRGIN OLIVE OIL FOR COATING SKILLET

Erbazzone / CHARD FRITTATA

Alda Beltrami, Reggio nell'Emilia, Emilia-Romagna

Serves 4 to 6

2 POUNDS TENDER
SWISS CHARD

SALT TO TASTE

2 LARGE EGGS

¼ CUP UNBLEACHED
ALL-PURPOSE FLOUR

¼ CUP BREADCRUMBS

1½ CUPS GRATED
PARMIGIANO REGGIANO

2 TABLESPOONS
UNSALTED BUTTER

FRESHLY GROUND BLACK
PEPPER TO TASTE

FRESHLY GRATED NUTMEG
TO TASTE

You can use any type of greens you like in this frittata in place of the chard. Just don't overcook the greens when blanching them. Sometimes a little cooked rice is added to this dish, and there are sweet versions as well.

Blanch the greens in lightly salted water, then drain and squeeze dry. Mince the greens. In a medium bowl, whisk the eggs then stir in the flour, breadcrumbs, and grated cheese.

Melt 1 tablespoon of the butter in a pan and add the minced greens. Sauté for 3 minutes. Stir the greens into the egg mixture. Stir to combine and season with salt, pepper, and nutmeg.

Melt the remaining 1 tablespoon butter in a skillet and add the egg mixture. Cook as you would a frittata: At first, every few seconds tilt the pan while pushing the more solid eggs from the edge into the center so that the still-uncooked egg mixture fills the space around the perimeter. When the bottom is firm but the top is soft, let cook undisturbed for 2 to 3 minutes until the bottom is browned. Flip the frittata, return to the pan, and cook until both sides are browned, an additional 2 to 3 minutes. Serve hot, room temperature, or cold.

Sformatino di porri con fonduta / LEEK FLAN WITH FONDUTA SAUCE

Enrica Berthod, Courmayeur, Valle d'Aosta

Fonduta is a cheese sauce most frequently made with fontina. To make fonduta, dice some fontina and place it in the top of a double boiler with milk to cover. Whisk over low heat until the cheese has melted and the sauce has thickened. You can also add an egg yolk or some flour to thicken the sauce. These flans can be made with cardoons in place of the leeks.

Preheat the oven to 325°F. Butter 4 ramekins and set aside. Melt the 2 tablespoons butter in a skillet over low heat, then add the leeks and onion and cook, stirring occasionally, until softened but not browned, about 7 minutes. Season with salt and pepper and set aside to cool. When the mixture has cooled, combine it with the basil, eggs, cream, and Parmigiano and puree in a blender or in a food processor fitted with the metal blade.

Fill the ramekins halfway with this mixture and cover tightly with aluminum foil. Set the ramekins in a baking dish and pour hot water into the dish to create a water bath. Bake in the pre-heated oven until the flans are set, 30 to 35 minutes. Unmold and serve each with some sauce.

Serves 4

2 TABLESPOONS UNSALTED BUTTER, PLUS MORE FOR BUTTERING RAMEKINS

1 POUND LEEKS, MINCED

½ YELLOW ONION, MINCED

SALT AND FRESHLY GROUND BLACK PEPPER TO TASTE

3 BASIL LEAVES

3 LARGE EGGS

1 CUP HEAVY CREAM OR WHIPPING CREAM

GRATED PARMIGIANO REGGIANO TO TASTE

FONDUTA FOR SERVING

Tartrà alle erbette con salsa al bleu d'Aosta /
INDIVIDUAL SAVORY HERB PUDDINGS WITH AOSTA BLUE CHEESE SAUCE

Ristorante La Clusaz, Gignod, Valle d'Aosta

Serves 4 to 6

1¼ CUPS WHOLE MILK

1¼ CUPS CREAM

FRESH HERBS TO TASTE, MINCED

11 OUNCES AOSTA BLUE CHEESE, CRUMBLED

6 LARGE EGGS

You can use any type of herbs you like to flavor these soft individual puddings. Be sure to reserve a few leaves and sprigs for garnish. Aosta blue cheese is a pale yellow cow's milk cheese with a smooth (not crumbly) texture. Like all blue cheeses, it has an assertive character.

Combine 1 cup milk and 1 cup cream and heat until it just starts to boil, then remove from the heat. When the mixture has cooled, place the herbs in the mixture and let them steep in the milk mixture in the refrigerator for 12 hours.

Preheat the oven to 175°F. Beat the eggs and combine them with the steeped milk mixture. Divide the mixture among individual ramekins. Set the ramekins in a baking pan. Pour hot water into the dish to create a water bath and cover with aluminum foil. Steam in the preheated oven until set, about 25 minutes.

While the puddings are baking, make the sauce. Dice the cheese and place it in the top of a double boiler with the remaining ¼ cup milk and the remaining ¼ cup cream. Cook, whisking constantly, until melted. Unmold the puddings and serve with the sauce.

Sformato di zucca e tartufo / SQUASH AND TRUFFLE FLAN

Osteria Ardenga, Diolo di Soragna (Parma), Emilia-Romagna

Serves 4

UNSALTED BUTTER FOR
BUTTERING PANS AND SAUTÉING

1 TABLESPOON BREADCRUMBS

4 CUPS (ABOUT 1 POUND)
DICED WINTER SQUASH

2 CLOVES GARLIC, MINCED

4 LARGE EGGS, LIGHTLY BEATEN

ABOUT ¼ CUP UNBLEACHED
ALL-PURPOSE FLOUR OR 00 FLOUR

¼ CUP GRATED
PARMIGIANO REGGIANO

1 BLACK TRUFFLE, SHAVED

SALT TO TASTE

FRESHLY GRATED NUTMEG
TO TASTE

Black truffle is less prized (and less expensive) than white truffle, but it has its charms. It is sometimes labeled Norcia truffle or Spoleto truffle.

Preheat the oven to 350°F. Butter 4 ramekins, coat with the breadcrumbs, and set aside. Steam the squash and with a food mill process into a puree. In a skillet, briefly sauté the garlic in butter over low heat until it begins to give off its aroma, then add the cooked squash puree and cook, stirring occasionally, until the squash begins to brown. Transfer the squash to a bowl and stir in the eggs and flour. (Add enough flour so that it is no longer runny, but not so much that it turns stiff. You may not need all of it.) Stir in the grated cheese, truffle shavings, salt, and a pinch of nutmeg. Transfer to the prepared pans and bake in the preheated oven until set, about 10 minutes.

Flan di topinambur / JERUSALEM ARTICHOKE FLANS

Osteria Boccondivino, Bra (Cuneo), Piemonte

Serves 4

UNSALTED BUTTER FOR
BUTTERING RAMEKINS

1 POUND JERUSALEM
ARTICHOKES

ABOUT 8 CUPS WHOLE MILK

3 LARGE EGGS

SALT AND FRESHLY GROUND
BLACK PEPPER TO TASTE

The milk should fully cover the Jerusalem artichokes when they are simmering—that will probably require no more than 8 cups, but you may be able to use a little less. A cheese sauce makes a nice accompaniment to these.

Preheat the oven to 325°F. Butter 4 ramekins and set aside. Thinly slice the Jerusalem artichokes and place in a pot. Add milk to cover by an inch or so and bring to a simmer. Simmer until tender, about 15 minutes. Drain the artichokes and set aside to cool.

In a bowl, beat the eggs with salt and pepper. Add the Jerusalem artichokes and stir to combine well. Divide the mixture evenly among the prepared ramekins. Set the ramekins in a baking dish. Pour hot water into the dish to create a water bath and cover with aluminum foil. Bake until set, about 30 minutes.

Flan di carciofi / INDIVIDUAL ARTICHOKE FLANS

Osteria I Santi, Mercogliano (Avellino), Campania

Romanesco artichokes are globe-shaped and have leaves streaked with purple. They tend to be extra meaty.

Prepare a bowl of cold water and add the lemon juice to it. Remove and discard the outer leaves and chokes of the artichokes, cut them into wedges, and soak the wedges in the lemon juice and water for 30 minutes.

Preheat the oven to 350°F. Butter 6 ramekins or 1 loaf pan and set aside. Sauté the garlic in olive oil. Drain the artichokes, pat them dry, and add them to the pan. Cook over low heat, stirring occasionally, until the artichoke stems are tender. Puree in a food processor fitted with the metal blade and allow to cool. Lightly beat the egg yolks. When the artichoke mixture is cool, combine it with the grated cheese, and 8 egg yolks. Season with salt and pepper. Beat the 8 egg whites to a stiff peak and fold them into the mixture. Divide the mixture among the prepared ramekins or transfer to the loaf pan and bake in the preheated oven until set, about 45 minutes.

Serves 6

JUICE OF 1 LEMON

5 ROMANESCO ARTICHOKES

BUTTER FOR BUTTERING PAN(S)

2 CLOVES GARLIC

EXTRA-VIRGIN OLIVE OIL FOR SAUTÉING

8 LARGE EGGS, SEPARATED

¼ CUP GRATED GRANA PADANO CHEESE

SALT AND FRESHLY GROUND BLACK PEPPER TO TASTE

Coste al brusch / CHARD WITH BEATEN EGGS

Rosina Idrame, San Damiano d'Asti (Asti), Piemonte

Many recipes call for stripping chard leaves of their white stems, but this one uses the stems. Reserve the greens for another use.

Tear the greens off the chard stems and reserve for another use. Wash and chop the stems and blanch them in lightly salted water until tender, about 4 minutes. While the chard stems are cooking, separate the eggs and beat the whites to stiff peaks. Beat the yolks separately and then beat them into the whites. Sift in the flour and beat again, then beat in the vinegar and ½ cup water. The egg whites will have deflated a great deal, leaving you with a batter.

Drain the cooked chard stems and place them in a pot with a small amount of oil. Cook, stirring frequently, over medium heat for 5 minutes. Turn the heat as low as it will go and pour in the egg mixture. Cook, stirring constantly, until the eggs solidify. Taste and adjust salt. Serve piping hot.

Serves 6

3½ POUNDS (4 TO 5 BUNCHES) CHARD

SALT TO TASTE

3 LARGE EGGS

2 TABLESPOONS UNBLEACHED ALL-PURPOSE FLOUR

½ CUP RED WINE VINEGAR

EXTRA-VIRGIN OLIVE OIL FOR SAUTÉING

Asparagi e uova / ASPARAGUS AND EGGS

Ristorante Leiter am Waal, Lagundo-Algund, Alto Adige

Serves 4 to 6

4½ POUNDS ASPARAGUS

SALT TO TASTE

1 TABLESPOON SUGAR

1 TABLESPOON
UNSALTED BUTTER

4 LARGE EGGS

1 TABLESPOON MUSTARD

JUICE OF 1 LEMON

EXTRA-VIRGIN OLIVE OIL
FOR DRESSING

WHITE WINE VINEGAR
FOR DRESSING

1 BUNCH CHIVES, SNIPPED

This is a useful technique for cooking asparagus, which can go from crisp to floppy very quickly. Simply cook them at a full boil for 2 minutes, then let them stand in the cooking water to finish cooking.

Peel the asparagus stalks. Place the asparagus in a pot with water to cover and add a pinch of salt, the sugar, and the butter. Bring to a boil and boil for 2 minutes, then remove the pot from the heat and let the asparagus cool in the cooking water for 30 minutes.

Meanwhile, place the eggs in a small pot, add water to cover, bring to a boil, and then simmer to the hard-boiled stage, 8 to 10 minutes. Peel the hard-boiled eggs and dice them. Remove the asparagus from the cooking water and place them on a platter. Sprinkle with the diced hard-boiled egg. Whisk the mustard and lemon juice with oil and vinegar to make a dressing and drizzle it over the asparagus and eggs. Scatter the chives over the asparagus and serve.

Asparagi e uova basocche / SOFT-BOILED EGGS OVER ASPARAGUS

Vecia Osteria del Moro, Pordenone, Friuli Venezia Giulia

Serves 4

8 LARGE EGGS

24 STALKS ASPARAGUS,
STALKS PEELED

SALT TO TASTE

JUICE OF ½ LEMON

1 TABLESPOON WHITE WINE
VINEGAR, PLUS MORE FOR
DRESSING ASPARAGUS

EXTRA-VIRGIN OLIVE OIL FOR
DRESSING ASPARAGUS

FRESHLY GROUND BLACK
PEPPER TO TASTE

Be sure to time the cooking correctly so that the asparagus are still warm when the eggs are cool enough to peel. The egg yolks should be creamy and liquid so that they spill out over the asparagus when cut with a fork.

Bring a pot of water to a boil and add the eggs. Boil for 4 minutes, then remove with a skimmer or slotted spoon and set aside to cool. Peel the asparagus stalks and cook the asparagus, standing vertically and tips upward, in a pot of boiling lightly salted water with the lemon juice and vinegar added to it for 10 minutes.

When the eggs have cooled, peel them, working carefully so as not to break them. Arrange the warm asparagus on a platter. Make a vinaigrette of oil and vinegar and drizzle it over the asparagus. Season the asparagus with salt and pepper and place the whole eggs on top. Serve immediately.

Asparagi con salsa Bolzanina /
ASPARAGUS WITH HARD-BOILED EGGS AND WATERCRESS
Ristorante Krone, Aldino-Aldein, Alto Adige

If you are fortunate enough to obtain fresh horseradish root, grate it yourself and toss it with a little vinegar to serve on the side. Just don't lean over the bowl while doing so—it will make your eyes water more than any onion ever has.

Peel the asparagus stalks from the top down and break off their woody ends. Tie them into 4 to 6 equal portions using kitchen twine. Bring a large pot of salted water to a boil, add 1 tablespoon butter, a pinch of sugar, and the white wine. Place the asparagus in the pot vertically, tips upward, and simmer gently, covered, until the asparagus is tender, 15 to 20 minutes.

Place the eggs in a small pot with water to cover and simmer for 7 minutes, then run under cold water. Peel them and divide the yolks from the whites. Mince both but keep separate. In a bowl combine the yolks with salt, pepper, the mustard, and the broth. Drizzle in the oil in a thin stream while whisking constantly. Whisk in the vinegar, the watercress, and lastly whisk in the egg whites.

Remove the kitchen twine from the asparagus and arrange the portions on serving plates. Melt the remaining 1 tablespoon butter and drizzle it on the asparagus. Sprinkle with minced chives and grated Parmigiano. Serve the egg mixture on the side and pass a small bowl of prepared horseradish, if using.

Serves 4 to 6

4½ POUNDS WHITE ASPARAGUS

SALT TO TASTE

2 TABLESPOONS UNSALTED BUTTER

1 PINCH SUGAR

2 TABLESPOONS DRY WHITE WINE

2 LARGE EGGS

FRESHLY GROUND WHITE PEPPER TO TASTE

1 TABLESPOON MUSTARD

2 TABLESPOONS VEGETABLE BROTH, WARM

¾ CUP VEGETABLE OIL

1 TABLESPOON WHITE WINE VINEGAR

1 TABLESPOON MINCED WATERCRESS, PLUS A FEW WHOLE LEAVES FOR GARNISH

1 TABLESPOON MINCED CHIVES

GRATED PARMIGIANO REGGIANO TO TASTE

PREPARED HORSERADISH (OPTIONAL)

Patate e uova in salsa verde / EGGS AND POTATOES IN GREEN SAUCE

Pier Antonio Cucchietti, Stroppo (Cuneo), Piemonte

Serves 4

8 SMALL POTATOES

4 LARGE EGGS

2 TABLESPOONS
EXTRA-VIRGIN OLIVE OIL

2 TABLESPOONS
UNSALTED BUTTER

1 MEDIUM YELLOW ONION,
THINLY SLICED

2 CUPS ROUGHLY CHOPPED
CHARD LEAVES

1 CLOVE GARLIC, MINCED

½ CUP PLUS 2 TABLESPOONS
VEGETABLE BROTH

SALT TO TASTE

¼ CUP CHOPPED
FLAT-LEAF PARSLEY

FRESHLY GROUND BLACK
PEPPER TO TASTE

Use a mezzaluna to chop the parsley—it helps preserve the flavor. If you can't find small potatoes (they should be about the size of eggs), you can use larger ones and cut them into quarters.

Bring a large pot of water to a boil and cook the potatoes until tender enough to be pierced with a fork. When they are cool enough to handle, peel them but leave them whole. Meanwhile, place the eggs in a small pot, add water to cover, bring to a boil, and simmer to the hard-boiled stage, about 10 minutes. Peel the eggs and cut them in half.

In a large skillet, combine the oil and butter and sauté the onion until golden. Add the chopped chard and the garlic and cook, stirring frequently, for 3 minutes. Add ½ cup broth, cover the pot, and cook over medium heat for 5 additional minutes. Add the potatoes and hard-boiled eggs to the skillet, season with salt, and cook, stirring frequently, for 5 additional minutes. Add the remaining 2 tablespoons broth to keep from sticking, if necessary.

Sprinkle in the parsley and stir gently so you don't break up the potatoes and eggs. Season with a generous amount of pepper and cook for a few additional minutes. Serve hot.

Uova in salsa / BAKED EGGS IN TOMATO SAUCE

Pino Osella, Carmagnola (Torino), Piemonte

Serves 4

4 CUPS TOMATO PUREE

8 LARGE EGGS

¼ CUP GRATED PARMIGIANO
REGGIANO TO TASTE

SALT AND FRESHLY GROUND
BLACK PEPPER TO TASTE

Use a high-quality Italian tomato puree for this recipes, as it's one of only five ingredients. You can also bake individual portions in small earthenware crocks. Be sure to serve some toasted bread with this dish.

Preheat the oven to 350°F. Heat the tomato puree and spread it in an even layer in a cast-iron baking pan or a skillet that can be used in the oven. Make 8 indentations evenly spaced in the tomato puree and gently place an egg in each indentation. Season with salt and pepper and sprinkle on the grated cheese.

Bake in the preheated oven until the whites are firm but the yolks are still soft, about 10 minutes. Serve hot.

Carciofi e uova in salsa ravigotta /
EGGS AND ARTICHOKES IN CAPER AND HERB SAUCE

Osteria Burligo, Palazzago (Bergamo), Lombardia

Ravigotta is a bright herb and caper sauce that elevates almost anything—try it on all kind of vegetables.

Mince the onion and process in a blender with the capers, a generous amount of herbs and salt and pepper. Continue to process while adding the vinegar and the oil in a thin stream. The result should be a thick sauce.

Trim the hard outer leaves and the chokes from the artichokes, but leave the artichokes whole. Bring a pot of salted water to a boil and add the wine, the lemon juice, and the bay leaves. Cook the artichokes until tender, then drain and set aside to cool. Place the eggs in a small pot with water to cover and cook to the hard-boiled stage, about 10 minutes.

Gently pry the artichokes open. Peel the hard-boiled eggs and cut into wedges. Arrange the artichokes in the center of a serving platter with the eggs around them in a ring. Pour the prepared sauce over the eggs and artichokes, garnish with minced parsley, and serve.

Serves 4

1 MEDIUM YELLOW ONION

¼ CUP SALTED CAPERS, SOAKED AND DRAINED

LEAVES OF AROMATIC HERBS SUCH AS PARSLEY, CHERVIL, CHIVES, AND TARRAGON, CHOPPED, TO TASTE

SALT AND FRESHLY GROUND BLACK PEPPER TO TASTE

2 TO 3 TABLESPOONS WHITE WINE VINEGAR

½ CUP EXTRA-VIRGIN OLIVE OIL

4 TO 5 ARTICHOKES

½ CUP DRY WHITE WINE

JUICE OF 1 LEMON

2 BAY LEAVES

4 LARGE EGGS

1 TABLESPOON MINCED FLAT-LEAF PARSLEY FOR GARNISH

Uova alla provatura / EGGS WITH PROVATURA CHEESE

Carla Magliozzi, Gaeta (Latina), Lazio

Serves 4

EXTRA-VIRGIN OLIVE OIL
FOR SAUTÉING

1 CUP DICED
PROVATURA CHEESE

4 LARGE EGGS

SALT AND FRESHLY GROUND
BLACK PEPPER TO TASTE

GRATED PARMIGIANO
REGGIANO TO TASTE

Provatura is a mild buffalo milk cheese from the southern part of the Lazio region. It is something like a cross between mozzarella and provolone. It originally evolved as a byproduct of checking the consistency of cheese during the cheese-making process and is sold in small balls, much like mozzarella. If you cannot find provatura in your area, mozzarella is an able substitute.

Film a skillet with a small amount of oil and place over low heat. Add the cheese and cook, stirring constantly to keep from sticking, until melted. Add the eggs on top of the cheese and continue cooking over low heat until egg whites are firm and egg yolks are creamy. Season with salt and pepper and sprinkle with grated cheese. Serve hot.

Cotolette di uova / EGG "CUTLETS" WITH TAPENADE

Marcella Cigognetti, Mantova, Lombardia

These vegetarian Milanese-style "cutlets" are crisp on the outside and creamy on the inside. Take care not to break the yolks of the poached eggs. Tapenade is a zingy sauce made with olives and capers. Marjoram is a must, but you can include any other herbs you like in it as well—parsley is always a good addition.

For the tapenade, chop together the olives, capers, garlic, and marjoram and other herbs. Drizzle in a thin stream of olive oil, stirring, until the mixture reaches the desired consistency. Set aside.

Poach 4 of the eggs. Drain and place on a wooding cutting board and carefully cut away any excess white to make them uniform.

Make a béchamel: melt the butter in a small pot. Add the flour and whisk constantly over low heat until it begins to turn golden, without letting any lumps form. Add the milk and nutmeg, whisking constantly. When you have a smooth mixture, whisk in the grated cheese. Continue cooking until cheese is melted and sauce is perfectly smooth and rather thick, about 5 additional minutes.

Gently spread a spoonful of béchamel (about ⅛ of the total) on top of each of the poached eggs and sprinkle each with 1 tablespoon of the breadcrumbs. Gently turn over the poached eggs and spread béchamel on the other sides and sprinkle each with 1 tablespoon breadcrumbs.

In a soup plate, beat the remaining egg. Place the remaining breadcrumbs in a second soup plate. Place the oil for frying in a pot with high sides and bring to temperature for frying. Dredge one of the eggs in the beaten egg, then in the breadcrumbs and fry until golden. Repeat with remaining eggs. Serve eggs hot, each accompanied by a spoonful or two of tapenade.

Serves 4

⅓ CUP PITTED BLACK OLIVES

2 TABLESPOONS SALTED CAPERS, RINSED AND DRAINED

1 CLOVE GARLIC

MARJORAM AND OTHER HERBS TO TASTE

EXTRA-VIRGIN OLIVE OIL FOR TAPENADE

5 LARGE EGGS

1 TABLESPOON UNSALTED BUTTER

2 TABLESPOONS PASTRY FLOUR

1 CUP WHOLE MILK, WARM

FRESHLY GRATED NUTMEG TO TASTE

⅓ CUP GRATED Parmigiano Reggiano

1 CUP BREADCRUMBS

OIL FOR FRYING

PANCAKES, FRITTERS, AND CROQUETTES

Fanzelti / BUCKWHEAT PANCAKES

Locanda delle Tre Chiavi, Isera, Trentino

Serves 4 to 6

3 CUPS BUCKWHEAT FLOUR

1½ TEASPOONS SALT

EXTRA-VIRGIN OLIVE OIL
FOR COOKING PANCAKES

These delicate buckwheat pancakes are served at home in place of bread in the Terragnolo Valley and are little–known outside the area.

In a bowl combine the buckwheat flour and salt. Add water in a thin stream while whisking constantly until you have a loose batter with no lumps. You will need about 2 cups of water.

Heat a skillet and brush it lightly with oil. When the pan is very hot, use a ladle to pour in enough batter to cover the bottom of the skillet in a thin layer. Cook, turning once, until mottled with brown spots on both sides. Set aside the pancakes in a warm place as they are finished and repeat with remaining batter, adding a little more oil to the pan when needed. Serve hot.

Subrich di patate / POTATO PANCAKES

Livia Borgata, Montegrosso d'Asti (Asti), Piemonte

Serves 6

6 MEDIUM YELLOW
POTATOES

SALT TO TASTE

3 LARGE EGGS,
LIGHTLY BEATEN

FRESHLY GROUND
BLACK PEPPER TO TASTE

½ CUP EXTRA-VIRGIN
OLIVE OIL

Subrich can also be made with cauliflower or other vegetables. Feel free to vary the recipe by adding a little minced parsley or any other item you like.

Boil the potatoes in lightly salted water for 30 minutes. They should be tender but not falling apart. Peel the potatoes and pass them through a potato ricer, letting them fall into a bowl. To the potatoes add the eggs, salt, and pepper and mix until well-combined.

Heat the olive oil in a pan with high sides and drop a few table-spoons of the potato mixture into the oil. (Do not crowd the pan.) Cook until golden, gently turning once, about 5 minutes per side. Repeat with remaining potato mixture. Serve hot.

Frittatine di spinaci / SPINACH PANCAKES

Palmira Giovannini, Bologna, Emilia-Romagna

These tasty little pancakes make a nice light main course, particularly when served with some good cheese and a salad. You can use chard in place of the spinach, or even carrots or onions.

Clean the spinach, then place in a pot with the water clinging to the leaves and cook, stirring, over medium heat until wilted, about 4 minutes. Drain, squeeze dry, and mince.

In a large bowl beat the eggs. Whisk in the flour and grated cheese, then the minced spinach. Season with salt and pepper and stir in 1 tablespoon olive oil.

Line a baking sheet with paper towels and set aside. Place an inch or two of oil in a large skillet and place over medium heat. When the olive oil is hot, drop in a few spoonfuls of the spinach batter. Do not crowd the pan. Cook, turning once, until browned on both sides, then remove with a slotted spatula to the prepared paper towel-lined pan to drain. Repeat with remaining batter.

Serves 4 to 6

1 POUND SPINACH

4 LARGE EGGS

¾ CUP UNBLEACHED ALL-PURPOSE FLOUR

2 CUPS GRATED PARMIGIANO REGGIANO

SALT AND FRESHLY GROUND BLACK PEPPER TO TASTE

1 TABLESPOON EXTRA-VIRGIN OLIVE OIL, PLUS MORE FOR PAN-FRYING

Cecina / CHICKPEA FLOUR PANCAKE

Antica Fattoria del Grottaione, Castel del Piano (Grosseto), Toscana

V

Serves 6

4 CUPS CHICKPEA FLOUR

SALT TO TASTE

EXTRA-VIRGIN OLIVE OIL
FOR PAN

FRESHLY GROUND BLACK
PEPPER TO TASTE

Cecina is highly adaptable and can be used to finish up leftovers. It makes even a simple meal special. A few rosemary leaves scattered on top add depth of flavor.

Preheat the oven to 350°F.

Place the chickpea flour in a bowl and whisk in 6 cups of water. Season with salt.

Pour a generous amount of olive oil in a baking pan large enough that the mixture will be less than ½ inch deep when added. Pour the batter into the pan and stir to combine well. Bake in the preheated oven until browned on top. Sprinkle with a generous amount of black pepper and serve hot.

Farinata / THIN CHICKPEA FLOUR PANCAKE WITH ROSEMARY

Osteria Puppo, Albenga (Savona), Liguria

V

Serves 6

2 TABLESPOONS SALT

6 CUPS CHICKPEA FLOUR

4 CUPS EXTRA-VIRGIN
OLIVE OIL

LEAVES OF 1 SPRIG ROSEMARY,
MINCED, OR 1 TABLESPOON
MINCED FRESH CHIVES

This thin flatbread is meant to be eaten hot. If you prefer an even crispier version, use about ¾ of the ingredients provided below. Be sure to check that a pan this large will fit in your oven—if not, make the farinata in two smaller pans and time accordingly.

In a large bowl combine 12 cups water and the salt. Sift in the chickpea flour. Whisk until well-combined, then set aside to rest for 5 minutes. Skim any foam off the top and discard, and then set aside to rest for about 5 hours. The warmer the weather, the less resting time required—in summer you can let it rest for 2 to 3 hours, but in the dead of winter it should rest for 6 hours.

Preheat the oven to 475°F. If your oven has the option of a top and bottom heat source, use both. Pour the oil into a copper pan 30 inches in diameter and swirl it to cover the surface. Whisk the batter briefly, pour it into the pan, and scatter on the minced rosemary. Mix again, then bake in the preheated oven until the bottom is browned (use a spatula to lift it carefully to check) and a brown crust has formed on top, about 25 minutes. Serve hot.

Testaroli pontremolesi / PANCAKE PASTA

Trattoria da Bussè, Pontremoli (Massa-Carrara), Toscana

Serves 2 to 3

2 CUPS UNBLEACHED
ALL-PURPOSE FLOUR

SALT TO TASTE

¼ CUP TORN BASIL LEAVES

1 CLOVE GARLIC

GRATED PARMIGIANO
REGGIANO TO TASTE

EXTRA-VIRGIN OLIVE OIL
FOR LOOSENING SAUCE

This is a specialty of Lunigiana, an area located in both Liguria and Toscana. Testaroli are thin crepes made on a griddle with a domed lid (always made out of a material that can withstand high temperatures) and cooked over an open flame. Testaroli have their own Slow Food Presidium. If you like a slightly spicier sauce, add a little grated aged sheep's cheese along with the Parmigiano Reggiano.

In a bowl combine the flour with a pinch of salt, then whisk in enough water to make a batter that is pourable but not overly liquid (like a crepe batter). Heat a griddle with a cover (see note) over an open fire. Pour a little of the batter on the bottom of the griddle and tilt to distribute evenly. Cover with the lid and place on the fire. After 5 minutes, lift the lid and see how it is doing—the surface should be dry and dotted with small holes. Remove and wrap in a cotton dishtowel. Repeat with remaining batter.

If the garlic has a green shoot in the center, remove it. Make a paste by processing the garlic and the basil in a mortar and pestle, then gradually adding the grated cheese. When the mixture has formed a paste, transfer it to a small bowl and whisk in enough olive oil to loosen the paste to the consistency of a sauce.

Bring a large pot of salted water to a boil for cooking the pasta. While the water is coming to a boil, cut the pancakes into diamonds with 2¾-inch sides. When the water is just about to boil, add the pancake pasta, remove the pot from the heat, and leave the pasta in the hot water until tender, about 2 minutes, but sometimes after just 1 minute if the pasta is extremely fresh. Drain in a colander, then divide among individual serving plates, alternating layers of pasta and the prepared sauce and sprinkling on a little more grated cheese as you go. Serve hot.

Kiffel / POTATO CROQUETTES

Antica Trattoria Valeria, Trieste, Friuli Venezia Giulia

Kiffel make an excellent antipasto. For a sweet version, see page 416.

Bring a large pot of salted water to a boil and cook the potatoes. When they are soft, drain them, peel them, and while still warm mash them with a potato ricer. Let the potatoes cool on a work surface until you can handle them, then mix them with the flour, butter, eggs, a pinch of salt, and the grated cheese, if using. Knead to form a soft dough with the ingredients evenly distributed. Form the dough into cylinders and cut the cylinders into 4-inch pieces. Curve each piece into a horseshoe shape.

Line a baking sheet with paper towels and set aside. In a pot with high sides, bring a generous amount of oil for frying to 275°F. Add the fritters, working in batches if necessary to keep from crowding the pot, and fry until puffed and golden, about 5 minutes. Remove with a skimmer or slotted spoon and drain briefly on the prepared pan. Serve very hot.

Serves 6 to 8

SALT TO TASTE

2 POUNDS POTATOES

2 CUPS UNBLEACHED ALL-PURPOSE FLOUR

5 TABLESPOONS UNSALTED BUTTER, SOFTENED

2 LARGE EGGS, LIGHTLY BEATEN

¼ CUP GRATED GRANA PADANO CHEESE (OPTIONAL)

EXTRA-VIRGIN OLIVE OIL FOR FRYING

Cuculli / POTATO CROQUETTES WITH MARJORAM AND PINE NUTS

Rosanna Orlandini, Genova, Liguria

Serves 4 to 6

2 POUNDS POTATOES

7 TABLESPOONS UNSALTED
BUTTER, CUT INTO PIECES

LEAVES OF 1 SPRIG
MARJORAM, MINCED

¼ CUP GRATED
PARMIGIANO REGGIANO

⅓ CUP PINE NUTS, CRUSHED

SALT TO TASTE

3 LARGE EGGS, SEPARATED

BREADCRUMBS FOR
DREDGING

EXTRA-VIRGIN OLIVE OIL
FOR FRYING

The name for these is a Genova dialect term for lively and funny children, who were often the biggest fans of these bite-sized fritters. There's even a nursery rhyme in the area that mothers used to recite while cooking these.

Bring a large pot of water to a boil. Boil the potatoes until soft and then peel them while they are still warm. Place them in a bowl and crush them with a fork or use a potato ricer, then add the butter and crush to combine. Add the marjoram, Parmigiano Reggiano, pine nuts, and a pinch of salt. Add the 3 egg yolks one at a time, stirring with a wooden spoon until soft and creamy between additions. Beat the egg whites to stiff peaks. Place the breadcrumbs in a soup bowl.

In a pot with high sides, bring a generous amount of oil for frying to the correct temperature. Use a spoon to create small balls of the dough—each about the size of a large walnut. Dredge the balls of dough first in the beaten egg whites, then in the breadcrumbs. Working in batches if necessary to keep from crowding the pot, fry them until puffed, soft, and golden on all sides. Sprinkle with salt and serve very hot.

Crocchè di patate / POTATO AND CHEESE FRITTERS ▷

Ristorante Costantinopoli, Pollica (Salerno), Campania

Serves 4 to 6

2 POUNDS POTATOES

3 LARGE EGGS,
LIGHTLY BEATEN

2 OUNCES CILENTO
GOAT CHEESE,
CUT INTO SMALL DICE

2 OUNCES PROVOLONE
CHEESE, CUT INTO
SMALL DICE

SALT AND FRESHLY GROUND
BLACK PEPPER TO TASTE

¼ CUP BREADCRUMBS

EXTRA-VIRGIN OLIVE OIL
FOR FRYING

Potato fritters are a classic street food snack in Campania, but they are also made at home. Cilento goat cheese is made from the milk of goats that graze in Cilento National Park and is unusually complex for a goat cheese. The cheesemaking process combines the use of both rennet and heat. The cheese has its own Slow Food Presidium.

Boil the potatoes and peel and mash them while they are still warm. In a bowl combine them with the eggs. Stir in both cheeses. Season the mixture with salt and pepper. Knead until well combined and form the mixture into oval croquettes. Line a baking sheet with paper towels. Place the breadcrumbs in a soup bowl. Place olive oil for frying in a pot with high sides and bring to high temperature. Dredge the prepared croquettes in the breadcrumbs and fry until browned on the surface but still soft in the center. Transfer to the prepared paper towels briefly to drain, then serve.

Pallotte cac' e ove / PAN-FRIED CHEESE CROQUETTES

Hostaria del Pavone, Vasto (Chieti), Abruzzo

Serves 6

ABOUT ½ CUP WHOLE MILK

14 OUNCES STALE BREAD

2 CUPS GRATED
PARMIGIANO REGGIANO

2 CUPS GRATED AGED
SHEEP'S CHEESE

2 CLOVES GARLIC, MINCED

LEAVES OF 1 SPRIG PARSLEY,
MINCED

FRESHLY GROUND BLACK
PEPPER TO TASTE (OPTIONAL)

4 TO 6 LARGE EGGS

EXTRA-VIRGIN OLIVE OIL
FOR FRYING

Abruzzo is home to numerous inventive dishes that combine eggs and cheese. These croquettes can be served as they are, or they can be simmered in tomato sauce.

Place the milk in a bowl. Soak the bread in the milk (you may need to add a little more to cover), then squeeze dry and crumble it into a clean bowl. Stir in both types of cheese, the garlic, and the parsley and season with black pepper if using (no need for salt). Lightly beat 4 eggs, add, and combine with the bread mixture. The mixture should clump together when you squeeze a bit in your hand. If it is too dry, add another egg, and then another, if necessary. Let the mixture rest for at least 3 hours and as long as 8 hours. Bring a large pot of several inches of oil to high heat for frying. Form the mixture into small ovals about the size of an egg. Flatten them slightly, then fry in olive oil until golden, working in batches to avoid crowding the pot if necessary and turning them to cook on all sides, about 10 minutes. Serve warm.

Frico con patate / CHEESE CRISP WITH POTATOES   ▷

Osteria dal Cjco, Castelnovo del Friuli (Pordenone), Friuli Venezia Giulia

Serves 4

1 MEDIUM YELLOW ONION,
THINLY SLICED

EXTRA-VIRGIN OLIVE OIL
FOR SAUTÉING

4 LARGE POTATOES,
PEELED AND DICED

SALT AND FRESHLY GROUND
BLACK PEPPER TO TASTE

11 OUNCES 3-MONTH
AGED MONTASIO CHEESE,
THINLY SLICED

Frico is the pride of Friuli Venezia Giulia, and for good reason—there are few foods more satisfying as this crisp and cheesy pancake. The versions of frico are endless and they may be more or less crisp, thicker or thinner, but all use local Montasio cheese, a pale yellow cow's milk cheese made in the mountains in the Carnia area that is included in the Slow Food Ark of Taste.

Thinly slice the onion. In a pot, sauté the onion in oil until it turns golden. Add the potatoes, season with salt and pepper, and add about ½ cup water. Cover and cook over low heat for 30 minutes.

Gradually stir in the cheese slices, allowing them to melt between additions. Skim off any fat and transfer the mixture to an 8-inch diameter nonstick skillet. Cook the frico until golden on both sides, flipping it once. Cut into 4 wedges and serve.

Frittelle di spinaci / SPINACH FRITTERS

Edda Servi, Venezia, Veneto

Serves 6

2 POUNDS BABY SPINACH

SALT TO TASTE

1 SMALL CLOVE GARLIC

2 TABLESPOONS
EXTRA-VIRGIN OLIVE OIL,
PLUS MORE FOR FRYING

FRESHLY GROUND
BLACK PEPPER TO TASTE

8 LARGE EGGS

¼ CUP RAISINS

¼ CUP PINE NUTS

Spinach fritters are a traditional Italian Jewish dish. For Passover, a sweet version is made using matzo meal and sugar.

Rinse the spinach, then place it in a pot with the water still clinging to the leaves. Add a pinch of salt and steam until wilted, 5 to 10 minutes. Drain, squeeze dry, and mince. Mince the garlic and sauté in 2 tablespoons olive oil in a skillet for 2 minutes. Add the spinach, season with salt and pepper, and sauté for 1 to 2 additional minutes to combine the flavors. Let the spinach mixture cool. In a medium bowl, beat the eggs. Beat in the raisins, pine nuts, and spinach mixture.

In a pot with high sides, heat a generous amount of olive oil for frying. Drop the mixture by spoonfuls into the oil, working in batches if necessary to keep from crowding the pot, and cook, turning gently, until both sides are browned.

Crema fritta / MILK FRITTERS

Trattoria Il Tubino, San Pietro in Casale (Bologna), Emilia-Romagna

Serves 6

4 CUPS WHOLE MILK

5 LARGE EGGS

½ CUP SUGAR

1 CUP PLUS 2 TABLESPOONS UNBLEACHED ALL-PURPOSE FLOUR

2 TABLESPOONS BUTTER

¼ CUP BREADCRUMBS

EXTRA-VIRGIN OLIVE OIL FOR FRYING

These fritters are often included in a mixed fry that may also incorporate fried artichokes, fried zucchini and zucchini blossoms, and fried stuffed olives. They make a unique snack at cocktail hour as well.

Scald the milk and set aside to cool slightly—it should be warm but not piping hot. In a small pot, beat 4 eggs with the sugar. Whisk in ¼ cup plus 2 tablespoons flour a tablespoon or so at a time, whisking to combine between additions. Add the scalded milk in a thin stream, whisking constantly. Bring to a boil while whisking constantly and whisk for 2 minutes, then remove from the heat and whisk in the butter.

Spread this mixture about ¾ inch thick on a clean, flat plate or platter and set aside to cool. Once it has cooled, cut it into cubes. Place the remaining ¾ cup flour in a soup bowl. Beat the remaining egg in a second bowl. Place the breadcrumbs in a third bowl. Bring a large pot of several inches of oil to high heat for frying. Line a baking sheet with paper towels. Pat the cubes dry and dredge them first in the flour, then in the beaten egg, and lastly in the breadcrumbs. Fry until golden and transfer to the prepared pan to drain briefly before serving.

Frisceu di erbe / BORAGE FRITTERS

Trattoria Chiapparino, Uscio (Genova), Liguria

Serves 4

4 LARGE EGGS

2 CUPS UNBLEACHED ALL-PURPOSE FLOUR

1 PINCH CREAM OF TARTAR

1 BUNCH BORAGE

OIL FOR FRYING

SALT TO TASTE

If you cannot locate the sweet herb borage to make these fritters, you can substitute a bunch of fresh chives or even other greens, such as raw lettuce or radicchio or cooked chard or nettles.

In a bowl, beat the eggs, then whisk in the flour and cream of tartar to make a batter. Set aside to rest for 30 minutes. Mince the borage and stir into the batter.

Line a baking sheet with paper towels. Place olive oil for frying in a pot with high sides and bring to high temperature. Drop the batter in by the spoonful. Fry fritters, in batches if necessary, until puffed and golden, about 5 minutes. Remove with a skimmer and transfer to the prepared pan to drain briefly, then salt and serve hot.

Sciatt / BUCKWHEAT AND CHEESE FRITTERS

Mariateresa Bettini, Teglio (Sondrio), Lombardia

Traditionally, *sciatt* (dialect for "frog," as these have a bumpy and irregular surface) are served on a bed of thin ribbons of raw chicory that has been dressed with oil and vinegar. Scimud goat's milk cheese hails from the Valtellina area near the Swiss border and is white and soft. Traditionally it was made with left-over milk for cheesemakers' families.

In a bowl, combine both flours with a pinch of salt and the grappa. Add sparkling mineral water in a thin stream, adding as much as you need to make a batter with a consistency a little thinner than sour cream. Cover and refrigerate for 3 hours. Cut the cheese into cubes, toss with the prepared batter, and set aside to rest for 1 hour.

Line a baking sheet with paper towels. Fill a pot with high sides with a generous amount of oil and bring to high temperature. Remove the cubes of cheese from the batter, letting any excess drip back into the bowl, and fry the cubes of cheese, working in batches if necessary. As the cubes brown, use a slotted spoon or skimmer to transfer them to the prepared pan and allow them to drain briefly. Serve hot.

Serves 4 to 6

1½ CUPS BUCKWHEAT FLOUR

⅔ CUP RICE FLOUR

SALT TO TASTE

2 TO 3 TABLESPOONS GRAPPA

ABOUT ¾ CUP SPARKLING MINERAL WATER

4 OUNCES YOUNG SCIMUD CHEESE

EXTRA-VIRGIN OLIVE OIL FOR FRYING

Polpette di zucchine / PAN-FRIED ZUCCHINI CROQUETTES

La Tradizione Cucina Casalinga, Minervino Murge (Barletta-Andria-Trani), Puglia

These can be made with winter squash when that is in season. You may want steam the squash briefly to soften it.

Grate the zucchini on the largest holes of a four-sided grater. Beat the eggs in a bowl, then stir in the grated zucchini, the flour, the breadcrumbs, and a pinch of salt. Stir to combine thoroughly. The mixture should be moist but not runny. Set aside to rest for 1 hour.

Line a baking sheet with paper towels and set aside. Form the mixture into small balls. Heat the olive oil in a skillet and cook the zucchini balls, working in batches if necessary to keep from crowding the pan, until browned. Drain briefly on the prepared baking sheet before serving.

Serves 4 to 6

1 POUND (ABOUT 3 MEDIUM) ZUCCHINI

2 LARGE EGGS

¼ CUP UNBLEACHED ALL-PURPOSE FLOUR

¼ CUP BREADCRUMBS

SALT TO TASTE

½ CUP EXTRA-VIRGIN OLIVE OIL

Cicoria impazzita / FRIED CHICORY

Osteria delle Spezie, San Salvo (Chieti), Abruzzo

Serves 4

SALT TO TASTE

1¾ POUNDS CHICORY GREENS

1⅔ CUPS UNBLEACHED
ALL-PURPOSE FLOUR

EXTRA-VIRGIN OLIVE OIL
FOR FRYING

Chicory is frequently paired with fava beans and it's nice to serve these crisp fried leaves alongside a creamy fava bean puree like the one on page 232 for variety of texture. Blanching chicory removes some of its natural bitterness.

Bring a pot of lightly salted water to a boil and blanch the chicory. Place the flour in a bowl with a pinch of salt and add about ½ cup water to make a batter the consistency of sour cream. Don't worry about making the batter perfectly smooth—any lumps will result in a crunchier texture when fried.

Chop the chicory. Place olive oil for frying in a pot with high sides and bring to high temperature. One by one, dredge the pieces of chicory in the batter so they are coated and add them to the hot oil. Use a slotted spoon or other utensil to spread them out so the pieces are open. Fry until golden and crisp, working in batches if necessary to keep from crowding the pot. Season with salt and serve hot.

Polpette di cicoria / PAN-FRIED CHICORY CROQUETTES

Ristorante La Piazza, Poggiardo (Lecce), Puglia

Serves 4 to 6

SALT TO TASTE

1 POUND WILD CHICORY

1 LARGE EGG, LIGHTLY BEATEN

1 TABLESPOON PLUS
1½ TEASPOONS GRATED AGED
SHEEP'S CHEESE

2 TABLESPOONS BREADCRUMBS,
PLUS MORE IF NECESSARY

FRESHLY GROUND
BLACK PEPPER TO TASTE

HEAVY CREAM OR WHIPPING
CREAM, IF NECESSARY

EXTRA-VIRGIN OLIVE OIL
FOR FRYING

Wild chicory has a sharper taste than its cultivated cousins, which include escarole, endive, and radicchio.

Bring a large pot of salted water to a boil and blanch the chicory leaves for 5 minutes. Drain and squeeze dry, then tear into small piece by hand and transfer to a bowl. Add the egg, cheese, and breadcrumbs and season with salt and pepper. If the mixture is too stiff to form a ball when you pinch off a piece, add about 1 tablespoon of cream at a time to make it more moist. If it is too loose, add some extra breadcrumbs.

In a skillet with high sides, bring a generous amount of olive oil to medium-high temperature. Form the chicory mixture into small balls, then flatten them slightly. Place olive oil for frying in a pot with high sides and bring to high temperature. Fry the croquettes in the olive oil until browned on all sides, working in batches if necessary to keep from crowding the pot.

Barbagiuai alle erbe /
FRIED DUMPLINGS STUFFED WITH GREENS, SQUASH, AND RICE

Ristorante Terme, Pigna (Imperia), Liguria

Look for a squash that weighs about 3 pounds in order to obtain the 4 cups of diced squash you will need once it is peeled and seeded. Any squash variety will work in these dumplings.

For the dough, place the flour with a pinch of salt in a medium bowl and add the 3 tablespoons olive oil. Stir in enough warm (not hot) water to create a soft, malleable dough. Cover and refrigerate. While the dough is chilling, prepare the filling. Blanch the chard in lightly salted water. Drain, squeeze dry, and mince. In a separate pot, boil the squash until soft, then drain and force through a sieve. Place the rice in a small pot with the milk and ½ cup water. Simmer until rice is cooked through and drain off any excess liquid. When the rice is cool, in a large bowl combine the rice, cooked greens, cooked squash, marjoram, eggs, and a generous amount of Parmigiano Reggiano. Season with salt, pepper, and nutmeg. Knead until thoroughly combined.

Remove the dough from the refrigerator. Cut off half of the dough, leaving the other half covered, and roll it out into a circle about 4 inches in diameter. Set aside and roll out the second half of the dough to the same size. As if making ravioli, arrange bits of the filling at regular intervals along one sheet of dough. Place the other sheet of dough on top of it and press between the portions of filling with your fingertips to make the two sheets of dough adhere. Using a pastry cutter, cut the dumplings between the portions of filling. Place olive oil for frying in a pot with high sides and bring to high temperature. Fry the dumplings in the olive oil until browned on all sides, working in batches if necessary to keep from crowding the pot. Serve hot.

Serves 4 to 6

4 CUPS UNBLEACHED ALL-PURPOSE FLOUR

SALT TO TASTE

3 TABLESPOONS EXTRA-VIRGIN OLIVE OIL, PLUS MORE FOR FRYING

1¼ POUNDS CHARD

4 CUPS DICED BUTTERNUT SQUASH OR OTHER WINTER SQUASH

1 CUP SHORT-GRAIN RICE

½ CUP WHOLE MILK

LEAVES OF 1 SPRIG MARJORAM, MINCED

2 LARGE EGGS, LIGHTLY BEATEN

GRATED PARMIGIANO REGGIANO TO TASTE

FRESHLY GROUND BLACK PEPPER TO TASTE

FRESHLY GRATED NUTMEG TO TASTE

Polpette di melanzane / PAN-FRIED EGGPLANT CROQUETTES ▷

Rosa Lazzaro, Sant'Andrea Apostolo dello Ionio (Catanzaro), Calabria

Serves 4

2 MEDIUM LONG EGGPLANT

SALT TO TASTE

LEAVES OF 1 SPRIG BASIL

1 CLOVE GARLIC

GRATED AGED SHEEP'S
CHEESE OR PARMIGIANO
REGGIANO TO TASTE

1 TO 2 EGG YOLKS

FRESHLY GROUND BLACK
PEPPER TO TASTE

BREADCRUMBS FOR
STIFFENING MIXTURE, IF
NEEDED, AND FOR DREDGING

EXTRA-VIRGIN OLIVE OIL
FOR FRYING

If you are confident that your eggplant is not bitter, you can skip the salting step.

Peel and dice the eggplant, salt it, and set it in a sieve to drain for 30 minutes. Squeeze the eggplant to remove any remaining liquid, then bring a pot of water to a boil and cook the eggplant until just soft, about 3 minutes. Drain and cool, then squeeze dry again and mince the eggplant with the basil leaves and the garlic. Combine that mixture with grated cheese and egg yolks. Season with salt and pepper and knead to combine. Form the mixture into balls, adding breadcrumbs if the mixture is too loose. Flatten the balls slightly.

Line a baking sheet with paper towels. Place the breadcrumbs in a soup bowl. Place olive oil for frying in a pot with high sides and bring to high temperature. Dredge the balls in the breadcrumbs and fry in the oil until browned. Remove with a skimmer to the prepared baking sheet to drain, then serve hot.

Medaglioni di melanzana / EGGPLANT MEDALLIONS

Maila Carpentieri, Udine, Friuli Venezia Giulia

Serves 4 to 6

2 LARGE EGGS

BREADCRUMBS FOR
DREDGING

EXTRA-VIRGIN OLIVE OIL
FOR FRYING

3 MEDIUM EGGPLANT

SALT TO TASTE

Eggplant can be cut in numerous ways for frying. In addition to these medallions, they can be cut into long strips, cubes with ¾-inch sides, or matchsticks. You can also cut them in half the long way or "butterfly" them by cutting them in half but leaving the two halves attached at the base.

Place the eggs in a soup bowl and beat. Place the breadcrumbs in another soup bowl. Line a baking sheet with paper towels. Place olive oil for frying in a pot with high sides and bring to high temperature. Slice the eggplant into rounds about ½ inch thick. Dredge the eggplant slices first in beaten egg and then in breadcrumbs and fry in the oil until browned. Remove with a skimmer to the prepared baking sheet to drain. Salt and serve hot.

Gnocco fritto di melanzane e taleggio con crema di topinambur /
TALEGGIO AND EGGPLANT FRITTERS WITH JERUSALEM ARTICHOKE PUREE

Trattoria Maria, Mondavio (Pesaro e Urbino), Marche

Serves 4 to 6

1 SMALL YELLOW ONION

EXTRA-VIRGIN OLIVE OIL
FOR SAUTÉING, FRYING,
AND DRIZZLING

14 OUNCES JERUSALEM
ARTICHOKES, PEELED AND
SLICED INTO ROUNDS

4 CUPS VEGETABLE BROTH

2 SPRIGS THYME

1 SPRIG MARJORAM

1 MEDIUM EGGPLANT

1 CLOVE GARLIC

4 OUNCES TALEGGIO

RICE FLOUR FOR DREDGING

2 LARGE EGGS

BREADCRUMBS FOR
DREDGING

Reserve a few thyme and marjoram leaves to scatter on the finished dish as a garnish, if desired.

For the puree, mince the onion and sauté in oil in a pot until golden. Add the Jerusalem artichokes. Add the broth, 1 sprig thyme, and 1 sprig marjoram. Simmer over low heat until soft, about 30 minutes, then remove and discard herb sprigs and puree Jerusalem artichokes and cooking liquid until smooth. Keep warm.

For the fritters, cut the eggplant into small cubes. Mince the garlic and the leaves of the remaining sprig thyme. In a skillet, sauté the eggplant, garlic, and minced thyme in olive oil for 10 minutes. Cut the taleggio into small pieces and sprinkle them in. Continue to cook, stirring frequently, until the cheese has melted completely. The mixture should hold together. Allow the mixture to cool, then shape into thick pieces about 1 ¼ inches long. Place the flour in a soup bowl. Beat the egg or eggs in a second soup bowl. Place the breadcrumbs in a third soup bowl. Place olive oil for frying in a pot with high sides and bring to high temperature. Dredge the fritters first in rice flour, then in beaten egg, and lastly in breadcrumbs and fry until golden, working in batches to keep from crowding the pan. Divide the puree among individual serving plates and place the fritters on top. Drizzle with a little oil before serving.

Carciofi ripieni al sugo / FRIED STUFFED ARTICHOKES IN TOMATO SAUCE

Elisabetta Antelmi, Agropoli (Salerno), Campania

Any leftover tomato sauce from this dish makes a perfect topping for pasta.

Fill a bowl with cold water and add the lemon juice. Trim the stalks and hard leaves and remove the chokes from the artichokes, dropping them into acidulated water as you do to keep them from turning brown.

Mince 1 clove garlic. In a bowl, combine the Parmigiano Reggiano, minced garlic, and minced parsley. Beat in the eggs. Drain the trimmed artichokes, dry them with a dishtowel, gently open them up, then stuff them with the egg mixture. Place olive oil for frying in a pot with high sides and bring to high temperature. Fry artichokes the hot oil, working in batches if necessary to keep from crowding the pan.

In a pot large enough to contain the artichokes, sauté a clove of minced garlic in extra-virgin olive oil, then add the tomatoes (break them apart with a wooden spoon) and their juices. Season with a pinch of salt, then arrange the artichokes in the sauce and cook for 30 minutes.

Serves 4

1 LEMON

4 ARTICHOKES

2 CLOVES GARLIC

1½ CUPS GRATED
PARMIGIANO REGGIANO

LEAVES OF 1 SPRIG PARSLEY,
MINCED

2 LARGE EGGS

2 CUPS CANNED PEELED
TOMATOES AND THEIR JUICES

EXTRA-VIRGIN OLIVE OIL
FOR FRYING AND SAUTÉING

SALT TO TASTE

Funghi fritti all'olio di lentischio / FRIED MUSHROOMS

Ristorante Letizia, Nuxis (Carbonia-Iglesias), Sardegna

Serves 6

2¼ POUNDS MIXED FRESH
MUSHROOMS, SUCH AS
BOLETUS SARDUS, PORCINI
MUSHROOMS, AND FIELD
MUSHROOMS

COARSELY GROUND
SEMOLINA FLOUR

MASTIC OIL FOR FRYING

EXTRA-VIRGIN OLIVE OIL
FOR FRYING

SALT TO TASTE

Boletus sardus and other wild mushrooms grow profusely on the island of Sardegna, where mushroom foraging is a popular hobby. Mastic oil (made from an evergreen shrub that grows in the Mediterranean) has an intense flavor and is rarely used on its own. Leave small mushrooms whole.

Trim the ends of the mushroom stems and wipe the mushrooms clean, keeping them as dry as possible. Cut into thick slices. Spread semolina flour on a work surface and gently toss the mushroom slices in the semolina. Fill a pot with high sides with several inches of a mixture of 1 part mastic oil for every 5 parts extra-virgin olive oil and bring to the correct temperature for frying. Meanwhile, line a baking sheet with paper towels and set aside. Fry the mushrooms until golden, turning them to cook them on all sides, and working in batches if necessary to avoid crowding the pot. As they are cooked, remove them with a skimmer to the prepared pan to drain briefly and season with salt.

Polpettine di finocchietto / PAN-FRIED WILD FENNEL CROQUETTES

Ristorante Andrea, Palazzolo Acreide (Siracusa), Sicilia

Serves 4

11 OUNCES WILD FENNEL

2 LARGE EGGS

½ CUP GRATED
TUMAZZO CHEESE

EXTRA-VIRGIN OLIVE OIL
FOR FRYING

SALT AND FRESHLY GROUND
CHILI PEPPER TO TASTE

Tumazzo is a seasonal cow's milk cheese made by being pressed in a basket. It is pale yellow with roughly textured rind.

Bring a pot of water to a boil and blanch the fennel, then drain and chop. Beat the eggs in a large bowl, then stir in the grated cheese and the fennel. Season with salt and pepper. Line a baking sheet with paper towels and set aside. Place several inches of oil for frying in a skillet and heat it but do not allow it to reach the smoke point. Using two soup spoons, form the fennel mixture into balls and drop them into the hot oil. Work in batches, if necessary, to keep from crowding the skillet. Turn the croquettes so they cook on all sides and as they are completely browned, remove with a skimmer to the prepared pan and let them drain and cool to room temperature before serving.

Munaceddi fritti / FRIED MILK THISTLE

Ristorante Mare Monti, San Giovanni Gemini (Agrigento), Sicilia

Serves 4 to 6

JUICE OF 2 LEMONS

1¾ POUNDS MILK THISTLE

SALT TO TASTE

½ CUP EXTRA-VIRGIN
OLIVE OIL

1 CUP SEMOLINA FLOUR

Milk thistle, also known as Saint Mary's thistle or *cardus marianus*, is related to cardoons and artichokes. It grows wild in dry places with lots of sun, which certainly describes the island of Sicilia.

Fill a large bowl with cold water and add the lemon juice. Clean the thistle and trim away any fibrous threads with a paring knife. If the pieces of thistle are very long, cut them into more manageable lengths. Place in the water with the lemon juice.

Bring a large pot of salted water to a boil and add the thistle. Boil until tender. Drain and set aside to cool.

Line a baking sheet with paper towels and set aside. Place olive oil in a cast-iron skillet and bring to high temperature. Dredge the thistle in the semolina flour and fry a few pieces at a time until golden on both sides. Use a pot lid to turn the thistle, if necessary. Season with salt. As the thistle is cooked, use a slotted metal spatula to transfer to the prepared baking sheet to drain.

Frittelle di alghe marine / FRIED SEAWEED

Ristorante La Guardiola, Diamante (Cosenza), Calabria

For a vegan version of this recipe, omit the egg whites, but chop the sea lettuce and drop spoonfuls of the batter with the chopped sea lettuce incorporated into the oil. Seaweed also makes a tasty salad when dressed with olive oil and lemon juice with minced garlic and a pinch of pepper.

Place ½ cup water in a bowl and whisk in the flour until smooth. Add a pinch of salt. In a separate bowl, beat the egg whites to stiff peaks. Fold them into the flour mixture. Line a baking sheet with paper towels. Place olive oil for frying in a pot with high sides and bring to high temperature. Dredge the leaves of sea lettuce in the batter and fry in the oil until puffed and golden, working in batches if necessary to keep from crowding the pot. Remove with a skimmer and transfer briefly to the prepared paper towels to drain, then season with a little salt. Serve hot and crispy.

Serves 4 to 6

¼ CUP UNBLEACHED ALL-PURPOSE FLOUR

SALT TO TASTE

2 EGG WHITES

EXTRA-VIRGIN OLIVE OIL FOR FRYING

16 4-INCH-BY-1-INCH LEAVES OF SEA LETTUCE

Frittelle di zucca / SQUASH CROQUETTES

Trattoria Zio Salvatore, Siderno Superiore (Reggio di Calabria), Calabria

Butternut squash and kobucha squash, which have a fairly dry texture, are both good choices for these crisp croquettes.

Bring a pot of salted water to a boil. Boil the squash until tender. Drain and set aside. In a bowl, beat the eggs. Whisk in the flour and parsley, the grated cheese, and the garlic, if using. Crush the cooked squash with a fork until fairly smooth. Stir the crushed cooked squash into the egg mixture.

Line a baking sheet with paper towels. Fill a pot with high sides with a generous amount of oil and bring to high temperature. Drop tablespoons of the mixture and fry until browned on all sides, working in batches if necessary. Remove the fritters with a slotted spoon or a skimmer, drain briefly on the prepared pan, and serve hot.

Serves 6

SALT TO TASTE

1 POUND PEELED AND SEEDED WINTER SQUASH, SUCH AS BUTTERNUT SQUASH

2 LARGE EGGS

¼ CUP UNBLEACHED ALL-PURPOSE FLOUR

LEAVES OF 1 SPRIG PARSLEY, MINCED

¼ CUP GRATED AGED SHEEP'S CHEESE

1 SMALL CLOVE GARLIC, MINCED (OPTIONAL)

EXTRA-VIRGIN OLIVE OIL FOR FRYING

Frittelle di Sant'Antonio / CAULIFLOWER FRITTERS

Laura Romanò, Tuscania (Viterbo), Lazio

Serves 6 to 8

1 HEAD CAULIFLOWER,
ABOUT 2 POUNDS

UNBLEACHED ALL-PURPOSE
FLOUR FOR DREDGING

GROUND CINNAMON TO TASTE

OIL FOR FRYING

SALT TO TASTE

January 17, the feast day of Saint Anthony the Abbot, is celebrated with sweet cauliflower fritters. The only difference is that they are sprinkled with a generous coating of sugar rather than salt after frying.

Break down the cauliflower into florets. Bring a large pot of water to a boil and boild the cauliflower until tender enough to pierce with a paring knife. Drain and pat dry. In a bowl, combine flour and cinnamon. Toss the florets with the flour mixture.

Line a baking sheet with paper towels. Fill a pot with high sides with a generous amount of oil for frying and bring to high temperature. Fry the florets, working in batches if necessary to keep from crowding the pan, until golden. Remove with a slotted spoon or a skimmer, drain briefly on the prepared pan, salt, and serve hot.

Polpette di verza / PAN-FRIED CABBAGE BUNDLES

Osteria della Villetta, Palazzolo sull'Oglio (Brescia), Lombardia

This recipe cleverly makes both a main course of cabbage bundles and a side dish of sautéed cabbage in tomato sauce.

Bring a large pot of salted water to a boil. Remove the outer leaves of the cabbage, leaving them whole, and boil for 5 minutes. Drain well in a colander. Core the remaining cabbage and cut into ribbons. Set aside.

Soak the bread in milk until crumbly, then squeeze dry and crumble into a bowl. Stir in parsley, season with salt and pepper, and drizzle in a little extra-virgin olive oil to moisten. Form the mixture into round balls and press lightly to flatten them a little bit. Wrap each ball of filling in a cooked cabbage leaf.

Place the flour in a soup bowl. Fill a skillet with high sides with a generous amount of oil for frying and bring to high temperature. Dredge the stuffed leaves in flour and pan-fry in the hot oil. As the leaves brown, they should adhere tightly to the filling.

In a separate skillet, sauté the onion and garlic in oil. Add the tomatoes, tomato puree, and reserved cabbage. Serve bundles and sautéed cabbage together.

Serves 4

SALT TO TASTE

1 SMALL HEAD SAVOY CABBAGE

SLICED WHITE BREAD FOR STUFFING

WHOLE MILK FOR SOAKING

LEAVES OF 1 SPRIG PARSLEY, MINCED

FRESHLY GROUND BLACK PEPPER TO TASTE

EXTRA-VIRGIN OLIVE OIL FOR DRIZZLING AND FRYING

UNBLEACHED ALL-PURPOSE FLOUR FOR DREDGING

¼ YELLOW ONION, MINCED

1 CLOVE GARLIC, MINCED

2 TOMATOES, CHOPPED

TOMATO PUREE FOR SAUCE

Panelle / CHICKPEA FLOUR FRITTERS

Ristorante Ai Cascinari, Palermo, Sicilia

Serves 4 to 6

1⅔ CUPS FINELY GROUND
CHICKPEA FLOUR

SALT TO TASTE

LEAVES OF 1 SPRIG PARSLEY
OR 1 FROND WILD FENNEL,
MINCED (OPTIONAL)

OIL FOR FRYING

There are special wooden stamps used to make these fritters. If you are lucky enough to own a set, use those rather than the plates. Panelle makers in Palermo's many *friggitorie*, which specialize in fried foods, never use olive oil for frying panelle but instead rely on peanut or vegetable oil. Panelle on a bun are one of the city's many street foods.

Place the chickpea flour in a pot and place over medium heat. Whisk in 2½ cups water and season with salt. Cook, stirring constantly with a whisk in the same direction, until the mixture thickens and begins to pull away from the sides of the pot. Stir in the parsley or fennel, if using, and remove from the heat. While the mixture is still hot, use a spatula to spread it evenly on small plates. Basically, you are using the plates in place of molds.

If you wish to prepare the panelle immediately, set the plates in the refrigerator. If you are not under a time constraint, you can allow the mixture to cool at room temperature. In either case, once the batter is cool and firm, cut it into triangles.

Place a generous amount of oil for frying in a pot with high sides and bring to high temperature. Working in batches to keep from crowding the pot, fry the panelle until golden and crisp, no more than 30 to 40 seconds. Drain and serve.

Fiori di trombetta ripieni / SQUASH BLOSSOMS WITH BEAN STUFFING

Marinella Badino Biancheri, Vallecrosia (Imperia), Liguria

Serves 4 to 6

4 MEDIUM POTATOES

¼ CUP SHELLED FRESH
WHITE BEANS, SUCH AS
CANNELLINI BEANS

2 LARGE EGGS

GRATED PARMIGIANO
REGGIANO OR AGED SHEEP'S
CHEESE TO TASTE

1 CLOVE GARLIC, MINCED

LEAVES OF 1 SPRIG PARSLEY,
MINCED

LEAVES OF 1 SPRIG
MARJORAM, MINCED

SALT TO TASTE

8 TROMBETTA SQUASH
BLOSSOMS

EXTRA-VIRGIN OLIVE OIL
FOR FRYING

Crookneck trombetta squash blossoms should be picked just before cooking. Open their petals gently and place them upside-down on a clean cloth to encourage any insects to leave the premises. Pinch out their pistils and remove any green leaves and stems. Rinse very gently, then let them drain, again upside-down, in a colander. If you need to use dried white beans, soak them overnight in water to cover, then rinse them before cooking. The stuffed blossoms can also be baked until golden brown.

Place the potatoes in a small pot with cold water to cover and boil until tender enough to pierce easily with a fork. Separately, boil the white beans until tender. Drain the beans.

Beat the eggs in a large bowl. Peel the cooked potatoes and crush the potatoes and beans with a fork or potato ricer. Add the beans and potatoes to the eggs. Stir in the grated cheese, garlic, parsley, and marjoram. Season with salt. Mix until well-combined. Stuff the blossoms with this mixture, then fold over the petals to close them.

Line a baking sheet with paper towels. Heat a generous amount of olive oil in a skillet with high sides and fry the blossoms until golden. Drain briefly on the prepared pan, then serve.

Caponet / STUFFED SQUASH BLOSSOMS

Osteria dell'Unione, Treiso (Cuneo), Piemonte

Seek out young, tender zucchini for this recipe. Often they can be found with their blossoms still attached. Blossoms can also be stuffed with a pea and basil puree.

Line a baking sheet with paper towels and set aside. Heat 3 tablespoons of oil in a skillet over medium heat and cook the zucchini, stirring frequently, for 15 minutes. The zucchini should be golden and cooked, but still crisp. Salt, then remove from the pan with a skimmer or slotted spoon and drain briefly on the prepared pan. Chop with a mezzaluna.

Whisk the egg yolks in a large bowl and stir in the zucchini, amaretti, cocoa powder, and sugar. Gently mix until well combined. Pinch off the pistils of the squash blossoms and shake over the sink, then rinse briefly. Gently stuff the blossoms with the zucchini mixture. Fill a skillet with high sides with a generous amount of oil for frying, bring to medium-high heat, and fry blossoms until golden, about 10 minutes. Season with salt and serve piping hot.

Serves 4

1 POUND (ABOUT 6 SMALL) ZUCCHINI, CUT INTO JULIENNE

3 TABLESPOONS EXTRA-VIRGIN OLIVE OIL, PLUS MORE FOR FRYING

2 EGG YOLKS

¼ CUP CRUMBLED AMARETTI COOKIES

1 TABLESPOON UNSWEETENED COCOA POWDER

1 TEASPOON SUGAR

12 SQUASH BLOSSOMS

SALT TO TASTE

PIZZAS AND SAVORY TARTS

Pizza vegana / VEGAN PIZZA

Barbara Torresan, Milano, Lombardia

Serves 4 to 6

2½ CUPS MILLET FLOUR

1 CUP OAT FLOUR

⅓ CUP RICE FLOUR

⅓ CUP FINELY GROUND CORNMEAL

1 PINCH SUGAR

2 MEDIUM ZUCCHINI

2 MEDIUM CARROTS

1 COOKED BEET

¼ CUP PLUS 2 TABLESPOONS EXTRA-VIRGIN OLIVE OIL, PLUS MORE FOR DRIZZLING

4 TO 5 CHERRY TOMATOES

6 TO 8 LEAVES TREVISO RADICCHIO

1 TEASPOON SALT

FRESHLY GROUND BLACK PEPPER TO TASTE

BALSAMIC VINEGAR FOR DRIZZLING

You can use a food processor fitted with the dough blade to make the dough. Place the flours and cornmeal in the processor, pulse a few times to combine, then drizzle in warm water until the mixture forms a ball. Process for 45 seconds and continue with the recipe.

Combine the flours, cornmeal, and sugar and stir in enough lukewarm water to make a soft, elastic dough. Shape the dough into a ball and set aside to rest for at least 30 minutes. Meanwhile, use a vegetable peeler to cut the zucchini into thin strips. Cut the carrots and the beet into very thin matchsticks.

Preheat the oven to 450°F. Press the dough very thin into a pan (or more than one pan). Brush the surface of the dough with ¼ cup plus 2 tablespoons olive oil and pierce it all over with a fork. Scatter the carrots, zucchini, cherry tomatoes, and Treviso radicchio on top of the dough. Drizzle with oil, sprinkle on the 1 teaspoon salt, and season with black pepper. Bake in the preheated oven until crust is speckled with dark spots and bottom is browned, 5 to 6 minutes. Scatter the beet on top of the pizza, drizzle with a few drops of balsamic vinegar, and serve hot.

Pizza de turco con cicoria / STUFFED CORNMEAL CRUST PIZZA

Ristorante Belsito, Serrone (Frosinone), Lazio

Serves 4

SALT TO TASTE

1 POUND CHICORY GREENS

EXTRA-VIRGIN OLIVE OIL
FOR SAUTÉING

2 CLOVES GARLIC

GROUND CHILI PEPPER,
TO TASTE

2⅓ CUPS CORNMEAL

Wild chicory greens are preferable for this pizza due to their sharp flavor, but the cultivated type will work in a pinch. Rather than being baked with a topping, this thicker crust is cut in half the long way and filled like a sandwich.

Bring a large pot of lightly salted water to a boil and blanch the greens in lightly salted water for 30 minutes. Drain, cool, then squeeze dry and chop. Heat olive oil in a skillet and sauté the garlic cloves in the oil. Add the greens and chili pepper and sauté until the greens have absorbed the flavor, 3 to 5 minutes.

Preheat the oven to 350°F. Bring 2 cups of water to a boil and lightly salt the water. With a cast-iron spatula, stir the cornmeal into the hot water until fully combined. Spread the mixture in a 13-inch-diameter pizza pan and bake in the preheated oven until firm to the touch. Cut the crust in half horizontally with a serrated knife. Place the spinach mixture on the bottom half, top with the top half, and cut into wedges.

Ciaccia al formaggio / FLATBREAD WITH SHEEP'S CHEESE

Isabella Dalla Ragione, Città di Castello (Perugia), Umbria

Making a well on a work surface out of dry ingredients and placing wet ingredients in the center is the traditional way of making dough. If you are uncertain about your ability to work this way without making a mess (sometimes the liquid leaks through the wall of the well), feel free to combine the ingredients in a large bowl and then transfer the dough to the work surface for kneading.

Dissolve the yeast in about ½ cup warm water and set aside until bubbly. In a bowl, combine the yeast mixture with ½ cup of the flour. Cover and set aside to rest for 1 hour. Form the remaining flour into a well on a work surface. Place the yeast mixture, the eggs, the butter, the cheeses, and the salt and pepper in the center of the well. Pull in flour from the sides of the well until a dough forms. Knead until the dough is soft and elastic.

Oil a pan with high sides. Place the dough in the pan, cover with a dishtowel, and set in a warm place to rise until doubled in size. When the dough is almost fully risen, preheat the oven to 400°F. When the dough is fully risen, bake in the preheated oven until lightly golden, about 1 hour.

Serves 8

1 TABLESPOON PLUS TEASPOON (TWO ENVELOPES) ACTIVE DRY YEAST

12½ CUPS UNBLEACHED ALL-PURPOSE FLOUR

12 LARGE EGGS, LIGHTLY BEATEN

2 STICKS PLUS 5 TABLESPOONS UNSALTED BUTTER, ROOM TEMPERATURE

2 CUPS DICED YOUNG SHEEP'S CHEESE

2½ CUPS GRATED AGED SHEEP'S CHEESE

2 TABLESPOONS PLUS 1 TEASPOON SALT

1 TABLESPOON FRESHLY GROUND BLACK PEPPER

EXTRA-VIRGIN OLIVE OIL FOR OILING PAN

Focaccia ortolana / FOCACCIA WITH MIXED VEGETABLES

Giuliano Guidi, San Costanzo (Pesaro e Urbino), Marche

1 BUNCH ASPARAGUS, TRIMMED

2 ARTICHOKES, HARD LEAVES REMOVED AND TRIMMED

2 TO 3 MEDIUM POTATOES

1 BUNCH WILD GREENS

1 TABLESPOON EXTRA-VIRGIN OLIVE OIL, PLUS MORE FOR MOISTENING FILLING AND BRUSHING

SALT TO TASTE

2¼ TEASPOONS (ONE ENVELOPE) ACTIVE DRY YEAST

3½ CUPS UNBLEACHED ALL-PURPOSE FLOUR

1 PINCH SUGAR

½ CUP GRATED PARMIGIANO REGGIANO

There is a longstanding tradition of foraging for wild greens (as well as hunting for mushrooms) in the Marche region. Use any type of wild greens you like in this recipe, or swap in cultivated greens if that's all you can find.

Bring a pot of salted water to a boil and blanch the asparagus, artichokes, potatoes, and greens separately until tender. Drain and cool. Peel the potatoes and mince the cooked vegetables together. Toss with enough olive oil to make a moist mixture. Season with salt.

Dissolve the yeast in a small amount of warm water until bubbly. Combine the flour, yeast mixture, 1 tablespoon olive oil, a pinch of salt, and sugar and knead in enough room temperature water to make a soft and well-combined dough. Transfer the dough to a bowl, cover with a damp dishtowel, and set aside to rise for about 2 hours.

Preheat the oven to 325°F. Divide the dough into two equal pieces. Roll each one out to a thin sheet using a rolling pin. Arrange one piece of dough in a low, wide cake or pie pan, spread the vegetable mixture on top, and sprinkle on the grated cheese. Top with the second sheet of dough and press the edges together to seal. Brush the top with a few drops of oil and pierce in several places with a fork. Bake in the preheated oven until golden brown on top, about 30 minutes. Serve hot.

Fucazza chiena cu la cipodda / FOCACCIA STUFFED WITH ONIONS

Ristorante Casale Ferrovia, Carovigno (Brindisi), Puglia

Senatore Cappelli is a variety of durum wheat. Type 2 flour is a less finely ground flour that is halfway between white flour and whole wheat flour. High-extraction flour is similar—it has had some of the bran and germ removed and some left in place. If you cannot find either of these—and they are admittedly hard to procure—substitute with all-purpose flour or a combination of 1 cup all-purpose flour and ⅔ cup whole wheat flour. Fiaschetto tomatoes are small oval tomatoes with their own Slow Food Presidium. Acquaviva red onions are extremely sweet. Sponsali are long, thin wild onions that resemble leeks. If neither is available, substitute standard red onions or the freshest and tastiest onions available in your area.

Slice the onions and sauté them in oil in a large skillet just until softened, then cover and cook over low heat for 15 minutes. Stir in the tomatoes, capers, and olives and salt to taste. (If your olives and capers are very salty, you may not need any.) Cook, stirring frequently, for a few minutes to combine the flavors, then set aside to cool. Bring a large pot of water to a boil and cook the potatoes. As soon as the potatoes are cool enough to handle, peel them and crush them with a fork. Combine the two flours and the crushed potatoes and form into a well on a work surface. Dissolve the yeast in a scant cup of warm water and add it to the center of the well along with 1 tablespoon oil and 2 ½ teaspoons salt. Knead into a soft, elastic dough, place in a bowl, cover, and allow to rest for 30 minutes.

Generously oil a baking pan. Divide the dough into two equal pieces and with your fingers spread the dough in the bottom of the prepared pan, stopping to let it rest if it resists. Spread the onion mixture on top, then stretch the remaining piece of dough to roughly the same size and shape as the first and place the second piece on top. Crimp the edges to seal and set aside to rest for 30 minutes.

Start a fire in a wood-burning oven or preheat oven to 400°F. Cook until browned on both bottom and top.

Serves 4 to 6

2 POUNDS ACQUAVIVA RED ONIONS OR SPONSALI ONIONS

1 TABLESPOON EXTRA-VIRGIN OLIVE OIL, PLUS MORE FOR SAUTÉING AND OILING PAN

¼ CUP CHOPPED FIASCHETTO TOMATOES

2 TABLESPOONS SALTED CAPERS, RINSED AND DRAINED

⅓ CUP PITTED OLIVES

2½ TEASPOONS SALT, PLUS MORE TO TASTE

2 MEDIUM POTATOES

1⅔ CUPS ITALIAN TYPE 2 FLOUR OR HIGH-EXTRACTION FLOUR

1¾ CUPS SENATORE CAPPELLI OR OTHER VARIETY OF SEMOLINA FLOUR

2¼ TEASPOONS (ONE ENVELOPE) ACTIVE DRY YEAST

Focaccia farcita alle erbe / FOCACCIA STUFFED WITH GREENS

Agriturismo La Cittadella dei Sibillini, Montemonaco (Ascoli Piceno), Marche

Serves 4

SALT TO TASTE

1 SMALL POTATO
(ABOUT 4 OUNCES)

1 SMALL ARTICHOKE
(ABOUT 4 OUNCES)

4 OUNCES WILD ASPARAGUS

4 OUNCES WILD CHICORY OR
OTHER FORAGED GREENS

3 TABLESPOONS
EXTRA-VIRGIN OLIVE OIL,
PLUS MORE FOR OILING PAN
AND BRUSHING

1 TABLESPOON PLUS
1 TEASPOON ACTIVE
DRY YEAST

5 CUPS UNBLEACHED
ALL-PURPOSE FLOUR

1 PINCH SUGAR

3 TABLESPOONS GRATED
PARMIGIANO REGGIANO

Feel free to play around with the vegetable mix in this stuffed focaccia—eggplant and zucchini can be used in place of asparagus and artichokes in summer. As for the greens, seek out chicory, wild radish, milk thistle, wild poppy leaves, and wild amaranth. Each will lend its own distinct flavor.

For the filling, bring a large pot of salted water to a boil. Peel and thinly slice the potato and boil until tender. Remove with a slotted spoon or skimmer. Trim the artichoke and slice thinly, then boil until tender. Remove with a slotted spoon or skimmer. Boil the asparagus until tender and remove with a slotted spoon or skimmer. Lastly, boil the chicory until tender. Let all of the vegetables cool, mince them together, and toss with 2 tablespoons olive oil.

For the dough, dissolve the yeast in a small amount of warm water and set aside until bubbly. Combine the flour, yeast mixture, 1 tablespoon oil, a pinch of salt, and the sugar with enough water to make a soft, elastic dough. Knead until smooth, then place in a bowl, cover with a damp dishtowel, and set aside to rise for at least 1 hour.

Preheat oven to 325°F. Lightly oil a wide baking pan with low sides. Divide the dough into two equal pieces and with your fingers on a lightly floured work surface stretch each to a little less than ¼ inch thick in a shape that will fit the prepared pan. (Let the dough rest for a few minutes if it resists.) Place one piece of dough in the pan, cover with the prepared vegetables Sprinkle on the grated Parmigiano. Place the second piece of dough on top and press around the perimeter to seal the two pieces together. Brush the surface with additional oil and pierce all over with a fork. Bake in the preheated oven until browned, about 30 minutes.

Pizzelle e Panzerotti / FRIED SMALL PIZZAS AND TURNOVERS

Antonio Rizzo, Napoli, Campania

Serves 6

2¼ TEASPOONS
(ONE ENVELOPE) ACTIVE
DRY YEAST

1⅔ CUPS UNBLEACHED
ALL-PURPOSE FLOUR

1 CUP TOMATO PUREE

LEAVES OF 1 SPRIG
BASIL, TORN

¾ CUP DICED AGED
SHEEP'S CHEESE

EXTRA-VIRGIN OLIVE OIL
FOR FRYING

These small turnovers and pizzas can also be baked in an oven. They will cook very quickly.

Dissolve the yeast in ⅔ cup warm water. Combine the flour with the yeast mixture and knead into a smooth and elastic dough. Divide the dough into 12 equal pieces. Form six of the pieces into balls and six into disks and set aside to rise for at least 3 hours.

Fill a pot with high sides with several inches of oil for frying and bring to high temperature. Roll out each ball of dough into a small pizza and fry, working in batches if necessary. Smear each one with a little tomato sauce and top with some of the cheese and the basil. Spread remaining tomato sauce on the 6 disks and distribute some of the remaining cheese on each one, then fold each disk in half and press the edges together to seal. Fry in the oil until browned, working in batches if necessary to keep from crowding the pan.

Arvolto con pomodori piccanti / FRIED DOUGH WITH SPICY TOMATOES
Locanda di Nonna Gelsa, Umbertide (Perugia), Umbria

Serves 4 to 6

SALT TO TASTE

4 CUPS UNBLEACHED
ALL-PURPOSE FLOUR

2 CLOVES GARLIC

EXTRA-VIRGIN OLIVE OIL FOR
SAUTÉING AND FRYING

1½ POUNDS PLUM TOMATOES,
PEELED, SEEDED, AND
ROUGHLY CHOPPED

MINCED CHILI PEPPER
TO TASTE

Adjust the amount of chili pepper to your taste. If you like your tomato sauce really spicy, use a whole pepper.

Add enough lightly salted water to the flour to create a soft, smooth dough. Divide the dough into equal-sized pieces by weight (5 to 6 ounces each) and shape each piece into a ball. Cover the balls of dough with a damp dishtowel and allow to rest for 10 minutes.

While the dough is rising, sauté the garlic in oil over medium heat. When the garlic begins to brown, add the tomatoes and cook until they begin to break down, about 10 minutes. Season with salt and the minced chili pepper.

Roll out the balls of dough one at a time. Their diameter should be just slightly smaller than the diameter of the pan you will use to fry them. Line several baking sheets with paper towels. Fill a skillet with high sides with several inches of oil and heat to high temperature. Add one of the disks of dough. When it begins to puff, carefully turn it over using tongs. When both sides of the disk are brown and puffed, transfer to the prepared baking sheets to drain. Repeat with the remaining circles of dough. To serve, arrange each disk of dough on an individual serving plate, cut into quarters, and top with the tomato sauce.

Torta Verde / SAVORY PIE WITH GREENS AND RICE

Francesca Ronco, Dusino San Michele (Asti), Piemonte

Nettle leaves are covered in fine stinging protrusions that disappear once the greens are cooked, so always wear gloves and work cautiously when dealing with raw nettles.

Blanch the spinach, chard, and nettles in a small amount of lightly salted water. Drain, squeeze dry, mince, and set aside. Place the broth in a small pot. Bring to a boil, then turn down to a simmer and keep at a simmer. Sauté the leeks and onion in olive oil until softened. Add the rice and cook over medium heat, stirring frequently, until the rice starts to color slightly. Add the wine and stir until the wine has been incorporated. Add the vegetable broth in small amounts, about ¼ cup at a time, stirring between additions until it has been absorbed. Continue until all the broth has been used and the rice is cooked through but still has a little resistance. Add the greens and remove from the heat to cool slightly.

Preheat the oven to 350°F. Beat the eggs in a bowl. Remove and reserve about 1 tablespoon beaten egg to use as an egg wash, then to the bowl add about ¼ cup Parmigiano and season with salt and pepper. Add the cooked rice mixture (which should have cooled by now so it doesn't curdle the eggs) and stir to combine.

Butter a tart pan and coat with about half of the breadcrumbs. Pour in the rice mixture. Brush the reserved egg wash on top, then sprinkle on the remaining breadcrumbs, remaining ½ cup grated Parmigiano, and the rosemary. Bake until browned on top, about 1 hour. Serve hot or warm.

Serves 6

1¾ POUNDS SPINACH

1¾ POUNDS CHARD

1 POUND NETTLES

SALT TO TASTE

2 CUPS VEGETABLE BROTH

2 LEEKS, THINLY SLICED

1 MEDIUM YELLOW ONION, THINLY SLICED

EXTRA-VIRGIN OLIVE OIL FOR SAUTÉING

1½ CUPS RICE

½ CUP WHITE WINE

6 LARGE EGGS

¾ CUP GRATED PARMIGIANO REGGIANO

FRESHLY GROUND BLACK PEPPER TO TASTE

1 TABLESPOON UNSALTED BUTTER

½ CUP BREADCRUMBS

LEAVES OF 1 SPRIG FRESH ROSEMARY

Torta di melanzane striate / GRAFFITI EGGPLANT TART

Barbara Torresan, Milano, Lombardia

Serves 4 to 6

¾ CUP PLUS 2 TABLESPOONS
MILLET FLOUR

1 CUP CHICKPEA FLOUR

⅓ CUP FINELY GROUND
CORNMEAL

¾ TEASPOON SALT, PLUS
MORE TO TASTE

1 TEASPOON XANTHAN GUM
(OPTIONAL)

¼ CUP PLUS 1 TABLESPOON
EXTRA-VIRGIN OLIVE OIL

2 MEDIUM GRAFFITI
EGGPLANT

2 MEDIUM YELLOW ONIONS

¼ CUP LOOSELY PACKED
BASIL LEAVES

½ CUP TOMATO PUREE

FRESHLY GROUND BLACK
PEPPER TO TASTE

MINCED FRESH OREGANO
TO TASTE

GROUND CHILI PEPPER
TO TASTE

Graffiti eggplant have striped skin and a very delicate flavor. The filling for this tart can also serve as a topping for pasta or crostini. To make the crust in a food processor, put the dry ingredients in the work bowl and add the liquid ingredients through the tube. Do not overwork.

Combine the millet flour, chickpea flour, cornmeal, ¾ teaspoon salt, and the xanthan gum, if using. Stir in 3 tablespoons olive oil and ½ cup water and knead into a well-combined dough, adding more water if it seems excessively dry. Shape the dough into a ball and set aside to rest in a cool place for at least 1 hour.

Meanwhile, dice the eggplant (no need to salt them) and thinly slice the onions. Heat 2 tablespoons of oil in a skillet. Sauté the eggplant and onions with the basil. When the eggplant is golden, add the tomato puree and cook for 5 additional minutes to thicken slightly. Season with salt, pepper, oregano, and a pinch of minced chili pepper.

Preheat oven to 350°F. Place a sheet of parchment paper on the work surface. Cut off a piece of the dough about the size of a large egg. Place the remaining larger portion of the dough on top of the parchment and with a lightly floured rolling pin roll out the dough evenly to a slightly larger diameter than the pan where you plan to bake the tart. Use the parchment paper to transfer the bottom crust to the pan and trim the edges. Transfer the eggplant mixture to the center of the tart. Roll out the reserved piece of dough, incorporating any trimmed scraps. Cut out decorative leaves and place this in the center of the tart, and make arched pieces of dough to form a ring around the perimeters. With a fork, gently seal this ring to the bottom crust. Bake in the preheated oven until crust is golden, about 40 minutes. If the decorations on top of the tart appear to be getting dark before the bottom crust is properly cooked, cover with aluminum foil.

Torta di trombette / TROMBETTA SQUASH TART

Marinella Badino Biancheri, Vallecrosia (Imperia), Liguria

Serves 6

1¾ POUNDS TROMBETTA
SQUASH

SALT TO TASTE

½ CUP RICE

2 TABLESPOONS EXTRA-
VIRGIN OLIVE OIL, PLUS MORE
FOR SAUTÉING, OILING PAN,
AND BRUSHING CRUST

2 CLOVES GARLIC, MINCED

1 MEDIUM YELLOW ONION,
MINCED

2 LARGE EGGS

1 CUP GRATED
PARMIGIANO REGGIANO
OR AGED SHEEP'S CHEESE

LEAVES OF 1 SPRIG PARSLEY,
MINCED

LEAVES OF 1 SPRIG
MARJORAM, MINCED

4 CUPS UNBLEACHED
ALL-PURPOSE FLOUR

Green trombetta squash have a dry flesh that makes them perfect for tarts like this, as they don't give off liquid that might make the bottom crust too damp. Trombetta squash first appear in Liguria from June to August as small zucchini-type squash, but then they grow as long as eighty inches long and they are still edible in that more mature stage.

Peel and seed the squash and grate it on the largest holes of a four-sided grater. Season with salt and set aside in a strainer to give off its liquid, about 20 minutes. Meanwhile, bring a pot of salted water to a boil and cook the rice as you would pasta, stirring frequently, until tender. Drain and set aside. Squeeze the grated squash to get out as much liquid as possible, then sauté in olive oil with the garlic and onion for 3 minutes. Set aside to cool. When the squash is cool, combine it with the eggs, cooked rice, grated cheese, and herbs. You can prepare this up to 24 hours in advance and it benefits from sitting.

To make the dough, form the flour into a well on a work surface and place 2 tablespoons oil, a pinch of salt, and ½ cup warm water in the center. Knead until you have a soft elastic dough and set aside to rest for 30 minutes.

Preheat the oven to 325°F. Oil a pan. Divide the dough into two equal portions and roll them out. Arrange one sheet of dough in the prepared pan, spread the filling evenly on top, place the second sheet of dough on the filling, and seal the edges all around. Brush the top of the tart with a little oil and pierce with a fork in several places. Bake for 30 minutes, then raise the oven temperature to 350°F and bake for 10 additional minutes.

Panada di carciofi / ARTICHOKE PIE

Antonia Mereu, Lunamatrona (Medio Campidano), Sardegna

The artichokes for this dish must be as tender as possible, as they are not cooked in advance.

Dissolve a pinch of salt in ⅔ cup water. In a large bowl combine 2 tablespoons oil with the salted water and drizzle in the semolina flour while stirring until all the semolina flour is incorporated. Knead into a compact dough, adding a little more water if the dough is too stiff to handle. Shape the dough into a ball, place in a bowl, cover with a dishtowel, and refrigerate for 1 hour. Meanwhile, trim the artichokes and cut them into thin strips. Toss with lemon juice to coat, then mince the parsley and garlic and toss with that. Add the remaining ¼ cup olive oil, salt, and pepper and toss again to combine.

Preheat the oven to 300°F. Divide the dough into two pieces, one slightly larger than the other. Roll out the larger piece and use it to line a cake or pie pan. Spread the artichoke mixture evenly on top, then roll out the second piece of dough and place it on top of the artichokes. Crimp around the edges with your fingers to seal the top and bottom crust. Bake in the preheated oven for 1 hour and 30 minutes.

Serves 4 to 6

SALT TO TASTE

¼ CUP PLUS 2 TABLESPOONS EXTRA-VIRGIN OLIVE OIL

2 CUPS FINELY GROUND SEMOLINA FLOUR

4 ARTICHOKES

LEMON JUICE TO TASTE

LEAVES OF 1 SPRIG PARSLEY

2 CLOVES GARLIC

FRESHLY GROUND BLACK PEPPER TO TASTE

Torta pasqualina / EASTER PIE WITH GREENS AND HERBS

Nina Colombo, Rapallo (Genova), Liguria

Serves 4 to 6

2½ CUPS UNBLEACHED
ALL-PURPOSE FLOUR

2 TABLESPOONS
EXTRA-VIRGIN OLIVE OIL
FROM LIGURIA, PLUS MORE
FOR SAUTÉING, OILING PAN,
BRUSHING DOUGH, AND
DRIZZLING

SALT TO TASTE

2 POUNDS CHARD, OR 10
ARTICHOKES, TRIMMED

3 BUNCHES BORAGE

½ CUP GRATED
PARMIGIANO REGGIANO

1 TEASPOON MINCED FRESH
MARJORAM LEAVES

1 LARGE YELLOW ONION

2 CLOVES GARLIC

LEAVES OF 3 SPRIGS PARSLEY

8 LARGE EGGS

10 OUNCES (1¼ CUPS)
RICOTTA

2 TABLESPOONS
WHIPPING CREAM

5 TABLESPOONS
UNSALTED BUTTER

FRESHLY GROUND BLACK
PEPPER TO TASTE

The whole eggs baked in the center of this Easter favorite are stunning when cut.

Form the flour into a well on a work surface and place 2 tablespoons oil and a pinch of salt in the center. Knead in enough water to form a soft elastic dough. Knead for 10 minutes, then divide the dough into 6 pieces and form each piece into a ball. Cover with a damp towel and set aside to rest for 1 hour.

Cut the chard and borage into thin ribbons and steam them. Drain, and squeeze dry, then combine with about half the grated Parmigiano Reggiano and marjoram and season with salt. Thinly slice the onion and sauté in olive oil until golden. Mince together the garlic and parsley. In a large bowl, beat 3 of the eggs with 1 tablespoon of the Parmigiano Reggiano and stir in the greens, the ricotta, the cream, the cooked onion, and the garlic and parsley mixture. Mix until well combined.

Preheat the oven to 375°F. Oil a cake or pie pan with high sides. Roll out one of the pieces of dough into a thin sheet. Place the sheet of dough in the pan. It should extend an inch or two over the side. Brush the surface of the dough with oil and repeat with another piece of dough. Top that second sheet of dough with a third piece, but do not oil the top of the third piece of dough. Spread the greens mixture on top of the dough and drizzle with a little oil. Cut about half of the butter into five pieces. Make 5 indentations in the filling. In each indentation place a piece of butter and then a whole egg, being careful not to break the yolks. Sprinkle the remaining grated cheese on top of the eggs and season with salt and pepper. Roll out one of the remaining pieces of dough and gently place it on top of the eggs. Brush with oil and dot the edges with a little butter. Roll out another piece of dough, place on top of the first and brush with oil and dot the edges with the remaining butter. Roll out the remaining piece of dough and place it on top. Fold the edges over to seal the tart. Brush the top with a little additional oil and pierce in a few places with a fork (being careful not to break the egg yolks).

Bake in the preheated oven until the top crust is a deep golden color, about 1 hour. Serve warm or cold.

Pizza di scarola / PIE WITH ESCAROLE, OLIVES, AND RAISINS

Trattoria La Chitarra, Napoli, Campania

Serves 6 to 8

A classic of Napoli and the surrounding Campania region, this pie cunningly combines savory, sweet, and spicy flavors.

DOUGH

2¼ TEASPOONS
(ONE ENVELOPE) ACTIVE
DRY YEAST

3⅓ CUPS UNBLEACHED
ALL-PURPOSE FLOUR

7 TABLESPOONS UNSALTED
BUTTER, SOFTENED

SALT TO TASTE

Dissolve the yeast in ¾ cup warm water and set aside until bubbly, about 5 minutes. Combine the flour, yeast mixture, butter, and a pinch of salt and knead until it forms a soft dough. Set the dough aside at room temperature, covered, until doubled in size. You can also prepare the dough one day in advance and refrigerate it overnight. If you do, remove it from the refrigerator at least 2 hours before baking to bring it to room temperature.

FILLING

SALT TO TASTE

2 POUNDS ESCAROLE

¼ CUP EXTRA-VIRGIN
OLIVE OIL

2 CLOVES GARLIC

¼ CUP BLACK GAETA OLIVES,
PITTED AND COARSELY
CHOPPED

1 TABLESPOON CAPERS,
RINSED AND DRAINED,

CRUSHED RED CHILI PEPPER
TO TASTE (OPTIONAL)

2 TABLESPOONS BLACK
RAISINS, SOAKED IN WARM
WATER AND SQUEEZED DRY

1 TABLESPOON PINE NUTS

For the filling, bring a large pot of lightly salted water to a boil and blanch the escarole. Drain, cool, and then wrap in a clean flat-weave dishtowel and squeeze very dry. Mince the greens. In a large skillet, heat the olive oil and sauté the garlic, stirring frequently, until golden. Add the olives, capers, and the chili pepper if using. Add the escarole, the raisins, and the pine nuts. Cook over medium heat, stirring occasionally, until the escarole is completely dry and not a trace of water remains. Taste and adjust salt. Drain off any excess oil and set filling aside.

Preheat oven to 425°F. Cut the dough in half. On a lightly floured wooden work surface, roll out half of the dough to a thickness of about ¹⁄₁₀ inch and use it to line a pan 12 inches in diameter with sides at least 1½ inches high. Pierce the surface in several places with a fork, then distribute the escarole filling evenly over the bottom crust. Roll out the other half of the dough and place it on top of the pie. Crimp the edges to seal. Pierce the top crust in several places with a toothpick and bake in the preheated oven until lightly browned on top, 50 to 55 minutes. Serve at room temperature or cold.

Casadinas / SHEEP'S CHEESE AND SAFFRON TART

Ristorante Ispinigoli, Dorgali (Nuoro), Sardegna

Casadinas may be sweet or savory. Wedges of this tasty tart make a wonderful start to a festive meal.

For the dough, combine the flour, the egg, a pinch of salt, and enough water to make a soft and elastic dough. Knead briefly, then shape into a ball, wrap in a clean towel, and set aside to rest for 30 minutes. Meanwhile, mince the cheese, calamint, and saffron together.

Start a fire in a wood-burning oven or preheat the oven to 350°F. Roll out the dough very thin (1.5 millimeters or 0.05 inch) and use it to line the bottom and sides of a cake or pie pan with high sides. Spread the cheese mixture evenly over the dough, then crimp the perimeter of the dough. Bake in the preheated oven until the cheese melts keeping close watch on the dough to be sure it doesn't dry out or begin to burn in spots, about 20 minutes.

Serves 4

2½ CUPS UNBLEACHED ALL-PURPOSE FLOUR

1 LARGE EGG

SALT TO TASTE

10 OUNCES YOUNG SHEEP'S CHEESE

LEAVES OF 1 SPRIG CALAMINT

1 PINCH SAFFRON

Torta con verdure / FLAKY PIE WITH GREENS

Gino Zampolini, Magione (Perugia), Umbria

Serves 4

2 CUPS UNBLEACHED
ALL-PURPOSE FLOUR

2 TABLESPOONS
EXTRA-VIRGIN OLIVE OIL,
PLUS MORE FOR SAUTÉING
AND BRUSHING

SALT TO TASTE

4 OUNCES SPINACH

4 OUNCES CHARD

4 OUNCES CHICORY GREENS

1 CLOVE GARLIC

Creating two layers of thin dough for the top and bottom crust of this pie gives it a crisp, flaky texture. The dough is very soft and tender. You can use any greens you like for the filling.

Shape the flour into a well on a work surface. Place 2 tablespoons oil and a pinch of salt in the center of the well, then pour in 5¼ cups warm water. Pull in the flour from the sides of the well until you have a crumbly dough, then knead until it is smooth and elastic. Shape the dough into a ball, wrap in plastic, and refrigerate for 30 minutes.

Bring a large pot of lightly salted water to a boil and blanch the spinach, chard, and chicory. Drain, squeeze dry, and chop. Mince the garlic. Heat a small amount of olive oil in a skillet and add the garlic. Sauté until golden, then add the greens and sauté for a few minutes. Set aside.

Preheat oven to 325°F. Divide the dough into 4 equal pieces. Roll out one piece of dough until it is extremely thin. Place in a cake or pie pan and brush with oil. Roll out a second piece of dough very thin and place it on top of the first. Spread the greens mixture evenly on top. Roll out a third piece of dough very thin and place it on top of the greens. Brush with oil, then roll out the last piece of dough very thin and place it on top. Crimp or fold the edges to seal. Bake in the preheated oven until browned, about 30 minutes. Cut into wedges and serve warm.

Broccolo in crosta / CAULIFLOWER TART

Graziella Chemotti, Vezzano, Trentino

Santa Massenza broccoli sprouts small heads of very tender white cauliflower, surrounded by large dark green leaves, similar to broccoli rabe. Both the leaves and the heads are edible. (*Broccolo* in Italian is often used interchangeably for broccoli and cauliflower.) Use standard cauliflower if you can't locate the Santa Massenza variety in your area.

Remove the leaves and reserve for another use, such as to make the strangolapreti on page 162. Bring a large pot of water to a boil and blanch the white florets until tender. Drain and allow to cool, then chop. Beat the eggs in a bowl. Beat in the cream and 1 tablespoon breadcrumbs and season with salt, pepper, and nutmeg.

Preheat oven to 400°F. Butter a pan with the 1 tablespoon butter and coat with breadcrumbs. Line the pan with the puff pastry, leaving enough overhanging the pan to fold over the top and enclose it completely. Pierce the puff pastry with the tines of a fork all over. Scatter the cooked vegetables over the crust evenly, then pour in the egg mixture. Fold over the overhanging puff pastry to cover and pierce the top surface with a fork in several places. Bake in the preheated oven until the top crust is golden, about 30 minutes.

Serves 6

1 POUND SANTA MASSENZA BROCCOLI

4 LARGE EGGS

1 CUP HEAVY CREAM OR WHIPPING CREAM

1 TABLESPOON BREADCRUMBS, PLUS MORE FOR COATING PAN

SALT AND FRESHLY GROUND BLACK PEPPER TO TASTE

FRESHLY GRATED NUTMEG TO TASTE

1 TABLESPOON UNSALTED BUTTER

11 OUNCES ALL-BUTTER PUFF PASTRY

Tortino di formaggio di malga ed erbette /
MALGA CHEESE AND GREENS TARTLETS

Signaterhof, Renon-Ritten, Alto Adige

Serves 4 to 6

2 CUPS UNBLEACHED
ALL-PURPOSE FLOUR

7 TABLESPOONS UNSALTED
BUTTER, SOFTENED, PLUS
MORE FOR BUTTERING PANS

2 LARGE EGGS

SALT TO TASTE

1 SMALL YELLOW ONION

4 CUPS LOOSELY PACKED
WILD HERBS, PLUS MORE
FOR SERVING

EXTRA-VIRGIN OLIVE OIL
FOR SAUTÉING

1 CUP DICED MALGA CHEESE

½ CUP WHIPPING CREAM
OR HEAVY CREAM

FRESHLY GROUND
BLACK PEPPER TO TASTE

FRESHLY GRATED NUTMEG
TO TASTE

Malga cheese takes its name from the huts in the Alps where it is traditionally produced. This cow's milk cheese uses skim milk left after churning butter, and the cheese in the Slow Food Presidium uses natural starter cultures.

Combine the flour with the 7 tablespoons butter, then work in 1 egg, a pinch of salt, and ⅓ cup water. Knead into a soft and well-combined dough. Cover and refrigerate for at least 30 minutes. Thinly slice the onion. In a skillet, sauté the 4 cups herbs and the onion in a little olive oil until herbs are wilted. Set aside to cool. Once the mixture is cool, combine it with the cheese.

Preheat oven to 350°F. Divide the dough into 4 to 6 equal pieces. Butter 4 to 6 individual tartlet pans, baking dishes, or ramekins. Roll out the pieces of dough and fit one into each pan and form into a crust. Top with a portion of the cheese and herb mixture. Whisk together the cream and the remaining egg and season with salt, pepper, and nutmeg. Pour the cream mixture over the cheese and herb mixture. Place the individual pans on a baking sheet and bake in the preheated oven until the tartlets begin to brown, 15 to 20 minutes. Cover with aluminum foil and bake until crust is cooked through, about 5 additional minutes. Unmold tartlets and serve each on a bed of herbs.

Baciocca con i funghi / POTATO AND MUSHROOM TART

Trattoria La Brinca, Ne (Genova), Liguria

Serves 4 to 6

SALT TO TASTE

1 POUND (3 TO 4) QUARANTINA POTATOES

1 MEDIUM ONION

EXTRA-VIRGIN OLIVE OIL FOR SAUTÉING

1⅔ CUPS PLUS 1 TABLESPOON UNBLEACHED ALL-PURPOSE FLOUR

1 CLOVE GARLIC

LEAVES OF 1 SPRIG PARSLEY

3 TO 4 CUPS SLICED MIXED WILD MUSHROOMS, SUCH AS PORCINI, CHANTERELLES, BLACK TRUMPETS, AND PARASOL MUSHROOMS

Quarantina potatoes grow in the interior of Liguria. They are white and fine-grained and grow nearly 1,000 feet above sea level. They are included in the Slow Food Ark of Taste.

Bring a pot of lightly salted water to a boil and cook the potatoes until tender. Drain the potatoes and as soon as they are cool enough to handle peel them and slice them thinly. Transfer the potatoes to a medium bowl. Thinly slice the onion and sauté in a small amount of olive oil until golden, then toss the onion with the potatoes. Dissolve 1 tablespoon of the flour in 2 tablespoons water with a pinch of salt. Pour over the potatoes and mix to combine. Mince the garlic and parsley. Sauté the mushrooms in a small amount of olive oil with the garlic and parsley just until softened, about 3 minutes.

Preheat the oven to 350°F.

Combine the remaining 1⅔ cups flour with a pinch of salt and enough warm water to make a soft, elastic dough. Roll out the dough and use it to line a pan with an inch or two of dough hanging over the pan. Arrange a layer of the potatoes on top of the dough. Cover that with a layer of the mushroom mixture, then continue, alternating layers, and ending with a layer of potatoes on top. Fold the empty border of the dough over the filling, pleating it decoratively. Bake in the preheated oven until golden, about 30 minutes, and serve hot.

Rotolo di spinaci / SPINACH ROLL

Adele Moretti, Bolzano-Bozen, Alto Adige

If you prefer, skip the melted butter and serve this with a light tomato and basil sauce instead.

Steam the spinach, squeeze dry, mince, and set aside. Bring a large pot of water to a boil and cook the potatoes until tender. Drain and as soon as they are cool enough to handle peel them and puree them with a potato ricer and set aside to cool completely.

Place 4 tablespoons of the butter in the top of a double boiler and melt, then add the egg yolks one at a time, whisking constantly. Whisk in the potato puree and season with salt and nutmeg. Transfer to a large bowl and allow to cool. In a separate bowl, combine the egg whites with a pinch of salt and beat to stiff peaks. Fold the egg whites and sprinkle the flour into the potato mixture, alternating between the two, adding a few spoonfuls at a time, and working gently so as to deflate the beaten whites as little as possible.

Preheat oven to 350°F. Line a baking sheet with parchment paper and spread the potato mixture a little less than ¼ inch thick on the lined pan. Smooth the top. Bake in the preheated oven until firm, about 10 minutes. Set aside to cool. Leave the oven on at 350°F.

Mince the onion and melt 1 tablespoon butter in a skillet. Sauté the onion until browned, then add the garlic, spinach, and the cream. Cook until the cream is reduced, then season with salt, pepper, and nutmeg and incorporate about half of the grated Parmigiano. Set aside to cool.

Place a piece of parchment paper on the work surface and flip the potato base onto it so that the underside is facing up. Carefully peel off the parchment that lined the pan. Spread the spinach mixture on the base and then very gently roll up, using the parchment paper underneath to help you if necessary.

Place the roll seam-side down on a clean baking sheet and reheat in the oven until warmed through. Meanwhile, melt the remaining 2 tablespoons butter. Slice the warmed roll and drizzle on the melted butter, sprinkle on the remaining Parmigiano, and serve warm.

Serves 4 to 6

1 POUND SPINACH

2 TO 3 MEDIUM POTATOES

7 TABLESPOONS UNSALTED BUTTER

3 LARGE EGGS, SEPARATED

SALT TO TASTE

FRESHLY GRATED NUTMEG TO TASTE

¼ CUP PLUS 2 TABLESPOONS UNBLEACHED ALL-PURPOSE FLOUR

1 SMALL YELLOW ONION

1 CLOVE GARLIC, MINCED

¼ CUP HEAVY CREAM OR WHIPPING CREAM

FRESHLY GROUND PEPPER TO TASTE

½ CUP GRATED ARMIGIANO REGGIANO

Crostata di cipolline / CIPOLLINI ONION TART IN A KAMUT CRUST

Osteria del Cucco, Urbania (Pesaro e Urbino), Marche

Serves 6 to 8

1⅔ CUPS KAMUT FLOUR

¾ CUP EXTRA-VIRGIN
OLIVE OIL

2 LARGE EGGS

2 POUNDS CIPOLLINI ONIONS

SALT TO TASTE

1 TABLESPOON MINCED FRESH
ROSEMARY (OPTIONAL)

Cipollini onions are small, squat, and sweet. For a vegan version of this dish, replace the eggs in the dough with about ¾ cup water. This kind of oil-based eggless dough is known as *pasta matta*, or crazy dough, in Italian. Similar tarts are made in this area with leeks, yellow bell peppers, and chestnuts.

For the dough, place the kamut flour in a bowl. Add ¼ cup olive oil. Lightly beat the eggs and add those as well, and mix with a fork until the mixture has the texture of sand. Knead very briefly to combine, then shape into a ball, wrap in plastic, and set aside to rest for at least 2 hours, but 3 hours are preferable.

Dice the onions, then either steam them or place in a pot with ½ cup water, cover, and cook over medium heat. In either case, the onions should be very soft but not browned. Drain off any liquid, season with salt and stir in the remaining ½ cup olive oil and the rosemary, if using.

When you are ready to bake, preheat the oven to 300°F. Divide the dough into two equal pieces and roll them out into thin disks. Line a cake or pie pan with one disk of dough. Spread the onion mixture on the crust, leaving a 1-inch border empty on all sides. (If liquid has collected in the onion mixture, as it sits, use a slotted spoon or skimmer to transfer it let any excess liquid drip off before you place it in the crust.) Place the second disk of dough on top and press with your fingers around the edges to seal. Pierce the top with a fork and bake in the preheated oven until golden, about 30 minutes.

Coccoi prena / SEMOLINA PIES WITH FRESH TOMATOES

Gianni Serra, Carbonia, Sardegna

The tomatoes for this dish should be quite ripe and juicy. If you already have a sourdough starter on hand, you can use it here to speed up the initial process. And if you enjoy the unusual taste of mastic oil, you can use it in place of olive oil in the filling. Just be sure to employ a light touch—too much mastic oil can be overwhelming. These can be shaped one of two ways: either as little circular pies that resemble galettes, or as half-moon turnovers.

Several days before you wish to bake the pies, make the starter. Knead together 1 ½ cups of semolina flour and ⅔ cup of all-purpose flour with about 1 cup of warm (about 85°F) water (preferably bottled mineral water). Knead until well combined, cover, and allow to ferment for two or three days in a warm (about 78°F) draft-free place.

Several hours before you plan to bake the pies, feed the starter by adding the remaining flours in two additions, incorporating enough water to keep the dough soft enough to knead each time and letting the dough rest for a couple of hours between additions.

Seed the tomatoes and chop them roughly, then toss them with salt and place them in a sieve to drain for 2 hours. Mince the garlic and tear the basil leaves, if using, into pieces. In a large bowl combine the drained tomatoes, basil, and garlic. Taste and adjust salt, season with pepper, and drizzle in a small amount of olive oil. Mix to combine and let the filling rest in a cool place for at least 1 hour.

By the end of the second rise, the dough should be at least doubled in volume. Divide the dough into equal-sized pieces, shape the pieces into balls, and set aside to rest for 1 additional hour.

When you are ready to bake the rolls, build a fire in a wood-burning oven or preheat your home oven as high as possible on the standard setting or to 400°F on the convection setting.

Generously oil and lightly flour 2 to 3 pizza pans and set aside. Roll out the balls of dough with a rolling pin. Arrange the rolled out dough on the pans and top each with an equal amount of

Serves 6 to 8

2 CUPS SEMOLINA FLOUR

1⅓ CUPS UNBLEACHED ALL-PURPOSE FLOUR, PLUS MORE FOR FLOURING PANS

1½ TO 1¾ POUNDS RIPE TOMATOES

SALT TO TASTE

3 TO 4 CLOVES GARLIC

3 TO 4 BASIL LEAVES (OPTIONAL)

FRESHLY GROUND BLACK PEPPER TO TASTE

EXTRA-VIRGIN OLIVE OIL FOR MOISTENING FILLING, OILING PANS, BRUSHING, AND DRIZZLING

Coccoi prena / SEMOLINA PIES WITH FRESH TOMATOES
continued

the filling. Pleat the perimeter of the dough so that it doesn't quite meet in the middle, leaving a hole in the center of each pie, or fold each circle of dough in half and press the edges together to seal.

Bake in the preheated oven until golden, about 1 hour. Brush with a little additional olive oil when you remove them from the oven, then allow to cool and serve warm or at room temperature.

Strudel di verdure / VEGETABLE STRUDEL
Ai Due Taxodi, Badia Pavese (Pavia), Lombardia

Serves 4 to 6

2 MEDIUM CARROTS

2 MEDIUM ZUCCHINI

1 MEDIUM EGGPLANT

½ MEDIUM YELLOW ONION

⅔ CUP SHELLED FRESH PEAS

EXTRA-VIRGIN OLIVE OIL FOR SAUTÉING

9 OUNCES SHORT-CRUST PASTRY DOUGH (SEE NOTE)

1 CUP RICOTTA

½ CUP GRATED GRANA PADANO

SALT AND FRESHLY GROUND BLACK PEPPER TO TASTE

Short-crust pastry, or pâte brisée, makes a wonderful crust for all sorts of tarts, pies, and strudels. To make about 9 ounces of short-crust pastry dough, combine 1¼ cups flour and ½ teaspoon salt in a bowl. Cut 8 tablespoons (1 stick) cold butter into small pieces and cut the butter into the flour until the mixture resembles sand. Sprinkle in 2 tablespoons of cold water and mix with a fork until the mixture forms a dough. Sprinkle in a little more water if necessary, but do not overwork. Knead a couple of times, shape the dough into a log, wrap in plastic, and refrigerate for at least 1 hour. This kind of dough freezes beautifully, so doubling the recipe is a great idea.

Preheat oven to 350°F. Cut the carrots, zucchini, eggplant, and onion into uniform dice a little less than ½ inch. In a skillet, sauté the carrots, zucchini, eggplant, onion, and peas in olive oil until softened, 3 to 5 minutes. Place a piece of parchment paper on a work surface and roll out the pastry dough to a rectangle on top of the parchment. Sprinkle the cooked vegetables over the dough. Drop spoonfuls of the ricotta on the vegetables, then sprinkle on the grated cheese. Season with salt and pepper. Use the parchment paper to roll up the dough, then twist the ends of the parchment paper to seal. Place the entire package seam-side down on a baking pan and bake in the preheated oven until dough is golden and dry to the touch, about 30 minutes. Allow to cool slightly before slicing.

CASSEROLES AND OTHER BAKED DISHES

Gattò di verdure / VEGETABLE CAKE

Barbara Torresan, Milano, Lombardia

Serves 4 to 6

BUTTER FOR BUTTERING PAN

4 MEDIUM CARROTS

3 MEDIUM ZUCCHINI

3 LARGE WHITE POTATOES

1 CUP RICOTTA

2 LARGE EGGS

1 TEASPOON MINCED FRESH THYME LEAVES

1 TEASPOON GRATED FRESH GINGER

1 TABLESPOON CURRY POWDER

SALT AND FRESHLY GROUND BLACK PEPPER TO TASTE

CRESCENZA TO TASTE

TALEGGIO TO TASTE

1 CUP PARMIGIANO REGGIANO SHAVINGS

Crescenza and taleggio are mild cow's milk cheeses from the Lombardia region. You can use any type of cheese you like, so feel free to use up any odds and ends you have in your refrigerator. You can also divide the mixture and the cheese among individual ramekins or other small baking dishes. The smaller cakes will cook in about 15 minutes.

Preheat oven to 400°F. Butter a baking pan. Steam or boil the carrots, zucchini, and potatoes until soft. Peel the potatoes, then puree the cooked vegetables together with a food mill. Combine with the ricotta and the eggs. Stir in the thyme, ginger, and curry and season with salt and pepper.

Spread about half of the vegetable mixture in an even layer in the prepared pan. Dot with pieces of crescenza and taleggio. (about half of each.) Spread half of the Parmigiano shavings on top in a single layer. Spread the remaining vegetable mixture on top and dot with the remaining crescenza and taleggio, then arrange the remaining Parmigiano shavings on top. Bake in the preheated oven until a brown, crisp crust has formed on top, 15 to 20 minutes. Serve hot.

Impasticciata / ESCAROLE AND MOZZARELLA CAKES

Hostaria de Dadà, Spello (Perugia), Umbria

Serves 4

2 HEADS ESCAROLE

SALT TO TASTE

1 (6-OUNCE) MOZZARELLA OR 6 OUNCES YOUNG CACIOTTA, DICED

½ CUP GRATED PARMIGIANO REGGIANO, PLUS MORE FOR SERVING

¼ CUP PLUS 2 TABLESPOONS EXTRA-VIRGIN OLIVE OIL, PLUS MORE FOR DRIZZLING

FRESHLY GROUND BLACK PEPPER TO TASTE

Escarole is a refreshing type of chicory popular all over Italy. It is not quite as sweet as spinach, but not as bitter as dandelion, and its leaves are tender enough to be eaten raw or cooked.

Preheat oven to 400°F. Mince the escarole as finely as you can by hand (discard any tough outer leaves and hard cores). Place the minced escarole in a bowl and season with salt. Stir in the mozzarella and ½ cup of the Parmigiano. Stir in ¼ cup plus 2 tablespoons of the olive oil. Divide the mixture among 4 single-serving earthenware baking dishes and bake in the preheated oven for 15 minutes.

Unmold the baked endive cakes and place on individual serving plates. Drizzle with olive oil and sprinkle with the grated Parmigiano. Season with pepper and serve.

Tortel di patate / BAKED POTATO CAKE

Paola Gottardi, Trento, Trentino

So venerated is the tortel di patate that a confraternity with 300 members meets annually to pay homage to it. Every town in the area prepares its own version. If you prefer a creamier texture, try boiling the potatoes, then mashing them with some cornstarch or potato starch, eggs, and grated cheese, or omit the eggs and use leftover buckwheat or corn polenta to bind the mixture. This dish is often accompanied by green cabbage cut into ribbons, dressed with a vinaigrette, and sprinkled with ground cumin, or a local cheese such as monteson. In Val di Non, it may be paired with Groppello di Revò, a red wine variety native to the area that has been saved from extinction.

Preheat oven to 350 to 400°F. Peel the potatoes and grate them on the largest holes of a four-sided grater. Place the grated potatoes in a bowl and drain off any liquid that collects in the bottom. Sprinkle on the flour and toss by hand to combine, then season with salt and pepper. Work gently so the mixture remains fluffy.

Generously oil a round, preferably copper pan with low sides. Gradually transfer the potato mixture to the pan without pressing down. Gently level the top of the potato mixture and bake in the preheated oven until golden and crisp on both sides, about 30 minutes.

Serves 6

2¼ POUNDS KENNEBEC OR OTHER STARCHY WHITE POTATOES

2 TABLESPOONS UNBLEACHED ALL-PURPOSE FLOUR

SALT AND FRESHLY GROUND BLACK PEPPER TO TASTE

EXTRA-VIRGIN OLIVE OIL FOR OILING PAN

Pinza di patate / YEAST-RISEN POTATO CAKE

Ristorante Aquila Nera, Frassilongo, Trentino

Serves 6

1 CAKE COMPRESSED YEAST
OR 2¼ TEASPOONS
(1 ENVELOPE) ACTIVE
DRY YEAST

4 CUPS UNBLEACHED
ALL-PURPOSE FLOUR

6 TO 7 MEDIUM POTATOES

SALT TO TASTE

EXTRA-VIRGIN OLIVE OIL
FOR OILING PAN

This cake is typically cooked in a round pan and cut into wedges. It is served cold, though it can be difficult to resist the temptation to taste it while it is still warm.

Place ½ cup warm water in a large bowl and crumble or stir in the yeast. Let sit until bubbly, about 5 minutes. Stir in the flour, adding a little more water if the mixture is too dry and crumbly, but keeping in mind that you will add the potatoes later and they contribute moisture. Knead until well-combined, then shape into a ball, place in a bowl, cover, and set aside to rise for 1 hour.

Meanwhile, bring a large pot of water to a boil and cook the potatoes until tender. Drain them and peel them as soon as they are cool enough to handle. Crush the potatoes, then place the prepared dough on a lightly floured surface and knead in the crushed potatoes, adding a little flour if needed and working in some salt so it is evenly distributed. The dough should be soft but not sticky.

Oil a baking pan. Roll out the dough and transfer to the pan. Sprinkle lukewarm water all over the surface. Cover loosely with a dishtowel and set aside to rise for 1 hour and 30 minutes. Preheat oven to 350°F while the pinza is rising. Bake in the preheated oven until the top is golden and crisp, about 30 minutes. Allow to cool completely before serving.

Polpettone di fagiolini carote e patate /
GREEN BEAN, CARROT, AND POTATO LOAF

Ludovica Sasso, Genova, Liguria

This vegetarian "meatloaf" cuts into neat slices that can be enjoyed hot, cold, or at room temperature.

Bring three pots of lightly salted water to a boil and separately cook the green beans, carrots, and potatoes until tender. Drain and mince cooked green beans, cut cooked carrots into dice, and peel the cooked potatoes. Soak the dried mushrooms in water for 1 hour, then carefully remove them, leaving any grit behind in the bowl, and squeeze them dry. Mince the rehydrated mushrooms.

Preheat oven to 350°F. In a pot, melt the butter with the 1 tablespoon oil. Add the onion and garlic and sauté over medium heat until they begin to color. Add the mushrooms, green beans, and carrots and sauté over low heat for 5 minutes.

In a bowl, crush the potatoes with a fork (or put them through a potato ricer). Add the green bean mixture, the eggs, the grated cheese, and the marjoram. Salt and season with pepper if desired.

Oil a loaf pan and coat with breadcrumbs. Transfer the mixture to the pan and smooth the top. Use a fork to draw a grid on the top. Brush with a little more oil and sprinkle with additional breadcrumbs. Bake in the preheated oven until a golden crust forms on top, about 30 minutes.

Serves 4

SALT TO TASTE

1 POUND GREEN BEANS

1 POUND (ABOUT 6 MEDIUM) CARROTS

1 POUND (ABOUT 3 MEDIUM) POTATOES

¼ CUP DRIED PORCINI MUSHROOMS

1 TABLESPOON UNSALTED BUTTER

1 TABLESPOON EXTRA-VIRGIN OLIVE OIL, PLUS MORE FOR OILING PAN AND DRIZZLING

1 MEDIUM YELLOW ONION, MINCED

1 CLOVE GARLIC, MINCED

6 LARGE EGGS, LIGHTLY BEATEN

1 CUP GRATED Parmigiano Reggiano

LEAVES OF 1 SPRIG MARJORAM, MINCED

FRESHLY GROUND BLACK PEPPER TO TASTE (OPTIONAL)

BREADCRUMBS FOR COATING PAN AND SPRINKLING ON TOP

Parmigiana di melanzane / EGGPLANT PARMIGIANA WITH TOMATO SAUCE

Osteria Nunzia, Benevento, Campania

Serves 4 to 6

3½ POUNDS (2 TO 3 MEDIUM) EGGPLANT

SALT TO TASTE

1 MEDIUM YELLOW ONION, MINCED

EXTRA-VIRGIN OLIVE OIL FOR SAUTÉING AND FRYING

3½ POUNDS PLUM TOMATOES, DICED

UNBLEACHED ALL-PURPOSE FLOUR FOR DREDGING

6 LARGE EGGS, LIGHTLY BEATEN

LEAVES OF 1 SPRIG BASIL

1½ POUNDS FIOR DI LATTE MOZZARELLA, CUT INTO SMALL DICE

½ CUP GRATED PARMIGIANO REGGIANO

Parmigiana should be served either at room temperature or completely cooled. In the Napoli area, the eggplant slices are dredged in flour but not egg before frying, and in some places it's traditional to include a small amount of melted chocolate between the layers.

Cut the eggplant the long way into slices about ¼-inch thick. Salt and place in a colander to drain. In a pot, sauté the onion in some olive oil until soft. Add the tomatoes and cook for 30 minutes, then process through a food mill to make a tomato sauce. Set aside.

Line a baking sheet with paper towels. In a pot with high sides, bring a generous amount of oil to frying temperature. Dredge the eggplant slices first in flour, then in beaten egg (reserve any leftover beaten egg), then fry in the hot oil until golden. Work in batches if necessary to keep from crowding the pan. Remove with a slotted spatula or skimmer and drain briefly on the prepared pan.

Preheat oven to 350°F.

Cover the bottom of a baking pan with some of the tomato sauce and a few of the basil leaves. Arrange some of the eggplant in a layer, overlapping slightly. Make a layer of mozzarella. Sprinkle with Parmigiano. Repeat layers in the same order until you have used up all of the eggplant and mozzarella and still have a little tomato sauce, a little Parmigiano, and some basil leaves. Mix together any remaining beaten egg (left over from the dredging) and the remaining tomato sauce and pour it over the top. Sprinkle on the remaining Parmigiano and basil leaves. Bake in the preheated oven until cheese has melted and the casserole is hot, about 30 minutes. Allow to cool before serving.

Parmigiana bianca di melanzane / WHITE EGGPLANT PARMIGIANA

La Bottega dell'Allegria, Corato (Bari), Puglia

Serves 4 to 6

1⅔ CUPS UNBLEACHED
ALL-PURPOSE FLOUR

4 LARGE EGGS

SALT TO TASTE

2 TO 3 MEDIUM EGGPLANT

EXTRA-VIRGIN OLIVE OIL
FOR FRYING

11 OUNCES CANESTRATO
PUGLIESE, GRATED

1 POUND SMALL MOZZARELLA
KNOTS, SHREDDED

LEAVES OF 1 BUNCH BASIL

Parmigiana of this type is "white" because it does not include tomato sauce. Mozzarella knots are small balls of mozzarella that are tied by hand. If you can't find them where you live, substitute with the small balls sold as bocconcini, or simply shred 1 pound of very fresh mozzarella by hand. Canestrato Pugliese is a sheep's cheese aged in baskets made of reeds. It is a DOP (Protected Designation of Origin) product.

Preheat oven to 350°F. Place the flour in a soup bowl. Beat the eggs with a pinch of salt in a second soup bowl. Cut the eggplant the long way into thin slices. In a pot with high sides, bring a generous amount of oil to high temperature. Dredge the eggplant slices first in flour, then in beaten egg, then fry in the hot oil until golden. Work in batches if necessary to keep from crowding the pan.

Place some of the eggplant in a layer in the bottom of a baking pan, overlapping slightly. Sprinkle with some of the canestrato, some of the mozzarella, and some of the basil leaves. Repeat layers in this order (you should have at least 2 layers of eggplant, but more is fine), ending with both types of cheese on top. Bake in the preheated oven until cheese has melted and top is browned, about 10 minutes.

Parmigiana di zucchine / ZUCCHINI PARMIGIANA

Trattoria La Bottegaccia, Simeri Crichi (Catanzaro), Calabria

Provola cheese, sometimes labeled provolone, is a mild cheese from southern Italy that melts to a smooth and stretchy consistency.

Cut the zucchini into strips the long way, salt, and set in a colander to drain for about 1 hour. Hard-boil the eggs, then peel and slice them.

Is a skillet, sauté the onion in olive oil. When it begins to turn golden, add the tomato puree and season with salt. Cook over low heat until thick, about 40 minutes.

Place the flour in a soup bowl. Line a baking sheet with paper towels and set aside. Fill a pot with high sides with the remaining ¼ cup olive oil for frying and bring to high heat. Dredge the zucchini slices in the flour and fry, turning, until golden on both sides. Remove and transfer to the prepared baking sheet.

Preheat oven to 350°F. Cover the bottom of a baking dish with a little of the tomato sauce and tear one or two basil leaves and scatter onto the sauce. Arrange some of the zucchini on top. Place a layer of hard-boiled egg slices on top of the zucchini and top the eggs with provola. Sprinkle on some of the grated Parmigiano. Repeat layers in this order until all ingredients have been used up, ending with a layer of tomato sauce on top. Tear remaining basil leaves and scatter on top.

Bake until top is golden and cheese has melted, 30 to 45 minutes. Allow to cool to just warm (not piping hot) before serving.

Serves 4

2 POUNDS (ABOUT 6 MEDIUM) ZUCCHINI

SALT TO TASTE

3 LARGE EGGS

1 SMALL TROPEA ONION, MINCED

¼ CUP EXTRA-VIRGIN OLIVE OIL, PLUS MORE FOR SAUTÉING

4 CUPS TOMATO PUREE

½ CUP UNBLEACHED ALL-PURPOSE FLOUR

5 TO 6 BASIL LEAVES

7 OUNCES PROVOLA CHEESE FROM CALABRIA, DICED

2 CUPS GRATED PARMIGIANO REGGIANO

Timballetto di friarelli e patate / FRIARELLI PEPPER AND POTATO TIMBALE

Ristorante Famiglia Principe 1968, Nocera Superiore (Salerno), Campania

Serves 4

11 OUNCES FRIARELLI
PEPPERS (SEE NOTE)

11 OUNCES (ABOUT 2
MEDIUM) POTATOES

1 CLOVE GARLIC

EXTRA-VIRGIN OLIVE OIL FOR
SAUTÉING AND DRIZZLING

SALT AND FRESHLY GROUND
BLACK PEPPER TO TASTE

1 CUP GRATED CACIORICOTTA
CILENTANO

5 TO 6 BASIL LEAVES

Friarelli are elongated sweet green peppers suitable for frying and baking.

Preheat oven to 350°F. Trim the peppers and cut into strips. Peel the potatoes and soak them in cold water for 10 minutes, then remove them from the water and cut them into julienne as well.

In a copper skillet, sauté the garlic clove in some oil. Add the potatoes and cook, stirring occasionally, for 5 minutes. Add the peppers and cook, stirring occasionally, for an additional 5 minutes. Season with salt and pepper. Vegetables should be tender but not falling apart.

Place a ring mold on a baking sheet, transfer the vegetables to the mold, and smooth the top. Sprinkle on the grated cheese. Tear the basil leaves and scatter on top. Drizzle on a little more olive oil and bake in the preheated oven until browned and set, about 20 minutes. Allow to cool slightly before removing the mold and serving.

Patate al forno / LAYERED ROASTED POTATOES

Mimma Tancredi, Potenza, Basilicata

Serves 4

1¾ POUNDS (5 TO 6 MEDIUM)
POTATOES

2 MEDIUM YELLOW ONIONS

2 TO 3 TOMATOES

EXTRA-VIRGIN OLIVE OIL
FOR DRIZZLING

SALT TO TASTE

BREADCRUMBS FOR TOPPING

GRATED AGED SHEEP'S
CHEESE TO TASTE

MINCED FRESH OREGANO
TO TASTE

Another tasty potato dish from this area calls for thinly slicing boiled and peeled potatoes and after they have cooled sautéing minced chili pepper in olive oil and pouring that hot mixture over the cool potatoes.

Preheat oven to 350°F. Peel the potatoes and cut them into slices. Thinly slice the onions and slice the tomatoes. Arrange a layer of potatoes in a baking dish. Drizzle with olive oil and season with salt. Make a layer of onions on top of the potatoes and drizzle with olive oil and season with salt. Top with a layer of the tomatoes and drizzle with oil and season with salt. Continue to arrange layers in this order, drizzling each layer with oil and seasoning with salt and ending with a layer of tomatoes, until you have used up the vegetables. Sprinkle breadcrumbs on top of the tomatoes, then grated cheese. Sprinkle on oregano. Bake in the preheated oven until potatoes are tender and top is browned, about 1 hour.

Pasticcio di Patate e Porcini / PORCINI AND POTATO CASSEROLE

Trattoria Castello, Serle (Brescia), Lombardia

Don't let the potatoes get overcooked when you're boiling them, as you want them to keep their shape and still be firm when they go into the oven.

Bring a large pot of water to a boil and cook the potatoes until just tender. Drain the potatoes and as soon as they are cool enough to handle, peel them and cut into slices 1/4 inch thick. Preheat oven to 350°F. Lightly oil a baking pan and arrange a layer of potato slices in it. Sprinkle on some of the garlic, chives, parsley, and oregano and drizzle with extra-virgin olive oil. Season with salt and pepper. Top with a layer of sliced mushrooms. Again, sprinkle on garlic, chives, parsley, and oregano and drizzle with oil, then season with salt and pepper. Continue layering the potatoes and mushrooms until you have used them up, ending with a layer of potatoes on top. Drizzle with oil and season with salt and pepper. You will need a minimum of two layers of potatoes and one of mushrooms, but if you have more that's fine. Cover the pan with aluminum foil and bake in the preheated oven until mushrooms are cooked and potatoes are completely tender, about 20 minutes.

Serves 6

5 MEDIUM WHITE POTATOES

EXTRA-VIRGIN OLIVE OIL FOR OILING PAN AND DRIZZLING

2 TO 3 CLOVES GARLIC, MINCED

1 BUNCH CHIVES, SNIPPED

LEAVES OF 1 SPRIG PARSLEY, MINCED

LEAVES OF 1 SPRIG OREGANO, MINCED, OR 1 PINCH DRIED OREGANO

SALT AND FRESHLY GROUND BLACK PEPPER TO TASTE

1½ POUNDS PORCINI MUSHROOMS, SLICED ¼-INCH THICK

Maüsc / BUCKWHEAT, POTATOES, AND GREEN BEANS CASSEROLE ▷

Oliana Maccarini, Berbenno di Valtellina (Sondrio), Lombardia

Serves 4 to 6

1 CUP BUCKWHEAT FLOUR

SALT TO TASTE

1 POUND WHITE POTATOES,
PEELED AND CHOPPED

10 OUNCES GREEN BEANS OR
YELLOW WAX BEANS, TRIMMED

13 TABLESPOONS (1 STICK
PLUS 5 TABLESPOONS)
UNSALTED BUTTER

1 SMALL YELLOW ONION, MINCED

3 TO 4 SAGE LEAVES

⅔ CUP CUBED BITTO CHEESE

⅔ CUP CUBED CASERA CHEESE

1 CUP GRATED
GRANA PADANO CHEESE

In place of the green beans, maüsc is sometimes made with borlotti beans or snow peas.

Combine the buckwheat flour with enough water to make a dough and roll out the dough about ⅛ inch thick. Cut into large pieces. Bring a large pot of salted water to a boil and add the buckwheat dough pieces, the potatoes, and the green beans. When all three items are soft, drain and then puree them through a food mill. Preheat oven to 350°F.

In a pot, melt the butter and sauté the onion and sage. Remove the sage and set aside. Add the buckwheat puree to the pot and cook, stirring frequently, until well combined. Sprinkle in all three types of cheese and stir to combine. Transfer the mixture to a cake pan where it will form a layer at least 1 ½ inches deep and smooth the top. Set the sage leaves on top. Bake in the preheated oven for 15 minutes. Scoop out with a spoon to serve.

Porri gratinati e uova al tegamino / BAKED LEEKS WITH FRIED EGGS

Osteria Burligo, Palazzago (Bergamo), Lombardia

Serves 4

SALT TO TASTE

12 SMALL LEEKS, WHITE ONLY

2 TO 3 TABLESPOONS HEAVY
CREAM OR WHIPPING CREAM

1 CUP GRATED
GRANA PADANO CHEESE

1 TABLESPOON
UNSALTED BUTTER

8 LARGE EGGS

Leeks and other onions are for more than just flavoring—they can also be the star of a dish. For this delicate main course, seek out young, tender leeks that look like scallions and use only the white parts and reserve the green for soup. Leeks tend to be silty, so cut a vertical slit in each and rinse well under running water. These go well with polenta.

Preheat oven to 350°F. Bring a pot of lightly salted water to a boil and boil the leeks until tender. Drain and cut each leek into 2 pieces. Divide the leeks among 4 individual baking dishes. Pour the cream over them, then sprinkle on the grated cheese. Bake in the preheated oven until well browned on top, about 10 minutes.

While the leeks are baking, melt the butter in a skillet and fry the eggs, leaving the yolks very soft. Season the eggs with salt and place 2 fried eggs in each individual baking dish on top of the leeks. Serve very hot.

Funghi al forno con patate / BAKED MUSHROOMS WITH POTATOES

Maria Assunta Cotini, Rovereto, Trentino

Serves 6

7 TABLESPOONS
UNSALTED BUTTER

SALT TO TASTE

1 POUND MIXED WILD
MUSHROOMS, SUCH AS
PORCINI OR CHANTERELLES

6 MEDIUM POTATOES

7 OUNCES SEMI-AGED
COW'S MILK CHEESE,
SUCH AS MALGA OR CASÈL,
THINLY SLICED

LEAVES OF 1 SPRIG
PARSLEY, MINCED

The potatoes used here should be neither purely waxy nor overly starchy. Yukon gold potatoes are a solid choice. The mushrooms should be exceeding fresh and firm. And the cheese can be one of several types found in Trentino, such as malga, made from the milk of cow's that graze freely in the region's lush pastures, or casèl. Whatever type of cheese you choose, make sure that it melts well.

Preheat oven to 350°F. Thickly butter the bottom and sides of a baking pan with some of the butter. Fill a bowl with lightly salted cold water and soak the mushrooms for a few minutes to clean them. Drain and gently pat dry with paper towels. Chop the mushrooms. Peel and thinly slice the potatoes. Make a layer of potato slices in the bottom of the prepared pan. Season with salt. Cover with a layer of the mushrooms. Season with salt. Make a layer of the cheese slices on top. Continue to make layers in this order, seasoning each layer lightly with salt and ending with a layer of potatoes. Set aside a little of the cheese. Pour ½ cup lukewarm water down the side of the pan. Sprinkle on the parsley, then cut the remaining butter into pieces and dot the surface with the butter. Bake in the preheated oven until cheese has melted and top is golden, about 40 minutes. Sprinkle with the reserved cheese and serve.

Patate gratinate / POTATOES WITH MELTED CHEESE

Enrica Berthod, Courmayeur, Valle d'Aosta

Starchy potatoes can stand up to even a longer aged fontina, which will be fairly sharp. In this area, boiled potatoes are also hollowed out and then stuffed with a filling made by crushing the potato interiors with minced onion and parsley. The Fêta di Trifolle celebrates the humble potato every year in August.

Preheat oven to 350°F. Butter a baking pan with the butter and set aside. Place the potatoes in a pot with cold water to cover, bring to a boil, and cook until tender. Drain and peel, then cut into thin slices. Arrange the potato slices in the prepared pan. Place the slices of cheese on top of the potatoes. Season with salt and pepper, sprinkle with a touch of nutmeg, and bake in the preheated oven until cheese has melted and browned, about 10 minutes.

Serves 4

1 TABLESPOON UNSALTED BUTTER

4 MEDIUM POTATOES

4 OUNCES FONTINA, SLICED

SALT AND FRESHLY GROUND BLACK PEPPER TO TASTE

FRESHLY GRATED NUTMEG TO TASTE

Pomodori arrosto / ROASTED TOMATOES

Paola Braccioni, Urbania (Pesaro e Urbino), Marche

Baking tomatoes causes their liquid to evaporate and intensifies their flavor. These may be served hot or cold.

Preheat oven to 350°F. Lightly oil a baking pan. Mince the garlic and fennel. Combine with the breadcrumbs and 3 tablespoons oil and season with salt. Halve the tomatoes horizontally. Place the tomatoes cut side down in the prepared baking pan. Roast in the preheated oven for 30 minutes.

Remove the pan from the oven, flip the tomatoes over, and sprinkle the breadcrumb mixture all over their cut sides, which should now be facing up. Return to the oven and bake until any liquid has evaporated, about 20 additional minutes.

Serves 4 to 6

3 TABLESPOONS EXTRA-VIRGIN OLIVE OIL, PLUS MORE FOR PAN

3 CLOVES GARLIC

LEAVES OF 1 SPRIG WILD FENNEL

2 CUPS BREADCRUMBS

SALT TO TASTE

8 TOMATOES

Fiori di zucchina al cacioricotta /
BAKED SQUASH BLOSSOMS WITH CACIORICOTTA CHEESE

Ristorante Peppe Zullo, Orsara di Puglia (Foggia), Puglia

Serves 4 to 6

EXTRA-VIRGIN OLIVE OIL
FOR OILING AND DRIZZLING

2 CUPS GRATED
CACIORICOTTA

1 LARGE EGG

LEAVES OF 1 SPRIG BASIL

SALT TO TASTE

30 SQUASH BLOSSOMS

½ CUP DRY WHITE WINE

Cacioricotta is made using a process that combines the steps for making ricotta with those for making traditional cheese with rennet. It can be fresh or aged, and for this recipe you want the latter type, though it shouldn't be aged overly long—just enough to make it firm for grating. To prepare squash blossoms, pinch out their pistils, then shake them over the sink to remove any grit. If they seem particularly dirty, rinse quickly and dry on paper towels.

Preheat oven to 400°F. Oil a baking pan large enough to hold the blossoms in one layer. Combine the grated cheese and the egg. Reserve a few basil leaves for garnish, then mince the rest and add to the cheese mixture. Season with salt and drizzle in a little olive oil. Stuff the blossoms with this mixture and place in a single layer in the prepared pan. Sprinkle the wine over the blossoms and bake in the preheated oven for 15 minutes. Garnish with reserved basil and serve hot.

Friggitelli alla verza / STUFFED PEPPERS

Ristorante Pietrino e Renata, Genzano di Roma (Roma), Lazio

Friarelli peppers (also known as friggitelli) are long, thin green peppers that are sweet rather than spicy.

Preheat oven to 350˚F. Cut off the stems of the peppers and seed them, but leave them whole. To make the stuffing, cut the cabbage into ribbons. Bring a pot of water to a boil and cook the cabbage until soft, then drain and place in a bowl. Moisten the bread with water and tear it into the bowl with the cabbage. Add the egg, grated cheese, thyme leaves, onion, and garlic. Season with salt and pepper.

Moisten the mixture with a little olive oil and mix until well-combined. Stuff the peppers with the mixture and arrange them in a baking pan. Top each pepper with 1 tablespoon tomato puree. Gently pour in ½ cup water at the side of the pan so that you don't douse the peppers. Sprinkle on the breadcrumbs and bake in the preheated oven until the water in the pan has evaporated and the peppers are heated through and browned on top, about 20 minutes. Allow to cool to room temperature before serving.

Serves 4

12 FRIARELLI PEPPERS

½ HEAD Savoy CABBAGE

1 2- TO 3-INCH SQUARE PIECE OF DAY-OLD BREAD, CRUSTS REMOVED

1 LARGE EGG, LIGHTLY BEATEN

½ CUP GRATED Parmigiano Reggiano

LEAVES OF 1 SPRIG THYME, MINCED

1 MEDIUM YELLOW ONION, MINCED

2 CLOVES GARLIC, MINCED

SALT AND FRESHLY GROUND BLACK PEPPER TO TASTE

EXTRA-VIRGIN OLIVE OIL FOR MOISTENING

¾ CUP TOMATO PUREE

BREADCRUMBS FOR TOPPING

Cialde di melanzane / EGGPLANT CUPS

Antonella Iadevaia, Cuneo, Piemonte

Serves 4

1 MEDIUM EGGPLANT

SALT TO TASTE

EXTRA-VIRGIN OLIVE OIL
FOR BRUSHING

GRATED PARMIGIANO
REGGIANO TO TASTE

These clever containers can be used to serve all sorts of things—great for finger foods at a cocktail party.

Slice the eggplant into thin rounds, toss with salt, and let drain in a colander for at least 1 hour. Preheat oven to 325°F. Line a baking pan large enough to hold the eggplant slices in a single layer with parchment paper. Dry the eggplant slices and brush them on both sides with olive oil. Arrange them in a single layer in the lined pan. Sprinkle on the grated cheese and bake in the preheated oven until golden, 10 to 20 minutes.

While the eggplant slices are still warm, set them in small round bowls or ramekins and use a spoon to push the center of each slice toward the bottom. Allow the eggplant to cool completely in the bowls, then remove gently so they keep their shape.

Zabbinata / ROASTED MIXED VEGETABLES

Osteria del Cacciatore, Castrofilippo (Agrigento), Sicilia

Serves 4 to 6

2 POTATOES

2 DARK GREEN ZUCCHINI

2 LIGHT GREEN ZUCCHINI

2 BELL PEPPERS

½ CUP CHERRY TOMATOES

LEAVES OF 1 SPRIG BASIL

EXTRA-VIRGIN OLIVE OIL
FOR DRIZZLING

SALT AND FRESHLY GROUND
BLACK PEPPER TO TASTE

MINCED FRESH OREGANO
TO TASTE

¼ CUP BREADCRUMBS

Zabbinata is as versatile as it is delicious—it can be served as a side dish or as a main course, and it is good hot or at room temperature. This is traditionally made in a wood-burning oven, but it tastes almost as good when baked in a standard indoor oven.

Preheat a wood-burning oven if you have one, or preheat a standard oven to 400°F. Peel the potatoes and chop. Chop both types of zucchini. Remove the seeds and white ribs from the peppers and chop those as well. In a baking pan combine the potatoes, zucchini, peppers, tomatoes, and basil leaves. Drizzle with a generous amount of olive oil and season with salt, pepper, and oregano. Sprinkle on the breadcrumbs and bake in the preheated oven until vegetables are soft, about 30 minutes.

Verdure ripiene / STUFFED VEGETABLES

Ristorante Nuovo Piccolo Mondo, San Remo (Imperia), Liguria

Serves 4 to 6

2 POUNDS VEGETABLES
SUITABLE FOR STUFFING,
SUCH AS ZUCCHINI,
ONIONS, BELL PEPPERS, AND
EGGPLANT

¼ CUP EXTRA-VIRGIN OLIVE
OIL PLUS MORE FOR OILING
BAKING DISH

3 MEDIUM POTATOES

4 OUNCES SNOW PEAS OR
GREEN BEANS

3 LARGE EGGS, LIGHTLY
BEATEN

½ CUP GRATED
PARMIGIANO REGGIANO

LEAVES OF 1 SPRIG
MARJORAM, MINCED

SALT TO TASTE

¼ CUP BREADCRUMBS

The vegetables for this dish should be young and tender. Some types of mushrooms are also suitable for stuffing. These improve as they sit and are delicious at any temperature—a great choice for feeding a crowd in summer.

First, prepare the vegetables to be used as containers. If using zucchini or onions for stuffing, blanch them (whole) for 5 minutes to soften. Drain any blanched vegetables. Scoop out the flesh of any zucchini and reserve it. Scoop out the centers of the onions and reserve, keeping the large external layers for stuffing. There is no need to cook peppers or eggplant. If using bell peppers, cut in half the long way, remove and discard seeds, salt the interiors, and set aside to drain. If using eggplant, cut in half the long way, scoop out the pulp while leaving the shell whole, salt cut sides lightly, and set aside to drain.

Preheat oven to 400°F. Lightly oil a baking dish and set aside. Bring a large pot of water to a boil and cook the potatoes until tender, then drain, peel, and crush with a fork or potato ricer. Blanch the snow peas and mince with any reserved zucchini and onion pulp. In a bowl, combine the minced snow pea mixture, potatoes, eggs, Parmigiano, marjoram, and 3 tablespoons olive oil. Season with salt. Mix with a wooden spatula until well combined. Fill the prepared vegetable containers with his mixture, placing them side by side in the prepared baking dish as you do. Sprinkle on the breadcrumbs and drizzle on the remaining 1 tablespoon olive oil. Bake in the preheated oven until browned on top, about 30 minutes.

Melanzane rosse di Rotonda ripiene /
ROUND EGGPLANT WITH WHITE BEAN AND PORCINI STUFFING

Ristorante Da Peppe, Rotonda (Potenza), Basilicata

The Rotonda area is known for orange-red eggplant, some with green streaks, that most likely came from Africa in the late nineteenth century. They resemble persimmons more than standard purple eggplant. The leaves of Rotonda eggplant are edible, and the flesh is fruitier than that of standard eggplant.

If using dried beans, soak them overnight, then drain them. Place the beans in a pot with water to cover, bring to a boil, then simmer until soft, about 1 hour. Drain and set aside. In a skillet, sauté the porcini in a small amount of olive oil with the garlic until soft. Discard garlic.

Cut off the cap of each eggplant and set aside. Use a paring knife to hollow out the eggplant, reserving the pulp. Bring a large pot of salted water to a boil and cook the eggplant shells for 10 minutes and remove with a slotted spoon or skimmer to drain. Boil the eggplant pulp for 5 minutes and drain. When the pulp is cool enough to handle, squeeze dry.

Preheat oven to 350°F. In a bowl, crush the eggplant pulp with a fork and combine with the porcini, beans, breadcrumbs, Parmigiano, and the egg. Stir to combine. Stir in the parsley and season with pepper, then stuff the eggplant shells with the mixture. Arrange the stuffed eggplant in a baking pan and place the reserved caps on top. Bake in the preheated oven for 7 minutes.

Serves 10

¾ CUP SHELLED FRESH POVERELLO BEANS OR DRIED WHITE BEANS

2 CUPS SLICED FRESH PORCINI MUSHROOMS

EXTRA-VIRGIN OLIVE OIL FOR SAUTÉING

1 CLOVE GARLIC

20 MEDIUM ROTONDA RED EGGPLANT OR OTHER ROUND EGGPLANT

SALT TO TASTE

2½ CUPS FRESH BREADCRUMBS

¾ CUP GRATED PARMIGIANO REGGIANO

1 LARGE EGG, LIGHTLY BEATEN

LEAVES OF 1 SPRIG PARSLEY, MINCED

FRESHLY GROUND BLACK PEPPER TO TASTE

Melanzane ripiene / STUFFED EGGPLANT

La Locanda di Nonna Mena, San Vito dei Normanni (Brindisi), Puglia

Serves 4

7 OUNCES STALE BREAD

2 MEDIUM EGGPLANT

ROCK SALT TO TASTE

EXTRA-VIRGIN OLIVE OIL FOR
PAN-FRYING AND SAUTÉING

½ ACQUAVIVA RED ONION

3 CUPS FIASCHETTO
TOMATO PUREE

LEAVES OF 1 SPRIG BASIL

SALT TO TASTE

1 CLOVE GARLIC

LEAVES OF 1 SPRIG PARSLEY

2 LARGE EGGS

2 CUPS GRATED AGED
SHEEP'S CHEESE

MINT LEAVES FOR GARNISH

Flat red onions from Acquaviva delle Fonti in the province of Bari are known for their sweetness, due in part to the fact that they grow in well-aerated, potassium-rich soil. They are celebrated every year at a local fair and also have their own Slow Food Presidium. Fiaschetto tomatoes also have their own Slow Food Presidium. They are small, extremely juicy, oval heirloom red tomatoes that all but disappeared before they were rediscovered by the Torre Guaceto Natural Reserve. Today there are two producers cultivating them in their native area.

Soak the bread in water until soft, then squeeze dry and crumble. Cut the eggplant in half the long way. Peel off a few strips of eggplant skin using a zester. Cut the flesh into cubes, leaving the shells intact. Toss the cubes with rock salt and set in a colander or sieve to drain. When the eggplant cubes have given up their liquid, fill a pot with high sides with a generous amount of olive oil, bring the oil to high temperature, and fry the eggplant cubes until golden. Fry the strips of peel until crisp. Set both aside separately.

Preheat oven to 325°F. Mince the onion. In a skillet, sauté the onion in a small amount of olive oil until it just begins to color. Add the tomato puree and basil leaves, season with salt, and cook, stirring frequently, until reduced, about 20 minutes.

Mince the garlic and parsley and in a bowl combine with the crumbled bread, the cooked eggplant cubes, eggs, and grated cheese for the stuffing.

Spread the tomato sauce in the bottom of a baking pan large enough to hold the eggplant shells in a single layer. Pan-fry the eggplant shells in a very small amount of oil, then fill them with the prepared stuffing and place on top of the tomato sauce. Bake in the preheated oven until set, 20 to 30 minutes. To serve, place the eggplant shells on a platter. Top with the tomato sauce from the pan, then garnish with mint leaves and reserved strips of fried eggplant peel.

Cipolle rosse ripiene / RED ONIONS WITH EGGPLANT STUFFING

Rosaria Salvatore, Tropea (Vibo Valentia), Calabria

Serves 4 to 6

2 MEDIUM EGGPLANT

SALT TO TASTE

1 POUND PLUM TOMATOES

EXTRA-VIRGIN OLIVE OIL FOR
OILING AND SAUTÉING

1 SPRING ONION

FRESHLY GROUND BLACK
PEPPER TO TASTE

LEAVES OF 1 SPRIG
OREGANO, MINCED

8 LARGE RED ONIONS

Save the onion pulp that you scoop out of these red onions for another use—it makes a tasty addition to all kind of vegetable dishes. The boiling mutes the sharpness of the flavor.

Cut the eggplant into small dice, toss with salt, and allow to drain for a couple of hours. Peel, seed, and chop the tomatoes.

Preheat oven to 400°F. Oil a baking pan large enough to hold the red onions in a single layer and set aside. Thinly slice the spring onion and sauté in olive oil in a skillet until it begins to brown, then add the tomatoes and the drained eggplant and sauté until tomatoes have collapsed and eggplant is browned, 5 to 6 minutes. Season with salt and pepper and stir in oregano. Bring a large pot of water to a boil and add the red onions (left whole). Cook the whole onions for 5 minutes, then drain. Slice off the tops of the onions and hollow them out. Stuff the onions with the eggplant mixture. Arrange in the prepared baking pan and bake in the preheated oven for 45 minutes.

Zucca al forno / ROASTED SQUASH

Barbara Torresan, Milano, Lombardia

Serves 4 to 6

1 WINTER SQUASH

LEAVES OF 1 SPRIG SAGE

LEAVES OF 1 SPRIG ROSEMARY

SALT TO TASTE

Honey TO TASTE

Winter squash comes in a rainbow of varieties. Choose one with firm, compact flesh for this dish. This can also be used as a stuffing for pasta or turned into a puree or even soup. Pureed winter squash with a drizzle of extra-virgin olive oil also makes an excellent sandwich filling that pairs well with ricotta, spinach, and a sprinkling of minced fresh thyme.

Preheat oven to 275°F. Peel and seed the squash and cut into medium-thick slices. Arrange the squash slices in a single layer on a baking pan. Mince the sage and sprinkle it on the squash. Sprinkle on the rosemary. Season with salt to taste, then drizzle on a little honey.

Roast in the preheated oven until browned, about 30 minutes.

Girelle di crespella gratinate / BAKED SPINACH CRÊPE PINWHEELS

Ristorante Silvio La Storia a Tavola, Cutigliano (Pistoia), Toscana

Serves 4 to 6

2 LARGE EGGS

1 CUP WHOLE MILK

1 CUP RICE FLOUR

1 POUND SPINACH

LEAVES OF 1 BUNCH
FLAT-LEAF PARSLEY

1¼ CUPS RICOTTA

2 CUPS GRATED
PARMIGIANO REGGIANO

SALT AND FRESHLY GROUND
BLACK PEPPER TO TASTE

FRESHLY GRATED NUTMEG
TO TASTE

7 TABLESPOONS UNSALTED
BUTTER, PLUS MORE FOR PAN

Be sure to make the batter for the crêpes far enough in advance that it can rest for a full hour. This is a very pretty dish that can be prepared ahead of time and baked just before serving, making it a good choice for serving a crowd.

Beat the eggs and milk in a bowl. Whisk in the flour so that there are no lumps. Set aside to rest for 1 hour. Meanwhile, prepare the filling. Rinse the spinach and steam in the water clinging to its leaves, then squeeze dry and mince together with the parsley leaves. Transfer to a bowl and combine with the ricotta and 3 tablespoons of the Parmigiano. Season with salt, pepper, and nutmeg.

Place a crêpe pan or other nonstick skillet over medium heat and make thin crêpes of the batter. Use about ½ cup batter at a time (depending on the size of the pan). Repeat until you have used up all of the batter.

Preheat oven to 350°F. Butter a baking pan and set aside. Melt the 7 tablespoons butter. Fill the crêpes with the spinach filling, spreading the filling to cover as much of the surface as possible, and roll them into cylinders, then cut the cylinders into slices about ¾-inch wide. Arrange the slices in the prepared baking pan, seam side down. Drizzle on the melted butter and sprinkle on the remaining grated Parmigiano. Bake in the preheated oven until browned, about 10 minutes. Serve hot.

Zucchine e fiori di zucca in salsa di pomodoro /
ZUCCHINI AND SQUASH BLOSSOMS IN TOMATO SAUCE

Ristorante delle Rose, Mongrando (Biella), Piemonte

Sometimes small zucchini are sold with their blossoms attached. To prepare the blossoms for cooking, pinch out their pistils, rinse gently, and set them upside-down on a clean towel to drain.

Preheat oven to 325°F. Peel, seed, and chop the tomatoes. In a small bowl, beat 2 of the eggs. Add about half of the ricotta, about ¼ cup of the Parmigiano, salt, pepper, and thyme. Transfer this mixture to a pastry bag and pipe it into the blossoms. Place the filled blossoms on a baking pan and sprinkle with another ¼ cup of the Parmigiano. Cut 2 tablespoons of the butter into small pieces and dot the blossoms with the butter, then bake in the preheated oven for 10 minutes. Leave the oven at 325°F.

Meanwhile, bring a large pot of lightly salted water to a boil and blanch the zucchini (left whole) until tender. Slice the zucchini in half lengthwise and scoop out the flesh. (Reserve for another use.) Lightly beat the remaining 2 eggs and the remaining ricotta. Crush the amaretti and stir them in. Stir in about ¼ cup of the Parmigiano and season with salt and pepper. Stuff the zucchini with this mixture and place in a baking pan that will hold them in one layer. Cut the remaining 4 tablespoons butter into small pieces and dot the zucchini with the butter. Sprinkle on the remaining grated Parmigiano and bake in the preheated oven for 10 minutes.

To make a tomato sauce, sauté the garlic cloves in extra-virgin olive oil. Add the tomatoes and the basil leaves and cook until reduced. Serve tomato sauce warm with blossoms and zucchini.

Serves 4

1 POUND TOMATOES

4 LARGE EGGS

¾ CUP RICOTTA

1 CUP GRATED PARMIGIANO REGGIANO

SALT AND FRESHLY GROUND BLACK TO TASTE

MINCED FRESH THYME TO TASTE

8 SQUASH BLOSSOMS

6 TABLESPOONS UNSALTED BUTTER

8 SMALL ZUCCHINI

5 TO 6 HARD AMARETTI COOKIES

2 CLOVES GARLIC

EXTRA-VIRGIN OLIVE OIL FOR SAUTÉING

6 BASIL LEAVES

SAUTÉS, BRAISES, AND GRILLED VEGETABLES

Patate in padella / SAUTÉED POTATOES

Anna Marcoz, Aosta, Valle d'Aosta

Serves 4

4 POTATOES

SALT TO TASTE

1 MEDIUM YELLOW ONION

1 LEEK

2 TABLESPOONS
UNSALTED BUTTER

Potatoes are eaten everywhere in Italy, but they are a true staple in the north. Look for locally grown potatoes in your area—they will be more flavorful and really add personality to this simple dish.

Scrub the potatoes and place them, unpeeled, in a large pot with cold water to cover by a few inches. Salt lightly, bring to a boil, then simmer until the potatoes are soft enough to pierce with a fork, but still holding their shape. Drain and as soon as they are cool enough to handle, peel them and slice them.

Mince the onion and the white portion of the leek. Melt the butter in a skillet and sauté the leek and onion until golden. Add the potatoes and cook, stirring frequently but trying not to break up the potatoes, until the potatoes are browned. Taste and adjust salt. Serve hot.

Pipi e patate / POTATO AND PEPPER SAUTÉ

Luisa San le, Monterosso Calabro (Vibo Valentia), Calabria

Serves 4

1½ TO 1¾ POUNDS (4 TO 5
MEDIUM) POTATOES

1½ TO 1¾ POUNDS
(4 TO 5 MEDIUM) ROUND
GREEN PEPPERS

EXTRA-VIRGIN OLIVE OIL FOR
PAN-FRYING AND SAUTÉING

10 CHERRY TOMATOES

SALT TO TASTE

In Calabria, peppers and potatoes are often paired. Round green peppers are the peppers typically used in this dish, but you can substitute red or yellow bell peppers if you prefer them.

Peel the potatoes and slice them thinly. Heat a couple of inches of oil in a skillet and cook the potato slices until browned but only about half-cooked, turning once and working in batches if necessary. Remove the potatoes with a skimmer as they are browned and reserve the oil. Cut the peppers into strips and fry them in the same oil. Wipe out the skillet and add a little oil for sautéing. Chop the tomatoes and add them to the skillet. Cook until they have collapsed and given up their liquid, then add the peppers and the potatoes are fully tender. Season with salt and remove from the heat to cool. Serve warm, but not piping hot.

Patugol / CRUSHED POTATOES WITH ONION AND CHEESE

Ristorante Mezzosoldo, Spiazzo, Trentino

This dish, which is something like a polenta made with potatoes, is endlessly adaptable. Good additions include ribbons of Savoy cabbage or chard, green beans, and chopped zucchini.

Bring a pot of salted water to a boil. Peel the potatoes and boil until tender. Remove the potatoes and pour off most of the cooking water, but leave about ½ cup in the pot. Return the potatoes to the pot and crush them in the pot along with the cooking water until they form a fairly smooth puree. Thinly slice the onion and in another pot or skillet, melt the butter and sauté the onions in the butter until golden. Stir in the grated cheese. Let the onion mixture cool slightly—it should be warm enough that the cheese is still melted, but it should not be piping hot—and then gradually add it into the potato mixture, stirring to combine well. Serve warm.

Serves 4

SALT TO TASTE

3 TO 4 MEDIUM POTATOES

1 MEDIUM WHITE ONION

7 TABLESPOONS UNSALTED BUTTER

1 CUP GRATED TRENTINGRANO CHEESE

Rösti / STOVETOP POTATO CAKE

Trattoria Altavilla, Bianzone (Sondrio), Lombardia

The trickiest part of this recipe is turning the potato cake once you have shaped it. You can either flip it like a pancake, using a spatula, or slide it out of the skillet and onto a plate, then turn the skillet face down over the plate and, holding the bottom of the plate firmly in place, flip both skillet and plate so that the uncooked side of the cake is now resting on the bottom of the pan.

Place the potatoes in a pot with water to cover and season with salt. Bring to a boil, then turn down to a simmer and cook until potatoes are tender. Drain the potatoes and when they are cool peel them and grate them on the medium holes of a box grater.

Melt the butter in a large skillet and sauté until soft and beginning to brown. Add the grated potatoes and cook, stirring gently with a wooden spoon, until browned, about 10 minutes. Then, press the potatoes and onions firmly into the pan to compact them into a cake. Cook, turning once, until browned on both sides and serve hot.

Serves 4 to 6

7 TO 8 POTATOES

SALT TO TASTE

2 TABLESPOONS UNSALTED BUTTER

⅓ CUP ONION CUT INTO JULIENNE

Caponata al miele di Zagara / SAUTÉED EGGPLANT AND PEPPERS WITH CAPERS, OLIVES, AND ZAGARA HONEY

Ristorante Don Camillo, Siracusa, Sicilia

Serves 4 to 6

2 LARGE GIARRATANA ONIONS

LEAVES OF 1 SPRIG BASIL

¼ CUP EXTRA-VIRGIN OLIVE OIL, PLUS MORE FOR FRYING

2 POUNDS PACHINO TOMATOES, HALVED

2 LARGE EGGPLANT

SALT TO TASTE

1 RIB CELERY

20 GREEN OLIVES, PITTED AND CRUSHED

¼ CUP PANTELLERIA CAPERS

½ CUP ZAGARA HONEY

½ CUP WHITE WINE VINEGAR

FRESHLY GROUND BLACK PEPPER TO TASTE

3 TABLESPOONS CHOPPED BLANCHED ALMONDS

1 TABLESPOON SLICED BLANCHED ALMONDS

The sweet white onions from the mountain town of Giarratana grow to a large size. A Slow Food Presidium is dedicated to them. Pachino tomatoes are an IGP (Protected Geographic Origin) product and originate in the town of the same name near Siracusa. They are small and spectacularly sweet. The capers that grow on the island of Pantelleria, south of Sicily, are large and meaty and are preserved in salt. They are part of the Slow Food Ark of Taste, as is Zagara honey, which is produced by bees that feed on citrus flowers.

Mince ½ onion. Sauté the minced onion and basil leaves in 1 tablespoon oil over low heat until softened, then add the tomatoes and continue cooking, stirring occasionally, until the tomatoes have given up their liquid and broken down. Process with a food mill into a smooth puree and set aside.

Cut the eggplant into ¾-inch dice. Soak in a bowl of cold salt water for a few minutes, then drain and pat dry. Line a baking sheet with paper towels and place several inches of oil for frying in a pot with high sides and bring to high temperature. Fry the cubes of eggplant, working in batches if necessary to keep from crowding the pan, in the oil until golden. Remove with a skimmer or slotted spoon and place on the prepared pan to drain.

Meanwhile, julienne the remaining 1½ onions and chop the celery. Blanch each, separately, in boiling salted water. Drain and set aside.

In a large skillet, heat 3 tablespoons olive oil and place over medium heat. Add the onions, eggplant, celery, olives, capers, and tomato puree and cook, stirring frequently, until thickened and combined. Whisk together the honey and the vinegar and stir this mixture into the caponata. Taste and adjust salt and pepper and remove from the heat. Let the caponata cool. Meanwhile, fry the chopped almonds in olive oil until golden. Serve caponata cold or at room temperature and garnish with the chopped and sliced almonds just before serving.

Ratatoia agrodolce / SWEET AND SOUR SAUTÉED VEGETABLES

Trattoria Tre Merli, Morano sul Po (Alessandria), Piemonte

Serves 4

2 YELLOW BELL PEPPERS

1 RED BELL PEPPER

2 MEDIUM YELLOW ONIONS

3 MEDIUM CARROTS

1 RIB CELERY

2 MEDIUM ZUCCHINI

1 CUP EXTRA-VIRGIN
OLIVE OIL

1 CUP WINE VINEGAR

¼ CUP SUGAR

10 WHOLE CLOVES

1 CUP TOMATO PUREE

SALT TO TASTE

Piemonte has a rich tradition of French-influenced cooking, including this ratatouille. In the Cuneo area, the vinegar and cloves are omitted, and sometimes cherry tomatoes and green beans are added to the mix.

Seed the peppers, cut away any white ribs, and cut into medium dice. Cut the onions, carrots, celery, zucchini, and peppers into medium dice. Keep the various vegetables separate.

Place the oil in a large skillet and place over medium heat. Add the onion and cook, stirring frequently, until soft. Add the carrots and celery and cook, stirring frequently, for 10 minutes, then add the zucchini and peppers and cook for 15 minutes. The vegetables should soften and color, but do not allow them to brown too aggressively. Adjust heat if necessary. Stir in the vinegar, sugar, cloves, and tomato puree. Season to taste with salt. Cook for an additional 10 minutes, then remove from the heat and allow to cool. Remove cloves before serving.

Melanzane al funghetto / GARLICKY SOFT EGGPLANT

Anna Cappellotto, Venezia, Veneto

Serves 4 to 6

4 LONG EGGPLANT

4 CLOVES GARLIC

EXTRA-VIRGIN OLIVE OIL
FOR SAUTÉING

SALT TO TASTE

Don't skimp on the olive oil for this dish, as it provides much of the flavor.

Quarter the eggplant. Cut a wedge off of each quarter from the center of the eggplant to remove the seeds, then slice the long way. Mince the garlic and sauté in a generous amount of olive oil until fragrant. Add the eggplant, season with salt, and cook, stirring frequently, until it browns. Cover and cook over low heat for about 5 minutes. Check the pan and if it seems to be drying out, add a few tablespoons of water. Continue cooking, covered, until the eggplant is extremely soft.

Peperoni con olive e capperi /
BELL PEPPER SAUTÉ WITH OLIVES AND CAPERS
Ristorante Il Sebeto, Volla (Napoli), Campania

Capers and olives add a piquant salty punch to this colorful dish. Use a combination of red, yellow, and orange peppers.

Seed the peppers and cut away any white ribs, then cut into julienne. Place the oil in a large skillet and add the garlic. When the garlic begins to color, add the peppers, capers, and olives. Season with salt and cook over medium heat, stirring constantly with a wooden spoon, until very soft, about 30 minutes. Be sure the mixture doesn't stick to the bottom of the pan; if it begins to stick, add a few tablespoons of water. Sprinkle with parsley and serve.

Serves 4

1½ POUNDS BELL PEPPERS

¾ CUP EXTRA-VIRGIN OLIVE OIL

1 CLOVE GARLIC

2 TABLESPOONS CAPERS, RINSED AND DRAINED

⅔ CUP PITTED BLACK AND GREEN OLIVES

SALT TO TASTE

¼ CUP MINCED PARSLEY

Peperoni verdi al tegame / GREEN PEPPER SAUTÉ
Ilda Cardinali, Passignano sul Trasimeno (Perugia), Umbria

Cooking vegetables low and slow really brings out their sweetness.

Slice the onion as thinly as possible. Place the oil in a pot and add the onion. Cook over low heat, stirring occasionally, until very soft, about 20 minutes. Seed the peppers and remove any white ribs, then cut into julienne and add to the pot with the onions. Cook, stirring with a wooden spoon, for 10 additional minutes. Add the tomatoes, season with salt and pepper, cover with a tight-fitting lid, and cook over low heat for an additional 30 minutes, shaking the pot occasionally to be sure the vegetables aren't sticking. Serve hot.

Serves 4

1 LARGE YELLOW ONION

¼ CUP EXTRA-VIRGIN OLIVE OIL

1 POUND SWEET GREEN PEPPERS

11 OUNCES PLUM TOMATOES, PEELED, SEEDED, AND CHOPPED

SALT AND FRESHLY GROUND BLACK PEPPER TO TASTE

Peperonata / SAUTÉED BELL PEPPERS

Ristorante Antica Barca, Cavenago d'Adda (Lodi), Lombardia

Serves 4

1 SMALL YELLOW ONION

1 RED BELL PEPPER

1 YELLOW BELL PEPPER

1 GREEN BELL PEPPER

1 EGGPLANT

EXTRA-VIRGIN OLIVE OIL
FOR SAUTÉING

¼ CUP CHOPPED
GREEN BEANS

2 TABLESPOONS CHOPPED
TOMATOES OR TOMATO PUREE

SALT TO TASTE

Peperonata is cooked and eaten all over Italy. The version from Piemonte has no tomatoes, while in Sicilia peperonata incorporates olives and potatoes. In the Cremona area of Lombardia, carrots take the place of the green beans and eggplant. Cooked peperonata can be transferred to sterilized glass jars and pressure-canned for 30 minutes for long-term storage.

Thinly slice the onion. Seed the peppers, cut away any white ribs, and dice. Dice the eggplant. In a large skillet, sauté the onion in olive oil until golden. Add the peppers, green beans, and eggplant. Stir to combine, then stir in the chopped tomatoes. Season with salt to taste and cook over low heat, stirring occasionally, until very soft.

Patao / SAUTÉED GREEN BEANS AND POTATOES

Ristorante San Sebastian, Valdaone, Trentino

Serves 4

2 POUNDS (ABOUT 6 MEDIUM)
STARCHY POTATOES, PEELED

1¼ TO 1½ POUNDS GREEN
BEANS, TRIMMED

SALT TO TASTE

1 MEDIUM YELLOW ONION

1 CLOVE GARLIC

11 TABLESPOONS (1 STICK
PLUS 3 TABLESPOONS)
UNSALTED BUTTER

1 CUP GRATED AGED CHEESE

7 OUNCES YOUNG
SPRESSA CHEESE

FRESHLY GROUND BLACK
PEPPER TO TASTE

This rich, buttery puree is often served with a refreshingly crisp salad of Savoy cabbage, which balances it beautifully.

Simmer the potatoes and green beans in a generous amount of salted water until very soft, about 40 minutes. Crush both the potatoes and green beans through a potato ricer to make a smooth puree.

Mince the onion and the garlic. Melt the butter in a large pot and sauté the onion and garlic until golden and fragrant. Add the potato and green bean mixture and stir to combine. While stirring, sprinkle in the grated cheese and then scatter in the spressa cheese a little at a time. Cook over low heat, stirring and being sure to reach all the way into the corners of the pot, until the cheese has melted. Season with salt and pepper and serve hot.

Fagiolini al pomodoro / GREEN BEANS SAUTÉED WITH TOMATOES

Trattoria Matteuzzi, San Casciano in Val di Pesa (Firenze), Toscana

You can also use yellow wax beans or a combination of yellow and green beans for this dish. The most important ingredient here is not a vegetable, but the earthenware pot used for cooking. This ensures that the vegetables cook slowly until they are meltingly soft.

Mince the onion and garlic, carrot, celery, and parsley. Tear the basil leaves. Place the onion, garlic, carrot, celery, parsley, basil, green beans, and tomatoes in an earthenware pot. Add a generous amount of oil, season to taste with salt and pepper, cover with a tight-fitting lid, and cook over very low heat until the green beans are very soft, 50 to 60 minutes.

Serves 4

1 SMALL YELLOW ONION

2 CLOVES GARLIC

1 CARROT

1 RIB CELERY

LEAVES OF 1 SPRIG PARSLEY

5 BASIL LEAVES

1¾ POUNDS GREEN BEANS, TRIMMED

1 POUND FRESH TOMATOES, CHOPPED, OR 4 CUPS CANNED PEELED TOMATOES AND THEIR JUICES, CHOPPED

EXTRA-VIRGIN OLIVE OIL FOR SAUTÉING

SALT AND FRESHLY GROUND BLACK PEPPER TO TASTE

Cornetti in salsa / GREEN BEANS WITH GARLIC AND OLIVE OIL

Ristorante Da Mario, Montegrotto Terme (Padova), Veneto

Beans can be divided into two groups: shelling beans, and beans with edible pods, which include green beans, yellow wax beans, flat romano beans, and others. Italians tend to cook their green beans to a very soft stage. Another dish from the Veneto calls for braising green beans in water and oil until they shrivel, then tossing them with a healthy splash of vinegar.

Trim the green beans by snapping off their ends. Bring a large pot of lightly salted water to a boil and add the beans. Boil until tender, about 10 minutes, but it will depend on their size. Meanwhile, in a skillet sauté the garlic in olive oil until browned. Add the green beans and sauté over medium heat, tossing, to season. Serve hot.

Serves 4

1½ POUNDS GREEN BEANS

SALT TO TASTE

1 CLOVE GARLIC

EXTRA-VIRGIN OLIVE OIL FOR SAUTÉING

Verdure ammollicate / POTATOES, GREENS, AND BREADCRUMBS

Trattoria La Collinetta, Martone (Reggio di Calabria), Calabria

Serves 4

6 OUNCES (ABOUT ½ BUNCH)
CHARD

6 OUNCES (ABOUT ½ BUNCH)
CHICORY

3 MEDIUM POTATOES

1 CLOVE GARLIC

3 TABLESPOONS EXTRA-
VIRGIN OLIVE OIL

SALT TO TASTE

½ TO 1 CUP STALE
BREAD CUBES

½ CUP GRATED AGED
SHEEP'S CHEESE

Chard and chicory provide some nice substance here, but feel free to swap in any greens available to you. You can make this spicy by adding a crumbled dried chili pepper when you add the garlic.

Steam the chard and chicory just to soften, then chop. Boil the potatoes until they are easily pierced with a paring knife, then drain, peel, and chop. In a large skillet, sauté the garlic in the olive oil. Add the greens and potatoes, season with salt, and sauté over medium heat, stirring frequently, until combined, about 3 minutes. Add the bread cubes and continue to cook, stirring frequently, until the bread has soaked up any remaining cooking liquid and breaks down. Sprinkle on the cheese and stir to combine.

Funghi trifolati / SAUTÉED MUSHROOMS

Ristorante Il Vecchio Mulino, Volterra (Pisa), Toscana

Serves 4

1½ POUNDS MIXED
MUSHROOMS

⅓ CUP EXTRA-VIRGIN
OLIVE OIL

2 CLOVES GARLIC

LEAVES OF 1 SPRIG CALAMINT

1 PIECE CHILI PEPPER,
CRUMBLED

SALT TO TASTE

LEAVES OF 1 SPRIG
PARSLEY, MINCED

You can also leave the mushrooms whole in this recipe—they will require 30 to 40 minutes to cook fully. This technique is delicious with all kinds of vegetables.

Coarsely chop any larger mushrooms. The smaller mushrooms can be left whole. In a large pot (the mushrooms will shrink drastically once cooked), combine the oil, mushrooms, garlic, calamint, chili pepper, and salt to taste. Cook over medium heat, stirring frequently, until the mushrooms have given up all of their liquid and it has evaporated, about 20 minutes. Remove and discard garlic, sprinkle with parsley, and serve hot.

Repouta / PRESERVED STEWED VEGETABLES

Lina Bionaz, Saint-Christophe, Valle d'Aosta

Resourceful Italians have dozens if not hundreds of ways of canning and preserving vegetables, especially in the north, where winters can be long and cold and small towns and villages may be isolated for long periods of time. Vegetables may be dried, brined, or, as here, preserved in vinegar. Serve these vegetables with cheese and some crusty bread.

Bring a large pot of salted water to a boil and add the lemon juice. Separately, blanch first the Savoy cabbage, then the chard, then the turnips, and finally the beet. Cook each just until tender but still crisp, remove with a skimmer, drain, and set aside to cool for 2 hours. Keep separate. (You can also cook all the vegetables in separate pots with a little lemon juice in each.)

Arrange the cooked vegetables in layers in sterilized jars suitable for canning, sprinkling each layer with salt, pepper, cloves, cinnamon, and chili pepper. Chop the leek and seed the bell pepper and cut it into wedges. Divide the pieces of leek and bell pepper among the jars. Press down as firmly on possible on the vegetables and pour into each jar enough vinegar to cover the vegetables complete and fill the jar. Hermetically seal the jars and keep in a cool, dry place. Let rest for 15 days before using.

Serves 6 to 8

SALT TO TASTE

JUICE OF ½ LEMON

2 POUNDS SAVOY CABBAGE, CHOPPED

2 POUNDS CHARD, CHOPPED

2 POUNDS TURNIPS, CHOPPED

1 BEET, CHOPPED

FRESHLY GROUND BLACK PEPPER TO TASTE

¼ TEASPOON GROUND CLOVES

¼ TEASPOON GROUND CINNAMON

GROUND CHILI PEPPER TO TASTE

1 LEEK, CHOPPED

1 BELL PEPPER

WHITE WINE VINEGAR FOR FILLING JARS

Verdure saporite / STEWED EGGPLANT, TOMATOES, AND BELL PEPPERS

Ines Diodori, Maratea (Potenza), Basilicata

Serves 4

2 EGGPLANT

2 MEDIUM YELLOW ONIONS

2 BELL PEPPERS

2 TOMATOES

2 CLOVES GARLIC

LEAVES OF 1 SPRIG PARSLEY

LEAVES OF 1 SPRIG BASIL

EXTRA-VIRGIN OLIVE OIL
FOR SAUTÉING

SALT TO TASTE

2 TO 3 SLICES DAY-OLD BREAD

Cook these vegetables at the lowest heat available on your stove, using a flame tamer if necessary.

Dice the eggplant. Thinly slice the onions. Seed the peppers, remove any white ribs, and cut into julienne. Dice the tomatoes. Mince the garlic, parsley, and basil together.

In a pot, sauté the onion in a generous amount of oil until soft, then add the eggplant, peppers, and tomatoes and cook for 10 minutes. Stir in the garlic and herbs and cook, stirring frequently, over low heat until very soft, about 1 hour. Season to taste. Toast the bread, cut into cubes, and scatter on top of the vegetables just before serving.

Ciaudedda / EGGPLANT STEWED WITH PEPPERS, POTATOES, AND ZUCCHINI

Ristorante La Tana, Maratea (Potenza), Basilicata

Serves 4

2 EGGPLANT

2 BELL PEPPERS

3 POTATOES

2 ZUCCHINI

20 CHERRY TOMATOES

¼ CUP PLUS 1 TABLESPOON
EXTRA-VIRGIN OLIVE OIL

1 CLOVE GARLIC

SALT TO TASTE

¼ TEASPOON MINCED FRESH
OREGANO

LEAVES OF 1 SPRIG BASIL

ABOUT ½ CUP VEGETABLE
BROTH (OPTIONAL)

Sometimes ciaudedda is made more substantial with the addition of beans, particularly fava beans. Serve with lots of toasted bread drizzled with olive oil.

Chop the eggplant and peppers. Peel the potatoes and cut into thick rounds. Slice the zucchini into thick rounds as well. Halve the tomatoes.

Place the oil and garlic in a skillet with high sides. Add the peppers and eggplant and sauté, stirring frequently, until browned, about 10 minutes. Add the tomatoes, potatoes, and zucchini, a generous pinch of salt, the oregano, and the whole basil leaves. Cook over low heat, stirring occasionally very gently so as not to break up the potatoes and zucchini, until vegetables are tender. If the pan dries out, add broth, if using, or water in small amounts to moisten.

Scarola stufata / STEWED ESCAROLE

Trattoria Le Quattro Fontane, Casagiove (Caserta), Campania

Escarole, a member of the chicory family, grows in loose heads. It is mild enough to be eaten raw as well as cooked.

Break down the escarole into individual leaves. In a pot, sauté the garlic in the olive oil until browned. Add the escarole leaves, cover the pot, and cook over low heat for 10 minutes. While the escarole is cooking, soak the raisins in warm water to cover for 5 minutes, then squeeze dry. Add the raisins, capers, olives, and pine nuts and check to be sure the pot isn't dry. If the escarole is beginning to stick to the bottom of the pot, add 2 tablespoons of water. Season with salt. Continue cooking, covered, until the escarole has given up all of its liquid and the liquid has evaporated, adding water occasionally if the pot seems too dry. This will take about 20 minutes total.

Serves 4

1 HEAD ESCAROLE

2 CLOVES GARLIC

3 TABLESPOONS EXTRA-VIRGIN OLIVE OIL

¼ CUP RAISINS

¼ CUP CAPERS, RINSED AND DRAINED

½ CUP BLACK OLIVES, PITTED

¼ CUP PINE NUTS

SALT TO TASTE

Verze sofegae / SMOTHERED CABBAGE

Livio Dal Farra, Limana (Belluno), Veneto

When cooked slowly, cabbage turns sweet and soft. Artichokes, eggplant, zucchini, and even beans are all delicious when cooked in this manner. A similar dish in the Jewish tradition of the Veneto calls for minced onion in place of the garlic.

Core the cabbage and cut into thin ribbons. Mince the garlic and rosemary. In a pot, melt the butter with the olive oil over low heat. Sauté the garlic and rosemary until they begin to color, about 3 minutes, then stir in the cabbage. Season with salt, cover with a tight-fitting lid, and cook for 1 hour. Stir in the wine and continue cooking, covered, until the cabbage is a deep, rich brown and has been reduced to one quarter its original volume, at least 1 additional hour.

Serves 4

1 HEAD Savoy CABBAGE

1 CLOVE GARLIC

LEAVES OF 1 SPRIG ROSEMARY

2 TABLESPOONS UNSALTED BUTTER

2 TABLESPOONS EXTRA-VIRGIN OLIVE OIL

SALT TO TASTE

¼ CUP DRY WHITE WINE

Crauti stufati / STEWED SAUERKRAUT

Italo Fassuoli, Trento, Trentino

Serves 10

1 MEDIUM YELLOW ONION

2 TABLESPOONS EXTRA-
VIRGIN OLIVE OIL

10 CUPS SAUERKRAUT

1 BAY LEAF

4 JUNIPER BERRIES,
LIGHTLY CRUSHED

2 TABLESPOONS CUMIN SEEDS

SALT AND FRESHLY GROUND
BLACK PEPPER TO TASTE

2 TABLESPOONS UNBLEACHED
ALL-PURPOSE FLOUR

Sauerkraut is made throughout the Dolomites: Green cabbage is cored and thinly sliced and then placed in wooden barrels with alternating layers of salt, cumin seed, wild fennel seed, and juniper berries. A wooden lid smaller in diameter than the top of the barrel is placed on top of each and then weighted down so that pressure is exerted on the cabbage and it ferments in its own liquid. It takes about a month for sauerkraut to be ready to eat. Sometimes turnips are fermented along with the cabbage.

Thinly slice the onion and sauté in the oil in a large pot over low heat until very soft. Drain the sauerkraut of most of its liquid, but not completely, and add to the pot. Add the bay leaf, juniper berries, and cumin seeds. Cook over low heat for 2 hours, stirring occasionally. If the pan begins to dry out, add a small amount of warm water. Season with salt and pepper and sprinkle in the flour. Stir to combine, then cook for 10 additional minutes. Remove bay leaf before serving.

Cavolo rapa soffocato / BRAISED KOHLRABI

Klaus Mair, Renon-Ritten, Alto Adige

Serves 4 to 6

4 KOHLRABI

6 TABLESPOONS UNSALTED
BUTTER

1 TABLESPOON SUGAR

1 TABLESPOON UNBLEACHED
ALL-PURPOSE FLOUR

SALT AND FRESHLY GROUND
BLACK PEPPER TO TASTE

¼ CUP HEAVY CREAM OR
WHIPPING CREAM

Kohlrabi, related to cabbage, can be eaten cooked or raw. Always peel off the tough skin on the outside of the bulbs.

Trim and dice the kohlrabi. Over medium heat, melt the butter in a pot, add the sugar, and cook, stirring constantly, until it begins to caramelize. Add the kohlrabi and sprinkle on the flour. Toss and season with salt and pepper. Cook, stirring constantly, until the kohlrabi is browned. Carefully add ½ cup cold water to the pot (it will splatter). Cover and cook over low heat for 1 hour, checking the pot occasionally and adding a little water if the kohlrabi is beginning to stick. Stir in the cream and cook, stirring, until reduced, about 5 minutes. Serve immediately.

Cianfotta di patate e carciofi / BRAISED POTATOES AND ARTICHOKES

Ristorante Europeo, Napoli, Campania

Aside from the main ingredients—potatoes and artichokes—you can adjust almost every ingredient in this dish to suit your tastes. This dish is easy to double.

Bring a large pot of water to a boil, boil the potatoes until tender enough to be pierced with a paring knife but still firm in the center. Drain the potatoes well, then peel and dice them. Prepare a bowl of cold water, add the lemon juice to the water, and trim and quarter the artichokes, dropping them into the bowl of water to keep them from discoloring. Chop the onion.

In a pot, heat olive oil for sautéing in a pot. Add the onion and potatoes. Drain the artichokes, squeeze as much water out of them as possible, and add them to the pot. Season with salt and oregano. Add the olives, capers, and parsley and stir to combine. Cover and cook over low heat until vegetables are very soft. Remove the cover from the pot and cook until any liquid in the pan has evaporated. Tear in calamint, stir to combine, and serve.

Serves 4

4 POTATOES

JUICE OF 1 LEMON

4 ARTICHOKES

1 MEDIUM YELLOW ONION

EXTRA-VIRGIN OLIVE OIL FOR SAUTÉING

SALT TO TASTE

OREGANO TO TASTE

¼ CUP PITTED BLACK OLIVES

¼ CUP CAPERS, RINSED AND DRAINED

2 TABLESPOONS MINCED PARSLEY

FRESH CALAMINT TO TASTE (OPTIONAL)

Patate silane 'mpacchiate ai funghi / BRAISED POTATOES AND MUSHROOMS

Ristorante Parco Pingitore, Serrastretta (Catanzaro), Calabria

Sila potatoes, which grow in the mountains, are yellow and very starchy, in part because have an exceptionally thick peel that keeps them from absorbing water.

Peel the potatoes and wipe clean with a dishtowel, cut into rounds. Slice the mushrooms. Place a generous amount of oil in a cast-iron or carbon-steel pot with high sides and bring to temperature for frying. Add the potatoes and cook until golden, 5 to 6 minutes, then add the mushrooms. Turn the vegetables gently, season with salt and chili pepper, and cook until potatoes and mushrooms are browned and almost cooked through. Remove from the heat and tear in the basil leaves. Transfer to a container with a tight-fitting lid and cover, then set aside and allow the potatoes to cook in the steam produced until completely tender.

Serves 4

1 POUND (3 MEDIUM) SILA POTATOES OR OTHER STARCHY POTATOES

9 OUNCES PORCINI MUSHROOMS

EXTRA-VIRGIN OLIVE OIL FOR SAUTÉING

SALT TO TASTE

GROUND CHILI PEPPER TO TASTE

LEAVES OF 1 SPRIG YOUNG BASIL

Umido di cipolline al cerfoglio / BRAISED ONIONS WITH CHERVIL

Osteria Bohemia, Soliera (Modena), Emilia-Romagna

Serves 4

1 POUND CIPOLLINI ONIONS

ROCK SALT TO TASTE

4 TABLESPOONS
UNSALTED BUTTER

¼ CUP EXTRA-VIRGIN
OLIVE OIL

½ CUP VEGETABLE BROTH

2 BAY LEAVES

BALSAMIC VINEGAR FROM
MODENA TO TASTE

LEAVES OF 1 BUNCH
CHERVIL, MINCED

The herb chervil is always used raw and never cooked, as it will lose its favor if exposed to heat. Since you want small, tender cipollini onions to remain whole, check for doneness with a toothpick.

Peel and trim the onions. Bring a large pot of salted water to a boil and cook the onions for 15 minutes. Drain and pat dry. Melt the butter with the olive oil in a large pot and sauté the onions until golden. Add the broth and the bay leaves. Cook for 2 to 3 minutes, then add the wine and cook the onions over low heat until tender. Drain, remove and discard bay leaves, drizzle onions with vinegar, sprinkle with chervil, and serve hot.

Scalogni glassati / GLAZED SHALLOTS

Riccardo Baiocchi, Carpi (Modena), Emilia-Romagna

Serves 4

20 SHALLOTS

1 CUP VEGETABLE BROTH

2 TABLESPOONS
UNSALTED BUTTER

1 TABLESPOON EXTRA-VIRGIN
OLIVE OIL

1 TABLESPOON HONEY

Honey predates sugar. Just keep a close watch on these shallots as they are cooking, as the honey can darken and turn bitter rather quickly.

Peel the shallots but leave whole. Place the broth in a small pot and keep warm. In a large pot, melt the butter with the olive oil and honey. Stir to combine. Add the shallots and stir to coat with the honey mixture. Cook over very low heat until tender, adding the broth to the pot a few tablespoons at a time to keep the pan moist.

Carote in agrodolce / CARROTS SIMMERED IN SWEET AND SOUR SAUCE

Elvira Menegon, Orgiano (Vicenza), Veneto

The sweetness of carrots and raisins contrasts nicely with the sharp vinegar in this dish. You can adjust both to suit your taste.

Soak the raisins in the wine. Slice the carrots into rounds and in a pot sauté in a generous amount of olive oil until browned. Season with salt. Cover the pot with a tight-fitting lid and cook over very low heat until carrots are tender enough to pierce with a fork. Drain the raisins and add to the pan along with the pine nuts. Pour off any excess fat and stir in the vinegar. Cook over low heat, uncovered, until carrots are soft. Serve hot.

Serves 6

⅓ CUP RAISINS

¼ CUP WHITE WINE

2 POUNDS YOUNG CARROTS

EXTRA-VIRGIN OLIVE OIL FOR SAUTÉING

SALT TO TASTE

¼ CUP PINE NUTS

3 TABLESPOONS WHITE WINE VINEGAR

Gobbi trippati / CARDOONS IN TOMATO SAUCE

Ristorante La Ribotta, Castagneto Carducci (Livorno), Toscana

Gobbo, or "hunchback," cardoons taste like artichokes. Look for cardoons that have been through a frost, as they will be the most tender. To trim cardoons, remove any leaves and peel off any fibrous strings. For the cheese here, an aged sheep's cheese from the Maremma area of Toscana is preferable, but Parmigiano Reggiano is an acceptable substitute. In some parts of the region, onion and a little ground cinnamon find their way into this recipe.

Prepare a bowl of ice water and add the lemon juice or vinegar. Chop the cardoons, then drop into the prepared acidulated water. Bring a large pot of water to a boil, drain the cardoons, and boil until tender, then drain, pat dry, and dredge in the flour. Place several inches of oil in a pot with high sides and place over medium heat. Add the cardoons and the garlic and brown. Season with salt to taste. When the cardoons are browned, drizzle in a small additional amount of oil and stir in the tomato puree. Cook briefly, but stir frequently to keep from sticking. Just before serving, sprinkle on the grated cheese.

Serves 4

2 TABLESPOONS LEMON JUICE OR WHITE WINE VINEGAR

1 BUNCH GOBBO CARDOONS

½ CUP UNBLEACHED ALL-PURPOSE FLOUR

EXTRA-VIRGIN OLIVE OIL FOR FRYING

4 CLOVES GARLIC

SALT TO TASTE

1 CUP TOMATO PUREE

1 CUP GRATED AGED SHEEP'S CHEESE OR PARMIGIANO REGGIANO

Baggianata / SUGAR SNAP PEAS BRAISED WITH TOMATOES AND BASIL

Nando Cellini, Viggiù (Varese), Lombardia

Serves 4

2 POUNDS SUGAR SNAP PEAS

1 CLOVE GARLIC

LEAVES OF 1 SPRIG PARSLEY, MINCED

5 BASIL LEAVES

1 POUND PLUM TOMATOES

EXTRA-VIRGIN OLIVE OIL FOR SAUTÉING

½ CUP RED WINE

SALT AND FRESHLY GROUND BLACK PEPPER TO TASTE

8 SLICES COUNTRY-STYLE BREAD

Sugar snap peas have a particularly herbaceous flavor that shines in this summer dish, but zucchini and eggplant can also be cooked in this manner.

Trim the sugar snap peas. Mince together the garlic, parsley, and basil. Chop the plum tomatoes. In a large pot, heat a generous amount of olive oil and cook the garlic mixture until it begins to color. Add the tomatoes and sugar snap peas. Stir to combine, then add the wine and cook until it has evaporated. Season to taste with salt and pepper and cook, covered, over medium heat for 30 minutes. Meanwhile, warm the bread in the oven. Serve the sugar snap peas hot with toasted bread.

Castraure in tecia / BRAISED BABY ARTICHOKES

Ofelia Facco, Cavallino Treporti (Venezia), Veneto

Serves 4

16 CASTRAURE OR OTHER BABY ARTICHOKES

EXTRA-VIRGIN OLIVE OIL FOR DRIZZLING

SALT AND FRESHLY GROUND BLACK PEPPER TO TASTE

Castraure are the first buds of the artichoke plant, harvested at the start of artichoke season. They can be cooked in this manner along with fennel and make a tasty salad when thinly shaved and dressed with extra-virgin olive oil. They can also be battered and fried.

Trim the castraure, gently open them somewhat, and arrange them vertically in a pot. Drizzle on a little oil and season with salt and pepper, then add enough cold water to cover the artichokes. Cook, covered, over low heat until the liquid has evaporated completely, about 20 minutes, shaking the pot occasionally to be sure the artichokes don't stick.

Carciofi alla romana / SLOW-COOKED STUFFED ARTICHOKES
Osteria Tram Tram, Roma, Lazio

Roman or romanesco artichokes are round and on the large side. They are a traditional favorite of the Jewish community that has populated the area in and around Roma for a good 1,500 years. Dropping trimmed artichokes in water with lemon juice keeps them from turning brown. You can also simply rub the cut side of a lemon all over the artichokes.

Fill a large bowl with cold water and add the lemon juice. Trim the artichokes: Remove and discard the hard outer leaves of the artichokes and peel the stem, if necessary, but leave the stem attached. Trim the tops and use a spoon to scoop out the chokes. Drop into the prepared lemon water and let them soak for 10 minutes.

Meanwhile, mince together the garlic, parsley, and calamint and season to taste with salt and pepper. Fill a pot with a couple inches of water—about ⅓ the height of the pot—and arrange the artichokes vertically with stems facing upward. Drizzle with a generous amount of olive oil and cook over low heat for 50 minutes. Serve hot.

Serves 4

JUICE OF 1 LEMON

8 ROMANESCO ARTICHOKES

2 TO 3 CLOVES GARLIC

LEAVES OF 1 SPRIG PARSLEY

LEAVES OF 1 SPRIG CALAMINT

SALT AND FRESHLY GROUND BLACK PEPPER TO TASTE

EXTRA-VIRGIN OLIVE OIL FOR DRIZZLING

Finocchi alla giudia / BRAISED FENNEL
Giuseppina Gagliardi, Roma, Lazio

Use young fennel for this dish, an ancient Jewish recipe.

Cut the fennel into wedges. Sauté the garlic in a generous amount of oil in a large deep skillet or a pot with a tight-fitting lid. When the garlic begins to turn dark, remove and discard it and add the fennel wedges to the pan. Cook, stirring frequently, for 15 minutes. Season with salt and add about ¼ cup water to the pan. Cook, covered, over medium heat until fennel is very tender and most of the water has evaporated.

Serves 4

8 BULBS FENNEL

1 CLOVE GARLIC

EXTRA-VIRGIN OLIVE OIL FOR SAUTÉING

SALT TO TASTE

Coste di bietole alla Veneziana / BRAISED CHARD STEMS

Ofelia Facco, Cavallino Treporti (Venezia), Veneto

Serves 6

STEMS FROM
3½ POUNDS CHARD

1 CLOVE GARLIC

LEAVES OF 1 SPRIG PARSLEY

2 TABLESPOONS
EXTRA-VIRGIN OLIVE OIL

SALT TO TASTE

2 TABLESPOONS WHITE
WINE VINEGAR

Turn to this recipe when you have used the chard greens for another purpose. The stems are equally delicious and have a pleasantly crisp texture that holds up well to both braising and frying.

Chop the chard stems. Mince the garlic and parsley. Place the chard stems in a pot, add water to cover, and bring to a boil. Simmer for 15 minutes, then remove any excess water, leaving enough cooking liquid to go about halfway up the chard stems. Add the oil, garlic, and parsley and season with salt. Cover and cook until the stems are soft enough to pierce with a fork. Simmer, uncovered, until all the water has evaporated, then stir in the vinegar and cook until that has evaporated as well.

Melanzane all'eoliana / GRILLED EGGPLANT WITH GARLIC AND CAPERS

Ristorante 'A Cannata, Santa Marina Salina (Messina), Sicilia

Serves 4 to 6

2 TO 3 MEDIUM EGGPLANT

EXTRA-VIRGIN OLIVE OIL FOR
BRUSHING AND DRESSING

1 CLOVE GARLIC

3 TABLESPOONS CAPERS,
RINSED AND DRAINED

MINCED CHILI PEPPER
TO TASTE

SALT TO TASTE

WHITE WINE VINEGAR
FOR DRESSING

Grilled eggplant acts as a sponge and soaks up all kinds of flavors. Capers from the island of Salina, one of the Aeolian Islands, have their own Slow Food Presidium and are a popular topping for grilled eggplant. In any case, always opt for salted capers over the ones preserved in vinegar. You can also sprinkle grilled eggplant with minced fresh oregano and mint.

Slice the eggplant a little less than ½-inch thick, salt, and set aside to drain in a colander. When the eggplant has given up its liquid, wash the slices and pat them dry. Brush the eggplant slices lightly with oil and grill them, turning once, until browned on both sides. Transfer to a platter.

Mince together the garlic and capers and sprinkle over the eggplant. Sprinkle on the minced chili pepper and season with salt. (Taste first, as the capers can be salty and the eggplant has been salted.) Make a dressing of vinegar and olive oil, whisk to combine, then pour over the eggplant and serve.

Cappelle di morecci in gratella / GRILLED MUSHROOMS

Osteria Bagnoli, Castagneto Carducci (Livorno), Toscana

Porcini mushrooms are delicious grilled because of their meaty texture. If you can't find calamint, use parsley in its place, and if you're really in a hurry, skip the marinating and just brush the liquid on the mushrooms while they're cooking. Don't overcook the mushrooms—they will take 6 to 8 minutes per side, but less if they are small.

Set aside 1 sprig calamint. Mince the remaining calamint leaves. Combine the vinegar, oil, and minced calamint. Season with salt and pepper. Pour the calamint mixture over the mushrooms and marinate for 30 minutes.

Preheat a grill. Remove the mushrooms from the marinade, reserving the liquid. Place the mushrooms smooth sides up on the grill. Grill, brushing the reserved marinade on them and using the reserved calamint sprig as a brush, until soft, 6 to 8 minutes. Turn and grill the other side, brushing the gills with any remaining marinade. Serve hot.

Serves 4

1 BUNCH CALAMINT

2 CUPS WHITE WINE VINEGAR

½ CUP EXTRA-VIRGIN OLIVE OIL

SALT AND FRESHLY GROUND BLACK PEPPER TO TASTE

4 LARGE PORCINI MUSHROOM CAPS

Capuss / STUFFED GRAPE LEAVES

Elena Salvaterra, Tione di Trento, Trentino

Serves 10 to 12

1¾ POUNDS CHARD

LEAVES OF 1 SPRIG PARSLEY

5 LARGE EGGS,
LIGHTLY BEATEN

5½ CUPS BREADCRUMBS

5 CUPS GRATED AGED
SPRESSA CHEESE

⅔ CUP RAISINS

FRESHLY GRATED BLACK
PEPPER TO TASTE

14 TABLESPOONS (1 STICK
PLUS 6 TABLESPOONS)
UNSALTED BUTTER

2 CLOVES GARLIC, CRUSHED

20 LARGE GRAPE LEAVES

SALT TO TASTE

EXTRA-VIRGIN OLIVE OIL
FOR DRIZZLE

If at all possible, pick your grape leaves just before using them. Look for fleshy leaves without any holes. If you can only find small to medium-sized grape leaves, use twice as many and sandwich each piece of filling between two of them. This dish is especially popular in August at the local San Bartolomeo festival, where the grape leaves are served cold, accompanied by a glass of wine.

Mince together the chard and parsley. Place in a bowl and stir with the eggs, breadcrumbs, and cheese. Stir in the raisins and season with pepper. Melt the butter in a large pot and cook the garlic until browned. Add the chard mixture and cook over very low heat, stirring constantly, until the mixture is thoroughly combined and dense.

Pull off a chunk of the filling mixture about the size of the palm of your hand and shape it into a diamond. Place the diamond on one of the grape leaves, fold envelope-style, and tie with kitchen twine. Repeat with remaining filling and leaves.

Bring a large pot of salted water to a boil. Turn down to a gentle simmer and add the leaves. Cook over low heat (if the water bubbles too briskly it will break open the packages) for 1 hour. Remove from the water with a skimmer and allow to drain and cool. To serve, remove and discard twine, then cut packets into slices and drizzle with a little olive oil.

DESSERTS

Crema di Cogne / CHOCOLATE ALMOND CARAMEL PUDDING FROM COGNE

La Brasserie du Bon Bec, Cogne, Valle d'Aosta

Serves 8

½ CUP BLANCHED
BITTER ALMONDS

½ CUP BLANCHED
SWEET ALMONDS

1 CUP WHOLE MILK

4 EGG YOLKS

1½ CUPS SUGAR

4 CUPS HEAVY CREAM

7 OUNCES GIANDUIA
CHOCOLATE, CHOPPED

Bitter almonds are difficult to track down in the United States. If necessary, replace the bitter almonds with sweet almonds and whisk in a few drops of almond extract along with the caramelized sugar. Gianduia is hazelnut-flavored chocolate.

Grind the almonds finely, but not until they turn into a paste. Combine the almonds and milk in a pot and cook over low heat for 20 minutes, never letting it come to a boil. Drain the milk and discard the almond solids. Let the milk cool to room temperature.

In a separate pot, beat the egg yolks with 1 cup sugar until thick and yellow. Add the cream and the milk, stirring with a wooden spoon. Place over very low heat and add the chocolate. Cook, stirring constantly, until the mixture just begins to boil, then remove from the heat.

Place the remaining ½ cup sugar in a small skillet and cook, stirring, over low heat until it turns fairly dark. Stir the caramelized sugar into the cream mixture and continue to stir until the mixture has cooled completely.

Biancomangiare di mandorle / ALMOND PUDDING

Caffè Sicilia, Noto (Siracusa), Sicilia

Serves 4

1 CUP BLANCHED
NOTO ALMONDS

¼ CUP WHEAT STARCH

¼ CUP SUGAR

Sprinkle some chopped almonds on this pudding as a garnish. Noto almonds are especially flavorful and have their own Slow Food Presidium.

Grind the almonds, but do not turn them into a butter. Place 1½ cups warm water in a pot and place over medium heat until warm but not hot. Remove from heat and whisk in the sugar, starch, and ground almonds. Press the almonds firmly to extract as much flavor as possible, then strain out the solids and discard. Bring the almond milk to a simmer over medium heat, then pour into one large mold or individual molds and refrigerate until firm, 3 to 4 hours. To serve, place a plate upside down on the mold or molds, then flip and lift off mold. Chop the reserved almonds and sprinkle on top as garnish.

Crema di castagne / CHESTNUT CREAM

Ristorante Luna Rossa, Terranova di Pollino (Potenza), Basilicata

The easiest way to peel a chestnut is to cut an X in the flat bottom of each with the tip of a paring knife. Once they are boiled, the shell and the peel should come away fairly easily. This chestnut cream makes a nice filling for a tart, or simply spread it on slices of toasted bread.

Place the chestnuts in a pot with 8 cups water. Bring to a boil and cook until tender. Remove a few at a time and shell and peel them. (The chestnuts are much easier to shell and peel while they are warm, so leave the unpeeled ones in the water.) Puree the chestnuts through a food mill.

Place the chestnut puree in a pot with high sides. Stir in the sugar and espresso. Cut the vanilla bean in half the long way and scrape the seeds into the pot. Cook over low heat, stirring frequently, until thick, about 30 minutes. Transfer the cooked cream to sterilized jars and cover them so that it cools slowly. Allow to rest a few days before eating.

Serves 6 to 8

2¼ POUNDS FRESH CHESTNUTS

1½ CUPS SUGAR

⅔ CUP STRONG ESPRESSO

1 VANILLA BEAN

Crema di Pistacchi di Bronte / BRONTE PISTACHIO PUDDING

Aldo Bacciulli, Catania, Sicilia

Shave some dark chocolate with a vegetable peeler and use it to decorate this tasty pudding. Delicately flavored Bronte pistachios, which have a Slow Food Presidium, are sold in many forms, including shelled, ground, and as a paste. Avola almonds are pointy and flat and are fruitier tasting than standard almonds.

Place the milk, cream, sugar, pistachios, almonds, and almond liqueur in a pot and bring to a boil, stirring constantly with a wooden spatula. When the mixture has reached a boil, remove from the heat and allow to cool, then whisk in the cornstarch, making sure there are no lumps. Puree smooth with an immersion blender or food processor fitted with the metal blade. Return to the pot and cook over very low heat, stirring, until the mixture is creamy and thickened. Transfer to individual serving dishes and refrigerate for at least 4 hours before serving.

Serves 4 to 6

2 CUPS WHOLE MILK

2 CUPS HEAVY CREAM OR WHIPPING CREAM

¾ CUP SUGAR

1 CUP BRONTE PISTACHIOS OR OTHER PISTACHIOS

¼ CUP AVOLA ALMONDS OR OTHER ALMONDS

2 TABLESPOONS ALMOND LIQUEUR

¼ CUP PLUS 2 TABLESPOONS CORNSTARCH OR OTHER STARCH

Crema al Mirto / MYRTLE LIQUEUR PUDDING

Marina Bendico, Capoterra (Cagliari), Sardegna

Serves 6

1 EGG YOLK

¾ CUP SUGAR

2 TABLESPOONS UNBLEACHED
ALL-PURPOSE FLOUR OR
POTATO STARCH

2 CUPS WHOLE MILK

2 TABLESPOONS MYRTLE
LIQUEUR

2 CUPS HEAVY CREAM
OR WHIPPING CREAM

In a bowl, whisk the egg yolk with ½ cup sugar, then whisk in the flour and milk until well-combined. Transfer the mixture to a small pot and bring to a boil over low heat, whisking constantly. Cook, whisking, until thickened, about 10 minutes. Remove from the heat, whisk in the liqueur, and set aside to cool.

Whip the cream to firm peaks with the remaining ¼ cup sugar. Fold the whipped cream into milk mixture and divide among 6 individual serving bowls. Chill in the refrigerator for at least 2 hours before serving.

Flam di cotogne e mele / QUINCE AND APPLE CUSTARD

Nando Ferrari, Trento, Trentino

In Trentino, this kind of custard may be savory or sweet. It is always gently baked at low temperature in a water bath.

Serves 4

1 QUINCE

2 REINETTE APPLES

4 EGG WHITES

4 TABLESPOONS SUGAR

2 TABLESPOONS UNSALTED
BUTTER

1 TABLESPOON UNBLEACHED
ALL-PURPOSE FLOUR

RASPBERRY JAM FOR
FINISHING

Preheat the oven to 300°F. Place the quince and the apples in a baking pan and bake until very soft, about 1 hour. Leave oven on at 300°F. Let the fruit cool, then peel and seed the fruit and crush smooth.

In a bowl, whip the egg whites to stiff peaks. Add the sugar and whip in, then fold in the cooked fruit.

Butter and flour a loaf pan with the butter and flour. Transfer the mixture to the pan, smooth the top, and cover with aluminum foil. Set the loaf pan in a larger baking pan and add water to the baking pan to come up the sides of the loaf pan. Bake in the preheated oven until set, about 1 hour. To serve, unmold onto a platter and slice. Serve a spoonful of raspberry jam with each slice.

Caffè in forchetta / COFFEE CUSTARD

Antica Fattoria del Grottaione, Castel del Piano (Grosseto), Toscana

While Italian pastry shops serve beautiful cakes and elaborate pastries, home-cooked desserts in Italy tend to be more like this humble spoon sweet. In the days before electric and gas ovens were commonplace, this would have been baked in a wood-burning stove that did double-duty heating the house.

Preheat the oven to 185°F. Beat the eggs and yolks with the sugar. Beat in the milk and espresso. Divide the mixture among 6 small ramekins. Set the ramekins in a baking pan and add enough water to come about halfway up the sides of the ramekins. Bake in the preheated oven until a crust forms on top, about 30 minutes.

Serves 6

5 LARGE EGGS

2 EGG YOLKS

1¾ CUPS SUGAR

4 CUPS WHOLE MILK

1¼ CUPS ESPRESSO, WARM

Fonduta di cioccolato / CHOCOLATE FONDUE

Ristorante Le Vieux Pommier, Courmayeur, Valle d'Aosta

This dessert obviously is modeled on fonduta, the famous cheese fondue topped with thin petals of truffle frequently served in this area. The fruit is a vehicle here, so use whichever type of fruit you prefer.

Melt the chocolate in the top of a double boiler. Add the cream and cook, stirring constantly, over very low heat until combined. Transfer the chocolate mixture to a fondue pot to keep warm. Cut the bananas, pineapple, and kiwis into bite-sized pieces. Trim the greens off the strawberries and halve if large. Serve the fruit and cookies and provide a long fondue fork to each diner for dipping the fruit into the chocolate mixture.

Serves 4

7 OUNCES DARK CHOCOLATE

2 CUPS HEAVY CREAM

2 BANANAS

4 SLICES PINEAPPLE

4 KIWIS

8 STRAWBERRIES

16 TEGOLE COOKIES (PAGE 410)

Budino di zucca e cioccolato / CHOCOLATE AND SQUASH PUDDING ▷

Antonio Rizzo, Napoli, Campania

Serves 4 to 6

3½ CUPS CUBED WINTER SQUASH

1 CUP RICE MILK

4 OUNCES DARK CHOCOLATE, CHOPPED

¼ CUP TURBINADO SUGAR

¼ CUP CORNSTARCH

GRATED ZEST OF 1 ORANGE

SALT TO TASTE

1 TEASPOON GRATED FRESH OR GROUND GINGER

The sweetness of winter squash is highlighted in this rich pudding. Garnish with candied orange peel and sliced almonds, or top with a little whipped cream.

Place the squash and ¾ cup of the rice milk in a pot and simmer over medium heat until the squash is soft and the rice milk has been completely absorbed. Crush with a potato ricer and transfer to a large pot. Stir in the remaining ¼ cup rice milk, the turbinado sugar, the chocolate, orange zest, cornstarch, a pinch of salt, and the ginger until smooth. Cook over medium-low heat, stirring constantly, for 30 minutes. The mixture should thicken.

Transfer the mixture to a large ring mold or individual bowls or molds and refrigerate for at least 3 hours before serving.

Fiocca / GRAPPA-FLAVORED WHIPPED CREAM

Letizia Palesi, Champorcher (Aosta), Valle d'Aosta

Serves 4

2½ CUPS HEAVY CREAM

¾ CUP CONFECTIONER'S SUGAR

1 TABLESPOON GRAPPA

4 OUNCES DARK CHOCOLATE

This simple dessert is often served alongside crisp tegole cookies (page 410). In Valle d'Aosta, it is made using extremely fresh cream from pastured cows that has a high fat content of at least 30 percent. Always chill your cream, bowl, and whisk or beaters well before attempting to whip cream.

Whip the cream to soft peaks, then continue whipping while gradually adding the sugar and then the grappa. Chop the chocolate and sprinkle on top.

Montebianco / CHESTNUT "MOUNTAIN"

Enza Vuillermin, Brusson, Valle d'Aosta

Serves 8

2 POUNDS CHESTNUTS

4 CUPS WHOLE MILK

2½ CUPS HEAVY CREAM OR
WHIPPING CREAM

1 VANILLA BEAN

2 TABLESPOONS RUM

1¼ CUPS SUGAR

1 PINCH SALT

12 WHOLE CANDIED
CHESTNUTS

This dessert is meant to resemble Mont Blanc, the tallest mountain in Europe at 15,781 feet. Candied chestnuts are almost always used for decoration, but you can also incorporate chopped chocolate, cherries in syrup, small strawberries, chopped candied fruit, and even small meringues. The options are endless.

Score the chestnuts. Bring a large pot of lightly salted water to a boil and blanch the chestnuts. Drain and peel off both the shells and the skin. Transfer the chestnuts to a pot with the milk (which should just cover them), sugar, and vanilla bean. Simmer for 45 minutes.

Drain the chestnuts. Remove and discard vanilla bean. Crush the chestnuts through a sieve or with a potato ricer and mix in the rum. Arrange the chestnut mixture on a large serving platter in the shape of a mountain. Chill in the refrigerator until serving. Just before serving, whip the cream to stiff peaks and arrange it on the "mountain" as if it were snow. Finish with the candied chestnuts and serve.

Polenta e mele / POLENTA WITH APPLES

Huber Kaser, Luson-Lüsen, Alto Adige

Serves 4 to 6

1 PINCH FRESHLY
GRATED NUTMEG

2 CUPS STONEGROUND
POLENTA

4 TO 5 APPLES

¼ CUP RAISINS

1 PINCH GROUND CINNAMON

2 TABLESPOONS SUGAR

Polenta is extremely flexible and can even be made into a sweet dessert. Leftovers make a tasty breakfast.

Place 4 cups water in a large pot and bring to a boil. Add the nutmeg and then add the polenta very gradually, letting it slip through your fingers in a thin stream. Cook, stirring constantly, until the polenta is thick and no longer tastes raw, about 45 minutes.

Meanwhile, core and peel the apples, dice them, and place them in a small pot with the raisins and 2 tablespoons water. Cook over low heat for 10 minutes. Stir in the cinnamon. When the polenta is cooked, stir the apple mixture into the polenta. Stir in the sugar and serve hot.

Panicielli / GRAPES WRAPPED IN CITRON LEAVES

Ristorante La Rondinella, Scalea (Cosenza), Calabria

Zibibbo grapes are small green grapes in the Muscat family. You can use this technique with other small green grapes as well. The fruit absorbs the refreshing scent of citron from the leaves, though the leaves themselves are not edible.

Dry the grapes in the sun. Preheat oven to 325°F. Place about 2 tablespoons dried grapes on a citron leaf and fold envelope-style. Tie with kitchen twine or esparto grass. Place in a single layer on a baking sheet and bake in the preheated oven for 10 minutes. Serve in the packets and let diners open them at the table.

Makes 12 packets

1½ CUPS SLIGHTLY UNDER-RIPE ZIBIBBO GRAPES

12 CITRON LEAVES

Crema di cotto di fichi / FIG REDUCTION

Ristorante Luna Rossa, Terranova di Pollino (Potenza), Basilicata

This syrup is traditionally drizzled on cartellate (page 422) and is also delicious over ice cream or any kind of spoon sweet. If at all possible, harvest figs for this recipe in the second half of August, as by then the fruit is quite sweet. The yield can vary widely depending on the type of figs you use and how ripe they are.

Peel the figs and place them in a large pot with 10 quarts of water. Cook until the figs are reduced at least by half, at least 5 hours. Transfer the cooked figs to a clean pillowcase. Tie the open end of the pillowcase closed and hang from a hook with a large bowl underneath to catch liquid and drain for 24 hours.

Place the liquid that has drained off the figs in a pot and cook over low heat for 4 hours, stirring occasionally and keeping a close eye on it to guard against burning. It will reduce to a thick syrup. Let the syrup cool and then transfer to glass jars or bottles.

Makes 4 to 5 cups syrup

11 POUNDS VERY RIPE FRESH FIGS

Amarene sciroppate / SOUR CHERRIES IN SYRUP ▷

Nuccia Barile, Termoli (Campobasso), Molise

*Makes about 8 cups,
enough to fill 2 quart jars*

2¼ POUNDS (7 TO 8 CUPS)
SOUR RED CHERRIES

2½ CUPS SUGAR

The sour cherries known as *amarene* (not to be confused with *visciole* and *marasche*, which are actually different varieties) are light red. In Central and Southern Italy they are made into liqueur and jam, as well as dried or preserved in alcohol. Always wipe cherries with a damp cloth rather than in running water, as they can easily absorb water and it will cause their flavor to dissipate.

Pull off the cherry stems and discard. In a large pot, combine 1 ¼ cups water and the sugar and bring to a boil. As soon as the liquid begins to boil, add the cherries and cook over low heat until softened, about 10 minutes. Transfer the cherries to sterilized jars and pour the syrup from the pot over them to cover. Seal the jars and process for 10 minutes in a water bath for longer storage.

Sorbetto di limone al profumo di basilico / LEMON AND BASIL SORBET

Laura Novellini, Fossano (Cuneo), Piemonte

Serves 4 to 6

3 ORGANIC LEMONS

1 CUP SUGAR

15 BASIL LEAVES

2 TABLESPOONS LIMONCELLO

Lemon sorbet infused with fresh basil makes a wonderful palate cleanser or light dessert. Use small, tender basil leaves, preferably Ligurian basil.

Place a low, wide aluminum or steel pan (such as an 8-by-8-inch baking pan) in the freezer. Peel off the zest from the lemons in strips. Be sure not to take off the white pith, which will make the sorbet bitter. In a pot, combine 2 cups water, the lemon zest, and the sugar. Bring to a boil and cook over medium heat for 10 minutes, stirring occasionally. Allow to cool.

Meanwhile, juice the lemons. In a mortar and pestle, crush the basil leaves with 2 tablespoons of the lemon juice. Combine the cooled syrup, the lemon juice, and the basil mixture. Strain the mixture (discard the solids) into the chilled pan. Stir in the limoncello and place in the freezer. After 15 minutes, use a fork to break up any frozen chunks. Continue to break up the mixture every 30 minutes until it reaches the desired consistency.

Gelato di more e mirtilli / BERRY FROZEN YOGURT

Camilla Forti, Milano, Lombardia

Serves 4 to 6

2½ TO 3 CUPS BLACKBERRIES
AND BLUEBERRIES

2 OUNCES DARK CHOCOLATE

1½ CUPS SOY YOGURT

3 TABLESPOONS SUGAR

ABOUT ¼ CUP SOY MILK,
IF NEEDED

1 PINCH GROUND CARDAMOM
OR GROUND GINGER
(OPTIONAL)

Juicy berries and dark chocolate quickly transform plain yogurt into dessert.

Place the berries and about three quarters of the chocolate in a blender and pulse briefly to blend. Add the yogurt and sugar and pulse again until smooth and creamy. If the yogurt you are using is very dense and you would like a creamier texture, add a little bit of soy milk and pulse again until smooth. Stir in the cardamom or ginger, if using. Divide the mixture among individual freezer molds and freeze until firm, about 8 hours.

To serve, unmold onto individual serving plates. Melt the remaining chocolate in a double boiler and drizzle the melted chocolate over the yogurt. Freeze again for 5 minutes, then serve.

Crostata con confettura di albicocche / APRICOT JAM TART

Alessia Battaglino, Bra (Cuneo), Piemonte

Serves 4 to 6

2 CUPS UNBLEACHED
ALL-PURPOSE FLOUR

3 TABLESPOONS CORNMEAL

¼ CUP HAZELNUT FLOUR

1 PINCH SALT

1 TABLESPOON CREAM
OF TARTAR

⅔ CUP RICE MALT SYRUP

⅓ CUP CORN OIL

ABOUT 3 CUPS APRICOT JAM

Look for high-quality jam to use in this tart. If you are lucky enough to have a jar of homemade preserves or jam, they will yield spectacular results. The exact amount needed to fill the tart will depend on the size of the tart you are making. While this recipe is for an apricot jam tart, you can obviously use any flavor you like—raspberry is also quite good.

Preheat oven to 350°F. Sift the flour, cornmeal, and hazelnut flour together in a bowl. Stir in the salt and cream of tartar. In a separate bowl (or measuring cup) whisk together the malt syrup and oil, then stir the mixture into the flour mixture until well-combined and no longer sticky. Cut off and reserve about one third of the dough for the lattice top. On a lightly floured work surface, roll out the remaining dough to a disk that will line the bottom and sides of your pie or cake pan. Set the disk in the pan and fill with the apricot jam. Smooth the top. Roll out the reserved dough and cut into strips, or simply roll the dough into thin ropes, and arrange the strips or ropes to form a lattice on top of the pie. Bake in the preheated oven until crust is golden and dry to the touch, about 30 minutes.

Semifreddo al torroncino con vincotto /
MASCARPONE AND NOUGAT SEMIFREDDO DRIZZLED WITH VINCOTTO

Ristorante La Locandiera, Bernalda (Matera), Basilicata

Nut-studded nougat (known as torrone) is sold in large bars and is especially popular at Christmastime. Look for the crisp type of nougat for this recipe, as it will be easier to chop than the soft type. With syrupy vincotto and light custard, this is a dessert fit for a special occasion.

Make vincotto: Combine the wine and 1 cup sugar in a saucepan and bring to a boil. Simmer for 1 hour. Add the figs and simmer for 1 additional hour. Set aside to cool.

Make a custard: In a small pot, beat 2 egg yolks with ¼ cup sugar until foamy. Add the milk and cook, whisking constantly, over low heat until thickened. Set aside to cool.

In a large bowl, whip the cream to stiff peaks. In another large bowl, whisk the remaining 5 egg yolks and the remaining 1 ¼ cups sugar. Beat the mascarpone into the egg yolk mixture, then fold in the whipped cream. Crush the nougat and fold it into the mixture, then transfer the mixture to a pan or container and freeze for at least 4 hours.

To serve, scoop out the semifreddo and accompany each serving with custard and drizzle with vincotto.

Serves 4

4 CUPS AGLIANICO RED WINE

2½ CUPS SUGAR

5 DRIED FIGS STUFFED WITH ALMONDS

7 EGG YOLKS

1 CUP WHOLE MILK

4 CUPS HEAVY CREAM OR WHIPPING CREAM

2 CUPS (ABOUT 1 POUND) MASCARPONE

1 300-GRAM BAR NOUGAT

Semifreddo al miele con purea di albicocche /
HONEY SEMIFREDDO WITH APRICOT PUREE

Ristorante Devetak, Savogna d'Isonzo-Sovodnje ob Soci (Gorizia), Friuli Venezia Giulia

Serves 4 to 6

⅓ CUP SUGAR

⅓ CUP ACACIA HONEY

4 EGG YOLKS

2 TABLESPOONS RUM

2 CUPS WHIPPING CREAM

2 TO 3 CUPS APRICOT PUREE

A semifreddo is a frozen mousse. If you prefer, you can freeze the mixture in a single large container and cut slices of it to serve, or simply scoop it out like ice cream. To make apricot puree, combine pitted and peeled apricots, sugar, lemon juice, and a touch of honey in a blender and puree smooth.

In a small pot combine the sugar with about half of the honey and 3 tablespoons water. Bring to a boil.

Meanwhile, in a large bowl, whisk the egg yolks with the remaining honey until smooth. Whisk in the rum and then whisk in the warm sugar mixture and whisk briskly until completely cool.

In a separate bowl, whip the cream to stiff peaks. Fold the whipped cream into the egg yolk mixture. Transfer to individual serving dishes and freeze until firm. To serve, unmold and top each with a dollop of apricot puree.

Crostata alla crema con nocciole / CUSTARD TART WITH HAZELNUTS

Silvana Richiero, Sommariva Bosco (Cuneo), Piemonte

Makes one 10-inch tart,
6 to 8 servings

1 VANILLA BEAN

⅔ CUP HAZELNUTS

2 CUPS UNBLEACHED
ALL-PURPOSE FLOUR

2 TEASPOONS BAKING
POWDER

1⅓ CUPS SUGAR

1 PINCH SALT

1 LARGE EGG

5 EGG YOLKS, DIVIDED

9 TABLESPOONS
UNSALTED BUTTER, ROOM
TEMPERATURE, CUT INTO
PIECES

2 TABLESPOONS PLUS 2
TEASPOONS POTATO STARCH

1½ CUPS WHOLE MILK

1 CUP HEAVY CREAM OR
WHIPPING CREAM

Piemonte is famous for its extremely flavorful hazelnuts, which appear in all kinds of tarts, cookies, and confections.

Split the vanilla bean and scrape out the seeds. Toast the hazelnuts briefly, then rub off their skins. Chop them roughly and set aside. Line a 10-inch pie pan with parchment and set aside.

For the crust, sift the flour into a bowl with the baking powder and ⅔ cup sugar. Add half the vanilla bean seeds and a pinch of salt and stir to combine. Shape the flour mixture into a well on a work surface. Place 1 egg and 1 egg yolk in the center of the well with the butter. Begin to pull in dry ingredients from the side of the well and incorporate them into the liquid. When you have a crumbly mixture, knead it into a soft dough, wrap in plastic, and chill in the refrigerator for 30 minutes.

Meanwhile, prepare the custard filling. In a pot, whisk the remaining 4 egg yolks with the remaining ⅔ cup sugar until foamy. Whisk in the potato starch, the milk, the cream, and the remaining vanilla bean seeds. Place over low heat and cook, whisking constantly, until the mixture reaches a boil and thickens. Remove from the heat and set aside to cool.

Preheat the oven to 350°F. Roll out the dough and use it to line the bottom and sides of the prepared pan. Spread the prepared custard evenly on top of the crust. Sprinkle the hazelnuts all over the custard.

Bake in the preheated oven until the crust is dry and golden and the custard is set, about 40 minutes. If the nuts on top are browning too quickly, cover loosely with foil. Remove from the oven and transfer to a cooling rack before serving.

Crostata del diavolo / HOT PEPPER AND ORANGE TART

Ristorante Sabbia d'Oro, Belvedere Marittimo (Cosenza), Calabria

Serves 6 to 8

¾ CUP BLANCHED ALMONDS

6 TABLESPOONS UNSALTED
BUTTER, PLUS MORE
FOR BUTTERING PAN

¾ CUP SUGAR

1 LARGE EGG

2 EGG YOLKS

FINELY GRATED ZEST
OF 1 LEMON

2½ CUPS UNBLEACHED
ALL-PURPOSE FLOUR

¼ CUP CHILI PEPPER
PRESERVES

½ CUP ORANGE MARMALADE

To make chili pepper preserves, use about 4 pounds bell peppers and 2 pounds red chili peppers. Seed both and remove any white ribs. Dice the peppers and toss them with 2½ cups sugar and let sit at room temperature for 4 to 5 hours. Transfer the peppers and sugar to a pot, add water just to cover, and cook over low heat for 1½ hours. Add another 2½ cups sugar and 3 tablespoons honey and cook for 2 more hours.

Preheat oven to 350°F. Chop the almonds but do not grind them to a paste. Set aside. Butter a pie or cake pan and set aside. Beat the 6 tablespoons butter and sugar until yellow and light. Beat in the egg, egg yolks, and lemon zest. Add the flour about ¼ cup at a time, beating to combine between additions. Roll out about two thirds of the dough into a disk and use it to line the pan. Spread the marmalade on the dough. Gently spread the pepper preserves on top of the marmalade, trying to keep the layers separate. Sprinkle on the almonds, then roll out the remaining dough, cut into strips, and make a lattice top. (Or roll into thin ropes and use those for the lattice.) Bake in the preheated oven until crust is golden and jam is set, about 40 minutes.

Torta sabbiosa / CRUMBLY "SAND" TART

Locanda delle Tre Chiavi, Isera, Trentino

Serves 4 to 6

2 STICKS PLUS 1 TABLESPOONS
(17 TABLESPOONS) UNSALTED
BUTTER, SOFTENED

1⅓ CUPS SUGAR

3 LARGE EGGS

1½ CUPS POTATO STARCH

2 TEASPOONS BAKING
POWDER

1 PINCH SALT

¼ CUP CONFECTIONER'S
SUGAR

The potato starch gives this buttery treat a crumbly texture that makes it perfect with a cup of coffee or tea.

Preheat oven to 325°F. Line a baking pan with parchment and set aside. Beat the softened butter with the sugar. Beat in the eggs one at a time, waiting for them to be incorporated between additions. Sift together the potato starch and baking powder with a pinch of salt and then gradually add the potato starch mixture to the butter mixture, incorporating between additions. Transfer to the prepared pan and bake until golden, 30 minutes. Allow to cool completely and sprinkle with confectioner's sugar.

Torta Greca / "GREEK" ALMOND TART

Pasticceria Franceschin, Mestre di Venezia, Veneto

This tender tart hails from the Castello *sestriere*, or neighborhood, of Venezia, which was once inhabited largely by Greeks and Albanians.

Preheat oven to 325˚ F. Butter and flour a pan and set aside. Melt 4 tablespoons butter and set aside to cool. Grind ⅔ cup almonds to a fine powder, combine with ¾ cup plus 1 tablespoon sugar and set aside. Combine ¾ cup flour, 7 tablespoons butter, and a pinch of salt and incorporate as much water as needed to make a soft dough. On a lightly floured work surface, roll out to a very thin disk—2 millimeters or 0.07 inch. Line the prepared pan with the dough, letting 2 to 2 ¼ inches of dough hang over the sides of the pan.

Separate the eggs and beat the yolks with the remaining 3 tablespoons sugar until frothy and light. Fold the ground almond mixture and the cooled melted butter into the egg yolks. In a separate bowl, whip the egg whites to stiff peaks. Fold the egg whites into the yolk mixture. Pour this mixture into the crust-lined pan, smooth the top, then fold over the border and crimp decoratively. Arrange the remaining 2 tablespoons whole almonds on top in a decorative pattern and bake in the preheated oven until filling is set and crust is golden, 35 to 40 minutes. Let cool, then finish with confectioner's sugar.

Serves 6

11 TABLESPOONS (1 STICK PLUS 3 TABLESPOONS) UNSALTED BUTTER, PLUS MORE FOR BUTTERING PAN

¾ CUP UNBLEACHED ALL-PURPOSE FLOUR, PLUS MORE FOR FLOURING PAN

⅔ CUP PLUS 2 TABLESPOONS BLANCHED ALMONDS

1 CUP SUGAR

1 PINCH SALT

3 LARGE EGGS

¼ CUP CONFECTIONER'S SUGAR

Strudel di mele / APPLE STRUDEL

Nando Ferrari, Trento, Trentino

Serves 8

3 CUPS UNBLEACHED
ALL-PURPOSE FLOUR

1 LARGE EGG, LIGHTLY
BEATEN

¼ CUP PLUS 1 TABLESPOON
EXTRA-VIRGIN OLIVE OIL

¼ CUP PLUS 1 TABLESPOON
PLUS 2 TEASPOONS BOILING
WATER

1 PINCH SALT

½ CUP GOLDEN RAISINS

2 POUNDS REINETTE APPLES

⅓ CUP WALNUTS

2 TABLESPOONS SUGAR

¼ TEASPOON GROUND
CINNAMON

FINELY GRATED ZEST
OF 1 LEMON

1 EGG YOLK

Always have the oven preheated and your filling prepared when you start to roll strudel dough, as this very thin dough can dry out quickly and become difficult to handle. The traditional way to measure the oil for this strudel dough is to use half of the eggshell as a measuring cup. If you would like to do this, simply reserve the eggshell after you have broken the egg and use 3 half-eggshells' worth of oil and 4 of boiling water. There are numerous variations to this recipe, and strudel can be made with a variety of different types of dough, but this is the classic Trentino version.

Place the flour in a bowl, form into a well, and place the egg in the center. Add the olive oil and boiling water to the center as well. Place a pinch of salt in the well, and then gradually begin pulling in flour until you have a firm but elastic dough. Gather the dough into a ball, cover the ball with a dishtowel, and set the dough aside to rest for 30 minutes while you make the filling.

Soak the raisins in warm water to cover until soft, then drain and squeeze dry. Peel, core, and slice the apples. Chop the walnuts. In a bowl, combine the walnuts and raisins. Stir in the sugar, cinnamon, and lemon zest and toss to combine, then add the apples and toss gently.

Preheat oven to 350°F. Line 2 baking sheets with parchment and set aside. Divide the dough into two equal pieces. Roll out half the dough into a very thin rectangle. Arrange half of the filling on the dough and roll it up jellyroll style. Firmly seal the two ends of the strudel by pressing with your fingers or with a fork, then transfer to one of the prepared baking sheets. Repeat with remaining dough and filling and place the second strudel on the second baking sheet. Lightly beat the egg yolk and brush it on the tops of the two strudels. Bake in the preheated oven until golden, about 1 hour.

Crostatine con lamponi / RASPBERRY TARTLETS

Sora Maria e Arcangelo, Olevano Romano (Roma), Lazio

Serves 8

Everyone seems to love an individual dessert. You can also make a raspberry coulis to serve alongside these tasty tartlets.

DOUGH

¾ CUP UNBLEACHED ALL-PURPOSE FLOUR

⅓ CUP SUGAR

1 TABLESPOON FINELY GRATED LEMON ZEST

4 TABLESPOONS UNSALTED BUTTER

1 LARGE EGG

1 EGG YOLK

FILLING

6 EGG YOLKS

¼ CUP PLUS 2 TABLESPOONS SUGAR

¼ CUP PLUS 2 TABLESPOONS UNBLEACHED ALL-PURPOSE FLOUR

4 CUPS WHOLE MILK, ROOM TEMPERATURE

1 LEMON

FINISHING

2 PINTS RASPBERRIES

FRESH MINT LEAVES

To make the dough, combine the flour, sugar, and grated lemon zest. Cut in the butter until the mixture resembles sand, then lightly beat the egg and yolk and stir them into the mixture. Knead, working quickly to avoid overheating the dough, until well-combined and soft. Shape the dough into a ball, wrap it in plastic wrap, and refrigerate it for at least 2 hours.

For the filling, in a bowl beat the egg yolks and the sugar. Gradually beat in the flour a little at a time and then beat in the milk. Cut off the zest of the lemon in one piece (do not grate) and add to the mixture. Transfer to a pot and cook over very low heat, stirring constantly with a wooden spoon, until thickened. Remove lemon zest and let the filling cool to room temperature.

Preheat oven to 350°F. Divide the dough into 8 equal pieces. Shape each piece into a disk and roll each disk out to fit a small tart or cake pan or mold. Bake in the preheated oven until golden and dry, about 20 minutes. Let the tart crusts cool, then fill them with the cream filling. Arrange the raspberries decoratively on top and finish with fresh mint leaves.

Stroscia / CRISP OLIVE OIL CAKE

Stefania Ricca, San Lorenzo al Mare (Imperia), Liguria

Serves 10

8⅓ CUPS UNBLEACHED
ALL-PURPOSE FLOUR

1 TABLESPOON PLUS
1 TEASPOON BAKING POWDER

1½ CUPS SUGAR

FINELY GRATED ZEST
OF 1 LEMON

½ CUP VERMOUTH
OR MARSALA

2 CUPS EXTRA-VIRGIN
OLIVE OIL

¼ CUP CONFECTIONER'S
SUGAR

The Italian love of olive oil is no secret. Still, most desserts use butter, even in Italy. This crisp cake is an exception. It is, in fact, too crisp to cut—diners reach in and break off pieces by hand.

Preheat oven to 375°F. Sift the flour and combine with the baking powder and sugar. Shape the mixture into a well on the work surface and place the lemon zest, vermouth, and olive oil in the center. Gradually pull the dry ingredients into the wet and stir until you have a crumbly dough, then knead briskly until well-combined.

Press the dough into a pan (there's no need to butter the pan because of the amount of oil in the dough) and bake in the preheated oven until golden and dry, about 1 hour. Let the cake cool completely, then sprinkle with confectioner's sugar and serve.

Torta di mele e pere / APPLE AND PEAR CAKE

Alessia Battaglino, Bra (Cuneo), Piemonte

Serves 4 to 6

1 CUP UNBLEACHED
ALL-PURPOSE FLOUR

2½ TEASPOONS CREAM
OF TARTAR

1 PINCH SALT

FINELY GRATED ZEST
OF ½ LEMON

¼ CUP CORN OIL

3 TABLESPOONS MAPLE SYRUP

ABOUT ¼ CUP RICE MILK

3 MEDIUM APPLES

1 MEDIUM PEAR

⅓ CUP SLICED ALMONDS

Plain and not overly sweet cakes studded with fruit like this are eaten all over Italy, not only for dessert, but also for breakfast and as a mid-morning or mid-afternoon snack.

Preheat oven to 350°F. Line a cake pan with parchment paper and set aside.

Sift the flour into a bowl and stir in the cream of tartar, salt, and lemon zest. Whisk together the oil, maple syrup, and ¼ cup rice milk and stir into the dry ingredients. You should have a fairly thick batter, but if it seems too dry, add a little more milk. Peel, core, and dice the apples and the pear and fold into the batter. Fold in the almonds as well. Transfer the batter to the prepared pan and bake in the preheated oven until the top springs back when pressed with a finger and a tester inserted in the center emerges clean, about 1 hour.

Torta di zucca / SQUASH CAKE

Trattoria La Vecia, Pontecchio Polesine (Rovigo), Veneto

The use of winter squash in desserts dates back to at least the nineteenth century. Amaretti cookies are almond cookies. They are also sometimes used in savory dishes.

Preheat oven to 350°F. Soak the raisins in warm water to cover. Halve the squash and scoop out the seeds and strings. Place on a baking sheet and roast until soft and easily pierced with a fork, 30 to 45 minutes. Leave the oven on. Peel the squash and puree in a blender. Combine with the flour, sugar, salt, and lemon zest. Drain and squeeze the raisins dry, then fold them into the mixture. Fold in the crumbled amaretti cookies.

Transfer the mixture to a cake pan and bake in the preheated oven until it is firm and a tester emerges clean, about 30 minutes.

Serves 6

3 TABLESPOONS GOLDEN RAISINS

1 WINTER SQUASH, 2 TO 3 POUNDS

2 TABLESPOONS UNBLEACHED ALL-PURPOSE FLOUR

3 TABLESPOONS SUGAR

1 PINCH SALT

FINELY GRATED ZEST OF 1 LEMON

¼ CUP CRUMBLED AMARETTI COOKIES

Torta di carote / CARROT CAKE

Trattoria All'Isolo, Verona, Veneto

For a festive carrot cake, double the recipe and make two layers, then stack them with a thin layer of peach or apricot jam spread between them.

Preheat the oven to 325°F. Butter a cake pan with the butter and set aside. Finely chop the carrots in a food processor fitted with the metal blade. Grind the almonds to a powder and set aside.

Separate the eggs and beat the yolks with the granulated sugar until light and foamy. Stir in the carrots, almonds, turbinado sugar, honey, and the orange juice. Beat the egg whites to stiff peaks and fold the egg whites, a little at a time, into the carrot mixture. Transfer to the prepared pan and bake in the preheated oven until the top of the cake springs back when pressed and a tester emerges clean, about 1 hour and 20 minutes.

Serves 4 to 6

1 TABLESPOON UNSALTED BUTTER

11 OUNCES (4 MEDIUM) CARROTS

1¾ CUPS BLANCHED ALMONDS

4 LARGE EGGS

¾ CUP GRANULATED SUGAR

¾ CUP TURBINADO SUGAR

1 TABLESPOON HONEY

JUICE OF 4 ORANGES

Krasko pecivo / NUT CAKE

Ristorante Devetak, Savogna d'Isonzo (Gorizia), Friuli Venezia Giulia

Serves 4 to 6

11 TABLESPOONS (1 STICK
PLUS 3 TABLESPOONS)
UNSALTED BUTTER,
SOFTENED, PLUS MORE FOR
BUTTERING PAN

2⅓ CUPS WALNUTS

⅔ CUP ALMONDS

1¼ CUPS SUGAR

4 LARGE EGGS

1¼ CUPS UNBLEACHED
ALL-PURPOSE FLOUR

1 CUP HAZELNUT FLOUR

2 TEASPOONS BAKING
POWDER

2 TABLESPOONS RUM

A slice of this satisfying cake—which reflects the Slovenian heritage of the Friuli Venezia Giulia region—is often served with the cherry plums that grow wild in the area.

Preheat oven to 325°F. Butter a loaf pan and set aside. Coarsely chop the nuts. Separate the eggs. In a bowl beat the sugar with the egg yolks and the butter until smooth. In a separate bowl, combine the flour, hazelnut flour, and baking powder. Gradually add the flour mixture to the egg yolks, incorporating between additions. Fold in the nuts. Whip the egg whites to stiff peaks and fold those in as well. Finally, fold in the rum. Transfer to the prepared pan and bake in the preheated oven until cake is firm to the touch and a tester inserted near the center emerges clean, about 1 hour. Serve warm or at room temperature.

Torta Rosata / ALMOND AND LEMON CAKE

Paolo Giangrande, Monopoli (Bari), Puglia

Serves 4 to 6

2 CUPS TORITTO ALMONDS
OR OTHER ALMONDS

1 TEASPOON BAKING POWDER

1 TABLESPOON WHOLE MILK

5 LARGE EGGS

1¼ CUPS SUGAR

FINELY GRATED ZEST
OF 2 LEMONS

Toritto almonds (named for the town in Puglia where they originated) boast their own Slow Food Presidium. Their creamy interior makes them a favorite for all kinds of baking and confections. They are frequently caramelized into brittle. At one time a wide range of almond varieties—many of them named for famous local figures—were grown around Bari.

Preheat oven to 350°F. Line a 9-inch cake pan with parchment paper and set aside. Toast the almonds and grind them to a powder. Dissolve the baking powder in the milk. Separate the eggs and beat the yolks with the sugar. Stir in the ground almonds little at a time, stirring to combine between additions. Stir in the milk mixture, then the grated lemon zest. Whip the egg whites to stiff peaks and fold into the yolk mixture. Transfer the batter to the prepared pan and bake in the preheated oven until the top is springy and golden and a tester inserted in the center emerges clean, 50 to 60 minutes.

Torta di nocciole / FLOURLESS HAZELNUT CAKE

Di Pietro, Melito Irpino (Avellino), Campania

The easiest way to skin hazelnuts is to toast them lightly and then rub them vigorously in a clean kitchen towel. Giffoni hazelnuts are an IGP (Protected Geographic Origin) item are round and uniform in size with a very thin skin that peels off particularly easily. Flourless nut cakes (perfect for those who have issues consuming gluten) are made all over Italy with different varieties of nuts.

Preheat oven to 300°F. Butter a cake pan with the butter and set aside. Toast, skin, and chop the hazelnuts. In a bowl combine the hazelnuts and sugar, then beat in the egg yolks until thick and well-combined. In a separate bowl, whip the egg whites to stiff peaks. Fold them into the egg yolk mixture, deflating as little as possible. Transfer the batter to the prepared pan and bake in the preheated oven until the top is springy and golden and a tester inserted in the center emerges clean, about 40 minutes.

Serves 4 to 6

1 TABLESPOON UNSALTED BUTTER

1⅓ CUPS GIFFONI HAZELNUTS OR OTHER HAZELNUTS

1 CUP SUGAR

5 EGG YOLKS

7 EGG WHITES

Torta caprese / CHOCOLATE ALMOND CAKE

Laura D'Amore, Salerno, Campania

Be sure to grind the almonds finely for this cake, but don't grind them to the point where they turn into a paste. You want them to be a fine powder. Using raw almonds rather than blanched almonds gives the cake a little more substance. This is another of Italy's wonderful flourless nut cakes.

Preheat oven to 350°F. Butter a cake pan and set aside. Beat the 2 sticks plus 2 tablespoons butter with ½ cup sugar until fluffy. Melt the chocolate in the top of a double boiler. Grind the almonds to a powder. Separate the eggs. Add the egg yolks to the butter mixture one at a time, beating to incorporate between additions. Beat in the chocolate and then stir in the almonds.

In another bowl, whip the egg whites with the remaining ½ cup sugar to stiff peaks and fold them gently into the yolk mixture. Transfer the batter to the prepared pan and bake until a tester inserted in the center emerges clean, about 50 minutes. Allow the cake to cool, then sprinkle with the confectioner's sugar.

Serves 4 to 6

2 STICKS PLUS 2 TABLESPOONS (18 TABLESPOONS) UNSALTED BUTTER, SOFTENED, PLUS MORE FOR BUTTERING PAN

1 CUP SUGAR

7 OUNCES DARK CHOCOLATE, CHOPPED

2 CUPS RAW ALMONDS

5 LARGE EGGS

¼ CUP CONFECTIONER'S SUGAR

Schiaccia briaca / DRUNKEN CAKE

Osteria La Botte Gaia, Porto Azzurro (Livorno), Toscana

Serves 4 to 6

½ CUP PLUS 2 TABLESPOONS
EXTRA-VIRGIN OLIVE OIL,
PLUS MORE FOR OILING PAN

⅔ CUP GOLDEN RAISINS

¾ CUP SUGAR

1 TABLESPOON HONEY

⅔ TO 1 CUP NUTS, SUCH AS
ALMONDS, WALNUTS, OR
HAZELNUTS

2½ CUPS UNBLEACHED
ALL-PURPOSE FLOUR

1 TEASPOON BAKING POWDER

2 TABLESPOONS ALCHERMES

¼ TO ½ CUP ALEATICO WINE

¼ CUP PINE NUTS

Sweet Aleatico wine turns this cake red, as does bright pink alchermes liqueur. A rustic dessert from the island of Elba, this has a dense texture.

Preheat oven to 400°F. Oil an 8-inch cake pan and line with parchment paper, then oil the paper as well and set aside. Soak the raisins in warm water to cover until soft, then drain and squeeze dry. Set aside a few raisins for garnish. Combine the remaining raisins, all but 1 tablespoon of the sugar, and the honey. Chop the nuts (almonds, walnuts, or hazelnuts) and add to the raisin mixture.

Combine the flour and baking powder and form into a well on the work surface. Place the nut and raisin mixture in the center of the well. Add ½ cup olive oil, 1 tablespoon of the alchermes, and the Aleatico wine. Begin to draw in the dry ingredients from the sides of the well. When you have a crumbly mixture, knead until the ingredients are well-combined and the dough is quite firm.

Transfer the dough to the prepared pan and press it so that it is even. Sprinkle on the pine nuts and the reserved raisins. Drizzle on the remaining 1 tablespoon alchermes. Drizzle with the remaining 2 tablespoons olive oil. Sprinkle the top with the remaining 1 tablespoon sugar and bake in the preheated oven until a tester inserted in the center emerges clean, 40 to 50 minutes. Cool to room temperature before serving.

Muffin di mirtilli con fichi / INDIVIDUAL BLUEBERRY FIG CAKES

Barbara Torresan, Milano, Lombardia

Rice cream is a great boon to vegans. To make your own, you can whisk together rice flour and water and cook over low heat until thickened, or soak rice in cold water to cover by several inches for 8 hours, then rinse and puree the soaked rice in a blender with fresh cold water until it is creamy.

Preheat oven to 375°F. In a bowl combine the farro flour, baking powder, and sugar. Drizzle in the oil and rice cream and stir just to combine. Do not overbeat. Fold in the blueberries. Dice the figs and fold those in as well. Line a muffin tin with liners and fill the liners with the batter. Bake until a tester emerges clean, about 20 minutes.

Serves 4 to 6

1½ CUPS FARRO FLOUR

1 TEASPOON BAKING POWDER

¼ CUP TURBINADO SUGAR

¼ CUP SUNFLOWER OIL

1 CUP RICE CREAM

1½ CUPS BLUEBERRIES

4 TO 5 FIGS

Torta di grano saraceno con confettura di mirtilli / LINGONBERRY JAM BUCKWHEAT LAYER CAKE

Osteria Nerina, Romeno, Trentino

You can use either blanched or raw almonds. The former yields a lighter cake, the latter a cake that's a little more rustic. If you can obtain raw Malga butter from the mountains, use it here.

Preheat oven to 350°F. Melt the butter and set aside to cool. Grind the almonds to a powder. Butter and flour a springform pan and set aside. Beat the melted and cooled butter with ¾ cup of the sugar until smooth. Separate the eggs. Beat the egg yolks into the butter mixture one at a time, beating to incorporate between additions, then beat in the buckwheat flour until combined, beat in the vanilla sugar, then fold in the almonds. Beat the egg whites to stiff peaks, gradually adding the remaining ½ cup sugar. Fold the egg whites into the batter. Transfer the batter to the prepared pan and bake in the preheated oven until a tester emerges clean, about 45 minutes. Allow to cool completely, then cut in half horizontally and spread the jam in between the layers. Sift the confectioner's sugar over the assembled cake.

Serves 4 to 6

2 STICKS PLUS 2 TABLESPOONS (18 TABLESPOONS) UNSALTED BUTTER, PLUS MORE FOR BUTTERING PAN

1¾ CUPS ALMONDS

FLOUR FOR FLOURING PAN

1¼ CUPS SUGAR

6 LARGE EGGS

1½ CUPS BUCKWHEAT FLOUR

1 TABLESPOON VANILLA SUGAR

1½ CUPS LINGONBERRY JAM

¼ CUP CONFECTIONER'S SUGAR

Torta di riso alle fragole con mousse alla vaniglia /
RICE FLOUR CAKE WITH STRAWBERRIES AND VANILLA MOUSSE

Risotteria Melotti, Isola della Scala (Verona), Veneto

Serves 4 to 6

DOUGH

6 TABLESPOONS UNSALTED BUTTER, SOFTENED, PLUS MORE FOR BUTTERING PAN

1¼ CUPS RICE FLOUR, PLUS MORE FOR FLOURING PAN

3 EGG YOLKS

2 TEASPOONS BAKING POWDER

⅓ CUP SUGAR

FINELY GRATED ZEST OF ½ LEMON

FILLING AND FINISHING

2 EGG YOLKS

¼ CUP PLUS 2 TABLESPOONS SUGAR

SEEDS OF ½ VANILLA BEAN

½ CUP WHOLE MILK

2 CUPS STRAWBERRIES

1 CUP WHIPPING CREAM

Don't overwork the dough for this tart's crust or it will get tough. It's okay if there are still bits of butter visible. This is the perfect finish to any summer meal.

Preheat oven to 350°F. Butter and flour an 11-inch round pan with high sides and a fluted rim and set aside. For the dough, form the 1¼ cups rice flour into a well on the work surface. Place the 3 egg yolks, the baking powder, the ⅓ cup sugar, and the lemon zest in the center of the well. Cut the 6 tablespoons butter into pieces and add those to the well. Begin to pull in flour from the sides of the well, and when you have a crumbly mixture, knead as little as possible until you have a smooth dough. Press the dough into the bottom and up the sides of the prepared pan. Bake in the preheated oven until golden and dry to the touch, about 20 minutes.

While the crust is baking, make a pastry cream for the mousse you will use as a filling. In a large pot stir together the 2 egg yolks, ¼ cup plus 2 tablespoons sugar, and the vanilla bean seeds until well-combined. Whisk in the milk in a thin stream. Place the pot over medium heat and cook, stirring frequently, until thickened. Do not allow the mixture to boil. Remove from the heat and set aside to cool. Slice 5 or 6 strawberries for finishing. Halve the remaining strawberries and set aside.

When the pastry cream has cooled, whip the whipping cream to stiff peaks and fold it gently into the pastry cream. Spread about half of the halved strawberries evenly over the crust. Spread about half the mousse over the halved strawberries. Top with the remaining halved strawberries. Spread the remaining mousse on top and smooth with an offset spatula. You can also create decorative lines in the top layer of mousse. Refrigerate the tart for at least 2 hours and decorate with the sliced strawberries just before serving.

Amor Polenta / POLENTA CAKE

Osteria Pane e Vino, Todi (Perugia), Umbria

Serves 4 to 6

1 STICK PLUS 6 TABLESPOONS
(14 TABLESPOONS) UNSALTED
BUTTER, PLUS MORE FOR
BUTTERING PAN

20 BLANCHED
BITTER ALMONDS

5 LARGE EGGS

1¼ CUPS SUGAR

1⅔ CUPS UNBLEACHED
ALL-PURPOSE FLOUR

1 CUP FINELY GROUND
POLENTA

¼ CUP WHITE VERMOUTH

2 TEASPOONS
BAKING POWDER

WHOLE MILK, IF NEEDED

Because cornmeal is very "thirsty," you may need to add a little milk or water after assembling the batter. This cake is traditionally baked in a cylindrical pan with ribs that lend it a characteristic shape, but you can use a loaf pan, too. If you cannot obtain bitter almonds, use blanched sweet almonds and add a few drops of almond extract to the batter. Slices of this cake are delicious with zabaione or pastry cream.

Preheat oven to 350°F. Butter a pan (see note) and set aside. Melt the 1 stick plus 6 tablespoons butter and set aside to cool. Grind the almonds to a fine powder. Separate the eggs. Beat the yolks with the sugar until foamy. In a separate bowl, whip the egg whites to stiff peaks. Fold the egg whites into the yolk mixture, then stir in the flour and polenta and then the melted butter, the vermouth, and the almonds. Sprinkle on the baking powder and stir to combine. If the batter seems very thick and dry, work in a little milk (or even water) at a time until it is a spreadable consistency. Transfer to the prepared pan, smooth the top with a spatula, and bake in the preheated oven until a tester emerges clean, 30 to 40 minutes. Let the cake cool in the pan for a few minutes, then unmold and allow to cool completely.

Laciada / SWEET PANCAKE

Trattoria Inarca, Proserpio (Como), Lombardia

Serves 3 to 4

⅓ CUP UNBLEACHED
ALL-PURPOSE FLOUR

1 PINCH SALT

EXTRA-VIRGIN OLIVE OIL
FOR FRYING

¼ CUP SUGAR

Laciada may be served as dessert or as a mid-morning or mid-afternoon snack. Even when your cupboards are bare, you probably have the ingredients to make this simple and satisfying sweet.

Line a baking sheet with paper towels and set aside. In a bowl, whisk the flour with 2 cups water until smooth. Whisk in the salt. Fill a skillet with at least 2 inches of olive oil and place over medium heat. When the oil is very hot but not smoking, add the batter, distributing it as evenly as possible with a spatula or the back of a spoon. Cook until browned underneath, then flip the pancake (use a pot lid or a large plate if necessary). Cook until browned on both sides, then transfer to the prepared pan to drain briefly. Cut the pancake into irregular pieces, sprinkle with the sugar, and serve hot.

Dolce di granturco al cacao / BAKED CHOCOLATE POLENTA

Trattoria La Sosta, Cremona, Lombardia

Serves 4 to 6

1 STICK (8 TABLESPOONS) UNSALTED BUTTER, SOFTENED, PLUS MORE FOR BUTTERING PAN

2 CUPS WHOLE MILK

1½ CUPS FINELY GROUND POLENTA

3 EGG YOLKS

1 PINCH GROUND CINNAMON

⅓ CUP SUGAR

1 CUP FINELY CRUSHED AMARETTI COOKIES

½ CUP PLUS 1 TABLESPOON COCOA POWDER

½ CUP HEAVY CREAM OR WHIPPING CREAM

¼ CUP CONFECTIONER'S SUGAR FOR FINISHING

Use finely ground polenta to make this cross between a cake and a pudding.

Preheat oven to 350°F. Butter a cake or pie pan and set aside. Place the milk in a pot and bring to a boil. As soon as it starts to bubble, add the polenta in a thin stream and cook, stirring constantly, for 20 minutes. Remove from the heat and allow to cool until just warm.

Briskly stir the egg yolks into the polenta mixture. Stir in the cinnamon, sugar, 1 stick butter, crushed amaretti, cocoa powder, and the cream. Stir briskly until thoroughly combined, then transfer the mixture to the prepared pan and bake in the preheated oven until firm, about 30 minutes. Sprinkle with confectioner's sugar just before serving.

Tisichelle / WINE AND ANISE SEED COOKIES

Trattoria La Tacchinella, Canzano (Teramo), Abruzzo

Makes 4 to 6 dozen cookies

1 CUP SUGAR

½ CUP EXTRA-VIRGIN OLIVE OIL

¼ CUP ANISE SEEDS

½ CUP TREBBIANO WINE

2 TO 3 CUPS UNBLEACHED ALL-PURPOSE FLOUR

Trebbiano is a fruity white wine cultivated in Italy since the Roman era.

Preheat oven to 325°F. Line a baking sheet with parchment paper and set aside. In a bowl combine ¾ cup of the sugar with the oil, anise seeds, and the wine. Add enough flour to make an elastic dough. Shape small pieces of the dough into ropes, then seal the ends together to form oval rings. Dredge the rings in the remaining ¼ cup sugar and place them on the prepared pan. Bake until golden on top, about 30 minutes.

Gubana / DRIED FRUIT AND NUT ROLL

Marco Pecile, Fagagna (Udine), Friuli Venezia Giulia

In Trieste, a similarly spiral-shaped Easter cake called a presnitz is made with a nut and candied fruit filing scented with ground cloves, cinnamon, and nutmeg.

To make the dough, place the flour in a large bowl. Cut the butter into pieces and scatter on top of the flour, then cut in the butter until the mixture feels like sand. Lightly beat the eggs with the grappa and add to the bowl. Stir with a fork until the mixture is combined, then knead until dough is smooth and well-combined. Wrap in plastic and set aside in a cool place.

Preheat oven to 350°F. Butter a round cake pan and set aside. For the filling, soak the raisins in the Marsala until soft. Brown the breadcrumbs in 2 tablespoons of the butter and set aside. Dice the figs and prunes. Shave the chocolate with a vegetable peeler. Chop the walnuts and almonds. Place the walnuts and almonds in a bowl and add the candied orange peel and citron peel, the diced prunes and figs, and the chocolate. Knead in the bowl until well-combined. Drain the raisins, squeeze them dry, and add to the mixture. Once the raisins are incorporated, stir in the pine nuts and grated lemon and orange zest. Add the egg yolk and knead to combine, then knead in the browned breadcrumbs. Separate the whole egg and beat the white to stiff peaks. Fold the egg white into the mixture.

Melt the remaining 2 tablespoons butter and set aside to cool. Roll out the dough to a rectangle of even thickness. Spread the filling evenly on the dough with a spatula. Roll the dough jelly-roll style, then form the roll into a spiral and place in the prepared pan. Lightly beat the egg yolk with the melted butter and brush the top with this mixture. Sprinkle with the sugar and bake in the preheated oven until golden, about 40 minutes.

Serves 6

DOUGH

2½ CUPS UNBLEACHED ALL-PURPOSE FLOUR

2 STICKS PLUS 2 TABLESPOONS (18 TABLESPOONS) UNSALTED BUTTER, PLUS MORE FOR BUTTERING PAN

2 LARGE EGGS

3 TABLESPOONS GRAPPA OR RUM

FILLING AND FINISHING

¾ CUP GOLDEN RAISINS

½ CUP MARSALA

1 TABLESPOON BREADCRUMBS

4 TABLESPOONS UNSALTED BUTTER

2 DRIED FIGS

2 PRUNES

1 OUNCE DARK CHOCOLATE

1½ CUPS WALNUTS

½ CUP BLANCHED ALMONDS

3 TABLESPOONS DICED CANDIED ORANGE PEEL

3 TABLESPOONS DICED CANDIED CITRON

½ CUP PINE NUTS

FINELY GRATED ZEST OF 1 LEMON

FINELY GRATED ZEST OF 1 ORANGE

1 EGG YOLK

1 LARGE EGG

¼ CUP SUGAR

Dolce di pere in sfoglia / LAYERED PEAR CAKE

Trattoria Al Ponte, Acquanegra sul Chiese (Mantova), Lombardia

Serves 6

6 FIRM ABATE FETEL
PEARS OR OTHER PEARS

2 TABLESPOONS PASSITO WINE

2 OUNCES DARK
CHOCOLATE, CHOPPED

1 PINCH GROUND CINNAMON

4 LARGE EGGS

½ CUP WHOLE MILK

3 TABLESPOONS SUGAR

2 TABLESPOONS RUM

3 TABLESPOONS UNBLEACHED
ALL-PURPOSE FLOUR

2 TABLESPOONS
UNSALTED BUTTER

7 OUNCES ALL-BUTTER
PUFF PASTRY

1 EGG YOLK

Sweet passito wine is sometimes called straw wine or raisin wine, because it is made from grapes that are dried on straw mats in the sun before being pressed. Abate Fetel pears are long and narrow and very aromatic. The variety was developed in France in the nineteenth century. You can make your own puff pastry dough (a time-consuming process) or purchase packaged puff pastry. For added crunch, sprinkle a handful of chopped blanched almonds on top of the tart after applying the egg wash and dotting with the butter.

Preheat oven to 325°F. Peel, core, and thinly slice the pears. In a pot, combine the passito wine, chocolate, and cinnamon and cook over low heat, whisking, until chocolate has melted. Add the pears and simmer over low heat, stirring occasionally, until pears are soft enough to pierce with a fork. Let the pears cool in any remaining liquid.

Combine the 4 eggs, the milk, the sugar, and the rum. Whisk in the flour until smooth. Heat a crêpe pan or sauté pan over low heat. Butter the pan lightly and pour in about one sixth of the egg mixture. Cook into a thin crêpe, turning once, and set aside. Repeat with remaining egg mixture to make six crêpes total (if you have to stack them, place wax paper between them to avoid sticking) and have used up the egg mixture, buttering the pan in between as needed with about 1 tablespoon butter total. Set the crêpes aside.

Roll out the puff pastry into a very thin disk and place it in a baking pan with the edges hanging over. Place one crêpe in the center and top with some of the pears, gently spreading them evenly with a spatula. Repeat layers of crêpes and pears until you have used up both. Fold the overhanging puff pastry on top of the cake. Lightly beat the egg yolk and brush the top of the cake with it. Dot with the remaining 1 tablespoon butter. Bake until puff pastry is crisp and golden, about 1 hour.

Tegole / TILE COOKIES ▷

Pasticceria Morandin, Saint-Vincent, Valle d'Aosta

Makes 10 to 12 dozen cookies

2⅔ CUPS HAZELNUTS

⅔ CUP WALNUTS

2⅔ CUPS SUGAR

¾ CUP PLUS 1 TABLESPOON UNBLEACHED ALL-PURPOSE FLOUR

5 EGG WHITES

¼ TEASPOON VANILLA EXTRACT

These delicious cookies—which traditionally were draped over rolling pins to cool so that they curved—can be varied by incorporating cocoa nibs along with the nuts.

Preheat the oven to 325°F.

Toast and skin the hazelnuts, then chop the hazelnuts and walnuts together. Combine the chopped nuts, sugar, and flour. Stir in the egg whites and vanilla. Fold the nut mixture into the egg whites. Transfer to a pastry bag fitted with a plain tip and, using a cookie cutter or round mold, pipe circles 1 to 1½ inches in diameter on nonstick baking sheets, leaving a generous amount of space between the cookies. Bake in the preheated oven until golden on top, 5 to 14 minutes.

Balocchi / NUT AND RAISIN COOKIES

Ristorante Il Moderno, Viterbo, Lazio

Makes about 6 dozen cookies

½ CUP EXTRA-VIRGIN OLIVE OIL, PLUS MORE FOR OILING PANS

2⅓ CUPS HAZELNUTS

¾ CUP GOLDEN RAISINS

4¼ CUPS UNBLEACHED ALL-PURPOSE FLOUR

1¾ CUPS SUGAR

2 TEASPOONS GROUND CINNAMON

½ CUP WHITE WINE

2 TABLESPOONS ANISE LIQUEUR

⅓ CUP PINE NUTS

These are soft nut cookies with just a hint of anise from the liqueur. Take care not to overbake them—they are meant to be soft.

Preheat oven to 350°F. Oil baking sheets and set aside. Toast and skin the hazelnuts, then chop them and set aside. Soak the raisins in warm water until soft, then drain and squeeze dry. In a bowl combine the flour, sugar, and cinnamon. Stir in the wine, liqueur, and oil. Incorporate the hazelnuts, pine nuts, and raisins. Add a little water if the mixture seems extremely dry.

Shape the dough into small balls and place them on the prepared pans. Bake in the preheated oven just until golden, about 15 minutes.

Amaretti / ALMOND COOKIES

Pasticceria Bria, Albenga (Savona), Liguria

Makes about 2 dozen cookies

⅔ CUP BITTER ALMOND FLOUR

½ CUP ALMOND FLOUR

1 CUP HAZELNUT FLOUR

½ CUP SUGAR

1 TABLESPOON AMMONIUM BICARBONATE

1 EGG WHITE

ABOUT 1 TABLESPOON HONEY

BUTTER FOR BUTTERING PANS

Amaretti may be hard or soft. These tasty cookies are great on their own and are also crumbled or crushed and incorporated into many dishes, both savory and sweet. You can make your own nut flours by grinding nuts in a food processor fitted with the metal blade. Just be sure to grind them just to a powder—go too far and you'll release their oils and end up with a paste. If you can't locate bitter almonds or bitter almond flour, use all standard almond flour and add a few drops of almond extract for a pleasant hint of bitterness. Ammonium bicarbonate can be found in gourmet and baking specialty shops and Greek grocery stores. Ammonium bicarbonate is smelling salts, so don't sniff the jar! The strong odor dissipates after baking.

Preheat oven to 350°F. Combine the almond flours and hazelnut flour with the sugar and the ammonium bicarbonate. Whip the egg white to stiff peaks and fold it into the mixture. Add enough honey to make a sticky mixture. (It may help to heat up the honey to liquefy it.) Combine thoroughly.

Butter baking sheets and shape the cookie dough into small balls. Place them on the prepared baking sheets and squash lightly with the palm of your hand. Bake in the preheated oven until dry to the touch, 7 to 8 minutes.

Spumini alle mandorle / MERINGUE KISSES WITH ALMONDS

Ristorante La Palomba, Mondavio (Pesaro e Urbino), Marche

Makes 4 to 6 dozen cookies

4 EGG WHITES

1¼ CUPS SUGAR

1⅓ CUPS BLANCHED ALMONDS, CHOPPED

Meringues need to bake at low heat. If you have a convection setting on your oven, that is helpful. Piping these with a pastry bag makes them look a little prettier.

Preheat oven to 200°F. Line baking sheets with parchment paper (or oil them lightly) and set aside. Whip the egg whites with the sugar with an electric mixer until they form stiff peaks, at least 3 minutes. Fold in the almonds. Drop meringues by the teaspoon onto the baking sheets, or transfer the mixture to a pastry bag and pipe them onto the baking sheets. Bake until dry to the touch, about 1 hour and 20 minutes.

Beccùte / CORNMEAL COOKIES

Marina Ferretti, Senigallia (Ancona), Marche

In the area around Ancona these are a Christmas treat, but elsewhere in the Marche they appear during Lent.

Preheat oven to 300°F. Soak the raisins in warm water for 30 minutes to soften. Drain and squeeze dry. Chop the walnuts, almonds and dried figs together and set aside. Shape the cornmeal into a well in a large bowl. Add the oil, raisins, pine nuts, chopped nuts and figs, sugar, salt, and pepper to the center of the well. Add a few tablespoons of boiling water to the center of the well. Begin to pull in dry ingredients from the sides of the well (use a fork rather than your fingers to avoid burning yourself), and continue to mix and add water in small amounts until you have a soft and well-combined dough. Shape the dough into small balls and place them on baking sheets or cookie sheets. Flatten the cookies slightly. Bake in the preheated oven until golden, about 15 minutes, and cool completely before serving.

Makes 2 to 3 dozen cookies

⅓ CUP RAISINS

⅓ CUP WALNUTS

⅓ CUP BLANCHED ALMONDS

3 DRIED FIGS

1¾ CUPS CORNMEAL

2 TABLESPOONS
EXTRA-VIRGIN OLIVE OIL

⅓ CUP PINE NUTS

1 TABLESPOON PLUS
1½ TEASPOONS SUGAR

1 PINCH SALT

1 PINCH FRESHLY
GROUND BLACK PEPPER

ABOUT 1 CUP BOILING WATER

Biscotti strudel / STRUDEL COOKIES

Marina Marini, Forlì, Emilia-Romagna

Vin santo is a very sweet dessert wine that not only is used as an ingredient in these rustic cookies, but also marries with them perfectly.

Preheat oven to 350°F. Butter and flour baking sheets and set aside. Soak the raisins in warm water until soft, then drain and squeeze dry. Combine the flour and the sugar. Stir in the vin santo and the olive oil, then stir in the raisins and pine nuts. Sift the baking powder over the dough, then knead until well-combined and firm. Pull off pieces of dough, roll them into balls, and place them on the prepared pans. Bake in the preheated oven until golden, 15 to 18 minutes.

Makes 4 to 6 dozen cookies

1⅓ CUPS RAISINS

4 CUPS UNBLEACHED
ALL-PURPOSE FLOUR

1 CUP SUGAR

¾ CUP VIN SANTO

¾ CUP OLIVE OIL

⅔ CUP PINE NUTS

1 TABLESPOON PLUS
½ TEASPOON BAKING POWDER

Ciambelline con il vino / WINE RING COOKIES

Maria Garzaniti, Guardavalle (Catanzaro), Calabria

Makes about 6 dozen cookies

4 CUPS UNBLEACHED
ALL-PURPOSE FLOUR

3 CUPS SEMOLINA FLOUR

1 TABLESPOON PLUS
½ TEASPOON BAKING
POWDER

2 CUPS SUGAR

1½ CUPS EXTRA-VIRGIN
OLIVE OIL

½ CUP RED WINE

FINELY GRATED ZEST
OF ½ LEMON

¼ CUP ANISE LIQUEUR

These eggless, not-too-sweet cookies can also be made with white wine rather than red, or with sweet vin santo in place of the liqueur.

Preheat oven to 350°F. Line baking sheets with parchment and set aside. Stir together the flours, the baking powder, 1¾ cups of the sugar, the oil, the wine, the lemon zest, and the liqueur and knead until well-combined. Drizzle in a little more olive oil if the dough seems too stiff. Roll the dough out evenly, cut into strips, and form the strips into rings, pinching the ends to seal them. If the dough crumbles, simply pinch it back together. Dredge the rings in the remaining ¼ cup sugar (or sprinkly with sugar if too fragile to move). Bake in the preheated oven until golden, about 20 minutes.

Bracalaccio / SWEET FRITTERS

Gino Zampolini, Magione (Perugia), Umbria

Serves 4

1⅔ CUPS UNBLEACHED
ALL-PURPOSE FLOUR

1 PINCH SALT

ABOUT 1 CUP EXTRA-VIRGIN
OLIVE OIL FOR FRYING

SUGAR OR HONEY TO TASTE

These fritters can be as sweet as you like—it all depends on how much sugar or honey you opt to use.

Line baking sheets with paper towels and set aside. In a bowl combine the flour and salt, then stir in ¾ cup water. You should have a fairly liquid batter. Place the oil in a heavy pot with high sides. It should fill the pot by at least 2 inches. Bring to high temperature for frying and drop in the batter by the spoonful, working in batches to keep from crowding the pan. The fritters should be a little less than ¼ inch thick. As they brown on one side, gently turn them and brown them on the other side. Remove browned fritters to the prepared pan to drain briefly, then sprinkle with sugar or drizzle with honey and serve hot.

Chiffel / CRESCENT PASTRIES

Ubaldo Balbi, Muggia (Trieste), Friuli Venezia Giulia

Be sure to use thick preserves, nothing watery or runny, in filling these little pastries. These can also be filled with pastry cream.

Make a starter by dissolving the yeast in the milk, then combining that mixture with about ¾ cup of the flour. Beat into a shaggy dough, form into a ball, place in a bowl, slash an X in the top, cover with a dish towel, and set aside to rise until puffed, about 1 hour.

While the starter is rising, knead together the remaining 1¾ cups flour, 3 eggs, the egg yolk, 2 tablespoons of the sugar, the salt, and the lemon zest into a soft dough. If the dough is very dry and stiff, knead in milk a little at a time. Knead in the 11 tablespoons butter and the starter. Knead until very soft and elastic, then form the dough into a ball, place in a bowl, cover, and set aside to rise in a warm, draft-free place for at least 2 hours. Knead the dough briefly again and then again shape it into a ball, return it to the bowl, cover, and set aside to rise for at least 8 hours, preferably overnight.

The next day, butter and flour baking sheets. Roll out the dough to a little less than ¼ inch thick and cut into triangles with 4-inch sides. Place about 1 teaspoon of apricot or peach preserves in the center of each triangle. Roll each triangle from the long end and form into a crescent. Repeat with remaining triangles. Arrange on the prepared baking sheets and allow to rise for about 1 hour. Meanwhile, preheat oven to 400°F. Lightly beat the remaining egg and brush the pastries with it, then sprinkle them with the remaining 1 tablespoon sugar. Bake in the preheated oven until browned, about 20 minutes.

Makes about 2 dozen pastries

1 TABLESPOON ACTIVE
DRY YEAST

ABOUT ¾ CUP WHOLE MILK,
WARM

2½ CUPS UNBLEACHED
ALL-PURPOSE FLOUR, PLUS
MORE FOR FLOURING PANS

4 LARGE EGGS

1 EGG YOLK

3 TABLESPOONS SUGAR

1 TEASPOON SALT

FINELY GRATED ZEST
OF ½ LEMON

11 TABLESPOONS (1 STICK
PLUS 3 TABLESPOONS)
UNSALTED BUTTER,
SOFTENED, PLUS MORE FOR
BUTTERING PANS

½ CUP APRICOT
OR PEACH PRESERVES

Knödel di albicocca / APRICOT POTATO DUMPLINGS

Ristorante Kohlern, Bolzano-Bozen, Alto Adige

Makes 8 dumplings, serves 4

14 OUNCES (ABOUT 2 MEDIUM) POTATOES

2 EGG YOLKS

4 TABLESPOONS UNSALTED BUTTER, SOFTENED

1¼ CUPS UNBLEACHED ALL-PURPOSE FLOUR, PLUS MORE FOR FLOURING WORK SURFACE

8 APRICOTS

8 SUGAR CUBES

SALT TO TASTE

¾ CUP BREADCRUMBS

1 TEASPOON GROUND CINNAMON

¼ CUP SUGAR

You can drizzle these dumplings with a little melted butter, or accompany them with a berry coulis and a dusting of confectioner's sugar, as well as any leftover cinnamon and sugar-flavored breadcrumbs. These dumplings can also be made with ripe plums.

Boil the potatoes, peel them, and puree smooth with a potato ricer. Combine with the yolks, butter, and 1¼ cups flour, then knead until you have a smooth, soft, well combined dough. On a lightly floured work surface, roll the dough into a thick sheet and cut it into 8 equal pieces.

With a paring knife, cut about halfway around an apricot. Extract the pit, leaving the two halves connected if possible. Slip a sugar cube into the indentation where the pit was and set aside. Repeat with remaining apricots. Wrap each apricot in a piece of dough and form the dough into a ball around the fruit with a smooth surface. (If you were unable to pit the apricots without cutting them in half, the halves should stay together once you've encased them in dough.) Bring a large pot of water to a boil, salt lightly, and boil the dumplings for 15 minutes.

Meanwhile, toast the breadcrumbs in a pan until golden. Remove from the heat and mix with the cinnamon and sugar on a small plate or soup bowl. Remove the cooked dumplings with a slotted spoon or skimmer and let them drain over the pot, then toss them in the sugared breadcrumbs.

Babà al rum / BABA AU RUM

Agriturismo Fattoria Terranova, Massa Lubrense (Napoli), Campania

Serves 6

1 ENVELOPE (2¼ TEASPOONS)
ACTIVE DRY YEAST

4 CUPS UNBLEACHED
ALL-PURPOSE FLOUR, PLUS
MORE FOR FLOURING PANS

7 TABLESPOONS UNSALTED
BUTTER, SOFTENED, PLUS
MORE FOR BUTTERING PANS

5 LARGE EGGS

1 PINCH SALT

½ CUP WHOLE MILK

1¼ CUPS SUGAR

¼ CUP PLUS
1 TABLESPOON RUM

Babà molds are tall and narrow so that the cakes rise high. In the Campania region, where they originate, these are often served with fresh fruit and pastry cream on the side.

Make a sponge: Dissolve the yeast in ¼ cup warm water, then combine with ¾ cup flour in a large bowl. Stir to combine, cover with a dish towel, and set aside until well-risen, about 45 minutes.

Form the remaining 3 ¼ cups flour into a well on a work surface. Place the yeast mixture in the center of the well with the 7 tablespoons butter, eggs, and salt. Pull in flour from the sides of the well until combined into a crumbly dough, then knead energetically for at least 15 minutes, adding the milk a little at a time as you do.

Butter and flour 6 individual babà molds. Divide the dough into 6 equal pieces and place them in the molds. Place the molds on a baking sheet. Cover with a dish towel and leave in a warm, draft-free place until the dough has risen to the rims of the molds.

Preheat oven to 350°F and bake the cakes until golden and risen, about 35 minutes. Meanwhile, combine 2 cups water with the sugar and rum and cook, stirring constantly, over medium heat until the sugar is completely dissolved. Gently unmold the cakes and soak them in the hot syrup. Remove the cakes from the syrup, drain briefly, and serve.

Zeppole / DOUGHNUTS

Locanda Pezzolla, Accettura (Matera), Basilicata

These donuts are rustic and filling due to the potatoes and the semolina flour. They make a satisfying mid-afternoon snack. For a savory version, simply omit the honey and sugar.

Stir the yeast into ¼ cup warm water. Meanwhile, bring a large pot of water to a boil and cook the potatoes until soft. Peel the hot potatoes and puree them. Combine the potatoes, yeast mixture, and semolina flour and knead at length until you have a smooth, moist, and well-combined dough. Shape the dough into a ball, place it in a terracotta container, cover with a kitchen towel and set aside in a draft-free place to rise until puffy, at least 30 minutes.

Pull off a piece of the dough about the size of a golf ball and shape it into a ring. Repeat with remaining dough. Place the olive oil in a pot with high sides and bring to high temperature for frying. Fry the donuts, working in batches if necessary to keep from crowding the pan, until dark golden brown. Drizzle with honey, sprinkle with sugar, and serve warm.

Makes about 1 dozen donuts

2¼ TEASPOONS (1 ENVELOPE) ACTIVE DRY YEAST

9 OUNCES (2 TO 3 MEDIUM) POTATOES

3 CUPS SEMOLINA FLOUR

1 PINCH SALT

4 CUPS EXTRA-VIRGIN OLIVE OIL

2 TABLESPOONS HONEY

¼ CUP SUGAR

Pan di ramerino / ROSEMARY BUNS

Salvatore Grieco, Firenze, Toscana

Makes 4 to 6 large buns

1 TABLESPOON ACTIVE
DRY YEAST

1 CUP WHOLE MILK, WARM

4 CUPS UNBLEACHED
ALL-PURPOSE FLOUR

½ CUP RAISINS

½ CUP EXTRA-VIRGIN
OLIVE OIL

2 TEASPOONS MINCED
ROSEMARY

½ CUP SUGAR

2 TABLESPOONS ANISE SEEDS

1 LARGE EGG

These rustic buns—not quite a dessert, more of a sweet snack—can also be made with sourdough starter in place of the yeast. There are also savory versions of these buns made in Firenze, especially during Lent.

In a bowl, dissolve the yeast in the milk. Add the flour and knead into a smooth dough, adding a little milk or water if it feels too dry. Shape into a ball, place in the bowl, cover, and set aside to rest for 1 hour. Meanwhile, soak the raisins in warm water until soft, then drain and squeeze dry. In a small skillet, heat the oil and sauté the rosemary in it until aromatic. Set aside to cool.

Knead the rosemary and oil into the dough, then knead in the raisins, ¼ cup plus 2 tablespoons of the sugar, and the anise seeds. Divide the dough into equal pieces, shape each piece into a bun, and set aside on a baking sheet to rise until puffy, about 45 minutes.

Preheat oven to 400°F. Slash an X in the top of each bun with a sharp knife. Beat the egg and brush it on the surface of the buns. Bake in the preheated oven until golden, about 20 minutes. While the buns are cooking, combine the remaining 2 tablespoons of sugar with ¼ cup water and cook, stirring constantly, over medium heat until sugar is melted. When you remove the buns from the oven, brush them with the syrup, then let them cool.

Cartellate / FRIED DOUGH ROSETTES

Ristorante Falsopepe, Massafra (Taranto), Puglia

Serves 4 to 6

1 ORANGE

2¼ TEASPOONS (1 ENVELOPE) ACTIVE DRY YEAST

¼ CUP EXTRA-VIRGIN OLIVE OIL

FINELY GRATED ZEST OF 1 LEMON

4 CUPS UNBLEACHED ALL-PURPOSE FLOUR

1 LARGE EGG, LIGHTLY BEATEN

½ TEASPOON SUGAR

1 TABLESPOON AROMATIC LIQUEUR

ABOUT 1 CUP ORANGE JUICE

PEANUT OR OLIVE OIL FOR DEEP FRYING

3 CUPS MILLEFIORI HONEY OR FIG REDUCTION (PAGE 381)

These festive pastries can also be decorated with sprinkles or chopped candied fruit, and in Puglia they are sometimes sprinkled with a little ground cinnamon. There are also versions that use white wine in place of orange juice.

Finely grate the zest of the orange. Juice the orange and reserve the juice. Dissolve the yeast in ¼ cup warm water and set aside. Place the ¼ cup extra-virgin olive oil in a small pot and heat over medium heat, then add the orange and lemon zests and heat until aromatic. Set aside to cool. On a work surface, make a well of the flour. Add the oil with the zests, the yeast mixture, the egg, the sugar, and the liqueur to the center of the well. Begin pulling in dry ingredients from the side of the well until you have a crumbly dough. Add the reserved orange juice that you squeezed, and then continue to add the additional orange juice a little at a time, kneading between additions, until you have a firm dough. You may not need all of the juice. Knead until smooth and well-combined. Shape the dough into a ball and set aside to rise for 30 minutes.

With a rolling pin or a roller pasta machine, roll out the dough into a thin sheet. Cut into long strips 1½ to 2 inches wide with a zig-zag pastry cutter. Take one strip and fold it in half the long way, pinching the long sides together at intervals so that you have a strip of little pockets. Shape the strip into a rosette. Repeat with remaining strips.

Place the oil for frying in a pot with high sides and bring to high temperature. Place the honey in another pot and heat it, but do not allow it to boil. Fry the rosettes, working in batches to avoid crowding the pan, until golden. As they are ready, remove them from the oil with a slotted spoon or skimmer and dip them in the warm honey, then transfer to a serving platter.

Crêpe con gelato / CRÊPES WITH ICE CREAM ▷

Giuliana D'Este, Ferrara, Emilia-Romagna

Makes 12 crêpes

3 LARGE EGGS

1½ CUPS UNBLEACHED
ALL-PURPOSE FLOUR

¼ CUP SUGAR

2 CUPS WHOLE MILK

3 TABLESPOONS UNSALTED
BUTTER, MELTED AND
COOLED, PLUS MORE FOR
BUTTERING PAN

2 TABLESPOONS RUM

3 PINTS ICE CREAM

Crêpes always make a big impression, and they're honestly not difficult to make. A drizzle of chocolate sauce and a handful of hazelnuts scattered on top and these are fit for company.

In a bowl, whisk the eggs until frothy. Sift in the flour and whisk until well-combined, then whisk in the sugar. Add the milk in a thin stream while whisking constantly, and continue to whisk until the batter is smooth and free of lumps. Refrigerate for at least 1 hour. Whisk in the 3 tablespoons melted butter and the rum until well-combined.

Butter a nonstick skillet lightly and heat over low heat. Add about ½ cup of the batter and tilt the pan to cover all surfaces thinly. Cook over low heat until the bottom is lightly browned, about 2 minutes, then flip and cook the other side. Remove and keep warm. Repeat until all the batter has been used up, buttering the skillet as necessary. To serve, place a scoop of ice cream in the center of each crêpe and fold.

Frittelle di mele / APPLE FRITTERS

Enza Vuillermin, Brusson, Valle d'Aosta

Serves 4

2 LARGE EGGS

½ CUP UNBLEACHED
ALL-PURPOSE FLOUR

½ CUP SUGAR

½ CUP WHOLE MILK

6 REINETTE APPLES

½ CUP GRAPPA OR MARSALA

OIL FOR FRYING

¼ CUP CONFECTIONER'S
SUGAR

If you have an apple corer, you can cut the apples into rings. Otherwise, quarter them, core them, and slice them into wedges. Reinette apples stay firm when cooked, but you can use other varieties as well. These are traditionally served in the area for the Feast of Saint Joseph, March 19.

Whisk the eggs, then whisk in the flour, sugar, and milk to make a smooth batter. Set aside to rest. Peel and core the apples and cut them into wedges or rings. Place the grappa in a bowl, toss the apples with the grappa and set aside to macerate for 30 minutes.

Drain the apples well. Place the oil for frying in a pan with high sides and bring to high temperature. Line baking sheets with paper towels and set aside. Dredge the drained apples in the batter and fry in the oil until golden, working in batches if necessary to keep from crowding the pan. As the apples are golden, remove them with a slotted spoon or skimmer and drain on the prepared pans. Sprinkle with confectioner's sugar and serve warm.

Frittelle di pane / BREAD AND JAM FRITTERS

Giuseppina Grossi, Arco, Trentino

Serves 4

½ LOAF DAY-OLD BREAD

¼ CUP FRUIT PRESERVES

ABOUT ½ CUP WHOLE MILK

2 LARGE EGGS

1¼ CUPS UNBLEACHED
ALL-PURPOSE FLOUR

1 PINCH SALT

1 TEASPOON SUGAR

EXTRA-VIRGIN OLIVE OIL
FOR FRYING

COCOA POWDER FOR
FINISHING

CONFECTIONER'S SUGAR
FOR FINISHING

Plum, apricot, and cherry preserves are all tasty on these simple fritters, a great way to use up leftover bread.

Cut the bread into slices a little less than ½ inch thick, remove the crusts, and shape each slice into a dense ball. Spread each ball with a little of the preserves. Dip the balls in milk to moisten, then set them in a soup bowl or an earthenware baking pan. Reserve the milk.

In a bowl, beat the eggs, then whisk in the flour, salt, and sugar. Whisk in enough of the milk to make a loose batter. Place the oil for frying in a pot with high sides and bring to high temperature for frying. Line baking sheets with paper towels and set aside. Dredge the balls of bread in the batter and fry until golden, working in batches if necessary to keep from crowding the pan. Remove with a slotted spoon or skimmer and drain on the prepared baking sheets. Sprinkle half of the fritters with confectioner's sugar and half with cocoa powder and serve warm.

Frittelle di farina di castagne / CHESTNUT FLOUR FRITTERS

Ristorante Il Poggiolo, San Marcello Pistoiese (Pistoia), Toscana

Makes about 3 dozen fritters

4 CUPS CHESTNUT FLOUR

1 PINCH SALT

¼ TEASPOON BAKING
POWDER

EXTRA-VIRGIN OLIVE OIL
FOR FRYING

Chestnut flour gives these fritters some heft. The recipe does not contain sugar, but you can sprinkle a little on the fritters if you like, or serve honey for dipping.

On a work surface, shape the chestnut flour into a well. Add ¾ cup room temperature water to the center of the well. Begin pulling in flour from the sides of the well and when you have a crumbly dough, knead until smooth and elastic. Add a little water if needed. Knead in the salt and baking powder until the dough is well-combined and no longer sticks to the work surface.

Pinch off a small piece of the dough and shape into a ball, then flatten slightly. Repeat with remaining dough. Place the oil for frying in a pot with high sides and bring to high temperature for frying. Line baking sheets with paper towels and set aside. Fry the pieces of dough until golden, working in batches if necessary to keep from crowding the pan. Remove with a slotted spoon or skimmer and drain briefly on the prepared pans. Serve hot.

Sciatt al cioccolato / CHOCOLATE BUCKWHEAT FRITTERS
Trattoria Altavilla, Bianzone (Sondrio), Lombardia

Serve these *sciatt*—local dialect for "frogs"—with a creamy vanilla sauce. These are the sweet version of the savory fritters on page 271.

In a bowl combine the buckwheat flour and all-purpose flour with the salt. Stir in the grappa and the beer and begin stirring in water a little at a time until you have a fairly thick batter. Chop the chocolate into squares and stir them into the batter. Finally, stir the baking soda into the batter.

Place the oil for frying in a pot with high sides and bring to high temperature for frying. Line baking sheets with paper towels and set aside. One at a time, remove a square of chocolate from the batter and fry until golden. Remove with a slotted spoon or skimmer and drain briefly on the prepared pans. Repeat with remaining squares of chocolate.

Serves 6 to 8

1¼ CUPS FINELY GROUND BUCKWHEAT FLOUR

¾ CUP UNBLEACHED ALL-PURPOSE FLOUR

1 PINCH SALT

2 TABLESPOONS GRAPPA

2 TABLESPOONS BEER

6 OUNCES DARK CHOCOLATE

¼ TEASPOON BAKING SODA

OIL FOR FRYING

Cotognata / QUINCE DIAMONDS
Rosella Donato, Imperia, Liguria

In the Veneto, quince paste is made with ground cloves and cinnamon and is called *persegada* (see page 435 for a recipe). For long-term storage, layer between wax paper in glass jars, ceramic jars, or wooden boxes.

Peel, core, and dice the quince, place in a pot with ¼ cup water and half of the lemon juice. As soon as the quince are soft, before they begin to fall apart, remove from the heat and puree with a food mill. Set aside to cool.

Weigh the puree. In a large pot, cook the cooled puree over low heat, stirring in 2 cups sugar for every 1 pound puree, along with the remaining lemon juice. Bring to a boil, then cook, stirring occasionally to keep it from sticking, until it is very thick and pulls away from the sides of the pot, about 30 minutes. Transfer to ceramic molds or spread, smoothing with a spatula, ¾ inch thick on a large platter. Allow to dry at room temperature in a cool and well-ventilated place. Cut into diamonds and toss each piece in confectioner's sugar until coated.

Serves 6

4½ POUNDS (8 TO 10 MEDIUM) QUINCE

JUICE OF 1 LEMON

ABOUT 6 CUPS SUGAR

¼ CUP CONFECTIONER'S SUGAR

Seadas / CHEESE TURNOVERS WITH HONEY

Ristorante Ispinigoli, Dorgali (Nuoro), Sardegna

Serves 6

7 OUNCES YOUNG SHEEP'S
CHEESE

1 ¾ CUPS SEMOLINA FLOUR

2 LARGE EGGS

SALT TO TASTE

4 TABLESPOONS UNSALTED
BUTTER, SOFTENED

3 TABLESPOONS GRATED
LEMON ZEST

EXTRA-VIRGIN OLIVE OIL FOR
FRYING

2 TABLESPOONS HONEY

Use the youngest sheep's cheese you can find for these—it should be stored in its own whey for a couple of days so that it becomes slightly acidic. You can use a food processor to make this dough, if you like. These days you can find seadas filled with ricotta, but the original recipe is this one.

Grate the cheese and set aside. Make the dough by combining the flour, the eggs, and the salt. Knead until very soft and smooth, adding warm water as needed. The dough should be soft. Gradually knead in the butter and lemon zest. Roll out to a thin sheet (but not overly thin—it needs to be thick enough to contain the filling). With a cookie cutter, cut the sheet of dough into disks 4 inches in diameter. Reroll dough to get as many disks as you can. Crumble the cheese and place a portion of the cheese on half of the disks. Top with the remaining disks and press all around the edges to seal.

Transfer the pies to a floured dish towel and pierce holes in their surfaces with a needle, pressing gently to expel any air trapped inside. Place a generous amount of extra-virgin olive oil in a pot with high sides and bring to temperature for frying. Fry the pies until golden, then drain briefly on paper towels. Drizzle with the honey and serve hot.

Baci di fichi e cioccolato / FIG AND CHOCOLATE KISSES

Trattoria La Collinetta, Martone (Reggio di Calabria), Calabria

You can skip the oven-drying step and make this with dried figs if you like. Just trim off any hard stems.

Makes 2 to 3 dozen pieces

2 POUNDS VERY RIPE FIGS

1 CUP BLANCHED ALMONDS

¼ CUP SWEET LIQUEUR

5 OUNCES DARK CHOCOLATE

½ TEASPOON EXTRA-VIRGIN
OLIVE OIL

Preheat the oven to 350°F. Halve the figs and place them on baking sheets. Bake in the preheated oven for 20 minutes. Let the figs cool, then chop them as finely as possible. Toast the almonds and chop those finely as well. Combine the chopped figs, chopped almonds, and the liqueur. Shape the mixture into small balls, each about the size of a walnut. Line baking sheets with wax paper or parchment paper. Place the chocolate and oil in the top of a double boiler and melt, whisk to combine, then coat the balls in the melted chocolate mixture. Transfer to the prepared pans and allow to cool completely at room temperature.

Cannoli di ricotta / CANNOLI WITH RICOTTA FILLING

Trattoria U Locale, Buccheri (Siracusa), Sicilia

Cannoli shells, which are shaped into tubes using metal molds, can be either fried or baked. To bake them, simply place the shells still on the molds on baking sheets and bake in a preheated 425°F oven until golden. Carefully remove the shells from the molds. (The metal molds will be hot from the oven.) Cool before filling. In addition to candied cherries, cannoli can be decorated with cocoa powder or chopped nuts. They tend to vary slightly from city to city. The most renowned cannoli in Palermo were at one time those made by the nuns at he convent of Santa Caterina, which were gigantic in size.

Drain the ricotta for the filling in a strainer set over a bowl for 24 hours.

For the shells, place both types of flour and the cornstarch on a work surface and shape into a well. Pour the 1 tablespoon oil into the center. Separate 1 egg. Reserve white and add 1 whole egg and 1 yolk to the center of the well, along with the sugar, salt, wine, and vanilla. Knead, gradually pulling in the dry ingredients, until you have a firm, smooth dough. Roll the dough into a thin sheet and use a cookie cutter to cut out disks about 4 inches in diameter. Oil cannoli molds. Dab the two opposite sides of one of the rounds with a little of the reserved egg white and wrap the shell around the mold to shape, sealing the edges where you brushed the egg white so the disk forms a tube. Repeat with remaining disks and molds. (Leave them on the molds.)

Fill a pot with high sides (or an electric fryer if you have one) with a generous amount of peanut oil and bring to high temperature. Line baking sheets with paper towels. Fry shells on the molds until golden. Work in batches if necessary to keep from crowding pan (or if you don't have enough molds). Remove from oil and gently slide the shells off of the molds and onto the prepared pans to drain.

For the filling, in a bowl combine the drained ricotta, sugar, and cinnamon. Stir with a fork at length until the mixture is creamy and dense. Fill the shells with the ricotta mixture. (A pastry bag is useful.) Add a candied cherry to each end, sprinkle with confectioner's sugar, and serve.

Serves 4

FILLING

1 POUND SHEEP'S MILK RICOTTA

¾ CUP SUGAR

¼ TEASPOON GROUND CINNAMON

CANDIED CHERRIES FOR FINISHING

½ CUP CONFECTIONER'S SUGAR

SHELLS

1 CUP SEMOLINA FLOUR

1¼ CUPS DI UNBLEACHED ALL-PURPOSE FLOUR

1 CUP CORNSTARCH

1 TABLESPOON EXTRA-VIRGIN OLIVE OIL, PLUS MORE FOR OILING MOLDS

2 LARGE EGGS

3 TABLESPOONS SUGAR

1 PINCH SALT

1 CUP RED WINE

¼ TEASPOON VANILLA EXTRACT

PEANUT OIL FOR FRYING

Nocciolini / MERINGUE HAZELNUT DROPS

Luigia Bevione, Monteu da Po (Torino), Piemonte

Makes about 12 dozen very small meringues

1⅔ CUPS HAZELNUTS

6 EGG WHITES

2½ CUPS SUGAR

These tiny treats, about ½ inch in diameter, were dreamed up in the early nineteenth century in Chivasso, in the province of Torino, by pastry chef Giovanni Podio and made famous by Ernesto Nazzaro (who trademarked the name noasetti for them in 1904) and Luigi Bonfante. They are still produced with Piemonte IGP (Protected Geographic Origin) hazelnuts. These days a machine often pipes them as little buttons onto strips of paper, but your handmade efforts, while not as uniform, are sure to be fantastic.

Preheat oven to 350°F. Line baking sheets with parchment. Toast, skin, and finely chop the hazelnuts. Whip the egg whites to very stiff peaks, then whip in the sugar. Fold the chopped hazelnuts into the egg whites. Transfer the mixture to a pastry bag fitted with a small tube and pipe into small mounds, each about the size of a hazelnut, on the prepared pans, leaving a couple of inches between them. Bake in the preheated oven until dry and golden, about 10 minutes.

Fichi e cioccolato / CHOPPED FIGS DIPPED IN DARK CHOCOLATE

Antonietta Gorga, Montecorvino Rovella (Salerno), Campania

Makes 4 to 6 dozen pieces

4½ POUNDS VERY RIPE FRESH FIGS

½ CUP SWEET LIQUEUR

11 OUNCES DARK CHOCOLATE

2 TABLESPOONS UNSALTED BUTTER

The best way to dry these figs is to bake them in a wood-burning oven where the fire is out but the oven is still warm. You can also incorporate some chopped toasted almonds into the fig mixture.

Preheat the oven to 350°F. Halve the figs and place them on baking sheets. Bake in the preheated oven for 20 minutes. Let the figs cool, then chop them as finely as possible. Combine the chopped figs and the liqueur. Shape the mixture into small balls, each about the size of a walnut. Line baking sheets with wax paper or parchment paper. Place the chocolate and butter in the top of a double boiler and melt, whisk to combine, then coat the balls in the melted chocolate mixture. Transfer to the prepared pans and allow to cool completely at room temperature.

Lonzino di fico / FIG AND NUT "SALAMI"
Gianfranco Mancini, Serra de' Conti (Ancona), Marche

This sweet "salami" is best made with dottato or brogiotto figs; the chunks of nuts really do resemble the pieces of fat in a salami, and the logs are wrapped in fig leaves and tied to fool the eye further. It pairs well with local cheeses and sweet wines and has its own Slow Food Presidium. Though this recipe gives instructions for drying the figs, you can also purchase dried figs (about 1 pound) and skip that step. The figs used to be dried in a bread oven after the bread had cooked and the fire had died down. For long-term storage, you will need to vacuum pack these.

To dry the figs, preheat oven to 200°F. Spread the figs on baking sheets and bake in the preheated oven until shriveled. Then set the figs in the sun so that they dry further.

Trim and roughly chop the figs and roughly chop the walnuts and almonds to pieces about the same size. Knead together the dried figs and nuts and knead in the mistrà. Shape the mixture into logs about 5 to 6 inches long and 1½ to 2 inches thick. Arrange the logs on a wooden board and allow to dry in a cool dry place for several days, turning them once a day. Wrap in fig leaves and tie with wool yarn.

Makes about 4 small logs

6½ POUNDS FRESH FIGS

¾ CUP WALNUTS

½ CUP ALMONDS

2 TABLESPOONS MISTRÀ OR OTHER ANISE LIQUEUR

FIG LEAVES FOR FINISHING

Gelo di fichi d'India / PRICKLY PEAR JELLIES
Ristorante Antica Filanda, Capri Leone (Messina), Sicilia

Prickly pears, the fruit of a kind of cactus, grow widely on Sicilia, where they are often turned into preserves. They are covered in thorns, so wear gloves when prepared them.

Seed the prickly pears and force them through a sieve to extract their juice. Measure the juice and combine with an equal amount of water. In a pot, combine the juice, water, the sugar, and the cinnamon stick. Place over medium heat and bring to a boil. Stir in the xanthan gum until well-combined, then distribute the liquid in molds (discard the cinnamon stick) and allow to cool until set, about 2 hours. Unmold the jellies.

Serves 4 to 6

12 PRICKLY PEARS

⅓ CUP SUGAR

1 CINNAMON STICK

2 TEASPOONS XANTHAN GUM

Colombine / SUGAR DOVES

Pasticceria Corsino, Palazzolo Acreide (Siracusa), Sicilia

Makes 16 to 20 pieces

1 CINNAMON STICK

3⅓ CUPS UNBLEACHED
ALL-PURPOSE FLOUR
OR 00 FLOUR

4 CUPS CONFECTIONER'S
SUGAR

You can shape these confections any way you like, but it is traditional to pinch a little of the dough into a kind of stem to represent the bird's head and neck.

Line baking sheets with parchment and set aside. Place the cinnamon stick in a pot with 2 cups water and bring to a boil, then set aside to cool. Remove and discard cinnamon stick. Combine the flour, the confectioner's sugar, and enough of the cinnamon-scented water to make a smooth dough. Pull off a piece of dough that weighs about 2 ounces and knead on the work surface with the palm of your hand for a few minutes, then shape into a dove (see photo). Repeat with remaining dough. Place the doves on the baking sheets and let them dry at room temperature for 4 to 5 days.

Preheat oven to 300°F and bake the doves until they exude sugar and it begins to caramelize, about 30 minutes. Let cool and store at room temperature in a container with a tight-fitting lid.

Aranzata de pompìa / POMPIA AND ALMOND SQUARES

Francesca Pau, Siniscola (Nuoro), Sardegna

Serves 4 to 6

9 OUNCES POMPÌA RIND

3½ CUPS BLANCHED
ALMONDS

2¼ CUPS HONEY

1 TABLESPOON SUGAR

Pompìa is a citrus fruit native to Sardegna that has a Slow Food Presidium. The fruit is almost inedible, but the peel is thick and flavorful and is often candied. These confections will keep for several months if wrapped tightly in parchment paper. Traditionally, each piece is served on a piece of pompìa leaf or a piece of lemon or orange leaf.

Cut the rind into wedges. Place in a pot with water to cover, bring to a rolling boil, and boil for 5 minutes. Drain the rind and dry on a kitchen towel, then cut into strips a little less than ¼ inch wide. Split and toast the almonds.

Place the honey in a pot and bring to a simmer. As soon as the honey starts to bubble, stir in the rind. When the mixture turns dark, stir in the almonds and cook over low heat, stirring frequently, for 2 hours. Stir in the sugar and cook, stirring constantly, for 5 additional minutes, then remove from the heat.

Brush a marble work surface with water and pour the mixture onto the work surface. Use an offset spatula to spread it evenly, a little less than ½ inch thick. Let the mixture cool completely, then cut into small squares.

Persegada / QUINCE CUBES

Francesca Ballarin, Venezia, Veneto

Lightly spiced quince cubes make a lovely after-dinner treat.

Serves 8 to 10

6⅔ POUNDS QUINCE

LEMON JUICE TO TASTE

SUGAR TO TASTE

GROUND CINNAMON TO TASTE

GROUND CLOVES TO TASTE

ROCK SUGAR FOR FINISHING

Place the quince in a pot with a generous amount water. Simmer over medium heat until the quince are soft, then peel and core them. Drain and wipe out the pot. Puree the quince by forcing them through a sieve, then return the puree to the pot and cook, stirring constantly, until thickened.

Weigh the puree. Add 2 cups sugar and ¼ cup lemon juice for every pound of puree. Add ground cinnamon and ground cloves to suit your taste. Cook over low heat for 30 minutes.

Allow the mixture to cool somewhat, then transfer to ceramic molds or a rectangular pan. Allow to cool and set, then cut into small cubes. Sprinkle the cubes with the rock sugar and when they are completely dry, transfer to a tin with a tight-fitting lid for storage.

INDEX

RECIPES BY REGION

EMILIA-ROMAGNA

FRIULI VENEZIA GIULIA

LOMBARDIA

PUGLIA

SARDEGNA

SICILIA

TOSCANA

TRENTINO

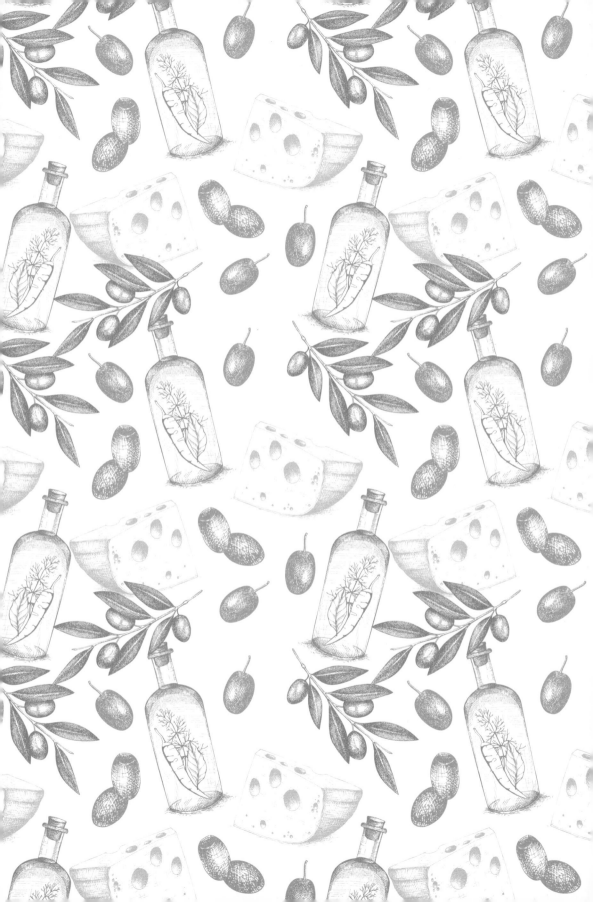